Social Anthropology
and Medicine

A.S.A. MONOGRAPH 13

Social Anthropology and Medicine

Edited by

J. B. LOUDON

University College of Swansea
University of Wales

1976

ACADEMIC PRESS
London · New York · San Francisco

A Subsidiary of Harcourt Brace Jovanovich, Publishers

ACADEMIC PRESS INC. (LONDON) LTD.
24/28 Oval Road,
London NW1

United States Edition published by
ACADEMIC PRESS INC.
111 Fifth Avenue,
New York, New York 10003

This volume derives mainly from material presented at a conference on social anthropology
and medicine sponsored by the Association of Social Anthropologists of the Commonwealth
held at the University of Kent at Canterbury, 5–8 April 1972

Library of Congress Catalog Card Number: 76-10489
ISBN: 0-12-456350-3

Printed in Great Britain by
J. W. Arrowsmith Ltd., Bristol

EDITOR'S PREFACE

This book is a result of the annual conference of the
Association of Social Anthropologists held in 1972 at
the University of Kent at Canterbury. The lapse of time
between the conference and the final preparation and pub
lication of the proceedings has enabled contributions to
be extensively revised. Sadly it must also be reported
that one of the contributors to the present volume, Mervyn
Jaspan, died before the work went to press.

Meyer Fortes, the begetter and convener of the
proceedings in Canterbury, whose editorial responsibilities I eventually assumed, has written a Foreword in
which he says a good deal about the thinking and planning
which he put into formulating the programme. With his
unofficial advisers he drew up an agreed rough set of
guidelines for potential contributors; one aim of these
was to attempt some demarcation of topics within a subject
area which might otherwise have become unmanageably and
unprofitably wide. Some aspects of the rationale behind
the guidelines are mentioned in the Foreword and in the
second part of the Introduction.

Although attempts were made to limit the theme
of the conference and also to guide the contributors to
some extent, they do not seem to have prevented the essays
being suitably diverse in approach. Indeed, they turned
out to be broadly representative of a number of different
points along the continuum of idealist-empiricist func-
tionalism which, however it may be dressed up, is characteristic of contemporary Anglo-French anthropology.
It may be noted here that, while most of the contributors
are professional social anthropologists, three (Gilbert
Lewis, N.J. Allen and myself) are professionally qualified
in both medicine and social anthropology, while two (Joyce
Leeson and Una Maclean) are qualified only in medicine,
though both - as their contributions show - are also highly sophisticated sociologists. A major source of satisfaction to me as a practising physician who later became
an anthropologist is the repeated emphasis on the ordinary, the common and the mundane in all the contributions
to this collection. In clinical practice, as experience
and confidence increase, satisfaction in the art and craft
grows with familiarity, so that common conditions and
regular complaints are almost greeted as old friends,
relatively undemanding, perhaps reassuring but inevitably,
as time passes, rather boring. Then, on reflection, they
may start becoming more mysterious than strangers. The

analogy with anthropological fieldwork is close: once
the excitement of the first six months is over, what
seemed exotic and extraordinary becomes familiar and
ordinary, then tedious and frustrating; this is when
what one has begun, like one's informants, to take for
granted can, with luck, grow puzzling and then profoundly
absorbing. Nothing can be more demanding intellectually
than the systematic analysis of everyday events, including the social process by which illness (which involves
elements both 'out there' and 'in here') is classified
and handled.

All the papers presented by contributors were
circulated beforehand to participants in the conference;
all but two are here reproduced in forms revised to some
extent by the writers or by myself or by both. M. Shokeid
wrote and presented a paper which he was unfortunately
unable to make available for publication here; and Jeanne
Bisilliat's essay appears in a translation by myself which
scarcely reflects the elegance of the original French
version presented. A large number of members and guests
of the Association took part in the conference and contributed to discussions. Meyer Fortes himself was unfortunately unwell for part of the proceedings; he and I
are grateful to Raymond Firth and Edmund Leach, both of
whom were prevailed upon at very short notice to take

the chair at some of the sessions.

The hard work done behind the scenes by those responsible for the domestic arrangements at ASA conferences is sometimes inadequately acknowledged. In this case warm thanks are due to John Davis for the characteristic aplomb with which he performed the arduous twin roles of unruffled host and flawlessly efficient stage manager. As Editor I am personally grateful for their patience, help and encouragement to Adrian Mayer, formerly General Editor of the ASA Monograph series, and Jean La Fontaine, who succeeded Meyer Fortes as Chairman of the Association. Finally, without Mrs M. Alfandary as dea in machina of this, as of a number of other anthropological publications, the last stages of production would not have been so painless.

MEYER FORTES

FOREWORD

The conference of which this monograph is a record came
about in response to a proposal I made to the Association
of Social Anthropologists when I was elected Chairman in
April 1970. I acted as the Convenor; but the programme
would never have been formulated without the advice of
Dr J.B. Loudon, Dr G.A. Lewis and Dr J. Woodburn; nor
would it have been achieved without the guidance and, in
due course, the editorial attention of Dr Loudon. I had,
indeed, from the outset reckoned on this, since, being
both an experienced physician and a professional anthropologist, in the tradition of Rivers and Seligman, he has
long combined his skills in field research and in theoretical work directed to the very theme of this conference.

       In proposing a conference on medicine and anthrop-
ology, I was influenced by considerations which had nagged
at me for some years. During the past twenty-five years
or so social anthropology was at first occupied primarily with the study of institutional forms and cultural

schemata operating within the framework of the social
system. More recently the emphasis has shifted to such
topics as myth and ritual, cognitive systems and modes
of thought, in studies dominated by concepts and paradigms borrowed from linguistic theory or technical philosophy. Understanding the human actor has been subor-
dinated to the theoretical analysis of the contents,
patterns and products of his actions. The analogy that
comes to mind is that of a science of flight for which
it is only the quantitative and physicalist variations
between the flight of eagles, barnyard fowls, sparrows
and jet liners that are relevant, whereas for the orni-
thologist there is a world of qualitative diversity to
be appreciated and understood here - differences between
the respective ecological niches of natural species, the
goals and tasks of species maintenance, innate and acquired capacities, and so forth, let alone the more fundamental differences between natural fliers and the arti-
facts represented by the jet plane.

As a layman, I think of medicine in the broadest
sense as being essentially concerned with the state of
the individual in the day to day processes of living, a
state which we evaluate by criteria derived from what
are conventionally labelled as the opposed poles of health
and disease. It seemed to me, therefore, that a con-

ference on topics of research that fall into this frame
of reference would be rewarding from the point of view
of re-focussing anthropological attention on the human
actor as such, rather than on abstract problems of, for
example, role and status or of the apparatus of custom
at the disposal of the actor. Health and illness apper-
tain peculiarly to individuals, and are, in essence, experienced, interpreted and acted upon by their individual
bearers (so to speak) even in the case of epidemics. We
need only remember that illness is signalled by pain or
at least discomfort, and health by various contrary ex-
periential signs, to become aware of this.

I am not saying that the concepts of health and
disease exhaustively categorise all the processes and
experiences of living. I do believe, however, that they
are heuristically satisfactory global concepts for dir-
ecting attention to the most critical determinants of
human existence; and they are the more pertinent because,
while identifying the individual experiencer, they also
invariably point to the social regulation and cultural
evaluation of the individual's circumstances and situation.

It is no innovation for anthropologists to give
particular attention to the role of disease in the life
of non-western peoples. Illness is the lot of mankind

everywhere. In the conditions of existence that are
common in pre-industrial lands, illness has always been
too conspicuous to be overlooked. Accounts of native
modes of treating disease, and of the beliefs and ideas
associated with them, appear regularly in the reports
of early travellers and other observers in these exotic
countries. Sigerist (1951, republished 1967) reviews
the history of the study of what he calls 'primitive
medicine' and shows how large a body of information was
already available to such writers as Tylor, Frazer and
their European and American contemporaries. He makes
a point (p. 166) of a comment by Ackerknecht (1945, reprinted 1971: p. 114) that to 17th century European observers American-Indian medicine would not have seemed
'strange or primitive'. Not only were such treatments
as cupping, bleeding, purging, herbal remedies, some
forms of surgery, and even exorcism, common to both, but
so also were some of the associated beliefs and mystical
theories about the causation of illness and the rules
of healthy living.

The gap that is nowadays accepted between western
medicine and non-European folk medicine is a product of
post-19th century medical science. And with this goes
an attitude that emerges in the works of the first medically qualified anthropologists to undertake field

investigations in the modern style. Take, for instance,
W.H.R. Rivers and C.G. Seligman, who were rising medical
research workers when they were converted to anthropology
as a result of the Torres Straits Expedition of 1898.
Both gave attention to ethnomedical problems in their
field studies. Curiously, however, they were both (and
more particularly Rivers) as obsessed as the lay ethnographers of their time and since with the questions about
the native theories of magical causality supposed to lie
behind some of their modes of treating diseases, and the
contrast with other forms of treatment that were, to all
intents, empirically sound. Preoccupied thus with the
patterns of causal ideas and beliefs he discerned behind
the medical practices of the peoples of the Pacific,
Rivers (1924: p. 52) concluded paradoxically that their
'art of medicine' was 'in some respects more rational
than our own, in that its modes of diagnosis and treatment follow more directly from the ideas concerning the
causation of disease', even though these are wrong from
the 'civilised' point of view. It was a simple step
from this conclusion to a special emphasis on the apparent psychological (as opposed to physiological) efficacy
of the magical medicine of tribal peoples, a step made
the more plausible by the absorption of Rivers in psycho-
pathological studies which resulted from his work with

shell-shocked soldiers in the 1914-18 war.

What is missing in this approach is a systematic correlation of objective pathology, as determined by western scientific and clinical methods, with the diagnoses and explanations of tribal 'leechcraft', as Rivers dubbed it. This would have been one way of testing how strongly a priori magical beliefs and ideas prevailed in the face of inescapable facts of nature accessible to the observation and understanding of a pre-scientific culture.

The orientation of which Rivers' work is an example was widely accepted in ethnomedical research and remains so to some extent at the present time. Transcultural psychiatry, for example, starting from premises not far removed from Rivers' notion of the internal rationality and therapeutic efficacy of the magical and religious framework attributed to ethnomedicine, is perhaps the most flourishing branch of ethnomedical research today (cf. Kiev 1972). But we see the same orientation in the proliferation of studies of social and cultural responses to illness and death defined as affliction or misfortune, from the emic point of view of a particular culture, as in the classical studies of Evans-Pritchard and, more recently, those of V.W. Turner. This reduces the study of health and disease to studies of witchcraft,

sorcery, magic, and in general curative or socially re-
adjustive ritual practices, with herbalist and empirically rational diagnosis, treatment and prophylaxis as
residual categories.

    This tendency appears even in the more sophistic-
ated, modern, studies in the field of ethnomedicine. An
impressive example is the book by Dr G.W. Harley (1941;
1970), who spent many years in Liberia as a medical missionary. In order to supplement his medical qualifications, he went to immense trouble to master the ethnographic and sociological literature and theories having
a bearing on African folk medicine. Harley does indeed
compare real pathology and appropriate treatment as determined by scientific western medicine, with native
Liberian Mano categories, diagnoses and modes of treatment. The resulting elucidation of the division in Mano
medicine between empirically rational procedures and
magical treatments facilitates an assessment of their
respective application in accordance with the native
classification of diseases (including accidents such as
snake bite) and in accordance with the people's knowledge
of aspects of anatomy, physiology and pathology as these
are known to western science and in so far as they are
accessible to the people's everyday experience. But,
as his unit of reference, Harley is primarily concerned

with the disease, not with the sick person; and it is
obvious that his chief interest is to track down the
magical and superstitious aspects of Mano leechcraft.
This is the more striking because the Mano are evidently
a people with a considerable knowledge of efficacious
herbal remedies and a respectable range of empirically
sound forms of treatment. It is a picture that could
be paralleled from elsewhere in West Africa.

It was the intention of the conference organisers
to direct attention to the person, in health and in disease, as the central concern for comparative study, in
contrast to states of illness and of health, as these
happen to be labelled in particular societies. We hoped
to address ourselves to such questions as: who, in a giv-
en social setting of family, household or community, is
identified as sick by what signs, when and for what supposed reasons, rather than such questions as: what are
the kinds of sickness that are recognized in that social
setting or society. Rather than considering the treatment of illness, this meant concentrating on the treatment (herbal, medico-magical, surgical or what you will)
of persons as they are perceived in a given culture in
terms of their physical and biological constitution, on
the one hand, and of their spiritual makeup, on the other.
And corresponding to this emphasis on the person as

patient we hoped also to pay special attention to the
healer as a person rather than to his craft in the abstract. The corollary to this is the possibility of
cross-culturally valid criteria and norms of health, as
seen from both the actor's and from the observer's point
of view. Ideas and beliefs about the relationship between 'body' and 'mind', 'individual' and 'society',
'man' and 'natural environment' (as we would phrase them)
come up in pursuing the problems of explanatory theories
invoked in activities aimed at ensuring health or in
procedures undertaken to prevent or cure illness.

Anyone acquainted with the ethnographical researches of the past half-century that bear on ethnomedicine will see that this programme follows many lines
first laid down in them. There have, however, been advances in theory and great extensions of ethnographic
coverage in the past twenty-five years; and a deeper
understanding of the problems brought to the fore in
those earlier researches is now possible, as the papers
here brought together demonstrate. Research in ethnomedicine is on the way to becoming a fashionable field
of anthropological activity. Associations and special
study groups concerned with this field are being established in many countries. The present volume, in my
opinion, opens up a number of new and promising lines

of research in this field; and it is a particularly good
augury that medically qualified anthropologists are now
coming forward, as is the case among our contributors,
to develop these studies. At the same time these papers
make it abundantly clear, and the discussions at our conference reinforced the impression, that medical qualifications are not, and never have been, indispensable for
research in ethnomedicine. What is important, in my
opinion, is to keep in mind the basic principle that our
primary concern as social anthropologists is with the
whole person as our unit of reference. This means looking at states of health and disease not as clinical entities in the abstract but as lived experiences of individuals, families, and communities.

        Such experiences, whether hurtful or not, are the
reflection of complex processes crosscutting several levels of existence - organic, individual and social. Every
system of medicine, including our own, serves the twofold
end of providing interpretations of these experiences
and of attempting to control the underlying processes.
It has to be effective, therefore, across all the levels,
often concurrently. Thus it confronts elements which
are pragmatically understandable and manageable, as at
the organic level; but it also confronts elements, at
the level of the life situations of individuals, which

are unpredictable, uncontrollable, sometimes mysterious
and even terrifying. Advanced as our own medical science
and technology may claim to be, it is still impossible
for us to predict exactly when disease will afflict a
particular individual, still less forecast the hour of
his death, pace all the actuarial virtuosity in the
world. As for control, the margin of chance has not
yet been eliminated. The process of aging cannot be
reversed nor the nine months of pregnancy halved or
doubled to suit individual convenience. So those rock-
bottom problems still remain with us which are often
adduced to account for the prevalence and possible success of the "magical" (in the widest sense) components
of pre-scientific medicine. The questions to which
Evans-Pritchard drew graphic attention in his study of
Zande witchcraft and magic - 'why me' and 'why now',
with their corollaries 'am I myself to blame' or 'am I
the victim of attack from the outside' - these questions
continue to be asked in the framework of western medicine, as Sigerist, for one, emphasizes (op. cit., p. 157)
and as some of the contributors to this volume illustrate.

Here, perhaps, lies the core of any anthropological study of a system of medicine, viewed as an institutional apparatus of defence against the incursion of

pain and the ever-looming threat of annihilation that
is the human lot.

REFERENCES

ACKERKNECHT, E.H. 1971. Medicine and ethnology:
   selected essays. Ed. H.H. Walser and H.M. Koelbing.
   Bern: Verlag Huber.

HARLEY, G.W. 1941. Native African Medicine: with
   special reference to its practice in the Mano tribe
   of Liberia. (New impression 1970). London: Cass.

KIEV, A. 1972. Transcultural psychiatry. Harmondsworth: Penguin Books.

RIVERS, W.H.R. 1924. Medicine, magic and religion.
   London: Kegan Paul.

SIGERIST, H.E. 1951. Primitive and archaic medicine
   (A History of Medicine, Vol. I) New York: Oxford
   University Press. (Reprinted 1967.)

SOCIAL SCIENCES, INTERNATIONAL ENCYCLOPEDIA OF THE.
   1968. New York: The Macmillan Co & The Free Press.

CONTENTS

CONTENTS

page

J. B. LOUDON

INTRODUCTION

The Torres Straits expedition of 1898, that
crucial enterprise in the development of British
social anthropology, was undertaken by men who, as
Evans-Pritchard (1951) remarks, being for the most
part natural scientists, "had been taught that in
science one tests hypotheses by one's own observations". Five of them - Rivers, Seligman, McDougall,
Myers and Haddon - were in due course elected Fellows
of the Royal Society. What is not always remembered
is that four of these (Haddon being the exception)
held medical qualifications. But none of them seems
to have had much, if any, first hand experience of
clinical medical practice as a physician, though
Rivers later worked as a psychiatrist in a rather
specialised field during the first world war. This
relative lack of direct practical experience of the
ordinary daily work and responsibility of treating
the sick, whether in their own societies or elsewhere, with all that is involved in learning the

hard way how and when to cut or not cut corners when
handling patients suffering from a wide variety of
mostly common conditions, may go some way towards explaining a fact to which Fortes draws attention elsewhere in this volume: namely, that Seligman and
Rivers shared with lay ethnographers of their own
time and since an obsession with magical theories of
causation as the basis for indigenous therapeutic
procedures, which led to "a special emphasis on the
apparent psychological (as opposed to physiological)
efficacy of the magical medicine of tribal peoples".

Doctors of medicine therefore happen to have
played a proportionately larger part in laying the
foundations of the fieldwork tradition of British
social anthropology than they have in later building
on them. It is true that in recent years a number
of medically qualified men and women have taken a
more than passing amateur interest in the discipline;
a few have become professionals, among them some of
the contributors to this volume. At universities in
what may be called the 'western' tradition a training
in medicine ideally involves a more or less balanced
mixture of science, humanity and art, of theory, fact
and practice, which might be thought to provide, for
the occasional adventurous spirit, as propitious a

springboard as any other for postgraduate work in
social anthropology. But, taking only the British
example, and allowing for differences in rewards and
career structures, it is surprising to me that, whereas between 1920 and 1955 at least a score of former
members of administrative and cognate branches of the
civil service in overseas territories of the Commonwealth joined the small band of professional anthropologists, in the same period no serious potential
recruits appear to have been attracted from among the
very large number of medical men and women with extensive first hand experience of cultures other than
their own. The generally high standards of professional and scientific competence set by what may
loosely be called the colonial medical services,
especially perhaps the clinical, pathological and
epidemiological research undertaken by members of the
medical services of India, of Malaya and of the Sudan,
may have had the effect of muting any maverick curiosity concerning the ideas and social systems of the
peoples among whom they worked. In addition, the
sheer scale and complexity of the health problems
confronting them were no doubt sufficiently challeng-
ing and daunting. But one conclusion to be drawn is
that, with a few noteable exceptions, these doctors

saw little direct relevance, for the practice of what
I shall call cosmopolitan clinical medicine, or for
the promotion of public health measures, or for the
solution of epidemiological problems, of more than a
quite superficial knowledge of indigenous concepts of
disease and illness, or of more than a nodding
acquaintance with the social relationships and technical procedures involved in indigenous modes of
treatment.

The exceptions among them shared with their
colleagues in other branches of the government and
administration of the territories concerned the reasonable expectation that at least some aspects of the
work of professional social anthropologists were
likely to be useful. The well-known pioneering work
in what used to be called 'applied anthropology'
therefore included a number of noteable contributions
in the health field; the names which spring to mind
as two of the most distinguished and formidable
trail-blazers are those of Margaret Read (1955; 1965;
1966) and Audrey Richards (1932; 1939; 1969). Since
the second world war studies of anthropological
aspects of disease and illness have burgeoned, particularly in the United States and under the auspices
of charitable foundations and international agencies.

Most of this work finds mention in the major reviews
of the field of 'medical anthropology' undertaken by
Polgar (1962), Scotch (1963), Fabrega (1972) and
Lieban (1973). I have no intention of producing here
yet another such survey. What is worth noting, however, is that, with a very few exceptions (which include Fabrega's essay), the largely unquestioned
assumption has been that studies by anthropologists
working in the health field are concerned with the
illumination of practical problems and primarily
intended to help towards their solution. Some
writers, such as Norman Scotch, are particularly concerned with problems regarding the role and status of
social scientists working alongside physicians in
population health studies. In all cases, however,
relevance for medical problem solving, whether direct
or indirect, short-term or long-term, tends to be
taken for granted.

The matter of relevance has recently sustained a
figurative extension of boundaries. In other words,
the chances are that this volume of essays will find
its way into the hands of a few established, if
eccentric, physicians. It may also catch the eye of
some of those students of medicine (and post-graduate
students in certain specialties) who have been made

aware of the existence of social anthropology through the medium of courses in the behavioural sciences which have been introduced in recent years to the curricula of certain medical schools. The word 'social' often seems to be avoided in the titles of these new developments; this may be because of the echoes it is feared might be set up in some medical minds; but the more distinctly biological connotation of the word 'behaviour' is in fact consistent with an emphasis which has long been evident in medical schools in Europe and America, and hence wherever cosmopolitan scientific medicine is taught.

Among university teachers in British medical schools these innovations appear to be most generally welcomed and supported by members of departments of psychiatry and of social or community medicine and public health. A number of the contributors to this monograph have extensive experience of teaching such courses at undergraduate and post-graduate levels. Faced by the pressure of other more traditional claims on an already congested pre-clinical and clinical syllabus, the emphasis in these new approaches is towards an integrated psycho-social orientation, the justification for which is its supposed relevance for clinical problems and for the kinds of issues of substance and communication which medical students may be expected to encounter when they qualify and begin medical practice.

The form these developments have taken is of course part of a much wider general change in contemporary expectations of universities. Although some members of the public, including a number of their elected representatives in local and central government, feel that too few students are having their energies directed towards the discipline of vocational training, there are many others who look to the universities to do more than just train people for the professions and for leading positions in government and industry. Higher education is regarded as more than just "a device for excluding the unworthy from the privileges of a governing elite" (Leach, 1968a); it is also expected to do something to bring about improvements in the well-being of mankind. In the case of training doctors in Britain, especially since the introduction of the national health service, these ill-defined humanitarian presumptions have been added to a notion which is by no means new but has become widespread, particularly (one suspects) among those who might have expected to have been 'private' fee-paying patients before 1948, and also among

members of the medical and para-medical professions,
including the social services. It is argued that
many if not most practising physicians would be better
at their jobs if they knew and cared rather more about
their patients as social and psychological beings,
even if gaining this knowledge and approach meant, of
necessity, that they were taught rather less about
them as diseased organisms which (it is hoped) will
respond favourably to treatment by various physical
and chemical procedures. Most commonly this argument
is not based on any objective assessment of the meaning of the word 'better' in this context; but it is
expressed in vague if forceful terms of people needing
to be regarded and treated as 'individuals' rather
than as 'cases'. The ideas here represented are more
important but less straightforward than they appear.

At one fairly superficial level they include a
reaction, even though often crude and muddled, against
the high and seemingly unassailable esteem accorded
to physicians, particularly those who specialise in
certain fields. At a deeper and more important level
the ideas arise from a diffuse disquiet about what is
loosely categorized as 'science'; they also relate to
a particular fear of becoming the victim of arrogant
medical engineers practising what has been termed

'assembly line medicine'. Linked with this fear is latent resistance to the notion of cure in the sense of "the imposition of discipline by force", of "compelling the unorthodox to conform to conventional notions of normality" (Leach, 1968b). Although the original context here was that of mental hospitals and penal institutions, no doubt with the shadow of forcible electro-convulsive treatment in the background, one does not need to go so far to find the same sentiments; they are encountered, for example, in child-care clinics, maternity outpatients, and labour wards.

As a corollary to these feelings and attitudes there is an ideal of what all doctors should be but few are. In contrast with the specialist, to whom "we are merely banal examples of what he knows all about", there is a kind of dream-physician - "that white-coated sage, never to be imagined naked or married", as the poet wrote, adding "begotten by one I should know better" (Auden, 1972). Other writers, more pretentious but less gifted and ironic, being themselves physicians, should also know better. Sacks (1973), for example, writes of "an ordinary medicine, an everyday medicine, humdrum, prosaic, a medicine for stubbed toes, quinsies, bunions and

boils, but all of us entertain the idea of another
sort of medicine, of a wholly different kind: something deeper, older, extraordinary, almost sacred,
which will restore to us our lost health and wholeness, and give us a sense of perfect well-being". Of
this contrast, which is the underlying theme of a
fascinating account of the effects of L-DOPA on those
suffering the dreadful sequelae of encephalitis
lethargica, one reviewer wrote that it is "tendent-
iously exaggerated. Between boils-and-bunion medicine
and the search for an ideal wholeness of being there
lies a wide and constantly increasing area of successful medical or surgical treatment for illnesses
that could be, and used to be, fatal or incapacitat-
ing" (Harding, 1973). In this argument, with the
emphasis both writers place on cure - whether of
quinsies or of the whole person or of those conditions for which treatments now exist where not so long
ago they did not - there is almost completely forgotten the matter of care.

In Britain and elsewhere during the second half
of the 20th century the gap has continued to widen
between the actual standards of the environment in
the 'care' sector of the health services and those in
the 'cure' sector. This is a situation which some

believe can only be modified by a serious attempt to
quantify value judgements and, for example, re-
allocate resources as between acute general hospitals,
on the one hand, and long stay hospitals for the aged,
the mentally ill and the mentally deficient, on the
other. "Most of us know the probability that we, our
relatives, and our friends may end our days in geri-
atric or psychiatric wards ..... cure is rare while
the need for care is widespread, and the pursuit of
cure at all costs may restrict the supply of care"
(Cochrane, 1972). It is of course only in a setting
of Byzantine complexity and grotesque inflation that
anyone can come to accept as inevitable a situation
where the annual division of the medical budget between 'cure' and 'care' (the latter including extensive domiciliary services) is not, as one might expect,
based upon expert calculations but rather on something
best described as administrative rule of thumb in the
dark. Hence the almost subversive suggestion that
what is done every year unconsciously and inaccurately
might be better if done consciously and on the basis
of serious attempts to measure and optimize outputs.

What immediately strikes an anthropologist is
the topsyturvy nature of the choices being made. In
small scale societies care is not usually a matter of

choice at all, certainly not between cure and care,
still less between domiciliary and institutional.
Care is institutionalised and domestic. Making due
allowance for the fact that many do not survive who
in an 'advanced' society end up in long stay hospital
wards, the aged, the depressed, the inadequate and
the backward provide "the acid test of the strength
of kinship sentiments", as the idle, ne'er-do-well,
weakling does among the Ndembu (Turner, 1968). If
such people are rejected without good cause the social
and moral order, based fundamentally on kinship
axioms, is radically challenged. By contrast, in
contemporary Britain, many such individuals can only
be cared for by, or with the assistance of, kinship
surrogates. If it is provided in a domestic setting
(including the euphemistic 'private home'), the relatives may be able to afford to see that adequate standards are maintained. But in the state system they
have no way of ensuring that as much is spent annually
on the care of a person suffering from senile dementia
as may, for example, be spent in a week on saving the
life and restoring the health of a twenty year old
drunken driver who crashes his motor bike into a lamp
standard.

It is quite unrealistic to imagine that many

medical students or many ordinary practising doctors
of medicine have much direct interest, academic or
otherwise, in these problems, however much they in
fact impinge upon their daily work. It would be fool-
ish to suggest that it is a waste of time to attempt
to draw some of these issues to their attention; but
it would be an illusion to think that instruction in
such matters is likely to deflect more than a tiny
minority from their principal aim and interest, namely
making a satisfactory living out of a job the satis-
factions of which depend on getting their teeth into
clinical problems and making decisions of a kind where
any division between cure and care is likely to seem
spurious or unhelpful. In the long run those who are
any good learn to cultivate a tolerant approach, warm
hands and a thick skin and to appreciate the truth of
one of Richard Asher's aphorisms: that it is a greater
medical triumph to leave the patient feeling better,
but thinking little of the doctor, than to leave him
feeling worse, but deeply impressed (Jones, 1972).

Most physicians in my experience have little real
interest in what they see as largely abstract notions
about the nature of illness, whether conceived of as
the loss of some vital principle or the intrusion of
some object or as the dislocation or disorder of

something which should be in order or in the correct
place. As for the notion of a deeper sort of medicine devoted to a sense of perfect well-being, the
hard-headed regard this as a muddled dream shared by
doctors who would be priests and laymen who would be
healers, without in either case having to soil their
hands and minds with the realities of blood, pus and
excrement with which birth, disease and dying are so
often associated. Mostly, of course, the daily round
is less dramatic and consists of a series of personal
encounters with individuals presenting a variety of
mundane complaints; the account by Berger (1967)
manages to convey the essence of its ordinariness in
a compelling way. It should not be forgotten, however, that there are some disorders of which the sufferer may be unaware and makes no complaint, conditions
discovered on examination for some other reason:
asymptomatic diabetes or early carcinoma of the cervix
uteri are obvious examples. But in most instances
the practitioner is confronted with seemingly
straightforward symptoms; coughs, headaches, backache,
chest pain, dyspnoea on effort, feelings of personal
inadequacy, early morning despair, insomnia, a sense
of impending doom. This is the basic stuff, the
ground upon which the social anthropologist must keep

his feet when attempting a more sophisticated analysis
of the central features of illness in any culture than
is usually undertaken by physicians themselves.

Here it is important to recognize and distinguish between specialist and non-specialist conceptions
of disease and illness; it is also sometimes even
more important to remember to distinguish between
degrees of refinement within conceptual levels.
Willis (1972), for example, draws attention to the
fact that "in Fipa society, as in our own, there has
long been a gulf between popular theories of causation
in the field of sickness and those held by the educated minority", while Barnes (1973) makes the more
general point that in our own culture "we tend to
assume that for ourselves no distinction between
formal science and informal ethno-science is needed".
He makes telling use of the notion of telegony as an
example of a doctrine abandoned by orthodox formal
science but, as anyone living in a Welsh agricultural
community could confirm, continuing to thrive tenac-
iously among stockbreeders. The fact that the notion
is sometimes extended to support beliefs about the
possible effects of human miscegenation is worth
exploration.

An important omission from the 1972 ASA confer-

ence, and hence from this volume, is that of any contribution dealing in detail with what Polgar (op.cit.)
has distinguished as 'professional', as opposed to
'popular', health cultures. It is particularly unfortunate that there was no discussion of the Ayurvedic and Unani medical systems of India (Marriott,
1955) or of traditional Chinese medicine, with its
distinction into 'scholarly' and 'folk' traditions
(Topley, 1970). Nor was any attempt made to tackle
the informal ethno-science of Western scientific cosmopolitan medicine. Admittedly this would be a particularly daunting task, demanding not only first-hand
ethnographic material to provide a basis for disent-
angling the ethno-science from the science, but also
at least some close acquaintance with a range of
scholarship embracing the history of medicine, of
scientific thought and of the development of a professional elite (including what Annan (1955) has entitled 'the intellectual aristocracy') in Western
Europe and North America, at least since the Hippo-
cratic renaissance in the seventeenth century, led by
Thomas Sydenham.

With idiosyncratic panache Foucault (1973) has
tackled some of the problems involved in unearthing
the basis of contemporary medical thinking and

procedures; but he wisely confined himself in the
main to the rediscovery in France round about 1804 of
the approaches of Hippocrates, Sydenham and John
Hunter and to the creation by Bichat and Laennec of
clinical medicine as we know it today. "The revival
of medicine", wrote Osler in 1904, "was directly due
to the French". Foucault is concerned to ferret
below the surface of the past and explore the murky
frontiers of thought and knowledge in disciplines
like clinical medicine where the basic concepts are
too dubious and imprecise ever to be truly scientific.
He does not set out to examine such crucial if pedes-
trian questions as those of recruitment to the medical
profession and the ambiguous position of the doctor
of medicine in a highly complex stratified society.
Nor is it grist to his particular mill to draw upon
that rich harvest of material, works of imaginative
literature, for information; although it is impossible
to believe that Le Médecin malgré lui, Le malade
imaginaire and Le médecin du campagne, for example,
are not part of his basic mental equipment.

On this side of the Channel it is no longer
possible for Bob Sawyer and Benjamin Allen to enter a
London teaching hospital and remain there until qualified to take over the practice of the late Dr.

Knockemorf. At the other extreme, it is as easy as
ever for temporary gurus to arise and devote themselves to the restoration of our lost wholeness; but
few are called, and fewer chosen, to make a lasting
impression. R.D.Laing is perhaps the most characteristic and likely candidate at the present time. The
appeal of such pied-pipers is partly a response to
the rat-race social and political climate of the day,
partly (and more importantly) a reaction against too
mechanical a form of medicine. In the 18th century,
for example, a medical and pre-Tylorian version of
animism and a closely allied doctrine known as vital-
ism, with their prophets Stahl, Hoffman and Barthez,
were for a generation acknowledged as benign alternatives to an increasingly materialistic orthodox
medical system. A little later Hahnemann, whose views
were made widely known in a a work published in 1810,
established in homoeopathy a system of treatment which
still survives and even thrives, sustained by the dis-
creet patronage of the present Royal House in Britain.
Although it is maintained that it has some rational
pharmacological basis, and certainly was when founded
a merciful relief from the bombardments of the Bruno-
nian school, homoeopathy was originally based on the
wholly magical principle of similia similibus curantur.

It is important to recognize that starry-eyed notions about ideal physicians are as central an element in a generally accepted 'scientific' medical tradition as are the accompanying doubts and suspicions regarding the honesty, benignity and professional competence of individual practitioners. A measure of scepticism maintains faith, by providing explanations for failures and for those healers who fall short of the ideal. However much the medical profession as a whole is ridiculed in any society, its members are also usually feared and sometimes respected. There is nothing new or paranoid in this proposition, as any Zande witchdoctor of experience and standing would doubtless confirm.

Being compelled to learn some of the basic facts of biology, physics, chemistry, anatomy and physiology does not necessarily mean that more than a tiny minority of medical students learn scientific ways of thinking. A fortiori basic courses in the behavioural sciences are unlikely to make many of them think sociologically or act with greater humanity than they would anyway when dealing with sick and frightened human beings. Becoming aware of the overwhelming importance of learning to listen and learning to expect and tolerate latent hostility in relation-

ships where its open expression is customarily suppressed are lessons best absorbed from example and
experience rather than from precept. At the same
time, having their attention drawn to the existence
of an ideal type of physician and to the fact that
human kind cannot bear very much reality may of course
help some medical graduates to steer clear of certain
pitfalls and too much gin. Given the range of ability
and predispositions from which the medical profession
in this country has to recruit, it is likely that on
the whole physicians tend if anything to be philos-
ophic realists and empiricists, any theories they
hold being largely dependent upon observation and ex-
periment. In this connection, however, Abercrombie
(1960) quotes from a statement in the report of a
committee of the Royal College of Physicians (1944),
as relevant now as thirty years ago, that the average
medical graduate "tends to lack curiosity and initiative; his powers of observation are relatively undev-
eloped; his ability to arrange and interpret facts is
poor; he lacks precision in the use of words". She
goes on to imply that physicians may learn "to make
better judgments" if they "become aware of some of
the factors that influence their formation ..... in
other words become more receptive or mentally more

flexible". Abercrombie herself contributed to the fascinating and complex issue of observer error in medicine strikingly demonstrated in relation to the reading by chest experts of such seemingly objective mechanical data as radiographs (Johnson, 1955).

If it is true that an essentially materialist philosophy is commonly associated with too mechanical a form of medicine, it should at least be possible to demonstrate to medical students that, even if they find it consoling to regard their patients as machines, they are much more complicated physical, psychological and social machines than they may imagine and that likewise being an efficient mechanic is a more subjective, imprecise and value-ridden business than they may at first believe. When, as is probable sooner or later, my senescent prostate needs to be dealt with and if I have to make a choice between a doctor who is notionally a plumber and one who is notionally a priest, give me an attentive plumber who knows his job; like most of us I think I can look after myself as a person in the world provided that someone else has the necessary technical skills to patch up the leaking tubes in the machine I inhabit.

There is no need to labour the point much

further. The character of the basic requirements and
the selection process for entry to medical schools is
largely governed by the market for members of a cosmopolitan profession, as are the conditions under
which they work when qualified. Much of the medical
curriculum continues to be dominated by the traditional so-called 'wet' sciences and by the modern
specialties dependent or built upon them. Attempts
to broaden and humanize the professional training by
introducing what can only be a superficial pre-
clinical acquaintance with appropriate aspects of
behavioural science are, in my opinion, likely to
prove misconceived, if well-intentioned, short cuts.
But there are no short cuts to becoming a reasonably
competent practising physician. It requires extended
initiation through an apprenticeship far more gruel-
ling than the process of learning about physiology or
pathology or sociology; namely, constant contact with,
and a measure of responsibility for, large numbers of
sick men, women and children. The expectation that
this experience can in some way be deepened or illum-
inated by behavioural science teaching is implicit in
the report of the 1968 Royal Commission on Medical
Education: "throughout the teaching in behavioural
sciences there should be a strong emphasis upon the

methods by which data are obtained /in order to/
demonstrate that human behaviour and social institutions can be investigated by the established methods
of science, that the techniques of observation and
measurement in these sciences yield data whose reli-
ability and validity can be systematically appraised,
and that concepts and theories about human behaviour
can and must be submitted to empirical verification".
These brave words, with their firmly biological flavour, smell of a sop to Cerberus. More often than not
such claims as these for the social sciences are
greeted with polite indifference by natural and physical scientists. Whereas they are ineffective as a
deterrent to that enthusiastic minority of converts
among medical teachers who embrace with innocent if
engaging warmth such disciplines as sociology or
social anthropology under the illusion that they will
help to provide "the empathy and self-awareness needed to understand people and their interaction". My
quotation is from a remark by a professional acquaintance of the kind whose kiss is death to those disciplines in medical schools and from whose ardour one
would wish them to be preserved. I feel sure that
their more discriminating friends in the medical
profession will understand.

Members of pre-clinical disciplines such as
anatomy or biochemistry, or of specialties with relatively little direct involvement in clinical care,
tend, for obvious reasons of time and availability,
to be responsible for decisions regarding the academic qualifications and personal qualities looked for
among medical school entrants, including what Ryle
(1936) referred to as "a scholarly heredity /which7
should, by Galtonian doctrine, be considered a very
distinct advantage". On the latest information
available, only a relatively small minority of those
holding office as Dean or Sub-Dean or the equivalent
at British medical schools are predominantly clinicians. At the same time, those medical teachers who
have the highest prestige and the most lasting influence among students are in the main those who, because of their overwhelming preoccupations with
clinical medicine and surgery, have less formal
responsibility for student affairs. One important
result of this may be the effect it has upon students'
concepts of, and attitudes towards, certain kinds of
medical problems, especially those in the less
prestigious aspects of clinical work such as
psychiatric geriatrics (Rawnsley, 1968).

As social anthropologists there are two

aspects of medical student selection of obvious possible interest to us. The first is the case of women
entrants to the medical profession; the second is
that of the effect of kinship on recruitment.

The position of women in medicine should, of
course be looked at comparatively, first in relation
to other professions such as the bar, engineering
and architecture, where there are important differences, second in relation to other societies such as
the U.S.S.R. where the proportion of women to men in
medicine and in the judiciary, for example, is very
different from that found in Britain. Here the position of women in medicine is a special example of
the ambiguity of current attitudes to sex differences
throughout our educational system, a system in which
"the difference between sex roles ..... distinguished
in some streams and denied in others is at first
sight ridiculous" (Leach, 1968a). Features of distinction and denial in the course of medical training
and practice are interesting. On the whole a female
candidate for entry to a medical school is expected
to be treated in the same way as a male candidate in
that there are no differences in the kinds of subjects required for admission or in the way in which
these subjects are taught. At the same time the

operation of a semi-official quota system means that
female candidates generally have to put up a better
performance at those same subjects in order to gain a
place. Once admitted, however, there are no differences; men and women medical students are regarded as
being just the same. In addition there is nowadays a
general expectation that most medical students, irrespective of gender, will get married sooner or later.
Once qualified, however, assumptions about there being
no differences are modified, particularly in relation
to the marital state of women. There are now many
more women, and many more married women, in general
practice than used to be the case; when due allowance
is made for demographic factors and to the larger
number of women medical graduates, this increase may
be related to the slight decline in the status of the
general practitioner in comparison with that of the
consultant, a change which is not related to the relative remuneration involved nor apparently affected
by the great increase in the number of consultant and
other specialist posts.

In specialist fields it is in general rare for
women, especially married women, to reach great emin-
ence; here, as elsewhere in the educational and professional fields, there are special escape-mechanisms

for exceptional cases. But it is clear that many
physicians, members of appointing committees and
many of the general public still expect there to be
certain areas of medical practice for which female
physicians, as women, are particularly suited; and
these areas often involve more in the way of care
than of cure. In other words, there are within
medicine itself certain quite clear preferences as
far as division of labour is concerned which to some
extent reflect those sex-role differences which operate in the world at large. In relation to illness
these differences may well reflect the fact that in
most if not all societies care of the sick in the
domestic sphere is generally carried out by women,
whereas cure is most often carried out by men, often
outside the domestic setting. And it is in the
domestic sphere that nature and culture coincide or
meet most closely, particularly in bed (or its equivalent); for the place we generally go to when we
first feel ill is the place where most of us expect
to have been conceived and to have been born and
where most of us expect (or hope) to die.

The second issue, that of the part played by
kinship ties in recruitment to medicine, is worth
consideration, however brief and superficial, because

of the considerable body of comparative material
concerning primitive societies where relationships
between succeeding generations of healers play a
crucial part in the maintenance of secret knowledge
and techniques as a form of exclusive property transmitted along lines of descent and affiliation.   In
Britain comparative material on other sections of
contemporary society includes such studies as those
by Lupton and Wilson (1959-61), Bell (1968) and Firth,
Hubert and Forge (1969).   There is some evidence,
particularly in relation to some of the long-
established medical schools in Britain, which suggests
that, other things being equal, the children of doctors may have certain advantages over other candidates for admission.   Whatever deeper meanings such
influences may have, in terms of creating and maintaining an elite within a stratified society, the
ostensible rationale of allowing kinship connections
to weigh in the choices made by selectors appears to
be in relation to 'common-sense' social concepts
rather than genetic notions.   The case has been made
out to me in terms of the process of socialization.
In other words, the domestic environment in which
such candidates have been reared are thought to
ensure that they are unlikely to have many illusions

— that is to say, illusions of the wrong kind — about
what is involved in the practice of medicine.

The art and craft of the physician is presented
as a straightforward combination of nous and practical
procedures, both based on laboriously acquired experience and knowledge of structures, functions, processes and techniques. The process of understanding
ordinary people and dealing with their ailments is
assumed to be firmly established on the application
of science but to have gone beyond a close link with
pure science, still less with behavioural science.
This view, contrary to popular belief, is certainly
not that of a mystique; indeed my medical informants
see their work as essentially down-to-earth, and are
anxious to stress that the children of doctors, if
favoured as candidates for entrance to medical
schools, are so precisely because they do not see
medicine as mysterious and because they are not
likely to be seduced by abstract models and ideal
categories.

At another level of interpretation certain
other points should be mentioned. One is the matter
of attitudes. It is assumed that medical students
who are the offspring of physicians have from childhood had daily acquaintance, at first and second hand,

of a small world in which patients and illnesses are
looked upon as unquestionably objective outside data
which inevitably play some part in the conversation
and other exchanges among members of the domestic
group. This is not simply a matter of gossip about
patients and illnesses; on the contrary, at one level
the importance of discretion and confidentiality in
relation to medical matters, and the informal
sanctions associated with them, are learnt commensal-
ly. In a local community the same is of course true
of the children of clergymen and policemen, to choose
two obvious examples. But in addition those children
of doctors who aim to enter the profession absorb
important attitudes regarding such matters as the
distinction between disease and its manifestation as
illness, between what is seen as genuine illness and
those complaints which are regarded as frivolous or
as evidence of malingering, between those problems of
a marginally medical kind which may or may not be
legitimately regarded as appropriate matters for the
professional concern of doctors.

Above all, perhaps, it seems to be felt (though
with what justification is another matter) that medical students who are the children of doctors have a
head start over those who are not in that they know

something at first hand of the true nature of clinical work. In a **very** important sense this contention
is not true. In the Western scientific medical tradition the transactions which take place between
physician and patient are essentially private and
usually dyadic. They consist in outline of a generally accepted series of stages, however modified in
particular circumstances, which are learnt by the
physician and generally accepted and expected by most
of those who consult him; they include listening to
the patient's complaints, identifying the leading
symptoms and their character, carrying out a physical
examination, attempting to make a diagnosis with the
aid of special investigations where necessary, giving
advice and treatment and comfort. Whatever advances
there may be in the technical aspects of the process,
the heart of the clinical situation is the consultation; this is so whether the transaction takes place
at the bedside or in the consulting room, in a Zulu
homestead or in Harley Street.

This last comparison is in fact a telling contrast. The essence of the consultation in a Zulu
household is that it takes place in public. At first
this is irksome for a non-Zulu doctor trained in cosmopolitan medicine. Surrounded by spectators who are

also participants from time to time, it is not easy
to take a systematic history, to conduct an orderly
physical examination, or to deliver a woman of a child
after protracted labour. With familiarity comes the
temptation to show off, to cover up mistakes or uncertainty or plain ignorance with a little harmless
conjuring; more dangerous is the temptation to act
when what the clinical situation demands is inaction.
In spite of oneself a little playing to the gallery
seems to become a necessary part of the job. Indeed,
as Turner (1968) shows, playing to the gallery in a
consultation is an essential part of the Ndembu
therapeutic situation. The actual social setting of
the transaction is all-important and it is vital that
those most closely involved should attend. Turner
reports an instance of the doctor upbraiding a headman for failing to ensure that sufficient people
turned up for an Ihamba performance, for it is in
terms of the widest social concerns of those standing
around watching that the Ndembu practitioner operates.
The social context is the clinical context, and vice
versa.

For most clinicians in Britain the social context within which the consultation takes place is
something that is taken for granted in several

respects. It is assumed that, as far as possible, a
responsible professional job is done irrespective of
the social and physical setting. Paradoxically it is
also assumed that relevant aspects of the social context are fully taken into account by doctors when
they make decisions and give advice; it is also
assumed in many instances that they are fully competent and able to do so. And again, however ill-defined
or uncertain the pathological or pharmacological bases
for action, it is assumed by most physicians that
everything they do or say in dealing with patients
has, or ought to have, an entirely rational basis:
that is, their transactions with patients are, or
should be, largely instrumental and free of anything
which might be identifiable as magical or symbolic.

To sum up, my contentions so far have been that
courses in the behavioural sciences, including that
modicum of social anthropology which may be included
thereunder, have less to contribute to the teaching
of medical students than some of my colleagues may
think to be the case; and that certain largely un-
spoken assumptions on the part of many physicians
practising cosmopolitan medicine - assumptions shared
to a considerable extent by the majority of their
patients in complex societies - constitute that aspect

of clinical work to which the social anthropologist
may most usefully direct questions. If there is anything in the study of what is for most of us our own
society to which we can bring a special kind of
approach and experience, it is the close and critical
examination of what is odd about what is taken for
granted, particularly about sacred cows. At the same
time, however immediate and localized, the approach
of the social anthropologist to such questions should
have a timeless and spaceless dimension. In relation
to medicine, as in other domains, the essence of the
approach lies in the patient analysis of universal
aspects of human experience and social organization
by means of scrupulous dissection of particular
instances rooted, directly or indirectly, in the
first hand observation of small-scale events. The
essays in this volume illustrate a number of variations on this theme and this approach.

        The most significant aspects of medicine as far
as the impact of social anthropology is concerned are
(i) modern public health and its applications, particularly in developing areas, and (ii) psychiatry,
especially what has come to be known as 'transcultural psychiatry'. The convenor of the 1972 conference

at Canterbury, together with his advisers, came to
the decision that it was essential to exclude those
two topics from the proceedings as far as possible,
in order to concentrate attention upon ethnomedicine,
that is, systems of thought and practice existing
outside the framework of what I have mostly called
cosmopolitan medicine.

We were more interested in papers based on
field research than essays confined to the review of
theoretical aspects of the theme. Contributors were
asked to avoid, as far as possible, concentrating too
closely on the topics of witchcraft, sorcery and
magic, although it was accepted that reference to
them was bound to occur in relation to some of the
papers. This avoidance was suggested because there
had already been an A.S.A. conference devoted to
witchcraft and it was felt that there are already
abundant publications on these and related subjects;
in addition, a great deal of the literature dealing
with the territory lying between the main fields of
anthropology and medicine tends, and is almost expected, to be overweighted in their directions.

On the more positive side, contributors were
invited to direct their attention, when presenting
field material, towards certain main areas of interest

which we felt were particularly thinly covered in
the literature.

First, it was suggested that questions needed
to be asked about notions regarding normality in relation to health and well-being and to deviations
from them. For example; what theories are encountered regarding the anatomy and physiology of the
human body and about the processes of conception,
birth, growth, maturation, senescence and death? To
what extent are comparisons made or parallels drawn
with the bodies of domestic and wild animals? How
far is it possible to identify notions of organic
systems comparable with those commonly employed by
modern scientific biologists?

Second, in regard to disease, what concepts are
found relating to aetiology or to what, in cosmopolitan medicine, is described and analysed as a pathological process? How far is disease viewed as an
external object of some kind by which the body is in-
vaded and are different classes of object associated
with particular complaints or with disorders affecting particular categories of person, such as children
or pregnant women? Or is disease seen rather as a
matter of internal disorder or derangement, of being
out of step with the environment? Given these two

possible models, which may be termed respectively
exopathic and endogenous, to what extent if at all is
there overlap between them in particular instances?
In the case of the endogenous model, is the relationship with the environment seen mostly in physical or
in moral terms? And how far is disease thought of as
an element in a wider system of beliefs regarding
such phenomena as contagion, pollution, sin and
death?

Third, are distinctions made within indigenous
systems of medical classification which correspond in
any way with those which it is useful to make between
the notion of disease and the notion of illness? In
this connection Gilbert Lewis is surely justified in
suggesting in his paper that it is wise to use external biological criteria as far as possible in
identifying particular diseases; the word 'illness'
may then be reserved to apply to those complaints involving physical or psychological changes which are
perceived by particular individuals or categorized in
particular cultures as indications of deviation from
health or from what is expected in terms of well-
being. This approach often encounters opposition.
It is, for example, maintained by some that indigenous
pre-scientific classifications of disease, and

indigenous notions about the causes, symptoms and
treatments of illness, have so many dimensions, which
flow over and into wider aspects of the general ordering of knowledge and experience, that it is impossible
to chart them against the conceptual grid of scientific medicine. This argument is consonant with a
wider and persisting debate, in social anthropology
and elsewhere, about whether attempts to understand a
culture solely in terms of the concepts, beliefs and
categories of its members does not make it difficult,
if not impossible, to gain understanding in any other
terms. A supposedly empirical discipline which gets
unduly concerned about epistemological worries is in
danger of losing its way. And there are certainly
some aspects of social anthropology where external
categories of more or less universal reference are
available which, if used with reasonable caution,
make possible comparative analysis over time and
space. Ethnobotany and ethnozoology provide obvious
examples; it is difficult to believe that many
anthropologists eschew the use of scientific identi-
fications of those plants and animals which figure
prominently in a particular cultural repertoire, however convinced they may be of the primarily subjective
nature of experience and of the undoubted necessity of

examining indigenous cognitive modes unsullied, as far
as possible, by the observer's own categories.

The same might be expected to apply to at least
some areas of ethnomedicine. But there is often a
marked contrast between the scepticism of some observers concerning categories employed in scientific
medicine and their insistence on the indigenous wisdom
distilled in pre-scientific herbal remedies or encap-
sulated in primitive healing techniques. The time is
long past when naive advocacy, however well-intentioned,
helps to gain due recognition for the undoubted skills
of healers operating in cultures other than our own.
Some supporters give the impression that personal
ideologies relating to concepts of health or to the
place of the medical profession in complex societies
affect their capacity to make objective comparisons.
On the other hand Horton (1973) has suggested that
anthropologists "should accept the fact that they cannot be effective anthropologists of traditional magico-
religious thought without at the same time being
anthropologists of modern scientific thought". If
this view is applied to the medical field, it seems
unlikely that much "effective" anthropology will be
produced, unless being an anthropologist of modern
medicine is thought of as a fairly superficial affaire

de coeur.

Some of the analytical confusions which may arise are indicated in a recent contribution to the culture-nature debate; Barnes (op.cit.) refers to "the inevitability of beginning cross-cultural comparison by matching alien cultures against our own", but reminds us that, as a scientific yardstick, our own culture is not above suspicion. But to insist, as I do, on the heuristic value of separating indigenous categories from external categories should not for one moment be thought to imply that modern cosmopolitan medicine is somehow immune to influence from informal ethnomedicine. Indeed, formal and supposedly scientific clinical medicine is itself shot through with informal and non-scientific elements. Notions which make up part of what may be termed the folklore of modern medicine abound in the textbooks and form part of a powerful tradition transmitted, with local variations and differing emphases, by precept and example from one generation of physicians to another. At the same time changes in ideas and practices, some (but not necessarily all) of which prove to be advances or improvements, often arise from another essential element in the same tradition; namely, the expectation that accepted bases for

clinical judgment are subject to continuous critical
examination. As in other branches of learning where
art and craft are at least as important a component
as scholarship, prolonged first-hand experience is
highly valued. This means that, although the young
and ambitious win their spurs in medicine by modifying or demolishing the tenets of their seniors, they
tend to do so with a measure of decorum not necessarily found in other disciplines.

The history of scientific medicine is therefore
strewn with crumbling shibboleths. But for the his-
torian to evaluate the medicine of the past solely
according to the extent to which it conforms with
present theory and practice would be as crass a
limitation on understanding as for the anthropologist
to apply the same criterion in making synchronic
cross-cultural comparisons. The fact must be faced,
however, that some clinical syndromes biologically
defineable as diseases are not necessarily regarded
as illnesses in all societies; and there are some
conditions, culturally defined as illness, which do
not easily fit any category of disease established in
external biological terms. Similar incongruences are
of course liable to be found as between specialists
and non-specialists in all cultures, and also between

different groupings in large-scale heterogeneous
societies.

An outstanding recent demonstration of the
value of making some such distinction between disease
and illness has been made by Topley (op. cit.). She
compares and contrasts what she is careful, "for
semantic reasons", to describe as two disorders or
complaints common among Chinese children in Hong Kong.
Haak-ts'an, "an emotional complaint" which she translates as 'injury by fright', is a condition regarded
by all her women informants as a disease, mostly
treated by various physical or medicinal remedies;
but, since it has no clear diagnostic label in modern
Western medicine, Topley, supported by Yap (1969),
considers it "a culture-bound disorder or syndrome".
Measles, on the other hand, which has a high mortality
rate in Hong Kong, was thought of by most informants
not as a disease but as a natural, necessary, inevitable but dangerous transitional condition. It is
held to be linked in various ways, particularly
through the notion of 'womb-poison', to a condition
affecting adult males which is unrecognized by
scientific Western medicine and is believed to result
from intercourse with a woman within the ritually
prohibited period of a hundred days after childbirth.

The child suffering from measles is regarded and
mostly treated in ways which closely resemble those
applied to persons and things undergoing a change of
social status, and which characteristically involve
ritual proscriptions; nevertheless some of the symptoms of measles may also be treated as physical
afflictions by medical means.

These distinctions in modes of treatment and
their relation to concepts of disease and illness,
bring us to the final topic to which contributors'
attention was drawn. When considering the work of
the healer and the duties and responsibilities expected of him or assumed by him, it is important to
know the extent to which healers are fulltime professionals and the criteria used in judging the
results of his ministrations. Are there, for example,
different grades of healer in particular societies,
and, if so, are the distinctions made in terms of the
modes of treatment employed or rather in terms of
different kinds of illness, distinguished by notions
of aetiology or by various combinations of signs and
symptoms? And who is mainly responsible for recognizing illness, identifying it and deciding upon the
appropriate choice of healer or therapy?

In this connection, and also in relation to the

difficulties of making distinctions between disease
and illness, and between illness and no illness
(within the system of categories employed in a particular culture), some of Turner's work on the Ndembu
is a rich and well-known source. The extended case
history of Kamahasanyi, already well on the way to
becoming a classic patient, illustrates the kind of
emphasis sought in contributions to this collection
of essays. In "The Drums of Affliction" Kamahasanyi
is described as an unusual and apparently somewhat
inadequate personality, a paradigm of victims of the
conflict between matrilineal and patrilateral allegi-
ances which is shown to bedevil the Ndembu body
politic. Physically, however, he was apparently
healthy enough; he cultivated his gardens, set plenty
of snares for game and could dance all night without
getting tired. But Turner also portrays him as a man
of weak character and strong emotions, conceited,
effeminate, probably sexually impotent, and craving
affection, attention and respect. Finding himself a
cuckold, ignored and despised, he took refuge in his
hut and developed a conglomeration of complaints
which most physicians would probably accept as commonplace psychosomatic symptoms: undue fatigue, palpitations of the heart, pains in the back, limbs and

chest. None of Kamahasanyi's relatives or neighbours
took much notice of his sufferings. "He was unable
to compel their attention by minor illness - what
Ndembu call musong'u hohu, 'just illness'. Such
complaints can be treated by herbalists or leeches
without recourse being sought to mystical notions"
(op. cit., p.154). Kamahasanyi then fell back on
claims that ancestral shades were troubling his
dreams. Partly because of his position in the
structure of kinship and political relations, he did
not need to step up the severity of his symptoms.
By invoking the idea that illness may be inflicted by
ancestors, a belief which "falls beyond the scope of
legitimate scepticism", he was able to make his minor
private troubles matters of dramatic public concern,
as Turner's account of cure by the performance of
ihamba ritual abundantly shows.

The essays in the volume speak for themselves.
As was hoped, most of them are concerned with the
illumination of neglected aspects of musong'u hohu,
'just illness', and therefore fill a gap in the
anthropological literature. Without having too much
recourse to mystical notions, they examine those
relatively mundane aspects of medicine which, especially for those (like most social anthropologists)

who have been forced to try to heal the sick, are
the most important in theory and the most common in
practice.

REFERENCES

ABERCROMBIE, M.L.J. 1960. The anatomy of judgment.
    London: Hutchinson.

ANNAN, N.G. 1955. The intellectual aristocracy in
    Plumb, J.H. (ed.) Studies in social history.
    London: Longmans, Green & Co.

AUDEN, W.H. 1972. Epistle to a godson and other
    poems. London: Faber & Faber.

BARNES, J.A. 1973. Genetrix: Genitor: Nature:
    Culture? in Goody, J. (ed.) The character of
    kinship. Cambridge: University Press.

BELL, C. 1968. Middle class families. London:
    Routledge & Kegan Paul.

BERGER, J. 1967. A fortunate man. Harmondsworth:
    Allan Lane The Penguin Press.

COCHRANE, A.L. 1972. Effectiveness and efficiency.
    London: Nuffield Provincial Hospital Trust.

EVANS-PRITCHARD, E.E. 1951. Social Anthropology.
    London: Cohen & West.

FABREGA, H. 1972. Medical Anthropology in Siegel,
    B.J. (ed.) Biennial Review of Anthropology, 1971.
    Stanford: University Press.

FIRTH, R., HUBERT, J. & FORGE, A. 1969. Families
    and their relatives. London: Routledge & Kegan
    Paul.

FOUCAULT, M. 1973. The Birth of the clinic. London:
     Tavistock Press.

HARDING, D.W. 1973. Review of Sacks (1973) q.v., in
     New Statesman, 7.9.1973.

HORTON, R. & FINNEGAN, R. (eds.) 1973. Modes of
     thought: essays on thinking in western and non-
     western societies. London: Faber & Faber.

JOHNSON, M.L. 1955. Observer error: its bearing on
     teaching. Lancet, ii, 422.

JONES, F. AVERY, (ed.) 1972. Richard Asher talking
     sense. London: Pitman Medical.

LEACH, E.R. 1968a. Culture and nature or la femme
     sauvage. (The Stevenson Lecture). London:
     Bedford College University of London.

-- 1968b. A runaway world? London: British Broad-
     casting Corporation.

LIEBAN, R.W. 1973. Medical Anthropology in J.J.
     Honigmann (ed.) Handbook of Social and Cultural
     Anthropology. Chicago: Rand McNally.

LUPTON, T. & WILSON, S. 1959-61. Kin connections
     and the Bank rate tribunal. Transactions of the
     Manchester School.

MARRIOTT, M. 1955. Western medicine in a village
     of Northern India in Paul, B.D. (ed.) Health,
     Culture and Community. New York: Russell Sage
     Foundation.

POLGAR, S. 1962. Health and human behaviour: areas
     of interest common to the social and medical
     sciences. Current Anthropology, 3: 159-205.

RAWNSLEY, K. 1968. Social attitudes and psychi-
     atric epidemiology in M. Shepherd and D.L. Davies
     (eds.) Studies in Psychiatry. London: Oxford
     University Press.

READ, M. 1955. Education and social change in
     tropical areas. London: Nelson.

-- 1965. The anthropologist's view in György, P. and Burgess, A. (eds.) Protecting the pre-school child: programmes in practice. London: Tavistock Publications.

-- 1966. Culture, health and disease: social and cultural influences on health programmes in developing countries. London: Tavistock Publications.

RICHARDS, A.I. 1932. Hunger and work in a savage tribe. London: Routledge.

-- 1939. Land, Labour and Diet in Northern Rhodesia: An Economic Study of the Bemba Tribe. London: Oxford University Press.

-- 1969. Characteristics of ethical systems in primitive human society in F.J. Ebling (ed.) Biology and ethics. London: Academic Press.

ROYAL COLLEGE OF PHYSICIANS. 1944. Report on Medical Education from the Planning Committee.

ROYAL COMMISSION ON MEDICAL EDUCATION. 1968. Report.

RYLE, J.A. 1936. The Natural History of Disease. London: Oxford University Press.

SACKS, W.O. 1973. Awakenings. London: Duckworth.

SCOTCH, N.A. 1963. Medical Anthropology in B.J. Siegel (ed.) Biennial Review of Anthropology, 1963. Stanford: University Press.

TOPLEY, M. 1970. Chinese traditional ideas and the treatment of disease: two examples from Hong Kong. MAN (N.S.), 5: 421-37.

TURNER, V.W. 1968. The Drums of affliction: a study of religious processes among the Ndembu of Zambia. Oxford: Clarendon Press.

WILLIS, R.G. 1972. Pollution and paradigms. MAN (N.S.) 7: 369-78.

YAP, P.M. 1969. Classification of the culture-bound reactive syndromes. Far East Med. J., 7: 219-25.

GILBERT LEWIS

A VIEW OF SICKNESS IN NEW GUINEA

The aim of this paper is to characterize a view of
illness held by villagers who speak the Gnau language
and live in forested hills of the Torricelli range,
in the West Sepik District, New Guinea.[1] My concern
is with their understanding of illness in general as
a kind of state or condition in which people find
themselves from time to time, rather than with their
understanding of the various particulars of different
illnesses or their specific causes. Indeed I shall
include very little on their beliefs about the causes
of illness.

Illness and health are clearly contrasted for
us as general concepts but we sometimes find it hard
to draw a strict line and say on which side a

1   The fieldwork upon which this paper is based was
     carried out from December 1967 to November 1969.
     I am very grateful to the Social Science Research
     Council for a generous grant, made to Anthony
     Forge who supervised the research, which enabled
     me to carry it out.

particular case falls. Health and illness indicate
either end on a continuum. Diseases show themselves
in diverse ways but we see something common to them
which allows us to put them within the general fold
of illness while we consent to exclude from it other
peculiarities occurring in people (such as gluttony,
menstruation, white hair, nostalgia and love-
sickness). Our view of what should be done when
someone is ill and of how he should behave is guided
by our understanding of the nature and significance
of illness. We rarely find it necessary to define
or specify the general and essential features of illness but they inform our responses to it. These
general features are implied in behaviour perhaps
more than they are formulated in words. They tend to
elude exact statement.

This is also true of the Gnau view which I will
try to characterize, and so I must describe the
behaviour of Gnau people in illness, particularly in
illness which they regard as serious or potentially
so. Part of my interest in this behaviour was prompted by the ways in which it did not conform to how I
expected a sick person to behave. The privileges of
questioning and of access to the sick person's body,
which I have taken for granted as a medical practit-

ioner in my own country, were not similarly given to
me among the Gnau. In part this was to be expected
from our mutual strangeness; but just as, with us,
the relations between doctor and patient are based on
common assumptions concerning the situation, so with
the Gnau the sick person and those who care for him
share certain assumptions and these do not provide an
identical basis to ours for the relationship between
patient and healer. That I deal with illness in general rather than in various particulars reflects an
aspect of their assumptions; that I deal with the
sick person and say little about the healer reflects
another aspect. The role of specialist in treatment
or expert healer is not sharply differentiated by
them; almost any adult may on some specific occasion
be considered the appropriate person to perform a
part in treating a sick person, although senior men
do most in treatment.

After describing the behaviour of someone sick,
I will examine some of the words by which they refer
to sickness. These words imply or suggest a link
between illness and death, and I go on to relate this
link to their view of the normal course of life and
the vulnerability of someone sick. One question lying behind my account of the Gnau view of illness is

to know how it corresponds to ours, whether we find
that they bring together a similar or different
assembly of human states to those which we include
within the domain of illness. The anthropologist who
intends to study illness in another society from his
own will want to decide what comes within the scope
of his inquiry. If he also aims to understand social
factors which influence the prevalence, course, and
outcome of illness there, or to show the problem of
disease and how it is faced in that society, he
should also in my opinion try to keep in mind a distinction between disease defined by external, modern,
medical criteria and illness as it happens to be
recognised in the society he studies. By preserving
this conceptual separation between social or cultural
views and medical or biological criteria, he will be
better placed to observe their interrelations. I
try to explain this distinction, though briefly, in
the later part of my paper, before coming back to a
final comment on what contrasts with illness, namely,
the Gnau view of health.

Illness to the Gnau: their main distinctions

The point of departure for a study of medicine in
another society will be the sick person, since it is

what happened to him that must be explained. What do
members of that society see as illness? While I was
among the Gnau I did not find or treat a wide variety
of ailments. I treated people when I was able to and
if they so wished; I was also brought pigs and dogs
to treat on occasion. In a most general sense nearly
all the conditions I saw, which we would hold to be
disorders of the body, are admitted under the heading
of things 'undesired': the word they use is wola.
This is the only word which will net or include all
these conditions. But wola is an adjective which
would correspond to our word 'bad'; I could gloss it
as 'ill', but it can also mean bad, evil, wretched,
harmful and forbidden, powerfully dangerous, and it
is also the only word they have for aged or old (although usually in this reference it is used with a
completed action marker bi - i.e. biwola). I wish to
note therefore that they lack a covering word which
would differentiate illness in general from other un-
desirables, as 'sickness' and 'illness' do in English.
It is quite common to read in ethnographies that a
particular people do not distinguish illness from
other afflictions or misfortune; later I will consider
in what sense this is so.

    But first it must be said that 'bad' or

'undesired' is not very different from the English
word 'ill'. We apply the contrasting concepts of
health and illness in everyday life and often we
apply them with naive certainty. The manner in which
they seem black and white, clear and straightforward
as general concepts, but yet at times prove obscure,
subtle and uncertain when we ask how they apply to
particular cases, resembles the application of other
judgements of value like ones of moral good and bad.
Long before medicine became scientific, health and
illness existed as concepts related to basic values
such as life and capacity for performance. Doctors
work with a knowledge of the range of normal functions
and the evidence of normal structure but the knowledge of different organs or systems varies greatly.

Medical science does not consist in elaborating
these normal standards to arrive at a general concept of illness any more than it feels it should
discover a single remedy for all its cases. The
doctor's function rather consists in ascertaining
what precise kind of state or event is presenting
itself, on what it depends, how it proceeds and
what will affect it. In the great variety of
states and events called 'disease' almost the only
common factor is that disease implies something

'harmful, unwanted and of an inferior character'
(Jaspers 1963: 780).

Thus with wola as their comprehensive term for ills
they differ little from ourselves. It may be worth
noting that the pidgin English 'sik' has been very
readily assimilated by them and even by speakers who
have only five or ten pidgin words in all: but they
certainly do not misuse sik for non-bodily misfortune.

When they applied wola to their ailments, I
noted that someone could say either that his part was
ill (a limb, tissue or organ), or that he himself was
ill. In trivial things, like a cut or sore, the man
is well, but a part of his skin is ill. In more
severe disorders, a crucial distinction is made by
the sick individual. It involves his perception of
himself, his body image, for he may say either that
it is he who is ill, or that it is the part which is
ill while he himself is well. This might seem to
read things into a mere form of words; but it was
indeed the supplication, repeated over weeks, of a
man each time he was brought forward to confront his
afflicting spirit, Malyi, that it was not he but his
joints only that were ill; and the figure Malyi would,
quivering, bow, bending at the legs, then rise tall
and stamp its foot in sign of acquiescence. The

simple phrasing of these supplications was of this
general form: 'I am a fit man (literally, a good man):
it is my knees and my shoulders that hurt, they are
ill - I am well. You must not kill me; it is only my
knees, not me, I am well'. It was also repeated and
called out by the other men who surrounded and supported him as he faced the spirit.

The distinction of illness of the self and not
only of a part of the body has far-reaching consequences for their behaviour when ill. They distinguish part of the wide field of things we call illness
with an intransitive verb which means 'to be sick' -
neyigeg - he is sick. He suffers in his person as a
whole. It applies to illnesses which are, for the
most part, ones we would call internal, ones accompanied by pain, fever, nausea, debility, or disturbances of breathing, of the bowels and so on. It does
not cover external ailments like skin diseases; nor
does it cover conditions which are long-standing
states of disorder, for example, limb deformities or
stunted growth or mental defect; nor insidious illness - it was not applied to a woman with a slowly
progressive nerve disease of paralysis and wasting
muscles, or to a man with gradual worsening heart
failure. Of these insidious diseases and the long-

standing disorders, they said that those who had them
were 'ruined', 'wretched', not that they were 'sick'
(neyigeg); they used the word biwola, the same word
as that for 'old', 'aged' (i.e. wola with its completed action marker). Ills of the body may therefore be
seen as ills of a part, or ills of the person; and
the ills of the person may either be a present critical state, or a completed finite condition.

Behaviour in serious illness

When someone is sick in the critical sense of neyigeg,
his behaviour is conspicuously changed. It is not
only altered by the physical effects of the disease,
but also by conventions for behaviour. He shuns
company and conversation; he lies apart, miserable in
the dirt or inside a dark hut, the door shut; he re-
jects certain kinds of normal food, tobacco and areca
nut; he eats alone; he begrimes himself with dust and
ashes. Further degrees of this behaviour are seen in
severe illness; more extreme restrictions of food are
applied, men discard the phallocrypt and lie stark
naked (although in all normal life, as when bathing,
they would always hide their naked penises).

The first thing to note about this pattern of
behaviour is that it involves a decision, and one

which the patient himself takes. The illnesses in
which this behaviour is assumed vary greatly in objective severity but if someone regards himself as
critically sick in his person, he adopts the behaviour. It is shown by both men and women. And he
keeps it up until he thinks he is safely well. An
ash-grimed man lies in the dirt and others say he is
ill. I might be urged to go and treat him, but on
some occasions the patient would tell me in a low and
confidential voice: 'I will be well tomorrow. I feel
all right and have felt so for a few days but I
stayed ill like this for a little more to be sure'.

Disease may be considered from the point of
view of the observer or the patient reflecting on
himself. As Charcot, the great 19th century neurol-
ogist, observed, 'There is a particular moment between health and sickness when everything depends on
the patient, the borderline between a discomfort
which is accepted and the decision "I am ill"' (quoted
in Jaspers 1963; 425). This borderline is sharply
defined by Gnau behaviour, and the decision is left,
except for children, to the patient. In marked contrast to ourselves they do not expect others, or
specialists, to discern for them whether or not they
are ill, or when they are better. That is not the

doctor's job.

What I have described represents a stereotype
of how a Gnau patient should behave. Clearly the
behaviour is patterned on common features of bad illness, and some people do not need to act or mime its
signs. The things which most mark it as conventional, rather than a spontaneous expression of subjective feeling, are the conspicuous and rapid griming
with dirt and ashes, the marked alteration in speaking voice, the disinclination to hold conversation,
the placing apart from others, even were it only to
lie outside in the sun where others anyway were gathered, and the consistent association of the essential
signs when shown. In addition to these, the other
signs mark an illness as more or less severe: the
grading of severity is shown in greater reluctance to
take part in conversation, the quavering thin voice,
withdrawal into a hut with shut doors, avoidance of a
wider range of foods, abandonment by men of all attire, including the phallocrypt; and eventually (and
this on the part of the patient's relatives) the
fencing off of a part of ground round the patient
with bamboo poles magicked with leaves and spells, so
that someone bearing ill to the patient will be
struck or a spirit barred off should one seek to pass

the magical barrier. The barrier also serves to
alert and keep away people who might be carrying
foods bringing dangers through the association of
spirits with food.

In general the type of behaviour is withdrawal
into a passive and wretched state; noisy, active or
agitated signs of illness are uncommon and when someone ill groans or shouts with pain, as occasionally
happens, it makes by contrast a more remarkable
impression on other people. Women sometimes provide
an exception to the general type of passive behaviour
in illness when they show bengbeng behaviour. Gnau
people say that this behaviour was first learnt in
the early 1950s when a cargo cult spread to their
villages. The behaviour was so characteristic of the
cult, and shown by men and women, that when the Administration came to suppress the cult and in the
course of doing this gaoled a few men, although none
from the Gnau villages, the interpretation of the
Gnau people was that the men were gaoled for bengbeng,
that the behaviour itself is forbidden by the Administration, carrying the penalty of gaol. Sometimes
bengbeng is accompanied by speech and revelations in
the persona of a spirit, but not necessarily. When
I observed it in women as an early and arresting

event in their illness, the chief features were
frantic and uneven breathing while rapid cries were
seemingly jerked out of them that rose and fell in-
continently with their uneven breathing (the cries
were often 'hus! hus! hus! hus!' or 'he! he! he!
he!'). If they sat, their bodies jerked in time to
the cries or they strode around chanting incompre-
hensibly, or spoke messages from dead spirits, or
warnings. The cries or jerks could crescendo to a
point of collapse called 'death', or else fade and
fall silent; the woman then sat blank and tired out
but in touch with her surroundings. I witnessed the
point of collapse once, but bengbeng without obvious
deep trance or collapse about fifteen times. In
Gnau theory, bengbeng is due to possession by a
spirit and the behaviour is not due to illness, nor
in itself an illness; it may however reveal illness.
Some women, after it had occurred, were regarded as
ill and behaved in the appropriate withdrawn manner.
They were treated, but the treatment was not for
bengbeng, which is not itself harmful, but for whatever it was that they were supposed to be afflicted
with or by.

Thus bengbeng to the outside observer can
appear as an additional way in which attention is

drawn to illness, although to the Gnau what shows the
illness is the withdrawn behaviour which follows:
that is the general rule of illness. The showing of
the withdrawn behaviour constitutes an appeal for
help, a demonstration which obliges others, particularly the patient's closest relatives, to find out
and treat his illness. As this was the appropriate
form of a request for treatment by the patient, it
was difficult to count requests for consultation in a
way that could be compared with those, for example,
of English patients. Actual requests or suggestions
that I should visit someone ill came from a variety
of people; if illness affected someone notable, or
was severe, I would be told to go recurrently through
the day or days of his illness by all sorts of people,
some of whom perhaps had not been to his hamlet since
he was ill, or did not know that I had already been.
People rely largely on the silent showing of illness,
and this works in a village where everyday life is
public and the spread of news within it rapid. People
quickly learn when someone is ill and if they have
any sense of obligation they come to find out what
the matter is and how they can help.

Communication with the sick person

In critical illness, sick people become inert and
withdrawn; others must take action to bring about
their recovery. I was sometimes baffled and exasper-
ated by this; few of those 'sick' themselves came
early or quickly for treatment at any time during my
stay. But a random succession of their relatives, or
of casual passersby, would tell me to go and see whoever it was. If I asked how the patient was sick,
they most often answered in generalities; or they
mentioned symptoms which were not confirmed by the
patient, or told me sites of pain which were diffuse
or proved inaccurate; or they occasionally said
wrongly that the patient, even when this was their
wife or father, had blood in the urine or had gone
deaf. The most common answer was, 'I don't know;
but he is very sick, sick all over'. Direct inquir-
ies of the patient were often frustrated because he
was showing rather than explaining how he was sick:
he lay listless, head hanging, and stared silently at
the ground; he indicated sites of pain with indis-
criminate gestures scattered over his body. A question to him was often answered for him by someone
watching, and the sick man would rarely then bother
to answer for himself or to correct what others said.

Illness is displayed rather than described. I
have emphasized this as it was one factor behind
their apparent indifference to recounting symptoms:
I could rarely get beyond learning that they were
sick and had pain and fever. Later I collected over
a hundred anatomical terms and assembled from descriptions of symptoms and illnesses a vocabulary
which was adequate to the precise and detailed description of pain in its varieties, and of functional
disturbances, and so on. Even though I knew the
language better, it was always rare and difficult to
obtain a subjective analytic account of symptoms
from an ill person during his illness. I would
emphasize that this list of words reveals a percept-
ual awareness of pain, weakness, nausea, and so
forth, which is in essentials like our own.

There is no ground to suppose that they fail to
suffer physically in illness as we do. For most
people in the world ill health has meant feeling ill,
suffering pain or incapacity and going in danger of
death or mutilation. Whether this state could be
traced to some structural change in the cells of the
body did not enter into consideration in deciding
whether a man was healthy or ill. Illness is recognized by the Gnau patient subjectively. It is

communicated to others in a conventional manner which
relies on non-verbal rather than verbal behaviour.
They have a verb meaning 'to examine something carefully or closely' (e.g. to look at the engraved pattern on an arrow shaft which might identify its maker)
but they do not apply the verb 'examine' to looking
at a patient; one just 'sees' or 'looks at' him (root
- nakel). The examining aspect of my medical approach
was only cautiously accepted by them.

The verbs for sickness and their implications

When they talk of the kind of illness, which with
them implies its cause, this is distinct from what
they say of the manner of illness, indicating constraint, suffering and limitation. If you wish to
know what kind of illness the patient has, you may be
told the names of one of the various agents causing
illness, but this tells you virtually nothing about
the clinical form or pathology of the illness. In so
far as the answer is concerned with the cause, it
corresponds to an aetiology, but as particular agents
are not, or rarely, held to produce specified symptoms
or signs of illness, one cannot deduce the kind of
illness from knowing its cause. By reference to the
manner of illness then, I mean description of its

observed form and kind as something roughly parallel
to what we would call its clinical description, or
else its pathology. It is in this respect that verbal distinctions about kinds of illness are lacking in
Gnau. As I have said, they have the necessary vocabulary to define the site and features of a disease
but they do not ordinarily refer to it to analyse and
define how someone is ill.

　　　　Instead this is indicated in general terms
through the discriminations of certain verbs. It is
characteristic of the language that these discriminations are made by verbs. Three verb roots can be
related to expressions for health and illness. They
are -p-, -t-, -g-, which are easier to grasp in third
person masculine present tense forms, viz:

nap - 'he lives'	nat - 'he sleeps'	nag - 'he dies'
and	and	and
nap - 'he stays'	nat - 'he lies'	nag - 'he is inert'

The live and sleep roots -p- and -t- are both used to
say of things that they 'exist', 'are somewhere',
'stay'; the root used depends on context as to the
more active or passive quality of staying (for instance as between nuts staying on the branch, and
nuts staying (put) in a bag). Only nap is used to

mean 'he lives'. Nag means 'he dies', but is used of
a man fallen unconscious, even though they know he
will come to in a moment, and get up. The root -g-
is also used for the moment when sago flour, being
mixed with boiling water and swirled round, suddenly
goes solid, it gells, it 'dies' (wag). The future
tense form of nag is neyig - 'he will die'.

Root	3rd masc. sing.	Verbs of sickness		
		reduplic.	Incompl. actn. marker	both
-p-	nap 'lives'			
-t-	nat 'sleeps'	natet	nambet	nambatet
-g-	nag 'dies'	nageg	nambeg	
	neyig 'will die'	neyigeg		

In Gnau, emphasis, exertion, repetitiveness can
be introduced into the action described in a verb by
reduplication of a component syllable, for instance:
nalep - 'he went', nalelep - 'he went on and on', or
napa'an - 'he stayed in the bush', napap a'an - 'he
stayed on and on in the bush'. In the verbs for
sickness we find a series of syllabic reduplications
of the verb roots for sleeping and dying. The basic
verb for 'he is sick' (neyigeg) is a reduplicated
form of neyig - 'he will die'. There are also forms

which incorporate the incompleted action marker,
-mb-. The reduplication of the root of the verb 'to
die' modifies its action rather than intensifying it
as is usual. The verbs for sickness are specific; I
learnt them to mean sickness as synonyms for neyigeg
without at first discerning distinctive meanings for
them or noticing their morphological relationships to
the 'sleep' or 'die' verb roots. Neyigeg is the verb
for 'he is sick': it does not by itself imply degree
of illness. Natet and nambet and nambatet are used
to suggest continuing illness, either severe or minor,
and they may be qualified adverbially. Nambeg and
nageg imply severe illness. The use of simple behavioural description to indicate more complex human
conditions, emotions or responses is characteristic
of Gnau idiom; for example, in a sentence such as
'they said to him "eat"; he sat', the words 'he sat'
are understood to mean 'he refused the offer'. The
form of verbs for sickness seems to link sleep, lying,
constraint, dying, the risk of death and sickness.

It is not easy to determine by questions in the
abstract whether one is right to infer such a conceptual link from the forms of verbs. If you turn to
look at Gnau food taboos you find that the sanctions
for many of them are given in terms of constraint,

implying illness: if you eat this or that which is
forbidden you will be heavy, you will be confined to
the village; by implication illness will take from
you activity, freedom and movement. They do not
usually specify how, although if you ask it is most
often said to be by breathlessness and weak and painful limbs. If now you look at the overall pattern of
food taboos you will find that at each stage of life
those foods which are forbidden are called wola.
There are two peaks of restriction when food taboos
are most complicated and extensive. One is from
birth to the age of about three to four years (objectively a dangerous period of their lives, judged by
Gnau infant and toddler mortality rates). The second
peak is from puberty until a man or woman has grown-
up children (the restrictions are most marked for a
couple with their first infant); after this time more
of the forbidden 'bad' foods are permitted until, in
old age, virtually all that was classed wola becomes
permissible. Thus the quality of 'bad' is not attributed to food as an absolute or inherent quality
(except where that which might be eaten is never
classed as 'food'), but as a quality relative to the
status, biological or social, of the person.

     I am trying to get at their view - implicit,

perhaps ill-defined or vague - of the relation of
sickness to the normal course of life. As they see
it, people develop to a stage of full maturity not at
but after puberty at about the time when they have
their first children. This is the stage when a person is fully entire or complete; the word they use is
nembli, meaning 'entire' in the sense, say, of a
sprig of nettle leaves before you have plucked off
any of the leaves. From this whole and untried state,
a person does things like having children, learning
to plant new things, shooting pigs; and in regard to
performing all sorts of activities like planting
something he had not planted before, or shooting a
cassowary, he is nemblin - 'whole', 'untried', in
that respect. The attitude towards achievement is
similar to that implied by the much more formal recognition given by Iatmul to achievement or first
performance through naven behaviour (Bateson 1936).
Progressively as the Gnau man proves himself in these
things, the restrictions protecting him are lifted.
Progressively he moves towards that eventual state of
old age which they call biwola. Thus his first child
is said to be nemblisa - the child of his 'wholeness', or of his whole blood. Each subsequent child
is relatively less the child of his whole blood than

the one before; and the taboos between siblings which
depend on birth order are phrased by reference to
this diminishing completeness of their source. As
the individual moves from maturity in this nembli
sense, he declines towards old age, biwolen, and he
is allowed more and more of the things which were
wola, which would before have endangered him with
illness, a premature decrepitude. Thus for a death
which comes in old age, they do not usually search
out an explanation by specifying some particular
cause.

The motives of Gnau behaviour in illness

Illness for the Gnau is a state in which many factors
may play a part. The conventions of their behaviour
when ill give a general uniformity to the outward
show of illness and tend to mask the different and
distinguishing signs of syndromes or symptom complex-
es. The sick appear most wretched and degraded; they
are cut off from normal life. They are well able to
describe the intention of this behaviour and they explain it in this general way: 'If you are ill you
are in danger of continued or aggravated illness from
which you could die. You are in danger of attracting
the attention of many spirits, and you are weak. You

must abstain from foods which you know spirits are
likely to be watching over, and especially if you
know which spirit is at work in your illness you must
not eat any of those foods with which it is particularly associated. If you ate them, it might say "Have
I not warned you already and you go eating my things
again?". You withdraw from normal activity and conversation because other people may bring with them
dangerous influences either from their sexual or ritual condition, or from spirits which follow or watch
over them, and may turn their eyes towards you or
smell you out in your weakness and turn aside to
strike you and compound your illness. Once ill you
are in greater danger of further and cumulative attack. You must appear wretched, for in this way you
may deceive a spirit into thinking that its aim,
which is your bodily ruin, has been accomplished and
it may leave you.'

The chief features therefore are the patient's
vulnerability, hence his need to avoid drawing
attention to himself and to appear wretched. Sympathy gatherings are held for sick people but the
patient does not participate in them, is often not
visible, nor do visitors go to see him. People
should not be loose-tongued in speaking a sick man's

name; in some circumstances it is forbidden. Sometimes I have seen a very ill man twitch with agitation and tremble because women crowded too close
around him. In many ways their behaviour when ill
resembles a _rite de passage_; it is indeed a life
crisis. The end of illness and the return to normal
life is marked by the patient going to bathe and wash
away the filth of his illness; the usual way they say
'I am better' is in fact by the implication of the
phrase 'I have washed'.

The form is close to that of a _rite de passage_,
containing elements of separation, marginality and
aggregation (e.g. the changes of attire, the withdrawal, silence, food abstention, the final purifying
wash). It is expressive and conventionalised. In
illness, the person passes through a crisis: as with
puberty or childbirth or death, the timing of the
events is, at least to our view, set by nature rather
than society. The word 'crisis' applies aptly to
illness with its accompanying threat of loss of life,
mutilation, or such damage as will deprive the sufferer of his independence and fitness to fulfil his
obligations and his hopes, or deprive him of his
previous status. The behaviour emphasizes marginality; withdrawal from danger, abstention from normal

life in the hope that it will protect the victim from
a bad or the worst outcome. But in contrast to the
rites for puberty, maturity, birth, marriage or
death, the crisis of illness is not usually among the
Gnau the prelude to assumption of a new social status,
but rather, by the illness itself, the victim is un-
fitted or forced from his usual position in society.
The conventionalised aspects of the behaviour in illness underline or signal this unfit state, an unwelcome change, to other people. If the patient survives
it, he hopes to return to his previous status, not
to some new one.

In some other societies, the illness is itself
the passport to a new status, or provided the possibility of achieving it: in the Ndembu cults of affliction described by Turner, certain rights of participation and certain roles are open only to those who
have passed through the illness and its treatment
(Turner 1968). An illness interpreted as possession
by pathogenic spirits is often 'the normal road to
the assumption of the shaman's calling' (I.M. Lewis
1971). Among the Gnau this view of affliction is
almost absent; but primacy in holding one large
ritual (that of Malyi), which was acquired by the
Gnau from a neighbouring tribe, is given to the line-

age descendants of the man who was first struck down
by the spirit and for whose treatment it was bought
and learned: his descendants are those who now direct
and officiate in the performance of this ritual. But
those who themselves have been struck down by the
spirit remain in their opinion at greater risk than
others from it, and take care not to approach the
spirit's image or to eat in the men's house where it
is housed, or to sing there for it when its full
ritual is performed.

The classification of illness

Apart from the general nature of illness, there is
the question of the classification of kinds of illness. I have already indicated that the Gnau do not
depend on observation of the physical signs or
symptoms of illnesses to discriminate between them;
in this they differ from Subanun, Zande, or Lunda
people and ourselves, who each have a more precise
scheme for illnesses, differentiated by their clinical signs.[2] In our system of medicine, signs or

---

2 Skin diseases must be excepted, for the Gnau make
   fine distinctions between different skin fungus
   diseases, and name variously some defects of the
   skin.

symptoms are the indicators of disease; the disease
can be inferred from these observations. Although
Gnau people could describe pains or physiological
disorders, such descriptions were rarely given by
patients.

A collection of descriptions of symptoms is not
the same as a set of disease names: it does not necessarily imply a classification - at least not in
the systematic or conceptual sense. The contrast or
distinction is that between percept and concept: one
can describe one's perceptions of illness without
necessarily organising these by some conceptual
scheme of kinds of illness. Classification is used
to organise knowledge and the selection of features
used in a classification is usually significant for
some purpose: the subject matter comes to be organ-
ised into a system. In studying the principles of
division in a classification we hope to discover
something of what others judge to be significant and
relevant.

The Gnau used a few verbs to differentiate the
severity of sickness; they also distinguish sickness
of the whole person from that of a part. However
they also classified illness further, not at the
level of its manifestations, but at that of its

causes. Once someone had become sick in the serious
sense of <u>neyigeg</u>, it was common for them to refer to
what had happened or was happening to him by naming
the cause. Treatment depended on identifying it.
Since in their view causes were not discernible from
the clinical signs, exact description or examination
of these was not relevant. Cause and remedy were to
be revealed by other evidence than that of the body's
state.

One might be tempted to say of the Gnau that
they have no word to distinguish illness from other
afflictions or misfortunes: the word <u>wola</u> does not.
On the other hand they have a verb (<u>neyigeg</u>) which is
quite specific for the critical field of illness.[3]
At what level of interpretation is it right to say
that some people do not distinguish bodily from other
affliction? I doubt that anyone intends to imply it
in the literal sense and suggest that they lack per-
ceptual sensory awareness of the boundary between
self and things outside themselves. Lévy-Bruhl proposed that primitive man's outlook on the world

---

3   The names for objects, events or kin relation-
    ships are easier to study and classify – or
    perhaps just more obvious – than verbs: at least
    it is nearly always nouns, occasionally adject-
    ives, which appear in the taxonomies analysed and
    drawn up by anthropologists.

differed from ours because various collective repres-
entations so ordered his understanding that he conceived there sometimes was a mystical participation
between himself and certain things of the outside
world. He did not argue that the senses or cerebral
structure of primitive man differed from ours.
Piaget, from his studies of child cognition, also put
forward the view that a child does not distinguish
clearly between his self and the outside world; the
physical world is not sharply divided off as material
and inanimate but instead is treated as thought it
were 'alive, responsive and willing'. Both have
suggested that people can have blurred views of the
distinction between a blow struck on one's self and
one which struck one's discarded clothing or a tree.
When it is said that illness is not discriminated
from other afflictions, what is meant, I take it, is
that the causes and explanations for both kinds of
misfortune are thought to be the same. However, the
outstanding and universal subjective property of illness is that it afflicts the individual person. In
behaviour, in the conventional withdrawal of the Gnau
patient, the personal crisis of illness is sharply
differentiated from other misfortune.

A clinical classification of disease as detail-

ed as the one described by Frake (1961) for the
Subanun of the Philippines provokes question of the
reason for so many names: he recorded 186 human disease names; 132 of these were single word labels for
diagnostic categories, the rest standard descriptive
categories like 'stomach ache' or 'swollen liver'.
One might expect that if diseases are named by reference to their clinical manifestations, then these
signs are significant either because they indicate a
cause or because they have a bearing on the treatment
to be used. In the reports of Evans-Pritchard on
Zande leechcraft (Evans-Pritchard 1937), and of Turner on Lunda medicine (Turner 1963), this seems to be
the case. In both examples they describe treatment
by specifics, by herbs and medicines whose appropriate composition depends on recognizing the kind of
illness by its symptoms. The fact that they have
herbal remedies, or some explanation for the nature
of symptoms, does not necessarily replace a set of
explanations or remedies on a different level, for
instance explanation by witchcraft. The analysis of
how such a system (involving explanation at different
levels) worked was of course a central theme of
Evans-Pritchard's first book on the Azande. Although
Frake was dealing with Subanun diagnosis, not treat-

ment, he mentions that 'everyone is his own herbalist' and that 'diagnosis - the decision of what name
to apply to an instance of being sick - is a pivotal
cognitive step in the selection of culturally appropriate responses to illness by the Subanun. It bears
on the selection of ordinary botanically-derived
medicinal remedies from 724 recorded alternatives'
(Frake 1961: 131).

In comparison the Gnau are poor as herbalists.
They rely on stinging nettle leaves as counter-
irritants, or small cuts over sites of pain. They
have some bark and sap dressings for cuts and sores,
and on these they also occasionally put white silt
from the river, lime, or urine. They prepare bark
poultices for painful joints, they chew ginger for
colds or sore throats (or another aromatic bark).
But in serious illness, only nettle leaves are commonly used. They use no specific herbs in the sense of
plants whose medicinal use depends on the clinical
signs observed. But there are many plants which must
be used in ritual treatment, although few are eaten
or rubbed or plastered on the patient's body: their
use is dependent on identification of cause and on
knowledge of the complex relationships between
spirits and plants.

Responsibility in assuming sick behaviour

I would like to go over some of the more striking
features of these observations. When a Gnau person
thinks his illness involves a threat to himself as a
whole, he behaves in a way that indicates this clearly to others. Sickness in this sense is thought to
be critical because the Gnau believe that it involves
a threat to life - the recognition 'he will die'
implied in the etymology of the verb neyigeg (which
perhaps I should note escaped me for a long time during my field work). The causes said to produce it,
such as spirits, destructive magic and sorcery, are
explicitly and conventionally held to cause lethal
illness, not just illness, and the outcome will be
death unless appropriate and effective treatment can
be performed. Once ill, the sick person is more
vulnerable to further attack and compounded illness.
His isolation and withdrawal from normal life contains an important element of prudence.

        The decision that his illness is critical rests
with the sick person. He is judge of when he is at
risk, and he discerns this mainly on subjective
grounds - his sense of being ill, but he may also
take into account the dangers he has exposed himself
to and any signs or revelations such as those of

dreams or strange events. Recognition of critical
illness is in principle held to be private to the
individual, not questionable or requiring legitimat-
ion or proof in objective physical signs in the clinical sense. However, children must at first depend
on the judgement of others when they fall ill and
people do assess by general appearance how seriously
ill someone else is, and also sometimes give advice
to others to be more careful; they may comment on or
question the severity of someone's illness when they
talk to other people about it. The conventions for
sick behaviour mask differences in the objective effects of various illnesses and make it hard to assess
severity. The intention to dissemble, to appear more
wretched and ill than one feels, to trick a spirit
into leaving, is an explicit element in this behaviour - again it is a matter of prudence. The outward
appearance of illness may be deceptive. This the
Gnau know, but they are not convinced that the way to
find this out is by inspection and examination of the
sick person. Malingering, the pretence of severe
illness, was mentioned to me a number of times as a
trick used commonly by those who secretly intended to
burst forth disguised as evil ancestors (mami wolen-
dem) during the night performance of a particular

dance ritual (<u>Wolpililyiwa</u>), and also occasionally by
those who planned a murder.

   If one accepts their opinion that the individual knows if he is critically ill and that others cannot really tell true from pretended illness by objective clinical signs, and if illness is also a legitimate ground for avoiding normal obligation, one may
ask what stops them from pretending illness often to
evade unpleasant duty? The question is connected
with the more subtle one of deciding whether their
conventions about illness tend to encourage the
valetudinarian, or to allow illness to become an in-
dulgence. The social isolation, starving, dirt and
abject lot of someone who is critically sick seemed
to me very discouraging. There are few comforts for
the sick. A man whose serious illness dragged on for
many weeks lay much of the time naked, silent, and
alone in a small smoky hut with the door shut and
therefore in the dark, hearing people's voices outside but not talked to; sometimes for part of the day
he had to lie in his excrement; late in his illness
he developed a toxic psychosis and was visited at
times by people who came to wail over him at his approaching death. His isolation and debility were
pitiful.

With the decision to behave as critically ill
comes dependence on others as well as exemption from
some obligations. The responsibility for providing
treatment, for searching out and bringing someone to
carry it out if necessary, rests with close kin primarily and then with the wider circle of co-villagers.
Occasionally the patient himself may perform some
small treatment ritual for himself; commonly he will
give some indication of what he thinks needs doing.
In part his behaviour while ill - his deceptive
wretchedness, abstinence from certain foods, for example - is intended to be protective and remedial,
self-determined treatment. But in general the sick
person must submit to the decisions of others, he
cannot fetch the ritual plants he needs. He appears
apathetic and miserable. If others decide to provide
some treatment, he submits, perhaps without knowing
the deductions which have led them to choose to do
it, for it is not necessarily discussed with him
beforehand. If his mother's brothers persuade his
own brothers that he has a better chance of recovery
if he is moved to their hamlet, then off he is taken.
The energy and urgency with which other people arrange
to treat someone who is ill, the gatherings in sympathy at the hamlet where he lies, provide an index

of their feelings and esteem, their sense of obligation, for him. In the case of at least one man, I
know the neglect and indifference shown by his relatives and neighbours was very bitter to him.

As inferences about the cause of an illness are
not thought of as arising from physical examination
there is no reason to pay special attention to clinical signs or to grant the healer special rights to
examine the patient's body. The patient waits for
people to treat him, for his relatives to arrange
this or to send for someone. He submits to treatment
rather than cooperates in it.

Problems of comparison: illness and disease

At the outset I said that only the word _wola_ would
cover all their ailments. The word means 'bad' and
can be used in many other and much wider contexts
than ailment: a man who has recently taken part in
ritual is _wolen_ in the sense of being dangerous to
others; a woman menstruating is _wola_, both dangerous
to men and vulnerable herself. Her withdrawal from
normal life, her purifying wash after her menstrual
period is ended, offer parallels to the behaviour of
someone sick in the _neyigeg_ sense; but she is not
spoken of as _neyigeg_, only as _wola_. The same would

apply to a woman in and after childbirth. The area
of ills of the person or self, not merely the part,
is the one circumscribed by neyigeg and it denotes
present active critical illness. The medical correl-
ates of neyigeg vary greatly; it may only be a headache. It excludes long-standing, slowly changing
disorders or completed ones;[4] instead they describe
people with these as biwola, as wretched, ruined or
old. These are not seen as critical destroying illnesses.

In attempting to compare the boundaries the
Gnau give to illness with our own, we may be led to
ask if our view has clear limits. Do we define the
field of medicine clearly? It may be futile or
frustrating to look for equivalents for medicine in
other societies if medicine is a vague concept and
peculiar to our own way of thinking.

In English, 'medicine' can be given the traditional meaning of the art of healing. There have been
sick people ever since man inhabited the earth. Or
medicine can be given the meaning it has come to have
now, that is, study of the diagnosis, treatment and
prevention of disease. The traditional sense, the

---

4   Perhaps rather similarly, we do not usually speak
    of mental defect or certain congenital anomalies
    as illnesses.

art of healing, implies that medicine is concerned
with sick people or patients, with conditions of man;
while the modern sense, study and control of disease,
implies rather study of a thing, disease. The change
of emphasis from conditions of people to a study of
disease entities is attested to in the history of
European medicine. It is associated especially with
Thomas Sydenham who repudiated the general supposit-
ion 'that diseases are no more than the confused and
irregular operations of disordered and debilitated
nature and consequently that it is fruitless to
labour to endeavour to give a just description of
them'. Instead he maintained that 'nature, in the
production of disease, is uniform and consistent.....
The self-same phenomenon that you observe in the
sickness of a Socrates, you would observe in the
sickness of a simpleton' (Sydenham 1676). Sydenham's
view has come to dominate nosology. Before him, disease had been considered as a deviation from the
normal in which a healthy man through the influence
of any number of factors - physical or mental - was
changed and suffered. We could, following Cohen
(1961), formulate this view as $A \xrightarrow{\downarrow\downarrow\downarrow} A'$ where A was a
healthy man. The later view was that disease was a
distinct entity. In the second view, when a healthy

man A fell ill, he became A + B, where B is a disease
(A $\xrightarrow{B}$ A + B). The view maintained that there were in-
numerable Bs, each with its individual and recogniz-
able characteristics. The recognition of disease
entities through patterns of symptoms and signs is
not of course restricted to Europe. Evans-Pritchard,
for example, wrote of the Azande: 'In such cases the
disease has to be diagnosed and named and a specific
remedy applied. This very naming and identification
of the disease objectifies and gives it a reality of
its own independent of witchcraft...' (Evans-Pritchard
1937: 508). But the Gnau view is not like that.

Our diagnostic nomenclature is largely a taxonomy by pathological anatomy: it classifies morphological form, not clinical function; disease, but not
people or illness; it is a classification by clinical
inference rather than one by clinical observation.
At the end of examination, the doctor covers over all
the clinical detail by giving a diagnostic label to
the patient's illness. I summarize the analysis of
Feinstein (1967) who, in his critique of clinical
judgement, calls for a clinician's nomenclature which
should classify a host, and an illness, and a disease.
Either the traditional view of medicine or the modern
one obliges us to look further - if medicine is the

art of healing, what is the state or process in man
that is to be healed? The answer is 'sickness'; then
what is 'sickness'? Or if we take the second view,
then we must define disease.

It is unusual to find a general concept of disease made explicit in medical writing: such writing
abounds instead with concepts of particular diseases.
From a biological standpoint, certain kinds of change
in any living species may be called disease. In
global perspective such changes may be seen to result
from varied causes such as genetic change, maladapt-
ion to environment, environmental change, the predat-
ory, parasitic, and competitive habits of different
organisms - bacteria for instance. The concept of
disease is focussed on the individual of a species.
The delicate spirochaete of syphilis must be precisely set conditions to live and these are given by the
human body: it is in terms of its effects on individuals of the human species that we call syphilis a
disease. We call it a disease because it alters the
physiological and psychological functions of the
individual man or woman and these functional changes
reduce the capacity of the affected individual to
survive or reproduce. These are the essential features of a biological view of disease. I assert then

that doctors recognize disease through particular disorders of physiological and psychological function.

Man, unlike trees or beasts, can reflect on and
talk about changes in himself. I use the word 'disease' to set it in a biological frame and I use the
word 'illness' to distinguish - perhaps artificially
to emphasize - that people recognize either in themselves or others certain changes of body or mind as
undesired, as ills, and that what particular people
so recognize may vary. I wish to contrast, on the
one hand, 'disease' defined by criteria of a biological nature, and applying generally to the human
species, with, on the other hand, 'illness' which
will be determined by the views of particular individuals or cultures - it is of a social and psychological nature. By using disease in the biological
sense we set bounds about the field relevant to our
inquiry. By reference to 'illness' we examine how
individuals perceive and interpret changes in their
condition. The reason for making this distinction is
to clarify what we are about if, for example, we wish
to examine the nebulous view that disease may affect
culture and culture affect disease. A social
anthropologist may quite well find that some diseases
are not regarded as 'illness' by those he studies;

he may find illness of the body apparently undifferentiated from other misfortunes such as a house
catching fire or drought failure. He may urge then
that medicine is a category like 'magic' or 'religion'
tainted by our particular conceptual bias, but this
would be hard to use in comparative study.

The sphere thought proper to medicine depends
on the conceptions of health and illness which prevail
in the society; these suggest for example what people
expect doctors to treat. In Samuel Butler's Erewhon
you find the problem in a nutshell:

In that country, if a man... catches any disorder,
or fails bodily in any way before he is seventy
years old, he is tried before a jury of his country
men, and if convicted is held up to public scorn
and sentenced more or less severely as the case may
be.... But if a man forges a cheque or sets his
house on fire or robs with violence from the person
or does any other such things as are criminal in
our country, he is either taken to a hospital or
most carefully tended at the public expense, or if
he is in good circumstances, he lets it be known to
all his friends that he is suffering from a severe
fit of immorality... and they come and visit him
with great solicitude, and inquire with interest

how it all came about, what symptoms first showed
themselves and so forth.

Erewhon was of course nowhere, but the problem it
suggests is this: should the medical ethnographer in
Erewhon concentrate on the management of embezzlers
or dyspeptics? In my view he should study the
dyspeptics.

The grounds for accepting that disease in modern medicine should be conceived in biological and
objective terms and lack any essential social features have been discussed - especially in reference to
mental illness and criminal responsibility (see P.
Halmos 1957: chap. 2; A.J. Lewis 1953; B. Wootton
1959: chaps. 7 and 8). I will not present the case
in detail here but only indicate some of the crucial
issues presented by the authors I have just referred
to. I think a strong case in favour of this view can
be made. If such a view is valid, then we have the
means to keep social well-being apart from health,
and disease separate from social deviance or maladj-
ustment: if we keep them distinct conceptually we are
better placed to observe their interrelations. But
even if disease criteria are in essence physiological
and psychological, we must often be highly dependent
on knowing the social and cultural background in

order to appraise the conduct and efficiency of these
functions. We cannot ignore social considerations
when we assess their adequacy but we are not bound to
consider whether the behaviour is socially deviant in
order to decide if disease is present.

The point of the argument is that some have
proposed social adaptation as a yardstick for health
or mental health. But how do we decide success or
failure in social adaptation? Who sets the criteria
or indications of maladaptation? If social disapproval plays a large part in deciding what is called
maladaptation then this will vary from group to group
who express the disapproval. Then the decision on
whether disease was present would depend on which
group expressed the disapproval. The demarcation of
health and disease would be shifting - for example,
with the state and saturation of the employment
market if the ability to hold a job were a criterion
of social adaptation and therefore of health. If
social adaptation is the criterion of health it is
possible that the valued and desired state, which
adaptation is to attain or maintain, may itself turn
out to be health: in so far as that is true social
adaptation will be a tautology for health. For these
chief reasons I think we are wise to accept external

biological criteria of disease, and to compare these
with the concepts of illness which prevail in a
particular society, rather than to depend solely on
sociological definitions of illness.

Health

In most of what I have written so far, my explicit
concern has been with illness, with the recognition
of disease. The uncovered side of the coin is health.
The biological view of disease, which I briefly presented, in effect implied that for practical purposes
health may be defined as the absence of identifiable
disease or infirmity - a negative view. But among us
health has much more commonly received recognition as
an ideal, for example by the World Health Organisat-
ion whose constitution begins: 'Health is a state of
complete physical, mental and social well-being and
not merely the absence of disease or infirmity'.
Ideals involve notions that go beyond what is to what
ought to be. Since their claim is to formulate what
ought to be rather than what is they cannot be verif-
ied in the sense of being shown to correspond to fact.
The doctor proceeds from knowledge of the range of
normal function and the evidences of normal structure;
but the knowledge of different organs and systems

varies greatly. The criteria of normality in medicine are both statistical and ideal. They are ideal
in the sense that the proper functioning of different
organs is conceived with the help of teleology – the
scientist tries to determine what the relationships
of different organs are, what purposes they serve; it
entails the notion of proper function adequate to a
purpose. Many of the most important functions of the
organism are those which regulate and integrate the
working of separate systems; some ideal of integration and balance, and the separate contribution of
different parts to this whole, comes to be involved
in judgements of adequacy. In practice the doctor
has no reliable positive indications of when ideal
balance is achieved; instead he considers healthy the
man who is free from any evidence of disease or infirmity. Health in the positive sense is an ideal,
'approached but not attained' (Polgar 1968).

In his article on health, Polgar distinguishes
this asymptotic view of health from two other kinds
which he terms the elastic concept and the open-ended
view. The elastic view holds that health is an accumulated resistance to potential dangers. The view
adopted is a preventive one which foresees illness as
likely to happen in some form. In the open-ended

view, health has no definite limits; put briefly,
health is anything better than death. The implicit
view of health which the Gnau would appear to hold
comes close to the elastic view in which illness is
part of living or a risk of living. There is a normal course of life in which vigour and strength to
resist illness waxes and then wanes; such a view
makes the deaths of infants and the old more ordinary
than those of people in their prime. Many of their
rules of behaviour, especially their taboos, are
phrased as rules of prudence by which health may be
preserved. As I went round the village during an
epidemic of influenza, I came to one man sitting in
his hamlet, where there were many lying scattered
about miserably in the dirt, and he said: 'I have not
got it. I am a hardwood post. I am well.' The idea
of resistance was expressed clearly and with pride.
Similarly the notion of variable resistance can be
deduced from the tentative, testing way people try
out the foods that were specially forbidden them when
ill, and the progressive way in which foods that were
once taboo become permissible after someone has shown
that he can do something, or has passed the stage of
vulnerability. In old age the most enduring food
taboos are lifted, but people argue uncertainly that

this is because the food will not matter if it debil-
itates them since enfeeblement and weakening are
natural to old age. The old are not expected to
maintain, or in the same way to husband their health;
old men have fulfilled their duties and should stand
aside to watch the young men kill their game. To
quote the words of a Gnau man as he invoked his ancestral dead at a hunting ritual for a grandchild:

Now we two have long been full grown men; no longer
will we kill pigs - no, these young men are growing
up to hunt, we now eat forbidden foods, we have
begotten children who are now grown up and adult...
Our children have borne children. The things of
hunting are for us no longer; we eat the (forbidden)
foods which scare game away. Shall we still kill?
These young men, they must kill; they, young men,
rise up and kill their game because they are still
men with the good smell, the smell of youth.

The notion of health as resistance still allows
it the quality of an ideal. It is desired and admired. Men and women take pride in good health. But
they imagine that the malicious spirits may sometimes
look on a vigorous person and say, 'there is a young
man, flaunting himself, I will make him shout with
pain', and strike him down in preference to a decrepit

unappealing old man. I can quote a tape-recorded
example of this kind of thinking, though it was expressed in joke. An old man retorted to a young man
who had teased him:

> When I am dead and you come along my path I will
> fasten tight around you - fine young man! You come
> along my path - I will strike you; and when the old
> dry yam-mami (i.e. an old man) comes along I'll let
> him be; that appetising one there, that's the one
> my eyes will rest on - aargh! strike him down, that
> one!

Conclusions

In discussing the behaviour of the sick person, I
have raised the question of comparison and the use of
a category such as 'medicine' in anthropology. It is
clear that not all societies agree about the conditions to be counted as illness. They hold various
views about the causes involved. I have asked
whether there were any clear external grounds to differentiate the sector of human misfortune we call
disease or illness, and argued that there were certain biological criteria for doing so. If these were
acceptable then we would have a basis for comparing
the social or cultural factors affecting its occur-

rence, recognition and treatment. If, on the other
hand, it were argued that social criteria necessarily
played a large part in deciding what was to be called
disease, then the decision would vary from group to
group; the demarcation of disease would shift and we
would be worse placed to analyse the interrelations
between disease and culture. In passing I would
point out that the biological standpoint which I ad-
vocate applies equally in our own culture, and puts
the onus on medicine in our society to show what
there is that is harmful to survival or reproduction
about some of the human conditions which our society
defines as appropriate for medical care. It may
equally oblige us to reconsider and to recognize that
sometimes what we call illness is only what we are
brought up to disapprove of. It is also true that,
with the development of medical knowledge, we have
been led to realise that the causes of some kinds of
condition or behaviour are biological, and not sin,
immorality or wickedness; and our treatment of such
conditions has sometimes thereby changed to become
more reasonable, effective and humane. To look at
another society and see how they delimit the field of
illness and how they treat it may bring us to a
clearer recognition of how far social forces or

convention determine responses to disease and affect
its outcome.

But apart from this comparative issue, I also
considered whether there was anything about disease
which might lead us to expect a universal recognition
of illness as distinctive in some way from other misfortunes. It has been argued that in some societies
illness is not distinguished from other forms of misfortune. The fact, often recorded, that the causes
of illness are the same as those for other kinds of
misfortune does not convince me that illness is not
distinguished. Among English people, there are some
ready to speak of bad luck causing illness; that bad
luck may show itself in illness or a lost bet does
not imply failure to distinguish the kinds of misfortune any more than the fact that fire may burn a
house or someone's skin implies the forms of misfortune are not distinguished. Why should the same not
be true of a spirit which causes crop failure and
human infertility? My point of departure was the
recognition of sickness in a person. The reason is
simple; for it is what has happened to him or her
that must be helped, healed or explained. If people
did not fall sick, as they do in every society, there
would be no need to find explanations or causes for

such misfortunes or to treat them. Illness is a distinctive form of misfortune by its outstanding characteristic. Some individual is directly harmed.
That individual, a self, is the subject, or for
others the human object, of the harm, having a private direct experience of it which cannot be equally
or identically shared by anyone else. Thus illness
is a misfortune sensed by the sick person in ways
which other misfortunes, like his house burning down,
are not. And since some diseases destroy or maim the
individual, having the power to alter or abolish a
living identified member of that society, it seems to
me unlikely that any society would fail to distinguish
at least part of the whole field of disease from
other misfortunes.

The discussion of whether illness can be distinguished from other kinds of misfortune is in part
obscured by an ambiguity when one speaks of illness,
arising out of its dual reference both to causal
entities and to the conditions of people. Illness
would not be known without the change in condition of
a person first occurring. The essential criteria of
the biological view of disease, namely, functional
changes that harm the capacity of an individual to
survive and reproduce, are matters of life and death,

and essential to the continuation of any society.
In the Gnau word for critical sickness (<u>neyigeg</u>) we
find recognition of this relationship to death; and
I think the great emphasis on the treatment of infertility and barrenness that is found, for example,
in the indigenous medicine of various West African
peoples, the stress on this as a major component of
medicine, becomes more readily understandable with
the realisation of what is involved in the biological
view of disease.

Once the condition is recognized, there follows
the question of its explanation and the question of
how illness is placed in a given cosmology.

REFERENCES

BATESON, G. 1936. <u>Naven</u>. Cambridge: Cambridge
    University Press.

COHEN, H. 1961. The evolution of the concept of
    disease <u>in</u> Lush, B. (ed.) <u>Concepts of Medicine</u>.
    Oxford: Pergamon Press.

EVANS-PRITCHARD, E.E. 1937. <u>Witchcraft, Oracles and
    Magic among the Azande</u>. Oxford: Clarendon Press.

FEINSTEIN, A.R. 1967. <u>Clinical Judgement</u>. Balti-
    more, Md.: Williams and Wilkins.

FRAKE, C.O. 1961. The diagnosis of disease among
    the Subanun of Mindanao. <u>American Anthropologist</u>
    62: 113-32.

HALMOS, P. 1957. Towards a Measure of Man; the
   frontiers of normal adjustment. London: Routledge
   and Kegan Paul.

JASPERS, K. 1963. General Psychopathology. Trans-
   lated from the German 7th Edition by J. Hoenig and
   M.W. Hamilton. Manchester: Manchester University
   Press.

LEWIS, A.J. 1953. Health as a social concept.
   British Journal of Sociology 4: 109-24.

LEWIS, I.M. 1971. Ecstatic Religion. Harmondsworth:
   Penguin Books.

POLGAR, S. 1968. Health. In the International
   Encyclopedia of the Social Sciences. New York:
   Macmillan and Free Press.

SYDENHAM, T. 1676. Medical Observations concerning
   the History and Cure of Acute Diseases (3rd Edition 1676) in The Works of Thomas Sydenham, translated by R.G. Latham, Vol. 1. The Sydenham
   Society 1848.

TURNER, V.W. 1963. Lunda Medicine and the Treatment
   of Disease. Rhodes-Livingstone Museum Occasional
   Paper No. 15. Livingstone.

-- 1968. The Drums of Affliction. Oxford: Clarendon
   Press.

WOOTTON, B. 1959. Social Science and Social Pathology. London: George Allen and Unwin.

MURRAY LAST

THE PRESENTATION OF SICKNESS IN A COMMUNITY
OF NON-MUSLIM HAUSA

The purpose of this paper is to show some of the variables that affect the generation and use of concepts
relating to sickness. The paper takes the form of a
field report, and thus raises not only the problems
involved in a field study, such us, for example, the
question of a 'biological base-line', but also the
complexity observable in the presentation of sickness.
I suggest that these are necessary preliminaries to a
discussion of Hausa concepts of sickness; that it is
important to delimit the times and the places when
particular concepts are, and are not, operative, and
when and where contradictory or supplementary systems
of thought are employed. Failure to use certain concepts seems to me as important as their use, and
studies of medical symbolism which omit the failures
are analytically defective. Built into a symbolic
system is appropriateness: it is this variable,

appropriateness, that is at the basis of this essay.
Included in an appendix, however, is an outline of
Hausa medical concepts which may elucidate some of
the terms used below and serve as material for comparison.

Field Study

The following data are based on field work in a community of Hausa peasants.[1] The plains of Hausaland
lie in the West African savannah, with six months (or
30-50 inches) of rain a year; the rainfall is sufficient to support densities of up to 400 persons per
square mile. Though the majority of the population
is rural, the area is noted for its large walled cities of considerable antiquity; Kano, for example, has
had iron furnaces since about the 7th century. The
cities have populations of 75,000 and more, while
many district headquarter towns contain 10,000 to
20,000 people. The urban and village population is

1 I am grateful to the Social Science Research
   Council for financing the research from 1968 to
   1971. One of the purposes of this study was to
   provide material for medical students in the
   Faculty of Medicine, Ahmadu Bello University,
   Zaria. I am much indebted to the Vice-Chancellor
   and to the Director of the Institute of Health at
   Ahmadu Bello University for their encouragement
   and hospitality throughout my work. A fuller
   account of Hausa medicine is in preparation.

Muslim and increasingly concerned with the proper
practice of Islam, including the seclusion of women.
Within Hausaland, on the margins of the Muslim areas,
are non-Muslim Hausa, the Maguzawa. For them there
is no seclusion of women, nor do they live in villages. Like most Hausa they are primarily farmers,
but, unlike the Muslims, only a few maintain a secondary occupation for the dry season. Owing to their
dispersed pattern of settlement on the margins of the
denser-populated Muslim areas, the Maguzawa live
among Muslim Fulani pastoralists. Although I did six
months' work on sickness among Hausa of all kinds, I
am presenting here only the data on the Maguzawa
with whom I lived for eighteen months. I will not be
comparing Muslim and non-Muslim Hausa: suffice it to
say that the differences between them do not seem to
be very great, though, because of purdah, Hausa women
are virtually impossible as a subject of study for a
male investigator.

Evenness in data was a prime concern. In a
matter as subjective as the assessment of sickness,
the fewer different judgements embodied in different
parts of the data the better. For this reason I
used neither assistant nor interpreter, except that
all the people with whom I lived were in effect

assistants and interpreters, and their judgements I
could compare with mine. Since one never knew when
someone would fall ill, I had to stay in the community almost continuously for the eighteen months. I
did not use questionnaires: earlier I had experiment-
ed with one for three months and found that the value
of the data was vitiated by variations in interview-
ing conditions, and that these variations were impossible to avoid, though easy to induce: for example,
medical histories varied with the time of day at
which the interview took place. The length of time
I spent in the community was important: after nine
months it seemed I had most of the data I wanted;
after eighteen months I had a largely different set
of data. People's confidence, their experience of
one's medical help, the chance occurrence of an interesting disease - these variables affect data, as
they do, mutatis mutandis, in all anthropological
studies; but possibly more so in sickness, since
sickness is a personal, often private, subject. It
is not that all the information given is wrong;
rather one often cannot know what item is wrong or
incomplete. And mere consistency is no guarantee of
accuracy.

A community studied without assistance is

inevitably small. I lived in a farmstead of some
120 people - 20 men, 40 women and 60 children. Outside this farmstead, I limited myself to other Hausa,
Muslim or non-Muslim, and to Fulani who lived in dispersed houses or camps nearby, a population of some
2,500. Clearly for the farmstead I might in theory
know almost everything; these data are the core of my
study, a single very extended case.

Though accuracy of data can become a fruitless
obsession, in a study such as this accuracy was always in jeopardy in one sector; namely, what (in
western scientific terms) exactly was the pathology
in any one person, whether sick or seemingly well?
Medically my judgement is simply that of an interested
anthropologist, and so worth little. In trying to
circumvent this problem, I was given great help by
the doctors and staff of the University hospitals:
they examined and treated all whom I brought in, and
they visited me at least once a month. Though people
were treated and cured, the treatment sometimes had
to be symptomatic: frequently neither the doctors nor
I ever knew precisely what was or was not wrong. Had
I therefore been medically qualified, my judgement
might have been better and more acceptable, but still
not adequate for statistical purposes. Without con-

siderable laboratory support accurate diagnosis in a
strictly medical sense is minimal; yet discussions of
indigenous concepts of sickness often involve western
terms for various diseases, and consequently imply
both a set of symptoms and the course the disease
takes.

Another feature of the study was my desire to
look, not just at those who were sick, but at the
whole population, and to concentrate on the patient,
or the potential patient, before he made any choice
of treatment or saw any healer. Healers in all their
variety took second place in this enquiry, as indeed
they do in practice: otherwise one studies a pre-
selected population. But, as I was myself classified
as in some ways a healer, my very presence constit-
uted an invitation to talk sickness. This was a constant, and controllable, factor. But on moral grounds
I also had, in effect, to spoil my case studies: I
could not let people die. In the event, some people
refused to go to hospital and sometimes I was too
late; I therefore saw a certain indeterminate number
of cases from start to finish.

In short, if accuracy, particularly statistical
accuracy, is required, a field study of sickness and
health presents considerable problems. Populations

and personalities of course differ, and much depends
on chance; an element of subjectivity, an element of
the unrepeatable, inevitably occurs. Yet in order to
make constructive comparisons, whether within one
study or with the results of other studies, what is
to be compared must be at a similar level of accuracy, preferably in both the anthropological and the
strictly medical data. But the time and personnel
required, the size and structure of the population,
and the number of cases studied, may make this impossible to achieve.[2] In my work I do not pretend to
have attained satisfactory accuracy in more than a
narrow area; instead I think the study has revealed
some of the limitations which are perhaps inherent in
this field.

Who gets sick?

Without going into the definition of 'sick' (leaving
it, for the moment, as those who cannot do their
normal day's work) the answer to this question is:
women and their children, not men. The average number of working days lost per man for the year was

2   The recent Johns Hopkins' report on the epidem-
    iology of Chad (Buck 1970) illustrates the limit-
    ations of the predominantly medical study.

approximately five, and represented two bouts of
fever. A number of minor complaints, such as toothache or headache, were common enough, but not sufficient to affect a man for a whole workday. Only
guineaworm, which can immobilise a person for a month
or more, was a major cause of work lost, and this was
confined to two farmsteads in a particular year:
otherwise occasional cases occurred randomly over the
area and over the years.[3] By contrast, women's ailments, enough to keep them at home for the day, were
far more numerous. Apart from fever or guineaworm,
they were more liable to chest complaints, pains in
their backs and limbs, and general ill health ascribed by them to genital disorders. Inguinal and
femoral hernias, surprisingly, were more common in
women; so were diarrhoea and conjunctivitis, in which
cross-infection with children was not unusual. Further, if a baby was ill, his mother might stay at
home, and it was sometimes rather difficult to tell

3   Guineaworm is very rarely fatal. But in the areas
    studied (including a village) it was the single
    most important disease, particularly as it was
    confined to the rainy season when labour is most
    in demand. An entire household might be incapac-
    itated. In the past guineaworm was even more
    common than it is now. The relationship of
    guineaworm with drinking water is well known
    locally. But infection does not affect all people
    equally, and an element of chance is seen to be
    involved.

who was staying home for what. Clearly an element of
malingering was involved, but not sufficient to
account for the differing incidence of sickness between men and women.

Both sexes agreed that women were more liable
to illness, and this quite apart from complications
of childbirth. Advanced pregnancy does not prevent
work, nor does morning sickness; women with either,
however, are apt to slow up, and after birth only for
some forty days is a mother entitled to a reduced
work-load if she wishes. Complications in labour are
a serious hazard, causing considerable fear in advance, but in the retrospective experience of the
people of the farmstead in which I lived only in one
of the previous 118 live births over the past twenty
years had a mother died - and she died last year of
post-partum heart failure, which was not attributed
to childbirth. As regards the incidence of illness
the death rate is somewhat misleading, since women
show a remarkable ability to survive puerperal sepsis
and very low haemoglobin levels, both of which may
leave them much debilitated. Children under five
years of age have both a high rate of sickness and
high mortality: half, on average, died before their
fifth birthday.

Briefly, then, the experience of people in the farmstead was that men rarely get ill; women get ill, but seldom seriously; young children very frequently get ill, and frequently die. Over the last twenty years they have buried 48 children, 4 women and 3 men in their prime, and 4 old people (3 women, 1 man). In 1971, there were 6 deaths (2 women in their prime, 4 children), 8 livebirths and 4 miscarriages (spontaneous abortions). One of the women died of cholera, which was new to Nigeria. My presence may have saved others among the women and children, including two in childbirth. I have no reason to think the farmstead I was in was particularly unhealthy - in fact rather the reverse; nor are the Maguzawa an unhealthy people. One anomaly, for which I found no adequate answer, was that more men died in their prime than did women during the eighteen months I was in the area. This did not seem to be due to better reporting of men's deaths; nor is it explained by the fact that I reduced the number of women dying in childbirth by about six by taking them to hospital. Women seemed not to die of, or not to catch, the diseases that killed men. The numbers involved are not great, however.[4]

---

4   Jaundice, spinal complaints and undiagnosed
    chronic ailments lasting over three months were
    the most common (the last two being possibly due

I suggest it is the experience of death and disease
as well as general concepts that mould attitudes; and
experience may vary widely, not only between men and
women but also from house to house, or from group to
group within a house, thus generating diverse concepts and behaviour.

I stress the imbalance between the sexes in
sickness because such an imbalance does not normally
appear in hospital returns or in figures such as
those published by the Ministry of Health (of what
was formerly Northern Nigeria). Conversely one does
not hear that the health of adult men is generally
inadequate by local standards. However, this inadequacy may account for anthropologists' prolonged
lack of interest in sickness, especially among some
rural peoples.

The presentation of sickness

Since women and their children are much more frequently sick than men, most of what follows describes
women's behaviour. Male behaviour in the face of
illness - what little I have seen of it - is char-

---

to tuberculosis). Epidemics of cerebro-spinal
meningitis have scarcely affected the area for ten
years; trypanosomiasis is absent now, as is smallpox. But malaria is holo-endemic.

acterized mainly by endurance and the occasional
application of herbs. To keep it in mind that I am
speaking of a woman patient or the mother of a
patient, I will use 'she' throughout.

The woman herself decides if she is sick, and
this is almost never disputed. Nor does someone say
'you look ill' or even 'you look well'. Health is a
personal matter: for an outsider to claim or suggest
she knows better about the inside of another is to
claim magical powers, and this no one wants to do.
In seeming contrast to this are the many terms for
the work-shy. Few, if any, of the terms actually
imply malingering, and all the terms are rarely heard
in practice since they are offensive. Some women are
known for their whining and their lack of character:
the words used are those that describe children's
whining, the readiness to give up. There seems to be
no immediate word for a hypochondriac: those whom I
personally regarded as hypochondriacal (and I sometimes explained this to their husbands or others)
were treated nonetheless with sympathy and their complaints taken as real. Hypochondria, with its distinction between physical and non-physical, is not a
feasible concept in the Hausa system. Feeling unwell, whether there are physical symptoms or not, is

a condition that can have an external cause. Work-
shyness is not classified as an illness but as part
of God-given character, and, as such, unchangeable,
incurable. It is a characteristic ascribed mainly to
men.

When a woman declares herself sick, she usually
names her trouble in describing her symptoms, but
commonly only when asked - that is, by neighbouring
women or by her husband. Sickness is not talked
about by the patient, though word may spread hap-
hazardly around the farmstead; haphazard because
there is no ordered system of who tells whom. Chance
encounters govern the spread of news, or, as often,
non-news. Misinformation is common if there is no
good reason to tell the truth; the questioner does
not have a prescriptive right to the proper answer if
her question is not itself proper. Leading questions
are assented to, and wrong interpretations allowed to
pass: in this way quite erroneous accounts of an illness may grow up within a small group. It does not
matter, as nothing comes of the talk; but scepticism
about such details becomes habitual.

Responses by people to news of someone's sickness depend on the report of its seriousness.
Sympathy should be shown by means of a visit, perhaps

days after the start of the illness, by which time
the patient may be cured. Late-coming, lateness in
hearing the news, even by close kin, requires little
excuse. Sympathy is part of the general intercourse
of the farmstead, an affirmation of good will; outside the farmstead it extends to kinspeople, affines,
and friends. Treatment is not expected: the only
cure the visitor offers is the prayer that God will
make the patient better again. At another level,
usually filled by persons closer to the patient either
spatially or in kinship, are those that suggest herbal
remedies. Some men and women are interested in herbal
cures in an amateur fashion; others have bought or
inherited remedies and the secrets of making them.
Herbs, like the symptoms they treat, are in the public
domain, though frequently the patient shows no interest in knowing what she is taking. Discussions of
symptoms are open, and people re-tell their stories
about similar cases, and often argue in a theoretical
way about what sickness is. Such talk is often separate from where the patient lies, and may result in
no action: the talk passes to another topic.

On still another level are those who feel responsible - the patient's mother-in-law, the husband,
perhaps a sympathetic co-wife or a busybody, possibly

the patient's kin from her own farmstead. At this
level in particular people discuss such causes as
'spirit-attack' or 'soul-attack' or witchcraft of
various kinds. (For definitions of these terms, see
appendix.) It is they who are likely to get the
medicines, to call in the specialist and pay for
treatment. In general, explanations and details such
as these are not discussed publicly. Within this
category, however, diagnoses of spirits as cause and
as treatment (curative or preventive) are more public
than diagnoses of soul-attack or witchcraft. Both
spirits and souls may require specialist treatment;
but soul-attack and witchcraft are personal in a way
spirit-attack is not, and so are treated more personally.

Should a married woman be chronically ill, she
returns to her parents' house: she is a charge on her
own kin, not on her in-laws. It is her kin who will
do everything for her, since a woman is ultimately a
stranger in her husband's house. In consequence her
brother and other kin are informed if anything is
wrong, though what is wrong may not be specified; in
this way the various levels of proper information
extend outside the farmstead.[5]

_____

5 I am omitting discussion of those who choose or

All three levels of involvement in a specific
case may be valid for a person, though only one may
be articulated at a time, depending on either of the
two discussants. Not that there is any particular
shame attached: rather, it is not an outsider's concern, and interest would be improper. Thus much of
the misinformation is allowed to pass uncorrected
whenever someone tries to cross the boundaries of his
expected level. This applies to other kinds of information, not merely medical, though its articulation is perhaps clearer here. Research by a transit-
ory outsider is particularly affected.

Perception of sickness: the public and the
specialist

Not all ailments are serious enough to fall into the
final category. There is an implicit decision which
determines what level of remedy is called for. The
availability of the remedy itself influences the
decision. Prognosis here is not concerned with
death, but rather with the time and skills required:

---

agree to go to the hospital or mission dispensary.
In general, in the area in which I lived, patients
had to be well enough to walk up to ten miles and
back; but occasionally the sick were taken as a
last resort. Pills, however, come into the second
category, along with herbs, as treatments for
particular symptoms.

remedial action is not to stave off death (which is
entirely God's responsibility and unpredictable), but
to cure the patient. Disease and death are distinct.
Prognosis concerns the chronicity of the disease: and
the criteria are largely empirical - if the pain is
very severe and if the symptoms refuse to disappear.

Time is particularly important since all diseases can be seen as chronic. An attack may last for
five or ten years, its form varying widely, the pain
moving about the body spasmodically active. There is
a tendency to use Occam's razor, to simplify, reducing a sequence of ailments to one cause and not to
multiple causes. A similar reduction is found in
treatment and in names of ailments: symptoms coalesce.
This is particularly true of the general public;
specialists prefer to proliferate causes, symptoms,
treatments, while the public seeks panaceas. Similarly, technical terms proliferate with dialect variations and synonyms, while general terms are few and
widely used without variation. It is of considerable
importance, then, to be clear whose concepts are
being reported - the public's or the specialists'.
These can differ, but the difference may not impair,
indeed may enhance, the working relationship between
public and specialists. Specialists of competing

theories, frequent enough in Hausa medicine (as in
western 'fringe' medicine), appeal to a common public. The most striking example is the dual attraction of spirit cures and modern medicine; another example is the use of Muslim written charms by non-
Muslims. The detail of ritual may hold different
meanings for the specialist and the public, especially if the public participating is young. Within
the household, then, there is a tendency to use
general terms for symptoms and diseases; but in any
discussion the more recondite words are used, though
often with limited understanding and consequent
argument.

The public does not necessarily spend much time
thinking about disease, just as it is apt not to
think much about cosmology. Working concepts are
few, yet sufficient. As the vast majority of ailments will disappear by themselves irrespective of
the medicines taken, the less done the better.
Though this attitude is not explicit, it is the basis
of the hopeful wait-and-see approach which is so
common; but this is in part dependent on the availability of treatment. That fortitude is a necessity
is endlessly stressed in daily speech. Only those
ailments that show no signs of clearing up require

specialist care, not because the general concepts
prove inaccurate but because the underlying causes
need more powerful treatment.

Specialists for our present purpose can be divided into two categories: those who will visit a
patient, and those who will not. Some, such as bonesetters, have to visit: so do those removing poison
from a patient's room. The spirit healers (who are
mainly women) do not visit; they are not dealing with
physical symptoms per se. In consequence those sent
to get medicine from a spirit healer may only have a
hazy idea of what is physically wrong with the
patient; they may not be aware of the 'when' and
'where' of the onset nor the exact site or history of
the pain. There is no question of proving the specialist's insight. The specialist can prescribe as
generally as her customers expect. Specialists who
visit usually have a cure for one specific ailment
and they determine if the patient has in fact got
that ailment. The specialist is called because the
particular symptom is thought to be present; the
specialist then agrees or does not agree with the
diagnosis - the test is visual. An extreme example
is the western medical specialist who diagnoses visually but is thought to have X-ray eyes.

Apart from the western specialist, no other healer invades the privacy of the person. In Maguzawa culture, for adults to touch each other is comparatively rare. (Handshaking is a Muslim Hausa practice.) With the exception of bonesetters, specialists do not touch the patient. In part this is linked to a fear of contagion which is itself based, I think, on the more general concern to preserve the margin of oneself in what is otherwise a very open society. Touch is a more dangerous level of contact than seeing; there is no 'evil eye' among non-Muslim Hausa. Speech, however, has powers of touching: hearing, tasting, feeling are the same; words can literally be soothing. Words rather than hands are used, and this reluctance to use hands limits diagnostic techniques as well as treatment (which may in fact be an advantage). Furthermore, inaccurate explanations are like clothes; they prevent direct contact in what is otherwise a nearly naked society. The healer is expected to prescribe despite the minimum of information given by the patient's kin. The healer has considerable latitude for his expertise: detailed explanations are seldom sought, and these, if given, are seldom critically examined. An implicit criticism of the healer may occur later if

not all the medicines are to be taken at once: for
some order of priority has to be worked out. Equally,
a diagnosis may be ignored. For example, a mother
went into spirit possession about 11 p.m. to diagnose
her daughter's illness, but by 11 a.m. the next morning, when the child died, there had been no attempt
to get the medicines necessary after the previous
night's diagnosis. Urgency in treatment runs counter
to the notions of death; urgency implies that death
is coming soon unless action is taken. But death's
coming is unknown, and pain, the other cause of urgency, is often disregarded since the patient is
either too weak or feels it is improper to show it.

The patient or those around her are ultimately
in charge. A specialist has no more rights over his
patient than has a tradesman over his customer. As
the specialist may rarely hear more of the patient
once he has given, or re-given, treatment, the relationship between them is brief. Instructions are not
always adhered to; how often the medicine is to be
taken begins now to follow western practice, but
quantities are not fixed. Only dietary restrictions
are specified, indeed these are frequently sought by
the patient. But prescriptions to eat certain foods
(of the sort prescribed by hospitals) are not classed

as medicine but as food. The two categories are
virtually exclusive.

Moral and ritual aspects

The patient is not blamed for her illness, nor is she
ashamed unless the disease is one classed as venereal.
No moral wrong is attached to being sick although
occasionally women's troubles or their children's
deformities may be ascribed to moral failure. But
there are alternative diagnoses of the cause if not
always of the sickness; and the diagnosis of the
cause can vary along lines of friendship or hostility.
If the patient recovers, the post facto diagnosis
will be altered if later circumstances point to a
better solution. But not everyone will adopt the
reinterpretation; indeed they may not know about it.
For most people the issue is academic until a dispute
arises in which they are themselves involved.

Witchcraft is a striking example of a wholesale
reinterpretation by the anti-witch party: yet even
here (and witchcraft is comparatively infrequent in
Hausaland) scepticism is to be found. The recent
cholera epidemic, the first in Nigeria, prompted
accusations of witchcraft. Not all who died did so
through witchcraft, however; rather, witches took the

opportunity of killing people under cover of the
epidemic.[6] If the patient dies, the case is closed
unless there is a lingering suspicion of witchcraft.
No post-mortems are done since no treatment is possible. If the grandmother, for example, keeps dreaming of her dead grandchild, something may be done such
as an offering of alms, but that is essentially an
individual action. No blame is laid on those who
failed to cure the patient or who failed to help.
Oncoming death is as irreversible as death itself.
Where large sums are involved in a cure, part payment
is usually made at the start of, and during, treatment, with most of the money paid after the cure has
been effected. Such payment-by-results make the
final instalment a form of alms or thanks which may
be left to the recovered patient's discretion.

        There is a certain ambiguity over payments in
that they are simultaneously both to the spirits and
to the specialists. Thus there is possibly an element of guilt, since a sign, of omission rather than
commission, may be implied. Maguzawa society is
not hierarchical or stratified (unlike Muslim Hausa),
and prayers to the spirits waver between requests and

---

6   As the conveners of the conference suggested, I
    will not discuss witchcraft here.

commands. Women, with their junior status, tend to
request; men, or women specialists who act like men,
tend to command. Though I do not have adequate evidence, it is possible that women feel more guilty than
men; women can expect more frequent times of danger
(such as childbirth), and difficulties at these times
may occasion guilt. The term for wrongdoing (laifi,
a word of Arabic origin) is not as internalised as
our usage of 'sin', and can be used quite lightly.
The patient, I believe, is concerned more with her
sickness than with her sin.

Accidents are an instance where ritual expiat-
ion might be expected to occur. Any fall from a tree
or a wound while axeing or hoeing can be seen as
caused by an angry spirit. In practice, wounds, like
bites from scorpions, snakes and mad dogs (all of
which are killed immediately), are treated without
any ritual. Bandages or powder are applied more to
keep flies off than to prevent spirits getting in.
Risks are constantly being taken with spirits. Each
individual has charms to protect him; if this protection fails, treatment is the individual's concern. By
contrast, for non-accidental wounds, and at crises
such as birth, circumcision and childbearing, ritual
concern is considerable and communal. On such

occasions the 'patient' is treated elaborately, and
there is comment if the ritual is poorly performed.
Ritual treatment is essentially preventive: failure
to treat results in disease at some later time. In
ritual there is all the certainty of armchair diagnosis; the 'patient', though in danger, for the present is well. In accidents and sickness, when the
patient is ill and the call is for curative treatment, there is less certainty and diagnoses have to
be put to the test. A further factor militating
against ritual in actual sickness is that the patient
may be too sick to take part; ritual is used later to
prevent a recurrence. Young children are least involved in ritual activity: sickness is too common,
death too frequent, and both are put down to causes
external to the child, such as the mother's sour
breast or the possessiveness of a dead kinswoman's
soul. (The mother and her surroundings are, however,
the object of ritual attention.) Though the baby has
its uvula and hymeneal tags cut, and some facial and
stomach marks incised, these operations are performed
by a Muslim specialist and are followed by no cele-
bration; unlike Muslim Hausa, Maguzawa have no naming ceremony.

      Ritual treatment, or prevention, through initi-

ation into a spirit possession cult, is given to
adults who are not ill, but who want to safeguard
against anything going wrong, especially if (for
example) a miscarriage has occurred and the woman is
worried. Loss or lack of children is the commonest
cause for seeking treatment by spirit possession.
Presentation of oneself for such treatment depends
more on the interest and the money that can be muster-
ed than on specific misfortune. Many, equally unfortunate, do not bother. The cure consists of getting
oneself in harmony with the disease spirits so that
they can touch one without causing harm. There is
seldom any great urgency to get initiated: the ritual
is performed at the slack season of the year, and the
numbers depend heavily on how good the harvest has
been. The patient pays most of the bill herself,
with contributions mainly from her own family and a
little from her husband. The patient herself decides
that she needs treatment. As the cure is expensive,
this is often not done till she is old enough to have
amassed the resources necessary; her brothers, too,
by that time, will be able to afford to help her. As
she is not in ill health, she requires cash, not
care; she spends the weeks of initiation in the
compound of the healer, the initiates together making

their food, fetching wood and water. The low success
rate for the treatment is recognized; the money now
tends to be spent on other goods and initiation becomes a short, comparatively cheap affair. In the
past initiation seems to have been more of an expression of a clan's continued interest in their
married daughter, and thus an opportunity to show
clan solidarity and wealth. Now, treatment has become
the concern of the individual rather than of the
clan. It seems likely that a similar trend is occurring in other forms of treatment, that previously
collective offerings to spirits were made in the
farmstead more often than they are now; to the old
this failure is seen as affecting the fertility and
health of women. Women therefore have to safeguard
themselves, and concern for health becomes increasingly personal.

Other changes are occurring in medical concepts:
there are new diseases and new treatments, which,
coming in from outside, may contradict earlier concepts. Change in Hausa medicine is not associated
only with western practices. There is evidence of
innovations purely within the Hausa conceptual world.
An historical approach to medical concepts is as necessary for the medical as for other fields.

Change in medical concepts

Change in medical concepts can be independent of any change in the actual epidemiology of an area. Equally, new diseases (such as cholera) need not disturb existing medical ideas. Diseases can have a nominal existence, appearing and disappearing according to social, not physical, factors. For example, there is a new disease - sank'arau - which people recognize as afflicting the neck, usually with symptoms of painfully enlarged neck glands. The government, however, introduced the term, based on good but rather recondite Hausa, to be used for cerebro-spinal meningitis: the word suggests the rigidity of a corpse. Meningitis is well known popularly, and possession dances portray it vividly, but it still has not got a clearcut name: sank'arau is not used for meningitis.[7] The government, in inventing a name for it, has instead invented a new disease.

Another new disease is gishiri ('salt'). A disease of the vagina, it is treated by incisions into the anterior wall of the vaginal orifice; the result may be a fistula with urinary incontinence.

---

7   This refers, of course, to the area in which I worked. The term is correctly used where the government, and the disease, are more in evidence; elsewhere the term may be known but not used by all.

A woman complaining of gishiri usually has nothing
clinically wrong: however, the symptoms that induce
her to cut herself, or be cut, are numerous. They
range from a vague feeling of malaise to backache
after a day's work, from tightness around the bladder
to obstructed labour. The complaint is known to be
new; its entry into the area where I worked can be
dated to about twenty-five years ago. Previously
neither the treatment nor the disease was known there.
The object of treatment is to let blood flow which,
in childbirth for example, may be achieved with
disastrous results. Clearly the original intention
was to widen the birth passage, and such operations
are not uncommon elsewhere in Nigeria, quite apart
from the hospital episiotomy. As an operation for
childbirth, the gishiri cutting is often done prior
to labour (sometimes at the first sign of uterine
contractions) as well as during labour. It has replaced the earlier complaint, linked to the 'show' at
the onset of labour and known as 'sweetness' (zak'i:
the term refers now only to the mucus, not to the
ailment). No one knows the origin of the disease,
though many will offer explanations for the name.
Where gishiri is unusual is in the fact that it has
become the omnibus complaint for women of childbearing

age irrespective of whether they are or ever have
been pregnant. Reportedly even a young virgin has
been treated for it. Given the rapid expansion of
the gishiri symptoms, there have been two trends in
treatment. Firstly, various healers began to offer
dramatic remedies, and from this starting point ex-
panded to treat other problems as well. Secondly,
the original treatment with a razor blade has become
as do-it-yourself as taking aspirin.

The existence of the new disease is not questioned, though its definition is blurred. It is not
venereal; indeed it is passed between women, from
cooking stool to cooking stool. That it is linked
with women's general concern over fertility and sex
is clear, but it may be as much the cause as the
result of such concern. With the loosening of clan
ties and the ease and frequency of divorce, it is
possible that women are feeling more dependent on
their ability to function well as bearers of children. But the distribution of gishiri complaints
among the women where I lived was related more to
their social ties with others who had gishiri than to
any specific problem: they caught it more by discussion than by anything else. Older women have never
had gishiri cutting done to them, but they often make

young women giving birth for the first or second time
have it done. Proximity, social contact between
mother-in-law and midwife, the fears of the woman as
childbirth approaches: through these the treatment
spread, and with it the new diagnosis.

Treatment ran counter to a number of Hausa medical norms. First, surgery of this sort is not usually practised: the antipathy to touching prevents any
handling, even of a baby in birth. Second, the aim
is to let blood. Although cupping is done to remove
'dead' blood, and although a good flow of menstrual
blood or even blood after delivery is regarded as
satisfactory, blood in gishiri cutting is being used
to flush the gishiri substance out (an alternative
outlet for gishiri is in urine). Normally loss of
blood is a bad sign; there is no 'excess blood'.
Blood instead is linked metaphorically to individual
character and the individual's relationship with
others. Third, gishiri meaning 'salt' (or occasionally salty exudation from a wall) is not usually
connected with bodily ailments of any kind, as is
mucus or sweetness (zak'i).[8] The variety of explanations for the origin of the term reveal an awareness

---

8 Though salt in food can be classed as sweet, it
   is not dangerously sweet.

that the word is a misfit.

I have given a rather detailed account of a new illness because it illustrates not merely change in concepts and treatment but also the rather haphazard spread of a diagnosis: how people can present themselves with seemingly little reference to particular symptoms and existing diagnoses but can catch a new disease in conversation and broaden its field of reference. Detailed observation has no place. I have not found, for example, anyone outside the hospital who has examined the vagina visually or digitally and can say exactly what gishiri is: this is not necessary so long as the patient says she has gishiri. On occasions, after cutting has proved fruitless, a mother-in-law will look and find, for example, that there is a cystocele (gwaiwan mata: used for prolapse generally) and she may then know that the cause is not gishiri; but observation in such cases was prompted by prior failure.

Gishiri does not involve spirits, but rather has displaced ailments that can be attributed to spirits and souls. There is some element of shame, though this may be linked to the site rather than the sickness, or to the fact that it is seen as infectious. As it is a purely female ailment, men, while

they accept its importance, are not well-informed
about it. The expansion of the _gishiri_ symptom is
therefore removing more and more of women's disease
outside the sphere of men.

I may by now have given the impression that
Maguzawa women are ridden by anxiety and that there
is in the farmstead an air of infectious suggestion
and fantasy. This is far from the truth. Rather,
considerable gaiety prevails, with levity about both
men and spirits; in contrast it is the life of the
men and boys that may be dull, hard and often lonely.
The children are always a matter of concern, but as
the fate of the child is seen not to be finally in
the mother's hands, there is little that can be done.
Once that has been done, there is only hope. For
women, sickness is a bar to achievement, and many in
fact work despite pain and potential damage.

Sickness and household size

I have suggested above that women and their children
account for the vast majority of cases of sickness,
and children for the majority of deaths; and that
men are largely peripheral to the day-to-day handling
of sickness. Clearly, in the days of warfare, hunting and encounters with wild beasts, men were more at

risk than they are now; their concern to ward off
death in those activities has since lapsed. At the
present time one factor in particular seems to affect
the participation of men in problems of health - namely the ratio of men to women-plus-children; the fewer
the women and children, the less they form a separate
unit. The ratio varies according to what stage in
the developmental cycle the farmstead has reached.

Maguzawa farmsteads can be divided roughly into
two groups: 'young' farmsteads and 'old' ones. By a
'young' farmstead I mean one in which the majority of
young males are between 15 and 25 years old, and
their parents are almost past child-bearing age; by
an 'old' farmstead I mean one where the majority of
males are about 35 to 45 years old, with parents
nearing senility. Old farmsteads are at their peak,
with a ratio of approximately 1 man, 2 women, and 3
children, 1 wife divorced and 3 children dead. A
young farmstead by contrast is closer to the ratio of
1 man, 1 woman, 1 child. An old farmstead is a dynamic centre able to provide itself and its neighbours with most of the specialisms required, not
least in the way of amateur herbalists and spirit
healers. For women in an old farmstead treatment is
close at hand; there is much discussion since more of

the women will have been initiated into the spirit
possession cult, and more will have had experience of
various diseases and their treatment. Death is a
more common occurrence; the chances of cross-infection
are higher. To the young, men or women, the larger
farmsteads are socially more attractive; infertile or
unhappy marriages will have dissolved, while a degree
of community has been built up. By contrast, young
farmsteads are more vulnerable to divorce, the senior
women are nearing menopause, and the tendency is to
drift away from the farmstead for social life and
special needs.

Behaviour by the patient and her kin can differ
not only in treatment but also in diagnosis according
to the relative age of the farmstead and the size of
the group she lives in. The most important example
of this is in witchcraft accusations, which, rare as
they are, seem to occur mainly in old farmsteads and
are one of the ways by which old farmsteads split, to
re-form into a number of young farmsteads. Witchcraft accusations, which take some five or more
years to emerge, add an extra dimension to diagnosis
and treatment; yet they encourage scepticism since
the community may be divided on the case and the
charge takes so long to be proved. Apart from

witchcraft, breaks in the unity of the farmstead by divorce and death, particularly the death of the head of the farmstead, eventually dissolve the old farmstead. Typically, the ancient grandmother then recedes into the background and her once constant medical attention slacks off. Instead a specialist is sought out, usually by the husband, or possibly nothing is done by way of treatment. In the young farmstead responsibility and care are shared more equally between husband and wife, and this applies not only in sickness but also in the fields. Malingering poses more of a problem. The woman in the young farmstead is more dependent on outside help, usually from her own kin if they are nearby. For her first child a woman is expected to show little concern, so that if no one is available in a young farmstead the mother returns to her parents immediately after childbirth (the child must be born in the husband's farmstead).[9] If return home is not practicable, the woman will have to rely on whatever kinship or bond friendship links she may have in nearby farmsteads.

9 Fulani and Muslim Hausa consider the practice of returning home de rigueur, at least for the first childbirth. Maguzawa, on the other hand, are governed in their practice more by convenience than by any clear rule, and no time period is set.

Conclusion

In conclusion, I have suggested on the basis of the
field evidence that women and children, particularly
in old farmsteads, form a self-sufficient community
of the sick and potentially sick. Not only do women
and children in old farmsteads outnumber men by 5:1
but they also individually suffer more disease. Consequently they discuss and treat more disease, and
experience death more closely, than do their menfolk.
Furthermore, the ritual means of healing have been
concentrated in the hands of women with the result
that religious expertise and activity of other kinds
tends to be dominated by women. Maguzawa women,
whether at work or at play, as girls or as wives,
always form a community within the farmstead separate
from men and boys; the handling of sickness accentu-
ates this separation. The patient is the arbiter of
her own health, but a newly-introduced diagnosis
(gishiri) has isolated men still further from control
over sickness and treatment among women. Ultimately
the men as masters of the house have general responsibility and authority, but in practice responsibility
in individual cases devolves upon the older women.
And in practice, of course, much depends on the personalities, and the disease, involved. But sickness

remains primarily an aspect of women's culture.

The divergence between men and women in the
handling of sickness is most marked among the Muslim
Hausa where it is seemingly recent in origin. In the
past Islam was not so widespread or so closely practised by Hausa men and the hazards of life for men
were considerably greater. Islam, basically a man's
religion and offering no ritual cures for sickness,
has provided Hausa Muslim men with a new religious
authority that the non-Muslim now lacks. Conversely,
Islam is inadequate for the needs of Muslim Hausa
women, and they persist in using non-Muslim ritual
in times of stress such as sickness. In so far as
women's misfortunes and interests differ from those
of men, so too will their religious emphases differ.
This difference has been developed among the Hausa
most conspicuously in their sickness behaviour.

A number of constraints affect the appropriateness of concepts concerning sickness, and their
articulation and distribution within a group. Vary
the constraints, both physical and social, and changes
occur. Historically this appears to have happened;
and, when other areas of Hausaland are considered,
some elements in the conceptual system are found to
alter, while other elements fail to be utilised.

The outline of Hausa concepts (such as the one I give
in the appendix that follows) can thus only be an
abstract, isolated from the social content which
affects the use, and in consequence the symbolic
value, of these concepts.

APPENDIX

Summary of Hausa medical concepts
(particularly among Maguzawa)

1. The body. An inner system coinciding with the
   stomach and faeces; an outer system which includes sensory perception, the heart, lungs, limbs,
   flesh, blood and urine. The inner system runs on
   solids, the outer one on liquids (including air).
   The outer is vulnerable to attack; apart from the
   womb (which is a special case), the inner system
   is not commonly attacked. The soul resides in
   the outer system, and leaves it at death to have
   a continued existence and to pose a threat to its
   living kin.

2. Elements. Hot, cold, sweet, sour are important
   for the rationale of a large number of treatments, but not for all. In particular, cold and

sweetness cause much illness in the outer and
inner systems respectively. For the outer system
smell is very important, as is sound, both of
which can be described in terms of taste (as an
English translation would make it appear). Incense and ritual washing cleanse the outer system, sourness the inner system; heat is curative
both inside and out. In practice the dichotomy,
inner and outer, etc., is not so consistent or
precise; the various pairs may split differently
at different levels.

3. Ailments. These may move about the body and may
last for years, reappearing in various forms and
with numerous symptoms. Terms therefore have a
wide field of reference. Amosani, for example,
in men includes most stomach pains, but especially hernia and hydrocele. The same symptoms in
a woman may be labelled amosani or kwantacce
(which describes a pregnancy that has 'gone to
sleep'). Ailments develop: amosani may turn into
hydrocele; kwantacce may become amosani. In men,
hydrocele (gwaiwa) is venereal in origin. Thus
the same physical symptoms, particularly those
affecting the trunk, may be labelled differently
depending on sex. Similarly, children's ailments

are liable to be separately labelled and ascribed
to a separate cause. Seasonal differences in
morbidity (in western terms) appear to exist but
are not much noticed locally: briefly, certain
obstetric and respiratory problems occur especially early and late in the wet season (i.e. when
hot and humid), while epidemics - e.g. meningitis,
measles - are confined to the dry season (i.e.
when fairly cold and dry). Apart from obstetric
and gynaecological problems there appear to be no
other clearly sex-specific diseases.

4. __Spirits, etc.__ Spirits are an invisible replica
of the human world outside the Maguzawa farmstead
and affect the prosperity of the Maguzawa, usually
adversely. Souls are dead Maguzawa, kinsfolk
reckoned bilaterally, who join the spirits in
their wanderings outside the farmstead. 'Soul-
attack' is an attempt by a soul to entice a living kinswoman or her child to join her in the
wandering; to entice another, the interfering
soul may employ a spirit. Similarly, a witch is
usually a live kinsman who acquires and employs
a spirit secretly for personal gain, but he has
to pay the spirit with blood. Spirits are also
publicly employed by the farmstead to prevent

communal loss. 'Spirit-attack', therefore, is
harmful interference by a spirit acting either on
his own or another's account. Death is not inevitable. An absence of evil spirits implies the
presence of good ones, but fundamentally health
is seen as a lack of ill health - all is well so
long as nothing attacks from outside. Islam in
some respects implies the reverse view, that man
is fundamentally bad and health is a special
blessing. As knowledge of Islam is widespread
among non-Muslim Hausa, there is a certain ambiguity in thought; at present Islam is much used
for its protective value in calling down blessing, and not yet used as a way inducing one to a
better life. Spirits are compatible with Islam;
witchcraft is recognized by Muslims, though not
by Muslim law.

5. Sickness. To be sick is to be in the grip of a
spirit. Spirits can grab a person by the arm or
squeeze his chest; they can shoot him, but the
weapon is merely an extension of the spirit. To
make the spirit let go is to cure the disease:
cures are effected by pleasing the spirit who is
holding the patient or by making the patient unpleasant to hold. In general, spirits affect

only the outer system. The **inner** system is upset
mainly by solids put into it, and treated by ex-
pelling them. Diseases are more or less caprici-
ous, but as there is in theory a disease for all
forms of abnormal (including antisocial) behaviour or results, the threat of disease may en-
force some aspects of morality. Mental sickness
is rare among Maguzawa (though it is on the increase through the use of amphetamines); when it
occurs, it can be seen variously as a soul or
spirit taking over the person or as the result of
'poison'. In general it seems that soul-attack
results in depression, spirit-attack in what
appear to be toxic confusional states, but the
possibility is publicly recognized that women
(particularly Fulani women) may mimic soul-attack/
depression to obtain their own ends. Seen as
quite distinct from disease-spirits are the effects of daily wear-and-tear. Their commonness
eliminates specialist treatment and specialist
diagnoses. The percentage of cases of sickness
actually ascribed to the workings of spirits or
souls is difficult to determine. It varies by
sex, experience and temperament. In general it
can be said that women may attribute some or all

their troubles to spirits or souls, while men may
attribute none. Women with many surviving children are as anxious as those with few or none.
But treatment for soul- or spirit-attack is much
less frequent; since once treatment has been
given, there only remain the regular symptomatic
remedies.

6. Treatment. Of two kinds: (i) herbal - a. commonly known, and b. private; (ii) spirit appeasement
- a. spirits, and b. souls. Herbal treatment is
mainly symptomatic and aims at curing ailments
with or without a spirit diagnosis. Men in particular are concerned with herbal, women with
spirit treatment; the former is more concerned
with temporary illnesses, the latter is in response to longer-term troubles. Herbal remedies
(mainly the bark and roots of trees and shrubs)
are based on a number of principles: some act as,
for example, purgatives of the inner system,
others as purgatives of the outer system (incense), while still others are for local application to wounds, swellings, etc. Spirit appeasement, other than through incense, is achieved
through sacrificial blood of chickens, goats,
sheep.

7. Surgery. Apart from the new gishiri treatment,
    surgery is limited to the Islamically sanctioned
    remedies - cautery and cupping (k'aho: 'horn');
    to circumcision (at age fourteen among Maguzawa),
    uvulectomy and the removal of the hormonally
    hypertrophied hymen (at the age of about ten
    days). Only cautery is done by Maguzawa them-
    selves, and it is the treatment of choice for all
    swellings. The other operations are all done by
    Muslim specialists at Maguzawa request. It is
    possible that more radical surgery was practised
    when warfare and hunting were more common.

8. Healers. Like other craftsmen, they mainly pur-
    sue their craft in the dry season; in the rains,
    they are farmers. They lack special influence
    and give no leadership in the community. In any
    crisis among a kin group remedies are often
    sought outside the group or neighbourhood. Thus
    although healers may be spaced only a mile apart
    throughout the countryside, their clientele may
    come from ten miles away. Healing is open to
    both sexes, with women predominating now in
    spirit treatment and men predominating in inher-
    ited technical skills like bone-setting, trade in
    herbs, and the prolonged treatment of frank

mental illness. Inherited expertise is highly
valued, but achieved skills are not excluded.

9. Fulani, etc. Hausaland has a poly-ethnic popul-
    ation of diverse historical origins. Medicine
    crosses ethnic divisions, with foreign traders
    hawking their local remedies to a ready public.
    Fulani pastoralists share the basic medical cul-
    ture of Hausaland, giving (for example) remedies
    for swellings caused by bush spirits and receiv-
    ing cures for spirit- and soul-attack. Muslims
    and non-Muslims alike patronise each other's
    special skills. In consequence there may not be
    consistency between ideology and practice in
    medical treatment, though the inconsistency may
    not be explicit on account of the patient's
    ignorance of the healer's ideology.

REFERENCES

BUCK, A.A. et al. 1970 Health and Disease in Chad.
   Baltimore, Md.: Johns Hopkins Press.

RUTH CARO SALZBERGER[1]

CANCER: ASSUMPTIONS AND REALITY CONCERNING
DELAY, IGNORANCE AND FEAR

Man's interpretation of human sickness has influenced
the direction of his search for aetiological factors
and for cures, as well as his attitude to the sick,
throughout the ages. Although interpretations may
differ in detail, it is possible to group them according to their underlying assumptions. The same assumptions can be found in the traditions of widely separated societies; interpretations based on different
assumptions may coexist in one society and be used in
different situations, not necessarily being mutually
exclusive; and interpretations based on certain
assumptions may be favoured at one period in the
history of a society, while those based on other
assumptions may gain supremacy at another.

1   The author was Calouste Gulbenkian Research
    Fellow of Lucy Cavendish College, Cambridge,
    while writing this paper.

The cause of, or the initiating factor in, human sickness has been sought either within the afflicted individual or outside him. In the Old Testament, Job's friends accuse him of having brought about his own misfortune, including his illness. In spite of his tragic circumstances, Job has the strength of mind to declare himself guilt-free and God triumphs over the attributions of automatic re-action and small-minded punitiveness. David Bakan (1968: 104), however, in a recent reinterpretation of the Book of Job, goes even beyond the accusations of Job's friends, declaring him guilty of a 'Laius complex', that is of infanticidal impulses towards his children, which cause him to be ill and his children to die. The belief that immoral intentions or behaviour result in sickness and even death, either directly or through the action of the supernatural – God, spirits, ancestors – is, of course, widespread. It has not only been found in pre-literate societies, such as the Nuer and Zulu, it also persists to some extent in our own society. In contemporary psycho-analytical interpretation of mental disturbance and of psychosomatic symptoms and diseases, particular stress is laid on the individual's own guilt, aggression and negative projection.

While in the first group of hypotheses concerning the cause of human sickness the individual is made
responsible for his choices - conscious or unconscious
- and hence for his sickness, in the second group he
is thought of as fated. The latter group is subdivid-
ed. When we attribute misfortune, including sickness,
to 'chance' or 'coincidence', no blame attaches to any
human being or personified supernatural power. A man
can also not be held responsible for the particular
distribution of the 'fluids' of his body with which,
according to Chinese and Greek tradition, he was born
and which may predispose him to develop a certain
character and fall victim to certain diseases. The
various hypotheses concerning the relationship between
physiological structure and the development of attitudes, interests and disease-proneness, are a continuation of this theme. In so far as the individual did
not choose his body and hence his character, he is
innocent; but in so far as he is a person with a particular character, having certain attitude and intentions and performing certain actions, he may accumulate guilt and develop sickness. Thus a man may be
said to be fated to become both guilty and sick.
According to Freudian doctrine, the whole of mankind
is fated to repeat the Oedipal tragedy in the uncon-

scious, paying in terms of unconsciously self-induced sickness for the failure to solve the Oedipus complex and to come to terms with the super-ego. The 'Oedipal principle' in the belief system of the Tallensi differs from this, since here the individual is held to choose his fate, and hence his misfortunes, before birth.

In the third cluster of reasoning about sickness, the afflicted individual is seen as a victim, in some cases chosen for religious privileges. Among the Arctic Tungus, the loss of one of man's three souls is taken to cause unconsciousness, and that of his second soul, death. In the Haitian voodoo, the trembling and convulsions preceding possession and trance are believed to be due to the invasion of a person's head by a spirit, which displaces one of the two human souls. The sick person may be held to have been attacked by a witch as, for example, among the Azande, the Zulu and Lugbara, or by a sorcerer, as among the people of Dobu, the Tangu of New Guinea and the Cewa of Northern Rhodesia. Witchcraft accusations can still be remembered in some sectors of our own society; they date back only one generation or two in the Fens of East Anglia. Some existential psychiatrists ascribe the 'disease' of the disturbed individual

in 'mental illness' to the attitudes of his family
and social group, who are making his position unten-
able. In the sphere of 'physical illness', the ignoring or rejection of ideas concerning the sick person's
'guilt' or 'fatedness' has made possible those spec-
tacular advances in medicine - discoveries, skills
and cures - which we in the West have witnessed since
the last century. Some of the most humane and compassionate attitudes to the sick are found among the
adherents to the view that sickness is caused by outside agents, by an individual's defence against attack
or by the insufficiency of his defences, and some of
the last compassionate among those who, like the
friends of Job, blame the sufferer for his affliction.

Assumptions about cancer

These differences in the interpretation of human sickness are also reflected in the studies of the disease
with which I am here concerned, namely cancer. Some
researchers emphasize the shortcomings of the individual who develops, or becomes 'host' to, cancer. His
guilt, anger, aggression, destructiveness, repression,
regression, despair, and hopelessness. Others draw
attention to factors of heredity, constitution and
immunity. Finally, there is the increasing amount of

knowledge about influences from outside in cases of
cancer: injury, viruses, radiation, pollution, carcin-
ogenic substances, and difficult and disappointing
life-situations.

The data which I shall now present and discuss
were collected by me during research undertaken in
East Anglia between 1967 and 1971 under the aegis of
the Cambridgeshire and Isle of Ely County Council.
What had given rise to the project was the County
Health Education Officer's dissatisfaction with the
results of cancer education programmes in schools,
youth clubs and adult groups, such as Women's Instit-
utes, as well as with the response to cancer screening
facilities offered at cervical cytology clinics. It
was assumed that if people continued to smoke, delayed
reporting cancer symptoms, and failed to attend the
clinics, this was because they had not grasped the
facts, because they continued to be insufficiently
informed about cancer - about the nature of the disease, about its symptoms, and about the chances of a
cure in cases reported and treated in time. It was
their ignorance, it was argued, which caused people
to be careless or to have irrational fears about cancer, instead of taking rational action to protect
themselves. This situation was interpreted as being

due to a failure in communication. The Health Education Officers were ready and eager to impart up-to-
date information about cancer, breast examinations and
cervical smears were available at cervical cytology
clinics, many lives could be saved in the hospitals if
patients presented themselves with pre-cancerous symptoms or at an early stage of cancer. Why were these
supplies and facilities not fully utilized by the general public? Why did people refuse to help themselves?
This was the starting point for my research.

Delay

In 1967 the number of cancer cases registered in the
Cancer Records Bureau of the East Anglian Region as
domiciled in Cambridgeshire and Isle of Ely was 877;
since three patients were entered for two primary
sites, the number of persons involved was 874. For
these, the time-lapse between the discovery and the
reporting of symptoms was as follows:

Same day to four weeks	319 Cases
1 - 2 months	115 "
2 - 3 "	42 "
3 - 4 "	66 "
4 - 5 "	24 "
5 - 6 "	23 "

6 - 7 months	37 Cases
7 - 8 "	8 "
8 - 9 "	10 "
9 -10 "	9 "
10 -11 "	6 "
11 " to one year	9 "
Several months or unspecified period under one year	27 "
1 - 2 years	47 "
2 - 3 "	24 "
3 - 4 "	7 "
4 - 5 "	5 "
5 - 6 "	4 "
6 - 7 "	1 Case
7 - 8 "	3 Cases
10 "	5 "
20 "	1 Case
30 -40 "	2 Cases
Many "	12 "
Not known or stated	42 "

A number of patients did not report symptoms, but were found to have cancer in the following ways:

Picked up during routine examination	13 Cases
Diagnosed while in hospital for other complaint or follow-up	5 "
Post-mortem examination	11 "

We can discount the last four categories, because these are patients about whose reporting we have no information and patients who were not aware of any cancer symptoms. We are then left with 806 cases. Of these, 319 were reported within the first month, 434 within two months, 589 within six months, and 695 within the year. Rational action about cancer symptoms, therefore, was far more prevalent than the Health Education Officer's anxiety about delay would have led one to expect: 39.6 per cent during the first four weeks, 53.8 per cent during the first two months, 73 per cent during the first six months and 86 per cent within the year. It was evident that a large number of people sought medical help within a reasonable time-span, once they had discovered that their bodies showed some abnormality.

Ignorance

My investigation into knowledge about cancer was carried out on two levels. I sent out a questionnaire with a mobile cervical cytology clinic which visited the rural areas of the County. The questionnaire was used in three villages and a factory, and 120 replies were returned. The aim of this exploratory venture was to get some idea as to which facts people had picked up, and how. The sources of knowledge most frequently given were newspapers, periodicals, books, conversations with others, and television; this was followed by experience of cancer in the family and among friends, and contact with medical people; radio, school and posters ranked lowest as information suppliers.

Seventy four respondents made statements concerning the nature and aetiology of cancer; these I have ordered into six groups, shown in the following table. Several statements could of course be made by any one respondent.

The impression gained from the replies, that cancer education had done a great deal to disseminate knowledge about cancer in the County, was confirmed by my field-work in East Anglian villages of both the traditional and the transitional type. People had seen, heard and read as much as they wanted to know about cancer. They were keen to collect money for cancer research, but did not feel impelled to stop smoking or to have a preventive test.

Thus the cancer registration cards, the questionnaire replies and villagers' comments all showed that the assumptions concerning ignorance about cancer and delay in reporting cancer symptoms had been

TYPE OF REPLY	NUMBER
1. Description of the nature of cancer (e.g. 'a breakdown in the renewal pattern of cells'):-	21
2. Statements concerning the aetiology of cancer:-	
a. Heredity:-	18
b. Psychological stress, e.g. 'tension, shock, worry':-	8
c. Carcinogenic agents, which act upon the body from outside or are internalized:-	
i. Radiation, causing leukaemia:-	2
ii. A virus:-	4
iii. Pollution:-	5
iv. Contact with carcinogenic substances:-	2
v. Swallowing carcinogens in food or drugs:-	5 18
d. Injurious collision between a previously healthy body and the external environment, e.g. 'a fall' or 'a gun-shot through the lung':-	23
e. Smoking, leading to lung cancer:-	13

erroneous: there was far more knowledge about cancer and far less delay than expected. On the other hand, attendance at the mobile cervical cytology clinic was indeed poor. In previous investigations of attitudes to cancer and reasons for delay, 'fear of cancer', based on ignorance about the facts and about curability, had been made responsible for keeping people away from breast and cervical examinations. This fear of cancer was held to be irrational, a 'cancer phobia'. It is this fear which I want to consider now.

Fear

Medically, cancer is a 'malignant tumour'. According to the Oxford English Dictionary, the adjective 'malignant' has the following connotations:

1. disposed to rebel;

2. having an evil influence;

3. keenly desirous of the misfortune of another or others generally; and

4. in the case of disease: virulent, exceptionally contagious or infectious.

Cancer cells are virulent cells. I have heard them described in a cancer education lecture as 'rebel cells, the Hippies among the cells'. In the minds of many lay people, the adjective 'malignant' when combined with 'tumour' has a strong moral flavour: it is an 'evil' tumour, bringing misfortune to its 'host' and to those who love him and are dependent on him.

'Phobia', according to the O.E.D., means 'fear, horror, or aversion, especially of a morbid character' and medically it is 'a persistent abnormal dread or fear of something'. 'Cancer phobia', therefore, is a morbid or abnormal fear or dread of a malignant (virulent and misfortune-bringing) tumour. 'Fear' - in Old English 'faer', danger or peril, 'Gefahr' in German - is 'the emotion of pain or uneasiness caused by the sense of impending danger, or by the apprehension of evil', 'a state of alarm or dread', 'anxiety for the safety of a person or thing' (O.E.D.).

Freud (1856, trans. 1936: 147) had the following to say about the relationship between danger and anxiety or fear:

> A real danger is a danger which we know, a true
> anxiety the anxiety in regard to such a known danger.
> Neurotic anxiety is anxiety in regard to a danger
> which we do not know.

Mowrer (1939: 563), writing about anxiety as a learned response, stressed its positive function:

> Anxiety is ... basically anticipatory in nature and
> has great biological utility in that it adaptively

motivates living organisms to deal with (prepare for or flee from) traumatic events in advance of their actual occurrence, thereby diminishing their harmful effects.

We could, therefore, ask: do people experience a true anxiety (Realangst) or fear of cancer, or do they suffer from a neurotic anxiety or cancer phobia? If it is a true anxiety, what is its positive function?

We have already established the fallacy of the belief that people were ignorant about cancer: both the questionnaire responses and my conversations with people in the villages showed that they were not. I found, and still find, that as soon as the topic of cancer comes up, people start talking about their own experience of cancer, in their family or among their friends; they talk about something they feel they know, a known danger. In order to show what this experience is, what is known, I shall describe three cases. To protect both the friends I made during my research and myself, I have compounded my cases from experiences with people in widely separated places. What matters here is not the correct portrayal of persons, but rather of social situations, actions and reactions connected with the occurrence of cancer.

Experience

The first case I shall call Mr Pearl. He was a man who had spent most of his life in the Midlands. He had known poverty in his youth but, with great diligence and many sacrifices, he managed to fulfil his life's ambition: to have a shop window in the centre of the city, where he exhibited jewellery made by himself. One day, just as he was about to lock up his shop as usual, he was hit over the head and fell down unconscious. When he came to, he found that burglars had made off with all the goods in the window - his life's work. He had not yet taken out an insurance policy, since he had not had enough money to spare.

After this, his wife began to suffer from asthma and became so nervous that they decided to move to the country. They settled in East Anglia, where Mr Pearl tried to build up a new existence. They had a son and a daughter, both married and living in Cambridge. One day the son, whom Mr Pearl himself had trained as a jeweller and who was ill, asked for his father's help to save his business. Mr Pearl obliged, travelling miles every day with his wife to work for his son and attending to his own work in the evenings and during the weekends. No sooner had he put his son's affairs in order than his daughter-in-law persuaded her husband

to sell his business and to take up more secure and
better paid managerial work in a large firm. The father
was deeply hurt by this. He felt that once more all
his efforts had been wasted - this time on training his
son and saving his business; and so, parents and children fell out.

Shortly afterwards, Mr Pearl developed such a bad
cough that he had to see his doctor. As his cough would
not yield to ordinary treatment, he was taken into hospital and X-rayed and treated there. Everybody assured
him that he would soon be well. He was sent home and
put on a massive dosage of drugs. His wife tried to
comfort him with promises of better health in the future.
Months passed and he did not improve. On the contrary,
he felt his strength declining to such an extent that
he was unable to use his hands for work; so he implored
his wife to tell him what was really wrong with him.
Mrs Pearl consulted the doctor, who said there was no
point in keeping the truth from the patient any longer.
She now admitted to her husband that he was suffering
from cancer of the lung. By the time I saw him, which
was a few weeks before his death, he was an embittered
man. He told me straight out that he had cancer. He
said:

The Bible doesn't give a man more than three score

years and ten. I have had this, so I should be content; but all my life I have wanted to make a necklace
for my wife and never had the time, and now my hands
are too feeble to hold a needle. This is what I reg-
ret. And why all this make-believe, all these promises in the hospital?

When I asked him what he thought had caused his condition, he replied: 'Worry; worries about my business,
and family worries'. He and his wife had been happily
married for very many years, so that when now he became
angry about his reduced state, Mrs Pearl put it down
to his mental anguish and physical pain. She was so
devoted to him that, in spite of the doctor's and the
district nurse's warnings concerning her own health,
she insisted on nursing him single-handed day and night.
The result was that she got so weak that she had to be
put to bed herself, and her husband was moved back to
the hospital. When the Pearls' daughter picked up her
mother to take her to her own home and called at the
hospital on the way, Mr Pearl had just died.

     The second case I shall call Eve Day. She is a
member of the largest and richest farming family in the
village. Her father, Isaac Day - a man with colossal
energy, great business acumen, and the ability to control others - had built up a farm of 750 acres. Eve

THE DAY FAMILY

(with the approximate ages, at the time
of Rachel's death, of those members of
the family who play the most prominent
parts in the account)

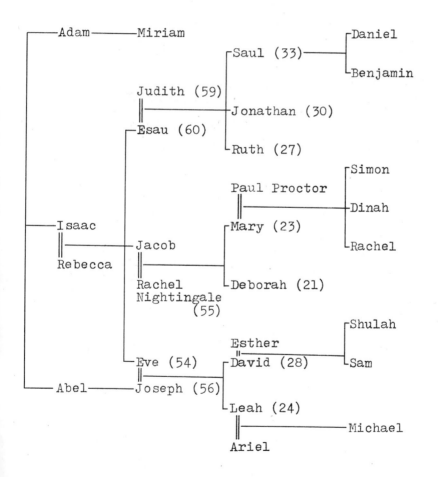

had married Joseph, who was farming land inherited from
his father, and they had a son and a daughter, David
and Leah.   David married Esther, a girl from the next
village, and the young couple helped Joseph with the
farm-work.   They, in turn, had two children, a daughter,
Shulah, and a son, Sam.   Leah was sent to Cambridge to
learn dress-making.   There she developed urban tastes
and no longer wanted to become a farmer's wife.   Against
her parents' advice, she married Ariel, a musician from
London.   Their backgrounds being so different, Leah and
Ariel quarrelled a great deal and soon after the birth
of their son, Michael, they separated.   Leah returned
to the village and used her dress-making skills to earn
a living for Michael and herself.

Eve was running her big farm-house, taking care
of her grandchildren when Esther and Leah wanted to be
free, and performing a number of duties which went with
her position in the village, such as providing Christmas decorations for the Church and Christmas gifts for
the inhabitants of the village almshouses.   She was
tired out by all her work and worried about her daughter's future when, early in the new year, she discovered
a lump in her breast.   She had been screened the previous autumn, during the mobile clinic's visit to the
village, and found to be all right.   She told me that

it was because a friend of hers had had cancer that she herself knew all about it, had noticed her own lump and gone to her doctor straight away. I knew that her mother, Rebecca, had died of cancer of the ovary, but she did not mention this to me. The doctor said that she must go into hospital at once. She did so and had the breast removed. She said that they had assured her it was so that she would have a better chance. She talked to me about friends who had survived for many years after an operation for cancer. While she was convalescing at home, she felt too weak to do much around the house, and this worried her; but she was grateful to Leah, Esther and Judith, her brother's wife, for their help and kindness, and to the hospital for giving her a special bra to wear, so that others would not notice the mutilation. Ariel, hearing about Eve's illness, visited her repeatedly. In this way he became known in the village; villagers stopped gossiping about him and instead accepted him as a kindly person. Eve improved and was able to come to her niece's wedding two summers later.

The third case, which in chronological order preceded Eve's by three years, was Rachel, Eve's sister-in-law and the wife of Jacob Day. She came from the next village and from a poor family, the Nightingales.

Her father had been a cobbler, sometimes in work and
sometimes out of it, but always jovial. Her mother
had kept her large family of ten children well-fed and
well-clad by her own work as a laundress; she was strict
and hard to please. Rachel, being the eldest, had to
help her mother to bring up the younger children. When
she had completed this task, she looked around for a
husband and found Jacob, the younger son of one of the
wealthiest farmers in the neighbourhood. The parents
on both sides objected to the relationship - the Nightingales because they thought Jacob would never marry
a poor girl, and the Days because they felt Jacob ought
not to. Rachel's motto for life, however, was that
one goes on trying until one succeeds. In the end both
sides were reconciled to the match; Rachel nursed Rebecca, her mother-in-law to be, through her terminal illness of cancer, and Jacob and Rachel were married.

The young couple had two daughters, Mary and
Deborah; they were both difficult births. Rachel soon
began to feel that she and her children were treated
as inferiors by the Day family. She tried to win them
over by knitting garments for her sisters-in-law and
their children, but to no avail. The more resistance
she met, the more she was determined to fight for justice for her family. Since her husband's brother Esau's

children, Saul, Jonathan and Ruth, were going to a private school, with old Isaac Day paying the fees, she
also sent her two daughters to a private school. Her
father-in-law took the hint and footed the bills.

Esau's wife, Judith, had brought up her first
son, Saul, with the idea that he would one day be lord
and master of all his grandfather's land and belongings.
When, after Isaac's funeral, his will was opened, it
was found that he had left 600 acres to be owned and
farmed jointly by Esau and Jacob, and 150 acres to be
owned by Eve and farmed by her brothers. Isaac's large
and ancient farm-house was to be inherited by his sons.
Jacob decided that Esau should have it for as long as
he lived. There were two other old and spacious farm-
houses in the Day family, left by Isaac. Eve and Joseph
moved into the one nearest the land inherited by Eve,
and Jacob and Rachel settled with their two daughters
in the other. Judith, however, was so outraged by the
contents of her father-in-law's will that, from the
moment it had been read, she never again spoke to Rachel. This was the beginning of the family feud between
Judith and her children on the one side and Rachel and
her daughters on the other; after twenty years it is
still continuing.

Judith became President of the Women's Institute

in the village and Rachel felt that the Days were dom-
inating village affairs and wished to exclude her from
taking part in them. She went to Church in her own
village, where her daughters were christened, and she
became a member of a women's guild there. She grew
flowers and vegetables for Covent Garden to have extra
money, with which to pay for Mary's training as a
secretary.

Meanwhile, hostilities between Judith and Rachel
grew. Rachel was infuriated by Judith's behaviour over
farm matters and saw it as new injustice added to the
old. To restore the balance, she felt she had to retaliate in kind. But as Rachel was very religious, she
found the situation a great strain: there was constant
conflict between what was right and what was just, and
between what was kind and what was just. To put an end
to these problems, she wanted the farm to be divided
between Jacob and Esau, but Judith would not hear of it.

Mary took her first secretarial job with a Justice
of the Peace, Paul Proctor, whom, in due course, she
married. It was hoped that Paul would take family affairs in hand and see to it that they were justly settled, but he said he did not want to become entangled in
the feud. Nine months after Paul and Mary had had
their first child, Simon, Rachel felt a lump in her

side. She had seen two of her brothers and two of her
sisters die of cancer - cancer of the bronchus, bowel,
rectum, and cervix uteri respectively - and had since
lived in dread of this disease. She had an operation
and the consultant told her that she would be all right,
but informed her family that she had a malignant tumour
in her womb, that it was too late to try and save her
by radiotherapeutic treatment, and that he did not give
her more than a few months to live. Rachel had felt for
some time that the work of looking after the big farm-
house was getting too much for her and in addition had
been very anxious about Mary's confinement. It had,
however, been a much easier birth than Mary's own; Mary
and Simon were fine, Rachel was now a happy grandmother
and therefore she was determined to recover. Again and
again she regained her strength, only to slip further
downhill; and so she lingered on for three years.

        Rachel bore her long illness with great fortit-
ude, singing hymns and always telling her doctor that
she would soon be quite well. However, she became weak,
more and more disfigured by the drugs she took, and so
heavy that Mary and Deborah could hardly lift her out
of bed. She lived in an unreal world, in which her
husband and daughters talked to, and acted towards,
her as though she were recovering; but outside the

sickroom they were preoccupied with thoughts about her impending death. Rachel had once told Mary that, if ever she was found to have cancer, she would not wish to live on, as she did not want to become a burden to her family. Mary, therefore, had to catch doctors and nurses as they entered the house to warn them that her mother did not know what was wrong with her; she told other people that her mother was unwell and they could not see her just now. Jacob, Mary and Deborah sheltered and hid their cancer patient from the outside world and so themselves became more and more isolated in their gloom and brooding. On the one hand, they tried to protect the patient; the village was not to know, so that the dreadful word 'cancer' would on no account reach Rachel's ear. Also, they did not wish to expose this disfigured woman to the eyes of outsiders. On the other hand, they wanted to protect themselves; they were reluctant to admit to the village that, on top of all the other injustices, this disaster had hit them.

Day after day Rachel's groans - her pain no longer being alleviated by drugs - filled the house and her family was wondering how long she would last, but pretending to her that she would recover. During this period, old Mrs Nightingale died. The family arranged the funeral quietly, without telling Rachel of her

mother's death. Mrs Nightingale had left a large and
much treasured album with photographs of the whole family to Rachel. One of Rachel's sisters brought it to
the house and said to Mary: 'It is yours'. This emb-
arrassed Mary greatly. Her mother was still alive; she
still had a mother, yet her aunt was treating her sister
as though she were no longer there, as though she were
already dead. This seemed like hastening her death by
thinking of her as dead; to Mary it seemed a wrong, evil,
forbidden thought. Thus the family lived in constant
preparedness for Rachel's death, their thinking concentrated on the subjects of cancer and death, but they
felt guilty about this and they tried to present to
Rachel and to the outside world a picture of unruffled
calm.

While Rachel was sinking, the mobile clinic arrived in the village for cervical screening. Mary was
visiting me when I asked her what she thought about it.
She burst into tears. She said that this was just what
her mother had, but she could not tell any one, neither
could she go to the clinic. Supposing her smear were
positive? Her mother needed her. And what would become
of her children, of Simon, who was clinging to her, and
her new baby, Dinah, in the pram outside? How could
any one leave such tiny children? Her sister could not

go either, for she was nursing her mother and looking
after her parents' household.

Discussion

It is at this point that I want to come back to the
question of delay, ignorance and fear. Not one of the
three patients delayed going to the doctor after discovery of the symptom. Once they had found their bodies
to be out of order, they consulted their doctor to be
reassured and cured. The question of cancer did not
arise in Mr Pearl's mind when he went to get a remedy
for his cough. Eve and Rachel Day associated their
lumps with something unpleasant, having experienced
cancer in their family; they went to their doctor to
hear that it was not cancer, not a malignant tumour but
a benign growth which could be made to disappear. Knowledge about cancer from experience sensitizes a person
to cancer and helps to make him or her act about symptoms once established. But preventive measures like
cervical screening and an examination of the breasts
fall into a different category. The person who undergoes screening believes that the results will either
allow her to continue to live as a normal member of
society, with the usual responsibilities of a daughter,
sister or mother, or condemn her to a life of suffering

and dependence on others — at home, in the hospital or
in a nursing home — and, possibly, to premature death.
The weeks between examination and the arrival of the
test results from the laboratory are agony for the ex-
aminees. When talking about cancer screening to the
lay public, doctor and health visitor stress that it
is a preventive procedure, that a woman can be cured
completely if found in a pre-cancerous condition and
that, where cancer has begun to develop, the earlier
the lesion is discovered, the better the chances of
total cure. But no doctor or health visitor can give
the patient a guarantee that the results of her examination will be negative or that there will be a lasting cure if they are positive. Not surprisingly, therefore, I found that the greater the amount of knowledge
about cancer from personal and tragic experience, the
less the delay in reporting symptoms once established
and the greater the reluctance to have a preventive
test.

     Three main lines of argument against examinations
were presented to me. The first, used by a school
teacher as well as by a farm-labourer's wife in a traditional village, was: 'Why should I make life more unpleasant for myself than it is? If I go to the clinic
and am found to have cancer, I shall worry. I might

be run over in two weeks' time. As long as I don't
know that I have cancer, I need not worry about it and
can enjoy myself until I die'.

The second argument was used by three women in
a transitional village. They looked upon the examination as provoking fate. They were feeling all right;
so why interfere? If they were destined to develop
cancer, they would do so at the appointed time, examination or no examination. The disease would make itself known; they did not wish to be prodded.

The third argument was Mary Proctor's. The reason for not visiting the clinic was concern for depend-
ents. Mary finally had the examination done just after
her mother's funeral. The worry about care for her
mother was over. She rang her doctor impulsively, not
wanting to give herself any time to think more about
it, wanting to get it over and wanting to know that she
was safe.

What had been taken for an irrational fear of
cancer or even cancer phobia emerged in my investigation as an anxiety about having to give up normal life
with just the ordinary worries, about interfering with
one's fate, and about becoming unable to shoulder one's
responsibilities to others. It was while fulfilling
their obligations to family and community that Mr Pearl

and Eve and Rachel Day got into states of exhaustion.
They did not, however, go to see their doctor until
they had tangible symptoms to present. One cancer patient found a lump in her breast while her daughter was
terminally ill with cancer; the mother guessed what
her own lump was, but postponed her visit to the doctor
until after her daughter's funeral. Here, the anxiety
about cancer kept the woman from seeking immediate medical advice and did not, therefore, help to protect
her. We can see, however, that it did have a positive
function if, instead of focussing on the mother, we
consider the daughter whom she was trying to serve as
long as possible. A person's anxiety about cancer,
while preventing him or her from having a diagnostic
examination, may, in the same way, serve his or her
social group, at least temporarily.

       Cancer falls into that group of diseases where
life is suspended in balance between being restored
or destroyed. The patient's kin and friends are not
immediately confronted by bereavement as in the case
of a fatal accident, but there is a period of time,
sometimes years, during which the family lives under
the threat of impending death. This situation of danger and need for care often influences strongly the
behaviour towards the patient of those who are con-

cerned for his or her welfare. As soon as Mr Pearl's children heard that he was suffering from cancer, they made up their quarrel with him and came to see him regularly in the country. The diagnosis of cancer had served to reunite the family.

Eve Day's children, too, rallied round her after her operation. Some work was found for Leah on the family farm, she and Ariel were reconciled and included in her parents' will, and Ariel has now joined his wife and son in the village.

When Rachel Day first discovered her lump, she was so worried that she drove over to the home of Mary and Paul in a neighbouring town every day. After a while, Mary felt that the best solution of the problem would be if she, Paul and their son Simon moved to her parents' house in the village and she looked after the two families. This she did. Eventually she had a second child, Dinah. Not only was the work now too much for her, there were also too many people in the house. So Jacob and Rachel moved into a bungalow nearby, Deborah gave up her job in London to look after her parents, and Mary and Paul inherited the large family home. The extended family was united in the village round the cancer patient.

Rachel had seen Mary happily married; her wish

was that Deborah should marry, too. One day she said
to Deborah: 'I have just seen my mother walk through
the door, as large as life; now I know I'm going to
die'. Her mother's death had still not been mentioned
to Rachel, but she felt that this apparition she had
seen, her mother's ghost, was calling her away from the
family she had founded. Her last words to Deborah were:
'I am sorry to leave you. See that your father gets his
rightful share of the farm'. It was, however, Mary who
was with Rachel when she died. Mary had wanted to be
there at that moment. She called her father and Deborah,
but they did not hear her. Mary was glad that the long
and hopeless struggle was over for her mother. She did
not feel that the corpse lying on the bed now was her
mother.

In the three cases described, members of the afflicted families rallied and reunited round their cancer
patient. As long as there is positive action around
the patient and all the conflicts are settled, there
is a feeling that all that could have been done has been
done for the patient. If the patient recovers, like
Eve Day, he or she lives on in a more congenial climate.
If the patient dies, like Mr Pearl, the fact is ultimately accepted without ill-feeling. It is in cases
where quarrels are not made up, where the conflict

continues and is inherited by the descendants, as in
the case of Rachel Day, that questions of ultimate meaning and justice may be raised and have to be answered.

In both examples, the Pearls and the Days, death
caused the disruption of relationships and the loss of
an irreplaceable relationship, that with a father or
a mother. But where the patient is involved in conflict
on behalf of his group, the feeling that he or she cannot be spared, that death has no right to take him or
her away, that life is unfair, is much stronger. 'My
mother was our right hand, she fought all our battles',
said Mary. 'What shall we do now?' Mary accepted death
as something happening to animals and to other people
in the bad world of the village outside, with which her
mother had been in conflict, but death had no business
to intrude into the sanctuary of the peaceful family
home.

Doctors and nurses came and went, without being
able to change the verdict: death. It was obvious that
no further help could be expected on a body-plane or
in the realm of science. All efforts at curing had
failed. What was needed was healing, which only God
could do; so that the ultimate responsibility lay with
God.

What tortured Mary was that God could allow such

a good person as her mother to die, while evil people
who had hurt her mother continued in good health. Had
not one of them wished her father dead during a recent
operation and while her mother was dying? What point
was there in being good, if the evil ones triumphed?
How could one go on believing in God? The only hope
was a life after death, when the good will be rewarded.
Mary felt for a time that, because of her mother's cancer, her whole world had collapsed. 'I thought that
I understood life; now I'm completely confused.' To
some extent she clung to dreams which could be interpreted as having been predictive, for these seemed to
provide some structure in an otherwise disorganized
reality; on the other hand, she dreaded these dreams
as being uncanny, belonging to a sphere which man should
not enter. The contemplation of the deaths in her family - her uncles' and aunts' deaths, the deaths of her
grandmother and of relatives of her husband, and her
mother's impending death - made her feel that her family
was doomed.

Not only Mary, but also people who were not so
near to Rachel, thought about her illness along lines
of morality. Miriam, a cousin of Esau, Jacob and Eve,
said to me, pointing to Rachel's bungalow: 'The poor
woman! They haven't said yet, but I think it's cancer.

And she's such a good woman; she hasn't deserved this'.
Misfortune, and particularly extreme misfortune, should
only come as a punishment; why else should men strive
to be good?

Mary felt so much identified with her mother that
at first it seemed to her as though part of herself were
ill and dying. From the moment her mother was dead,
however, she knew that she had to act and that from now
on she had to carry the responsibilities her mother had
had to relinquish, in addition to her own. She made
all the funeral arrangements. Deborah cried and said
she wished she were with her mother, and she could not
face the funeral. Mary did not want to go either, but
said she must. All her relatives, including those who
had never once written to her mother or visited her
during her long illness, would come to the funeral to
make a good impression on others and get their names
into the local paper; her mother's enemies would feel
that they had won. Therefore, she, Mary, must go to
represent her mother.

The funeral, which took place in Rachel's home
village, was attended by many members of the Nightingale
and Day families, including Esau and Judith, Eve and
Joseph, and Miriam, and by friends. Deborah and a
friend meanwhile prepared tea in Jacob's bungalow.

Only the Nightingales and friends came to this tea;
none of the other Days - Esau's and Eve's families or
Miriam - appeared. And the feud continued.

Deborah went on holiday, and when she came back
she took a job in the village and managed her father's
household. Two years later she was married at the
Church in her mother's village and she put flowers from
her bridal bouquet on her mother's grave. Mary had another child, whom she called 'Rachel' after her mother.
'Something pleasant for my father and for the family',
Mary said; and the christening took place at her mother's Church.

Mary and Paul bought farmland at a village auction
and in this way established themselves as farmers. Next,
Paul persuaded Esau and Judith that it was unwise to
risk a high death-duty on the farm, in case Esau and
Jacob died. So an agreement was reached at last for
the farm to be divided and to be made over to Esau's
and Jacob's children. That half of the farm which goes
to Saul, Jonathan and Ruth has to support them and their
parents, as well as Saul's wife and children. Moreover,
their family home is to go to Jacob after Esau's death.
Mary and Deborah, on the other hand, have husbands who
earn their living in town, and money made from farming
will be additional income for them. 'It would have been

worth while for Judith and her children to offer us
friendship; we could have let farmland to them. Why
are people so envious, instead of enjoying life?' asks
Mary now, and Paul explains: 'I believe in just dealings - an eye for an eye'. So Rachel won in the end,
after her death, though not quite in the way she had
planned. For Jacob's land will belong to his daughters, Mary and Deborah; he will farm it and they will
get the rent. But Rachel's premature death from cancer
has been avenged, the tasks which she could not complete
have been brought to a happy end and, in the eyes of
her children, justice has been established.

It is easier for a social anthropologist than for
those involved in the struggle, like Mary, Deborah and
Paul, to see that 'justice' may be a matter of interpretation. From Judith's point of view the situation
looks very different. For Judith had been thinking
along traditional lines, where the eldest son, if he
was a good farmer, inherited his father's farm and the
younger son had to build up his own farm by his labour
or go into the Church, the army or the navy. Mary says
she is too busy to work out whether life makes sense
again, but in fact life presents a much more inviting
vista to her now.

Conclusion

Sir Francis Chichester prefaced the first chapter of
one of his autobiographical books (1964) with the prayer: 'From death before we are ready to die, good Lord
deliver us'. One of the things people find most dis-
turbing when faced with the possibility of death is
that they might be cut off from life before their tasks
have been accomplished. Eve wanted to see an acceptable solution of her daughter's marriage problems so
that she would be reintegrated into the village community. Mr Pearl wanted his family relationships to be
repaired and himself to be reinstalled in his former
social position. Rachel wanted her husband to be sole
owner of half his father's farm, to which he was entitled, and her children to be accepted as equals by
the Day family and as being of independent farm-owner
status by the village. All three wanted to see a moral
order established or re-established. Not everyone is
as fortunate with cancer as Eve Day and Sir Francis.
The 'catastrophe', as Loudon (1966) terms it, is felt
to be the loss of life before the person is ready to
die, before he or she has achieved his or her aims in
life.

I have heard only one cancer patient indicate
that having the disease might in some way be his own

fault. Eve thought that she had developed the growth because of a weakness in her constitution. Mary felt that her mother's, her uncles' and her aunts' cancer must have been due to the physical environment in which they grew up. Mr Pearl saw his cancer as the result of worry, cased by adverse events in his life for which other people were responsible. Sometimes a doctor is blamed for having made the right diagnosis too late. Only once have I witnessed a humble acceptance of a younger person's death from cancer and that was by a Jewish father. During the mourning period for his daughter, he gave a short address to his friends and, translating the words of Job from the Hebrew burial service, said: 'The Lord gave, and the Lord hath taken away; blessed be the name of the Lord'.

REFERENCES

BAKAN, D. 1968. Disease, Pain and Sacrifice. Chicago and London: University of Chicago Press.

CHICHESTER, F. 1964. The Lonely Sea and the Sky. London: Hodder and Stoughton.

FREUD, S. 1936. The Problem of Anxiety. Translated from the German by H.A. Bunker. New York: Psycho-analytic Quarterly Press and W.W. Norton & Company.

LOUDON, J.B. 1966. Religious order and mental dis-
    order: a study in a South Wales rural community in
    Banton, M. (ed.) The Social Anthropology of Complex
    Societies (A.S.A. Monograph No. 4). London: Tavis-
    tock Publications.

MOWRER, O.H. 1939. A stimulus-response analysis of
    anxiety and its role as a reinforcing agent.
    Psychological Review 46.

VIEDA SKULTANS

EMPATHY AND HEALING:
ASPECTS OF SPIRITUALIST RITUAL

This essay deals with responses to pain and sickness
among Spiritualists, and therefore may not be unambig-
uously eligible for inclusion in this symposium. I
would argue, however, that religion is concerned with
suffering and, therefore, that health and illness must
of necessity be among the objects of religious attention. If ritual is excluded, this exclusion is made
at the cost of understanding the full meaning of sickness and pain for the patient. Spiritualism is one
field where ritual matters and health matters are in-
extricably interwoven.

Before presenting the ethnographic material, the
level at which sickness is being considered must be
indicated. A theme in everyday thought as well as in
theoretical discussion is one which recognizes a distinction between real pathology and socially defined
sickness which may or may not have a basis in real

pathology. From the point of view of the sufferer this
is a meaningless distinction, since the experience of
pain need not be affected by its basis, or otherwise,
in real pathology. The Spiritualist sufferer is concerned with his experience of pain irrespective of
whether this has a basis in physiological disorder or
psychological and social conflict. To ask whether
spirit healing works in terms of removing the pathology
is to alter the focus of attention. Spirit healing
works insofar as Spiritualists claim no longer to have
pain and insofar as they do not present themselves for
treatment.

Given this approach to sickness, the term 'sociosomatic' illness is particularly useful with regard to
my material. Illness which does not have a basis in
real pathology has usually been labelled psychosomatic.
I would argue that in very many cases this is an inappropriate label for which the term 'sociosomatic' could
be substituted with greater descriptive accuracy. Reproductive disorders among women are typically among
those most readily described as being of psychosomatic
origin. I have argued elsewhere that statements about
reproductive disorders and menstrual processes are symbolic statements about social roles and relationships
(Skultans 1970). Menorrhagia, for example, can in many

instances be looked upon as a 'housewife's sickness'.
It is, therefore of sociosomatic rather than psychosomatic origin.

Returning to Spiritualists, very many of their
complaints are interwoven with difficult social or marital situations. This is born out by the way in which
illness is presented within the Spiritualist group as
one among a number of difficulties with which Spiritualists have to contend. This heterogeneity in the presentation of misfortune is echoed in an eclecticism in
explaining sickness. No one explanatory model predom-
inates. Social, psychological and organic possibilities
are considered as exerting a causal influence on sickness. Similarly, there is an eclectic approach to
treatment. Spirit healing, herbal remedies, psychological insight, suggestions for social manipulation
of difficult situations are each considered as methods
worth trying.

This eclectic or 'sociosomatic' approach to sickness finds its focal point of expression in the Spiritualist concept of 'aura'. Everybody is thought to have
an aura. It is half-physical, half-spiritual, rather
like a rainbow which surrounds a person's body. Although not visible to the uninitiated it can be seen
by 'sensitives' or those who are spiritually developed.

A person's aura is like a barometer which measures social, psychological or physical balance and imbalance.
This balance and harmony or their lack are reflected
in colour. A good aura is white, blue or purple. A
bad aura is a dark colour, especially red. The colour
of the aura can be affected for the worse by an imbalance or state of conflict at any level, whether it be
at the level of social conflict or strain or at the
level of organic pathology. Blue is described as the
'healing colour' and is especially highly valued. The
aura of a healthy and well-balanced individual who is
at peace with himself and others is blue. Occasionally,
when members of a Spiritualist group are in tune with
one another and are temporarily freed from misfortune,
a blue light is seen surrounding the circle.

In summary, this paper concerns Spiritualism in
South Wales and the response of Spiritualists to pain
and sickness. Spiritualists lend themselves particularly well to this study since they consider themselves
beset by a variety of disabilities and are preoccupied
with the problem of the meaning of suffering and its
communication.

General Ethnography

There are three Spiritualist churches in Swansea and

numerous 'home' or 'developing' circles. It is difficult to give an accurate assessment of the total Swansea Spiritualist population, but I would put it at
around four hundred. Of these most are working class,
about three-quarters are women, middle-aged and older.

    The 'home' or 'developing' circle is the most
widespread and important form of Spiritualist meeting.
Both terms are literally descriptive. The latter term
refers to the group's functions; the former to its setting. Circles are run by mediums of long-standing and
high reputation. The circle meets regularly, often in
the home of the medium. Its aims are to develop the
latent and nascent mediumistic powers of its members
and thus produce fully-fledged mediums. In view of its
intimate setting the circle can be seen as a private
rehearsal for the grand début which takes place at a
Spiritualist service. This form of organization is
a reflection of Spiritualist ideology which has as one
of its basic tenets the belief that everyone possesses
psychic power in a latent if not fully developed form.
(This belief is, of course, consistent with the fact
that most people never develop their mediumistic potential at all.) Entrance to such circles is difficult to
obtain. Frequently this is achieved by making one's
psychic gifts known publicly and especially to well-

established mediums associated with the coveted circle.
Continued and regular attendance is, it is thought, essential if good results are to be attained. Developing
circles should never be large and the optimum number
is thought to be about twelve. One of the underlying
premises of developing circles is that progress in mediumistic performance achieved by one member affects
every other member of the group in a positive way.

Although there is a written tradition of thought
about Spiritualism and official doctrine is available
at any one of the Spiritualist headquarters, its influence at the local level is insignificant. Practice and
belief seem to be determined by local needs and inspiration rather than being documented by a central authority. This is explained in part by an explicit emphasis on individual inspiration and in part by an inherent weakness in organizational and co-ordinating abilities. This lack of influence of official doctrine is
apparent in that few Spiritualists are aware of which
national organization, if any, their church belongs to;
let alone do they know the doctrinal differences consequent upon such membership.

Religious beliefs and practices are learnt from
other more developed mediums, usually in the context
of the developing circle. In fact, there is a stigma

attached to learning about Spiritualism, especially
mediumship and healing, from published material. The
true path to Spiritual power, as, indeed, to much therapeutic art, is through regular contact with and encouragement from a small number of more advanced adepts.
Spiritualist women in Swansea are frequently the daughters of Spiritualist mediums. Thus, first introduction
to the movement takes place in childhood but a regular
link is not established until later on in adulthood,
usually after marriage.

Does Spiritualism deal with a peculiar sector of
illness?

Much of Spiritualist activity is concerned with healing
and giving advice about sickness. I shall describe
this more fully later in the paper. Before turning to
the details of these activities, however, a summary of
the types of complaints managed by Spiritualism and its
relationship with orthodox medicine is necessary.

Unlike Christian Science, Spiritualism does not
attempt to assert its supremacy over orthodox medicine.
Spiritualists are seldom discouraged from seeing their
doctor and are seldom given advice which contradicts
that of the doctor. Indeed, Spiritualism does not see
itself as an alternative to orthodox medicine but rather

as its complement. It fills in the gaps and smooths
over the inadequacies of more orthodox treatment methods. Thus it does not deal with a peculiar sector of
illness. It has a contribution to make towards the
management of all sickness. Most frequently, however,
spirit healing aims to increase a person's overall vitality, zest and resistance towards disease and the
strains and stresses of life. In other words, one need
not have a specific complaint to be able to benefit
from spirit healing. However, healing is also given
for specific complaints which have either been previously diagnosed by a doctor or are diagnosed within the
Spiritualist setting by spirit. In such instances
spirit healing is always thought to help, in that it
alleviates pain, and sometimes it is thought to cure.
There are many first-hand accounts of such cures.
Blindness, stomach ulcers, kidney stones have disappeared, it is claimed, by spirit healing. Thus within
the context of Spiritualist ideology there is a tradition of curing and ready evidence for its success.
Whether or not such cures would be recognized by 'scientific' medicine did not form part of my research
interests, in that I was concerned with whether Spiritualists themselves considered themselves to be cured.
Thus success was judged by their self-assessment of

health.

The Spirit World

At this point perhaps an account of the structure of
the spirit world should be introduced in order to bring
out its relationship to earthly suffering. Two words
are frequently used. 'Spirit' is a word commonly used
to refer to the mystical, the non-empirical: it is used
in such contexts as, for example, 'I am getting a message from Spirit', or, 'Spirit is very strong with you',
or, 'Spirit is protecting you all the way'. Inter-
changeable with the word 'Spirit' in some contexts is
the word 'Power'. Thus one can correctly say: 'The
power is very strong with you'. However, it would not
be correct Spiritualist usage to say either: 'I am getting a message from Power', or 'Power is protecting
you all the way'. These examples show that 'Power' can
be used as a synonym for 'Spirit' only in contexts where
it is most closely related to and intermingled with
human beings. Thus where Spirit is thought of as a
discrete entity, distinct from human beings, it cannot
also be referred to as 'Power'. However, in contexts
where a person has already become an instrument of
Spirit it is usual and correct to use the term 'Power'.
In such contexts the word 'Power' is not only convent-

ionally correct, it is also literally true. Messages
which are agreed to come from Spirit are axiomatically
true and, therefore, confer great power and prestige
on the medium.

There is a similarity with Middleton's account
of the Lugbara conceptualization of Spirit in terms of
its remote and immanent aspects. The Lugbara words
refer to Spirit in its remote aspects as being creative
and infinite and to Spirit in its immanent aspects as
being the cause of pestilence, droughts and famine
(Middleton 1960). The parallel between the spiritual
categories of Swansea Spiritualists and those of the
Lugbara is not complete but it is there nevertheless.
Although Power is not necessarily conceptualized as
evil and hence is not the complete equivalent of the
Lugbara term, nevertheless there is a distinct value
for Spirit in its immanent aspect. However, it is only
in its immanent aspects that Spirit can be bad or produce illness. In other words, the badness of bad spirits is only manifest on those occasions when they possess a person.

Spirits are hierarchically organized, there being
a continuous upward movement from the time of death.
Communication is usually with the spirits from the lower
ranks of the hierarchy. Communication between human

beings and the lower spirits constitutes a link of mutual interdependence. Immediately after death, spirits
find themselves at a 'loose end' in the spirit world
and still feel strongly attached to their 'earth conditions'. They are in a state of transition between
the living and the dead. This state is ambiguous and,
hence, dangerous. Spiritualists are able to help spirits who are trapped in the meshes of their previous
existence by performing as mediums and acting out conditions of affliction. Through mediumship such spirits
can be released from the previously painful conditions
to which they were bound. Acting as instruments of
Spirit, Spiritualists can provide the stage on which
the circumstances of dying can be re-enacted. The medium becomes possessed or 'takes on the condition' of
a dying person so that, in effect, a death scene is re-
enacted in the midst of the Spiritualist circle. Thus
the spirit in question is freed from the scene of his
earthly pain and suffering and allowed to move upwards
in the spirit world. Without the ready help of Spiritualist mediums, spirits would remain forever fettered
to this life. This aspect of Spiritualist activity is
known as 'rescuing' or 'rescue operations'. Most difficult 'rescue operations' are notoriously those which
involve the spirits of deceased mediums.

However, the link between the spirit and physical
world is one of mutual interdependence and help flows
both ways. Human beings are dependent upon Spirit for
help. This help takes the form of advice about health
problems, emotional problems, protection in the face
of difficulties and, most important, the power of healing. Such advice is not expected to come from the spirits of the immediately departed: it has been shown that
they are themselves helpless. Neither is it thought
to come from those spirits who have progressed far in
the spirit world: they are no longer concerned with
human beings and their material problems. Help is
thought to come from those spirits occupying an intermediate position in the spiritual hierarchy. They are
neither so involved in 'earth conditions' as to need
help themselves, nor so distant as to be completely
unconcerned. Perhaps the easiest way of indicating the
scope of the spirit world is to list the categories of
spirits which it contains:

1. There is a vast array of spirits who have ascended
into the higher realms of the spirit world. No communication exists with these spirits and, hence, they
are seen as an undifferentiated spiritual mass in which
little interest is expressed.

2. The second category in order of spiritual prestige

involves all those spirits who return to give advice.
These range from the permanent and reliable spirit-guide
to the casual spirit visitor with a single item of advice.

3. A third large-sized category of spirits covers
those who, whilst not malevolent, are themselves in need
of comfort and help as a result of some particularly
distressing 'earth conditions' they have experienced
and are unable to remove.

4. A fourth slightly smaller category includes all
spirits who have died a violent or painful death. These
are the spirits who call the 'rescue operations' of
mediums into action. Contact with these spirits requires a high degree of skill and control.

5. A final category, constituting a sub-category of
category four, contains all those spirits, malevolently
disposed, who actively inflict sickness.

Tambiah (1970: 316) refers to this final category
as those who have 'unnaturally escaped society'. He
explains the evil nature of these spirits in the following terms:

The belief in the violent spirit is thus a magnified
and dramatized conceptualization of a free-floating
malignant force, which, however, does not find an
expression as systematized cult behaviour. It rep-

resents the theoretical extreme of the concept of an
unfulfilled life, the notion being transferred into
the notion of an uncontrollable evil.

Thus it can be seen that the scope of spiritual categories is such as to provide an adequate mirror for the
varieties of human distress. The range is between distressing conditions which can be managed with little
active display of emotion, and those evoking strong
emotional responses and acting-out behaviour. It is
of interest that in the latter case the distress is
located in the spirit world and the human agent is seen
as taking on the role of a competent and generous helper.

Ritual auctions: Illness as currency[1]

When asked, most Spiritualists admit to physical disabilities. However, they do not regard this as unusual.
Sickness, whether chronic, temporary or recurrent, is
interwoven with the Spiritualists' expectations of life.
From this there stems a theme of sadness running through
all Spiritualist activities. Spiritualists consider
themselves different from others not in claiming more
sickness for themselves, but in their management of it.

---

1. I am grateful to Dr. Basil Sansom for suggesting
    this analogy to me.

Thus each occurrence in the medical and emotional history of a Spiritualist is a proper object of attention
for the entire Spiritualist group.

An analogy using the idea of an auction will help
to make clear the concerns of Spiritualist circles.
The central importance of illness emerges from questions
which such an analogy suggests. The questions to be
asked include the following: What is the bidding for?
Who are the auctioneers? In what currency is the bidding
made? What rules govern bidding? At Spiritualist meetings bidding is for attention and status and all Spiritualists participate in the bidding. However, the
participants are both auctioneers and bidders. Within
the space of an evening Spiritualists both bestow concern and attention on others and demand it for themselves. The currency is in terms of physical or emotional complaint. However, there are well-defined norms
which specify what can and cannot be put up for auction
and the manner in which this must be done. Conversation
at meetings has as its focus the body and onslaughts
on its well-being. Bidding for attention which becomes
too frequent is critically received. However, a reserve
is set below which bidding for attention is not toler-
ated. Physical impairment is thus almost a pre-
condition of eligibility for group membership. There-

fore, the degree and nature of participation by members
in the activities of the group is controlled.

Illness and pain

Much has been written by sociologists but little by
anthropologists about the presentation of illness. Discussion has usually been under the heading of the theory
of illness behaviour. Sociologists have aimed to identify social factors which are relevant to the way in
which sickness is perceived and which determine the subsequent behaviour of the sick person. Medical sociologists have tried to show how behaviour in sickness is
connected with a number of factors other than those relating to the severity or intensity of pain. For example, the values placed on endurance and self-control
as opposed to the ready dramatization of pain have been
cited (Zola 1966; Zborowski 1952). Behaviour in sickness has also been related to the social role of the
sick person and the way in which the sickness can be
accommodated to current obligations (Robinson 1971).
Such considerations as these have directed attention
away from the problem of pain and unease popularly regarded as being at the very heart of sickness. No doubt
this is an attempt to focus attention away from the
physical to the social and cultural. However, in the

course of this shift of attention a very large area belonging to the cultural, namely, the structure of pain
experience, has, in fact, been relegated to the biological. Perhaps another reason why the connection between
pain and sickness has been neglected is because it is
too close and uncomfortable. It is the case, however,
that little has been written about the influence which
the structure of pain experience has on the presentation
of sickness. The problem of examining the cultural and
linguistic conventions which determine the perception
and expression of pain has been left on one side. More
importantly, there is no systematic study of how the
perception of pain is reflected in subsequent definitions, management of sickness and healing procedures.

Privacy and pain

The aim of this paper is not merely to demonstrate a
general concern which Spiritualism has with pain, suffering and its management, but to indicate the precise
topography and content of Spiritualist pain experience
and to relate this to their group activities. One approach is to consider certain key Spiritualist rituals
and thereby infer the underlying attitudes to pain. A
more direct approach considers overtly-expressed ideas
about pain.

Spiritualist thought is diffused with anxieties about communication, that is, the inability to convey the precise quality of an experience to others and the sense of isolation when faced with pain and suffering. The activities of Spiritualist groups express these anxieties. Moreover, the development of mediumistic powers is one of the ways in which the quality of communication between people is improved. It is a way of penetrating the 'inner world' of others as well as the spirit world. One way of becoming aware of the Spiritualist experience of pain and the anxiety about its communication is by briefly considering a philosophical controversy about pain. The problems are definitional: should pain be defined as a sensation or an emotion? Jeremy Bentham (1970) treated both pains and pleasures as sensations. F.H. Bradley (1888), on the other hand, regarded pains as emotions. Pain, he thought, contributes the feeling-tone to an experience.

How pain is defined determines pain behaviour. Thus given our own linguistic conventions, pain defined as a sensation cannot be shared. One can <u>have</u> a pain, itch or throb, but one cannot be said to <u>know</u> it and neither can anyone else. Pain defined as emotion, however, relates to suffering. It can be communication and hence shared. This philosophical digression in the

middle of an anthropological text is justified if it
reveals a variety of definitions of pain and, hence,
ways of handling pain.

The teaching of Spiritualist mediums involves
an implicit awareness of such definitional controvers-
ies. On the one hand they are taught to become possessed or 'to take on a condition'. On the other hand,
they are taught to become 'impressed' or 'to listen to
Spirit'. In possession or taking on a condition, the
condition which is taken on is usually a painful one,
such as, for example, backache, migraine, stomach ache.
This is the condition suffered by one of the members
of the Spiritualist group or by a spirit whilst it was
on the 'earth plane'. However, according to Spiritualist theory, this condition may be experienced not only
by the sick person but also by the healer and any other
Spiritualists who are 'sensitives'. By 'taking on conditions' pains can be shared in much the same way as
visual or auditory objects can be shared. The pain
acquires some of the properties of a physical object,
which several people can see, hear or feel at the same
time, provided they are favourably situated. Pains
taken on by 'sensitives' resemble the blurred contours
of physical objects seen in a dim light.

'Listening to' or becoming 'impressed' by Spirit

is a more complex activity. This procedure requires
an active response on the part of the developing medium
as opposed to a passive surrendering of one's conscious
personality. It is a way of transmitting information
and advice from Spirit to human beings. Such information and advice relates broadly to the fields of physical sickness and interpersonal relations.

These two types of activities can broadly be described as representing the overtly therapeutic and the
didactic elements in Spiritualism. More advanced Spiritualists usually acquire a 'spirit-guide', that is, a
spirit whose connections are confined to one particular
Spiritualist. Such guides are frequently, though not
necessarily, thought to be the spirits of deceased doctors and preachers. As such the healing powers which
they are able to confer upon individual Spiritualists
are especially strong. These spirit-guides resemble
the Tallensi ideas about 'good destiny'. Like the good
destiny a spirit-guide is not acquired before adolescence. Similarly, it makes its presence felt to the
medium through a series of minor accidents (Fortes 1959:
41-55).

What I hope this description of ritual activities
brings out is the basically solipsistic nature of the
Spiritualist world-view. Spiritualists see each other

as being rather like Ryle's (1949: 13) 'ghost in the
machine', each living 'the life of a ghostly Robinson
Crusoe'. This epistemological outlook is one which,
at the emotional level, produces feelings of loneliness
and isolation. It is also one which inclines towards
seeking help from a mystical source in order to ease
communication and overcome epistemological barriers.
Most knowledge of others is gained by 'taking on a condition' or by 'listening to Spirit'. 'Taking on a condition' means complete identification with the other,
in the sense of having their feelings and emotions.
The implication is that any other form of acquiring
knowledge of the states of mind of others by more empirical, everyday methods is bound to be incomplete,
imperfect and, hence, disappointing.

The privacy felt to enclose one's inner world becomes especially hard to tolerate where illness or emotional hardship is involved. This may be because these
are situations which most urgently require guidance or
rules for understanding and acting, a feature which is
conspicuously absent from a private world. However,
these attitudes are not only implicitly revealed in certain ritual activities of Spiritualists; they are also
openly acknowledged. Spiritualists admit to turning
to Spiritualism 'out of pain and sorrow' and the need

to share these.

This view of pain, which puts it in a domain of logically enforced privacy, is one which has implications for the classification of pain and sickness as types of misfortune. Gilbert Lewis argues elsewhere in this volume that sickness is a distinctive kind of misfortune in that it is contained within the body and threatens the continued existence of the self. I would argue that it is pain which has this distinctive quality, not sickness. Pain isolates and is difficult to communicate. Sickness, by contrast, breaks down this isolation in that diagnoses of sickness enable the individual to see himself as one of a category of sick people.

This difficulty in tolerating the epistemological privacy of pain and the response of Spiritualism to pain is particularly interesting and unusual when considered in the light of psychiatric thought. Loss of psychological privacy, in the sense both of sharing thoughts, emotions and feelings and having them controlled by others, is taken as indicative of a loss of sanity. 'The loss of the experience of an area of unqualified privacy, by its transformation into a quasi-public realm, is often one of the decisive changes associated with the process of going mad' (Laing 1971: 36). This area

of 'unqualified privacy' is, according to Laing, a reflection of the preoccupation with 'the inner/outer,
real/unreal, me/not-me, public/private lines' (ibid:
34). Traditional psychiatry refers to the loss of the
privacy of experience and, hence, of ego boundaries and
the identity of the self in terms such as 'ideas of
passivity', 'ideas of reference' and 'ideas of influence'. Such terms are indicative of the psycho-pathol-
ogical condition of the individual. By contrast, Spiritualism encourages such states of mind and they are
achieved by mystical means.

The comparison is striking both in terms of the
similarities and the dissimilarities which it shows.
On the one hand, there is a similarity between the type
of experiences sought by Spiritualists and thought patterns diagnosed as 'schizophrenic' by psychiatrists.
On the other hand, opposed values are placed upon such
experiences according to the context in which they appear. (Difficulties in the interpretation of experiences of loss of privacy become most acute when the
same person is both a Spiritualist and a psychiatric
patient.) Loss of psychological boundaries in the context of the Spiritualist circle seem particularly interesting when seen as a variation of the theme of loss
of bodily boundaries. Values placed on bodily bound-

aries and their concomitants in social structure have
received much attention (Douglas 1971). However, the
boundaries of the 'self' and the experience of self have
been neglected.

The management of illness

The way in which Spiritualists experience pain and illness can be shown in more detail by describing the way
in which actual physical complaints are dealt with.
The responses to illness can be roughly grouped under
three activities, although each response has elements
which it shares with the others. The activities may
be distinguished as follows: 'Taking on conditions';
'Healing'; 'Message giving'.

    'Taking on conditions' has already been mentioned
in relation to the training of Spiritualist mediums.
It provides the back-bone or element of continuity for
all other Spiritualist activities. It is the mystical
insight into the ordinarily hidden pains of others.

    By the response of 'healing', Spiritualists refer
to 'the power of healing', the greatest gift which Spirit can bestow on human beings. Most healers are men,
although women can, in principle become healers too.
Spirit healing involves the mystical discovery and
identification of pain and sickness. It penetrates

other bodies and unearths information otherwise available only to the patient.

It is believed that the healer is only an instrument or receptacle of the healing art of a spirit, frequently the spirit of a deceased doctor. The healer himself usually knows that this possession has taken place by a peculiar tingling sensation in his fingertips. When this sensation is present the healer should place his hands on to that part of a woman's anatomy to which he is guided by Spirit. The patient knows that she is receiving this healing power by the intense heat which emanates from the healer's hands and which penetrates her body. This power, although it has physical attributes such as cause the sensation of heat to be felt, is itself non-empirical. The presence and the efficacy of the power are established ex post facto, when health has, in fact, been restored.

At the level of empirical description, spirit healing involves the laying on of hands by the healer on to that part of the body which is understood to be the cause of pain. Usually the healer's hands move in gentle stroking motions. Sometimes the healer shakes his hands after each stroke, thus symbolically discarding the sickness that has been drawn out of the patient's body. At sessions which are specifically and

exclusively devoted to spirit healing several healers
work at the same time. Healers wear white coats and
stand or kneel by the patient who is seated on a chair.
Each healer has a plastic bowl of water by his side in
which he washes his hands after giving healing to each
patient. In return, the patient, when he or she feels
the healer's hands being placed upon him, says either
'Thank you' or 'Bless you'. Very frequently, women
will murmur: 'Oh, that's wonderful', or, 'I can feel
the power coming'.

The range of complaints treated by spirit healing
is very wide; they vary both in their degree of severity
and in duration. The efficacy of spirit healing is very
highly valued. It is believed that the discomfort of
chronic complaints such as rheumatoid arthritis can be
alleviated through spirit healing; also that acute conditions such as ulcers, growths and kidney stones can
be completely removed.

The activity described as 'message giving', insofar as messages from Spirit relate to pain and sickness,
performs a labelling or diagnostic and explanatory service. The content of messages is obtained by 'listening
to' or becoming 'impressed' by Spirit. This activity
is a complex one since it demands an active and creative
response on the part of the listener. Part of an

aspiring medium's education involves training in the
presentation of messages. It is thought that messages
should be spiritual not 'material'. They should aim
to sum up a person's situation or condition in a highly
symbolic or eidetic form.

All Spiritualist meetings involve a continuous
reinterpretation and reassessment of feelings, motives
and relationships, especially insofar as these affect
members' well-being or lack of it. This endless sifting
of experience recalls Kafka's description of the Day
of Judgement as a 'court in standing session'.

Messages from Spirit define conditions involving
pain and suffering in such a way that they can be managed and handled. The sense of privacy and isolation
felt by Spiritualists to be a necessary corollary of
pain gives rise to the demand that the sickness be seen
as part of a more general pattern, that it be explained
by being seen as one instance of a recurring series of
events. In other words, that the painful event be defined and given a symbolic meaning. Detailed probing,
both in the course of ordinary conversation and in the
course of delivering messages, is made about physical
ailments. Such probing is especially apparent during
'the unorganized phase' of the illness (Balint 1964: 2).
Frequently it aims to locate the sources of tension in

a person's social relationships insofar as these might
be responsible for the lack of physical well-being.
The establishment of a definitive reality is a mutual
undertaking made by the healer and the sufferer and
bears a close resemblance to the process, described by
Balint, of bargaining for a diagnosis in terms of 'offers and responses' (ibid: 21-36).

Perhaps an example of the management of pain and
distress with reference to one particular woman which
brings into play the major Spiritualist activities can
be described at this point. Ethel is a woman in her
middle forties who has been a member of a developing
circle for the past five years. She is married to an
electrical engineer and has four adolescent children,
the eldest of whom is married. The family lives in a
large detached house in the suburbs of Swansea. Ethel's
marital history is a tale of endurance in the face of
conflict and despair. Her husband is, according to
Ethel, irresponsible with respect to money, inconsiderate and inconsistent towards the children and sadistic
towards herself. Throughout their married life he has
been preoccupied with his involvements with other women.
Ethel characterizes him as an aggressive and selfish
man, utterly insensitive to the feelings of others.
Apparently Jim is not altogether oblivious of her

opinion of him, since he eventually agreed to consult
a psychiatrist at a psychiatric hospital in Swansea.
This man spoke to Ethel and told her that there was nothing at all wrong with her but that her husband was
'schizoid'. Since this consultation Ethel's life has
been slightly easier, for she has realized that her
husband is a 'sick man' and that he is suffering from
an 'illness'. It is therefore her duty to stick by him
and to help him even though her help may be rejected.
Ethel's outlook is such that she now regards helping
her husband regain his 'health' as her life's task and
she approaches it with fervour. Despite her stoicism,
however, her situation is not a happy one.

Ethel brings to the meetings her feelings of terrible loneliness, meaninglessness and despair. These
feelings find frequent expression both during possession
and during her non-mystical states of consciousness.
Thus on one occasion, for example, Ethel had a very intense and uncontrolled fit of crying. It was not entirely clear whether or not she was in a state of possession. She turned to Mr Forde sitting on her left
who had quite clearly 'gone' and was 'under control'
by Sing Lee. What should she do? She had 'this heavi-
ness, pain and depression'. Should she take pills?
Sing Lee said she should not, that it was 'mental' and

that pills would never remove the conflict. Upon hearing this Ethel was convulsed with heart-rending sobs.
She screamed: 'Oh, my God help me!' and 'I don't want
to be alone!' Mr Jones got up and laid his hands on
her shoulders. Mr Forde, still 'under control', held
her hands. The rest sang and prayed. All uncrossed
their knees 'so as not to break the power'. In this
instance, uncrossing symbolized the need to open up or
the need for co-operation and help. This was done, with
the exception of Mrs Russell, a competitive woman, who
sat with her knees crossed. She was asked why she did
not help in this obvious and simple way but replied:
'Ask a silly question, get a silly answer'. Subsequently, she said that she herself had buried her brother
and her brother-in-law that very week, but she did not
bring the condition with her. In other words, her attitude implied that she begrudged the help that Ethel was
getting and was, therefore, unwilling to take on the
role of healer herself. However, other members of the
circle showed a readiness to identify with Ethel. This
was especially apparent in the healing which the two
men gave Ethel.

Conclusion

The perception of pain and suffering as being, first,

essentially private and hence divisive, and, second,
an integral part of life, especially woman's life, influences not only the specific procedures developed for
handling illness but also the setting in which these
occur. In this context it is significant that most
meetings, especially those which encourage the development of mediumistic powers, form an actual physical
<u>circle</u> of sitters.

Like all good symbols the circle is significant
at a number of different levels of meaning. First, at
the level of social structure it reflects the ideal of
equality between the 'sitters' expressed in the frequently repeated maxim: 'We all rise together'. This
equality is with respect to access to spiritual power,
since it is thought that everyone possesses mediumistic
power in a latent, if not manifest, form. Spiritualists
themselves way: 'The circle has no beginning and no
end: it is perfect. That is why we sit in a circle'.
It is thus consciously thought of as a symbol of spiritual perfection. However, it is also an apt reminder
of the permanence and continuity of suffering and pain.
Thus in one sense the circle can be seen as a reconcil-
iatory device. For, on the one hand, there is an explicit emphasis on continued spiritual progress summed
up in the principle of 'eternal progress open to every

human soul', whilst on the other hand there is a conspicuous lack of any real change in the lives of Spiritualist women. Spiritualism can, therefore, be seen
as a ritual of reconciliation. The supportive and the-
repeutic nature of the groups is underlined by the fact
that there is little, if any, interaction between members of a Spiritualist group outside that group.

    To conclude, I want to suggest a cross-cultural
approach, bearing in mind the associations suggested
by my Spiritualist material. Is there a correlation
between the degree of privacy or publicity felt to surround pain and a corresponding emphasis on mystical or
secular methods of diagnosis and cure? The notions of
privacy and of its essentially ruleless nature have not
been singled out as significant concepts in understanding and explaining responses to illness and misfortune.
Consideration of them is needed.

REFERENCES

BALINT, M. 1964. The Doctor, his Patient and the
    Illness. London: Tavistock Publications.

BENTHAM, J. 1970. An Introduction to the Principles
    of Morals and Legislation, (ed.) J.H. Burns and
    H.L.A. Hart. London: Athlone Press.

BRADLEY, F.H. 1888. On pleasure, pain, desire and volition. *Mind* XIII, 2.

DOUGLAS, M. 1970. *Natural Symbols*. London: Barrie & Rockliff.

FORTES, M. 1959. *Oedipus and Job in West African Religion*. Cambridge: Cambridge University Press.

LAING, R.D. 1971. *The Self and Others*. Harmondsworth: Penguin Books.

MIDDLETON, J. 1960. *Lugbara Religion*. London: Oxford University Press.

ROBINSON, D. 1971. *The Process of Becoming Ill*. London: Routledge & Kegan Paul.

RYLE, G. 1949. *The Concept of Mind*. London: Hutchinson.

SKULTANS, V. 1970. The symbolic significance of menstruation and the menopause. *Man* (NS) 5, 639–51.

TAMBIAH, S. 1970. *Buddhism and the Spirit Cults in North-East Thailand*. Cambridge: Cambridge University Press.

ZBOROWSKI, M. 1952. Cultural components in responses to pain. *Journal of Social Issues* 4, 16–30.

ZOLA, I. 1966. Culture and symptoms: an analysis of patients' presenting complaints. *American Sociological Review* 31, 615–29.

RONALD FRANKENBERG AND JOYCE LEESON

DISEASE, ILLNESS AND SICKNESS: SOCIAL ASPECTS
OF THE CHOICE OF HEALER IN A LUSAKA SUBURB

Lusaka is the capital of Zambia and the largest town in
the country. It was said in 1969 to have a population
of roughly a quarter of a million. About 15,000 of these
were believed to be non-African; Matero township and the
adjoining squatter compound which we studied had a population of 80,000. Many traditional healers practise in
Lusaka; later we will attempt to estimate the number.
Africans come from all parts of Zambia, Malawi and further afield, to live and (hopefully) to work in the town.
Nyanja-speaking people from the Eastern Province predominate, but there are also many Tonga, Bemba, Lozi and
members of other language groups and cultures. On the
first day in office as acting Director of the Institute
of Social Research, one of us had to seek to resolve a
dispute about which of the Institute's drivers had caused, by witchcraft, the death of one of his colleagues
from a brain tumour. He was unsuccessful. When he

himself later broke a leg, each member of the Institute
staff called to reassure him of lack of malice towards
the Director. These experiences, the number of ng'angas
in Lusaka, and encounters in British universities and
elsewhere, where personal multiplex frustrating antagon-
isms are as frequent (and as infrequent) as in central
Africa, lead us, while accepting Marwick's (1963) association of personal relations with witchcraft, to doubt
the converse in this statement:

A final common element in the contexts of Cewa Sorcery
should not escape us because, like Chesterton's post-
man, it is so familiar that it is invisible. In all
the cases I have recorded and possibly in all cases of
believed witchcraft and sorcery that have ever been
recorded, the relationship between the characters involved has been a personal one, one in which they have
exposed in their mutual interaction not merely single
facets of their personalities but all facets. Their
relationships have been what Gluckman calls multiplex
(1955: 19) and what some sociologists call total as
opposed to segmental (e.g. Coser 1955).

This last point may provide the answer to the
question why beliefs in witchcraft and sorcery, in
the form in which they exist in many contemporary non-
literate societies, have disappeared from our own

society. We may attribute their disappearance, neither to the growth of religion nor entirely to the rise of rationalism, but rather to the development of a society in which a large proportion of our day to day relationships are impersonal and segmental ones in which tensions may be isolated and compartmentalised, and expressed in forms very different from those of a society small enough in scale to be dominated by the ideas of personal influences.

It is at once too simple in its view of London (for example) which contains Bethnal Green, and Zambia which contains Lusaka. It is also too simple, as Horton (1967) and Douglas (1970b) have sought to show us, and as we suspect from doctor/patient relations as well as from attitudes to disease and misfortune in the rational industrial West, in suggesting the nature of differences in modes of thought. To do this we have to turn, as Marwick (1970) does, to Horton's work. We shall later echo the latter's footnote and Bradbury's (1959) review of Fortes' Oedipus and Job when we suggest that the Zambian traditional healer's view and understanding of disease is closer to ours than is that of many of our clinical colleagues. We would accept Horton's suggestions that Western industrial man has a mastery of things in contrast to the mastery of social relations of the

ng'angas in particular and Africans in general. The
new-found enthusiasm for contraception among British
general practitioners, now that all they have to do is
to give out pills, is a case in point (Cartwright 1970).
We should take issue, however, with his (to us) over-
ready acceptance of psychosomatic causes for disease.
We feel the necessity for a clear distinction between
psychic and social factors.

However, we find ourselves in the paradoxical
position that while we can readily accept the analysis
in Part I of his paper of the role of theory which scientific thought and African mystical beliefs have in
common, and most of his distinctions in Part II, we
cannot, given the situations in Lusaka, find his major
distinction useful on its own. Horton (1967) writes:

What I take to be the key difference is a very simple
one. It is that in traditional cultures there is no
developed awareness of alternatives to the established
body of theoretical tenets, whereas in scientifically
oriented cultures, such an awareness is highly developed. It is this difference we refer to when we say
that traditional cultures are 'closed' and scientifically oriented cultures 'open'.

We shall see that sick Africans in Lusaka had a wide
choice of options and that they behaved empirically.

They were determined to get the best of all worlds.

We shall suggest that patients' relations with
western doctors are to be seen in terms of membership
category, but that they relate to ng'angas as individuals. In the case of the chronic sick, they move in
both cases (if the treatment is successful) towards a
situation were both personality and membership of
group are important.

Characterising ng'anga practice

Douglas (1970b), Turner (1964), Van Velsen (1964), and
others have long since demolished the deterministic
model of beliefs even in village African society. There
is always a choice of norms available to the actor to
cope with the emergencies of life. In Lusaka, the paths
open to the sick in their search for help are of bewild-
ering complexity. They include, of course, dyadic consultation with kin; with white, Indian, or fellow African employer; with fellow employees of diverse tribal
and linguistic origin; with neighbours and friends. In
Lusaka, however, as elsewhere, if disease, a pathological entity, is to pass through psychological consciousness - illness - to social recognition - sickness - it
has to be legitimated. Legitimating agents here again
(as elsewhere) are organized in a professional or semi-

professional way. The choice available includes 'western' doctors operating privately, or through government
hospitals or clinics, and nurses, medical assistants
and the like. Also available, however, are a variety
of 'traditional' healers known collectively as sing'anga
or manganga in Nyanja and Bemba respectively, to whom
we shall colloquially refer as ng'angas. This paper
is concerned with the social characteristics of such
ng'angas and secondarily with their patients.

The ng'angas were encountered during the course
of a more general and comprehensive survey of health
behaviour in two areas of Lusaka carried out by one of
us (J.L.), in the presence and with the occasional col-
laboration of the other (R.F.), during 1967 and 1968.
Two sample populations, one in a municipal housing area
(1,000 households) and one in a squatter compound (600
households) were intensively studied during this period,
and a number of surveys carried out. During the course
of these surveys we heard about, met and interviewed,
some thirty-three ng'angas as well as over a thousand
patients. These were by no means a random sample of
those practising in the town. We first met the most
well known, such as those who practised herbalism either
in Lusaka central market or Matero township market, and
those to whose houses we were attracted at the weekend

by the sound of drumming as they 'danced' the victims
of spirit possession. These introduced us to their
associates and friends, and sick patients introduced
us to further practitioners. We certainly failed to
identify others, especially part-time practitioners,
even in the research area where we conducted several
detailed censuses. Any estimate of numbers is bound
to be low. On the other hand, some were transients,
others died or moved away during our two years research,
so that the thirty-three that we knew were never simultaneously present. Ten of them lived in one or other
of our research areas which had a combined population
of about 8,000 in 1967. Another twenty lived nearby.
Matero and the squatter compound together, with a total
population of about 80,000, had thirty ng'angas known
to us.

It is at least clear that traditional healers are
more numerous and more readily available than any other
source of primary 'official' medical care, for at the
time of our study there was one private doctor available
in Matero, one government clinic and one (later three)
sub-clinics. Other private doctors and an outpatient
clinic were available in central Lusaka four or five
miles away. In an earlier paper one of us (J.L.) compared the patients attending each source of medical

care and this is repeated here to put the ng'anga into
perspective.

At the private doctor's, as at the clinic, 45
per cent of the patients were young children, at the
outpatients department the number was 25 per cent, but
at the ng'angas' only 9 per cent of the total. Our
present results confirm that 63 per cent of the adults
attending ng'angas were women, as were about half of
those attending the clinic and less than half at the
outpatients. So it seemed that sick children were taken
predominantly to the clinic or private doctor, sick men
went to hospital or clinic, whilst women used all the
services, but were more likely to be found at the
ng'angas than were the others. Morbidity and mortality
were, as one would expect in this kind of society, heavily concentrated on children: 1,361 out of 2,006 recorded Lusaka deaths in 1967 were of children under five
years of age, i.e. 68 per cent of the total for that
year.

It is possible to comment on these findings at
several levels. Firstly, men who become ill during the
day are more likely to be near hospital or a private
doctor than are women. They are in general more mobile,
and more likely to be able to cope socially with busy
Indian doctors unable to speak Bemba, Nyanja, or other

relevant languages. Men are, in general, more likely
to know, and less likely to fear, African medical assistants who are usually the first line of medical care
at both hospital and clinic.

Secondly, as we shall see, the ng'anga's patients
tend to be a population of survivors - the patient and
the illness have survived western medicine. Most children who attend the clinic or a private doctor will have
acute illness and, therefore, are likely either to die
or be cured, so that the occasion for consulting a
ng'anga does not arise.

Thirdly, the ng'anga's speciality is in handling
the social disturbance caused by disease (or for that
matter other misfortune or potential misfortune). To
understand this fully it is necessary to reproduce
(Frankenberg 1968) a now modified model of what happens
when people fall sick. It is our contention that this
model reflects more closely the so-called traditional
pattern of actions than the so-called western pattern
(cf. Horton 1967: 63 fn.3).

It will be, or should be, a commonplace to sociologists, anthropologists, and ng'angas, if not to the
products of western medical schools, that becoming sick
is a social process. Implied in it is not only a physical unwellness, but the recognition by significant

others that all is not well and the consequent readjust-
ment of patterns of behaviour and expectations. The
first stage of sickness as a social phenomenon is,
therefore, the communication of the fact to another,
or others, by voluntary or involuntary, verbal or non-
verbal, signs. Once the symptoms and the sickness have
become social property, the now established social fact
will disturb previously existing social relations in
some way or other. Indeed, as in the case of barrenness
to be discussed below, the disturbance of social relations, the failure to fulfil the expectations of a role,
may be precisely and simultaneously the non-verbal sign
and the sickness. More usually this is a temporary
disturbance of equilibrium, allowing a man not to work,
and perhaps entailing a quarrel as to whose fault the
sickness is. Sometimes and in some (especially chronic) diseases, the disturbance may be more fundamental;
it may require in some societies, and at some times,
immediate and perhaps prolonged (e.g. Turner's cults
of affliction) ritual expressive action to restore or
rebuild social relations. Death nearly always has this
effect (Loudon 1961). In either case, social relations
will be affected at a number of levels - the immediate
family at the very least, often a wider group of kin,
a village and other social groups. Sometimes the

sickness of an individual (e.g., the Pope, the President of the USA) may be of very wide or even of world import and lead to national and international rituals. In all cases, men in society will take legitimating action which may be local or cosmopolitan, instrumental or expressive (cf. Middleton 1967: ix).

The levels at which social relations are affected provide us with dimensions of difference between ng'anga and western doctor, although the differences are often of emphasis rather than absolute. One may discern parallels between elaborate procedure for the collection, preparation and consumption of a herbal medicine, and such western rituals as retiring to bed and 'three times daily after meals'. These dimensions may be presented diagrammatically as in the accompanying Table 1.

Thus people act to show their concern by rallying round the sufferer or rejecting him. Both western doctors and ng'angas often act as entrepreneurs of concern organization. Acting is organized to remove the symptoms or eliminate the disease (physically) or to remove the social disturbance that taking cognizance of them has caused. It will be remembered that Goffman (1963) analyzes the deliberate ignoring of chronic symptoms to avoid the disturbance of social relations that their recognition would cause. This is analogous

Table 1

	LOCAL	COSMOPOLITAN

positive
 	
EXPRESSIVE.
	Visits from kin.
	Casting out
	  spirits.
		Telegrams.
		Letters of
		  sympathy.
		National days
		  of prayer.

negative	Casting out patient.	Custodial institutions.
disease (pathology)	Herbs, 'African injection'.	Treatment in rational bureaucratic way – western medicine.

INSTRUMENTAL:
ACTIONS TO
  REMEDY.
  illness
    (psychology)
	Private 'magic'.	Bedside manner.

sickness
  (social)
	Reconciliating
	  rituals.
		Social case
		  work (if
		  anything).

to the conversion of symptoms of disease into legitim-
izing signs of adepthood in 'cults of affliction'.

As hinted above, this can be achieved within an
intimate framework of neighbours, fellow tribesmen, or
fellow Africans, or within a less intimate one whose
relationship to the sufferer is not as an individual
but as the incumbent of a role, or a member of a group
– doctor or nurse. Again, this may be expressed diag-
ramatically, in Table 2. This helps us to see why all

Table 2

	WESTERN MEDICINE	TRADITIONAL
CATEGORY (INTER-ROLE	Doctors. Nurses, etc. Medical Assistants. Acute - quick cure.	Herbalists. Market ng'angas.
INTER-PERSONAL	Medical Assistants (friends or lovers).	Locality ng'angas. Chronic - incurable. Non-medical.

doctors are regarded as equally good or equally bad, whereas ng'angas in general are regarded as villains and only a specific ng'anga as good. Indeed, as Turner has pointed out in relation to Muchona (Turner 1967: 134) and Douglas in relation to Nuer prophets (1970b), it is the socially undesirable character of ng'angas in general which is part of their effectiveness. This helps to explain also our later finding that sick ng'angas themselves go to western doctors for treatment.

In the case of chronic illness, patients will only continue in treatment if the western doctor or auxiliary establishes a permanent personal relationship in addition to the professional one. Among traditional healers, the formation of a group of adepts, a spirit possession cult of affliction, moves the chronic patient

in the other direction towards formal role-structured
relationships.

These considerations should clarify the sharp
distinction which is made by western doctors (at least
in Zambia, though in advanced industrial countries the
distinction is less sharp, especially under the influence of psychoanalysis - see Balint 1957; Wootton 1963;
Horton 1967: 56) between medical and non-medical problems. Their instrumental concern with physical symptoms
outside social context is at once their strength and
the source of their ineffectiveness. On the other hand
the ng'angas have the opposite virtue and fault, and
no misfortune which disturbs social relations is seen
as outside their competence. In the normless (because
over-supplied with norms), loose, changing social groupings of Lusaka, they have a special importance (as Douglas might have predicted) in coping with sexual misfortune. In terms of body openings, western medicine is
focussed on mouth and anus - nutrition and hygiene; and
traditional medicine on genitals - impotence and birth.
Just as Mary Douglas sees the hippies and secularists
as repeating Ituri Pygmies at a new level, so we might
see the obsessions of middle-class America (in its pre-
Portnoy pre-oral phase) as returning to those of the
emerging African town.

Since we inevitably see ng'angas in dialectical opposition to western doctors we can define a view of their behaviour by contrast here (before proceeding to more detailed consideration of the data) by tabulating this opposition (see Table 3). In the rest of the paper we shall seek to show that the social characteristics and origins of the ng'angas we interviewed were consistent with a behaviour pattern derived from this tabulation.

Social characteristics of Lusaka ng'angas

There were twenty-seven men and six women. Although they included a few young people, twenty-seven (more than 80 per cent) were aged over forty years. In this they differed considerably from the general population of the area, of whom only about one quarter were over forty years. The distribution of area of origin of the ng'angas was generally similar to that of the general population, with a preponderance of Eastern Province people in both.

The ng'angas had not only lived longer on average than the population they lived amongst but they had also lived longer in towns in general, and in Lusaka in particular. Nineteen (57 per cent) had lived in a town for more than twenty years, as compared with about 25

Table 3

Doctors	Ng'angas
Indian or European.	African.
Bureaucratic.	Informal.
Specialised locales.	Home.
Payment in advance (or not at all).	Payment by results.
Cheap.	Expensive.
Defined illness.	Misfortune.
Acute.	Chronic.
Injections) deep invas- Surgery) ion of body	Scarification) superfic- Inhalations) ial in- vasion of body
Mechanical & manufact- ured drugs.	Herbal remedies.
Ignorance of local language. Ignorance of local social idioms.	Knowledge of languages. Awareness of local social idioms.
Physiological aetiologies.	Social aetiologies.
Consulted first.	Consulted by survivors.

per cent of the men in the general population, and nine of them (27 per cent) claimed to have lived in Lusaka itself for more than twenty years, which was only true of about 8 per cent of all males. It must be admitted, though, that in the case of two of them it would be

more accurate to say that they now lived in Lusaka, and
that they had lived in the same place for many years -
Lusaka having gradually engulfed them.

Another difference, perhaps associated with age,
was the relatively low level of education. Half the
men, and all the women, were unschooled, as compared
with one-fifth of the men and half the women in the
general population; and only 12 per cent of the male
ng'angas, and none of the female, had completed primary
education, compared with 34 per cent of men and 7.5 per
cent of the women of the area.

The practice of ng'angas

These traditional healers could not be said to belong
to a school of medical practice, unlike some of their
counterparts in other parts of the world, such as those
who practise Ayurvedic medicine, or acupuncture and
moxibustion. There is no written body of knowledge or
beliefs (cf. Horton 1967: 180), no systematic means of
instruction; they are in fact a heterogeneous collection, with no unanimity of theory or practice, although
of course they share some common features.

Two 'ideal types' of practitioner can be described
- the herbalist and the witchdoctor. The first may be
regarded as a development of a traditional role of

elders in village society, the equivalent of the 'wise women' of the English village in days gone by, who knew some local herbal remedies for common complaints. Six of the sample resembled this pattern, and all but one of these had learned his craft entirely by apprenticeship. Another two had served a different sort of apprenticeship, one as an assistant to a white herbalist, the other as a first-aider.

The second type of practitioner has mystical powers which enable him to diagnose and treat, or even prevent, a variety of misfortunes, including illness and death. His powers are derived from spirits or gods who visit him in dreams or in a trance, or guide him by other signs. In some cases he may not know what the diagnosis and treatment is even after he has pronounced it, for the spirits are speaking through him whilst he is in a trance, and an assistant listens, interprets where necessary, and relays the information to those consulting him. He has no need to ask the trouble, or to examine – indeed he has no need to see the patient at all. Twenty ng'angas tended towards this type, three others were Muslim (unlike their patients) and used holy books for guidance, whilst the remainder combined questioning the patient with magical treatments. In practice, however, it was seen that careful observation and skilled questioning, or more subtle ways of getting clues, were employed by the ng'anga or his assistants to supplement the supernatural guidance. In addition many (15) had been apprenticed to other healers, making twenty-five (75 per cent) who had received some training. A further four said they had relatives who were ng'angas, but made no mention of consciously learning from them. Overall, eighteen (54 per cent) felt they owed their powers to being possessed by spirits, but few of these had also been apprenticed. A further indication of the importance of training is that only five out of thirty-three respondents did not and would not think of training others.

Some of these ng'angas were very busy people, with a stream of patients always waiting to see them; these were all full-time ng'angas, with the exception of one who had a craftsman's job and left young relatives to do the consultations while he was at work. Fifteen, three of them women, were full-time, and of these we knew nine who were consulted often and one other who had fewer patients; the remainder were transients, or newcomers who had not yet established themselves when seen. Four other ng'angas were full-time, but sold things as well, not only herbs but also groceries or fruit. Three of these had many patients, and the

fourth just a few each day. Six more had no other employment, but were really old people who were past working anyway and who made a little money as a ng'anga with
those few patients, mostly neighbours and relatives,
whom they could attract. All the other eight were employed, one tailoring on his own account, the others
as employees. They include the man mentioned above,
who left relatives in charge, and three others who devoted most of their weekends to their ng'anga work, all
in the field of spirit possession. The others seemed
to see a few patients in the evening or on Saturday or
Sunday.

Methods of diagnosis

Ten ng'angas, including the eight herbalists, relied
on questions and/or examination in coming to a diagnosis, although one of these used dreaming as well.
The other twenty-three employed mystical techniques of
various sorts, some of them most ingenious, and many
combined several methods. Becoming possessed by spirits
as a result of a particular routine such as dancing,
listening to singing or donning appropriate dress was
the main diagnostic method of six ng'angas; in some
cases the patient joins in, if indeed his trouble is
due to these spirits, and the process of diagnosis

merges into treatment. Seven other ng'angas communed
with their spirits by dreaming at night, and for one
of them this must have involved sixty or more dreams
per night, if all the day's cases were to be covered.

Throwing bones, according to Gelfand (1964) a
popular Shona practice, was not common, only three (two
Rhodesian) doing this. Gourd rattles and magical horns
were more popular, being used by five ng'angas. Modern
aids were quite common, six ng'angas using mirrors, and
three using a divining apparatus seemingly operated by
magnets. The three Muslim healers consulted holy books
for guidance. Perhaps the most fascinating technique
involved consulting the spirit on a sort of 'hot line'
via a horn transmitter-receiver connected by a cord to
a shrine.

Modes of treatment

A similar wide range of treatment was found, from the
herbalists' simple remedies to the elaborate rituals
necessary to placate angry spirits - in the latter case,
as already mentioned, the diagnosis merges imperceptibly
into treatment as the patient begins to take up the
rhythm of the drums and dance, or to pass into a trance
as appropriate. The use of herbs was almost universal,
all but two prescribing them. Herbs are important in

spirit ceremonies, being used to wash in and wear, as well as to consume. For most purposes roots are more favoured than leaves; some are dug locally, others are specially imported from far away places, such as Mecca in the case of the Moslems, but from all over Africa in the case of the more travelled of the others. The efficiency of many of the remedies is not something inherent in the plant; seen as all important were the mode of preparation, and the circumstances, including the frame of mind of those fellow consumers who were present, when it was taken.

The two exceptions who did not prescribe herbs were Dr M. and Mr R. Dr M. had received first-aid training in the mines in South Africa, and he used only chemists' medicines and dressings. He had formerly been a minister of the local evangelical church, but had lost the job after a conviction for illegal administration of injections. Mr R., a new neighbour of ours, was the leader of a religious sect which not only disapproved of herbs but also in fact ascribed many troubles to people's belief in and use of them. But both these men did, however, put special herbs in the water they used to cleanse sufferers.

An interesting treatment was one that a Moslem healer used, and which it appears was once widespread

in Europe. Having identified the appropriate prescription in his holy book, he copied it out in special ink
on to the bottom of a plate. A little water was added
to dissolve the ink, and the prescription was thus made
up and swallowed on the spot. Neither the antiquity nor
the religious significance of this was known to most of
his patients who were not themselves Moslem.

Theories of disease

In each interview, we attempted to discuss several diseases which interested us, seeking to discover if the
disease was known to the ng'anga and treated by him;
and if so, what he believed to be the cause of the disease and the right way to treat it. There were many
difficulties in doing this; it took some time, and as
anyone will know who has tried to interview doctors in
Britain, time spent on talking to questioners may not
seem time well spent if patients are waiting. Appoint-
ments made often came to nought because of unexpected
calls of a professional or family nature, and some of
the ng'angas were only in the area for a short time.
Although some had generalised theories of causation,
thinking most troubles to be due, for example, to off-
ending spirits or to ignoring taboos, others were not
greatly interested in causes in general, although they

may be concerned in particular cases. As all Azande,
most anthropologists and some doctors are aware, causation of a disease is a complex question: whilst the
presence of the tubercle bacillus is a necessary cause
of clinical tuberculosis, it is not a sufficient explanation for the occurrence of the disease in a particular
person at a particular time. A further difficulty arises in translation, when the vernacular terms used or
their popular translation may unwittingly imply not only
symptoms but also aetiology - as mashave, spirit possession, does. In other cases, the answer was a sociological one, 'it depends'; as we shall see, many things
could either be 'natural' or otherwise.

Sexual problems

The commonest problems ng'angas meet, and those that
many of them claim to be specialists in, were those involving sexual function and sexual organs. Twenty-eight
per cent of the 1,123 ng'angas' patients interviewed
by our research assistants complained of genito-urinary
disease and/or infertility. Twenty-three (70 per cent)
of the ng'angas said barrenness was a speciality of
theirs, and eight (24 per cent) said the same of venereal disease or 'women's diseases'. This emphasis may
be the outcome of several tendencies. Undoubtedly human

fertility, and its symbolic relationship to crop and
livestock fertility, has been of central concern to mankind through most of history (and should be today, although in a different sense). The traditional practices
may be more appropriately described in some instances
as ensuring fertility rather than treating infertility.

At the individual level, if the adoption of the
sick role is a result of inability to fill normal roles,
then infertility in a woman is clearly a most important
problem, making her socially sick, since in traditional
African society child bearing is a most important function. And the high incidence of venereal diseases, with
often inadequate treatment and contact tracing, ensures
that many women are infertile, with or without other
gynaecological complaints. Yet another factor is the
unlikelihood of obtaining rapid effective treatment for
infertility from the hospital or private doctor, a cir-
cumstance, as we shall see, which often leads to consultation with a ng'anga. The problem is reclassified
as one which modern medicine cannot treat, and is,
therefore, probably regarded as an African disease
which ng'angas understand.

Less than half the ng'angas would give a 'cause'
of venereal diseases, but nearly all those who did were
well aware of the mode of transmission. Twenty-six of

the twenty-eight who answered the question treated venereal diseases, although one said he might refer syphilis, and two that they might refer gonorrhoea, to the
hospital.

Almost every ng'anga believed that barrenness
could be due to either natural or mystical causes. A
common answer, which was hard to classify as one or the
other, was that male impotence is caused by the umbilical cord being allowed to fall on the penis when a baby
boy is born. Incidentally, it seemed to be assumed by
all but one practitioner that a man is only barren if
he is impotent, so that if intercourse is not followed
within a fairly short time by pregnancy, the woman must
be barren. Thirty were recorded as willing to treat
impotence in men, and thirty-one treated barrenness in
women. With the two exceptions mentioned above, all
used herbs, and one (for women) and two (for men) used
dancing too.

Spirit possession

The only other sizeable speciality apart from sexual
problems was in spirit possession, claimed by eight
ng'angas (24 per cent). Many other symptoms or diseases
were mentioned, but only by one or two practitioners.
They included enuresis, epilepsy, coughs, palpitations

and skin diseases.

Twenty-five answers were recorded about spirit possession. In two cases spirits were specified as coming from God, but most of the others knew of various spirits, each tribal group having its own, but with some spread to others, especially, for example, to people who marry into a tribe. All twenty-five were prepared to treat: twenty-two used herbs, sixteen used dancing (that is, they conducted a mashave ceremony), three used prayers, and six had other methods of treatment. One spirit dancing that we observed showed clearly the development of social concern, as Zambian participants had learnt Shona songs and drum rhythms specifically to help a Shona woman.

Malnutrition and other common conditions

For reasons which will be obvious to anyone familiar with the health problems of developing countries, we were interested in the ng'angas' knowledge of malnutrition in childhood, and we tried to discuss with them the two extreme types, kwashiorkor and marasmus. Information was available from twenty-one ng'angas, and only two of these seemed not to recognize the syndromes as we described them. However, only two had any understanding of the relationship to nutrition, and a majority

believed that the cause lay in the behaviour of the
parents, who had broken taboos, or otherwise deserved
punishment.

Most ng'angas had few child patients, but even
if they had more it might seem at first glance that
they were unlikely to contribute much to controlling
this mass problem, since they did not understand its
nature. However, their observations were relevant, for
in some circumstances parents' behaviour clearly does
contribute directly to the development of malnutrition
in childhood. Premature weaning follows early resumpt-
ion of sexual relations if another pregnancy occurs;
and this puts the child at high risk of malnutrition.
Inadequate protein intake, the basic cause of kwashiorkor, may be due to the father's income going on beer
and barmaids, or to the mother, for some other reason,
failing to buy nutritious food for all the family, or
failing to ensure that the weanling, who is most in
need, gets his share. The intervention of ng'angas in
these sort of circumstances could be beneficial, especially if their advice included appropriate dietary prescriptions. Several ng'angas did propose improved diets,
although not always explicitly - one required that his
powerful herbs be dissolved in reconstituted powdered
milk, thus giving the child the best of both worlds.

Coughs and diarrhoea were further cases in point of how things could be either one thing or the other. Every ng'anga thought that both of these troubles could be natural, but for coughs, half, and for diarrhoea, one quarter, said that they could also be caused by breaking taboos, bewitchment or other mystical factors. A special cough, coughing blood, which was how we described tuberculosis, was a little different. Just over half thought it was 'natural', and a half described it as due to breaking taboos, with only three thinking it could be either. A frequent taboo mentioned was that of sleeping with a menstruating woman, or one recently aborted — a cause one assumes would only apply for men, although one ng'anga thought the woman also put herself at risk for TB by such behaviour.

Payment of the ng'anga

In this respect at least, most of the ng'angas remained traditional. Only five out of thirty answering (16 per cent) demanded cash for each consultation. Seven relied on payment by results - patients paid when cured, or could take any money paid back if they were not cured. The others either collected a small initial payment, the rest to be paid on cure, or else gave a price for the treatment, and then continued to give advice and

medicines for as long as they were needed. It should
be noted that spirit dancing is an expensive, as well
as a time-consuming, form of treatment. Even if the
ng'anga is not paid, the drummers must be; and provis-
ions, such as beer or other refreshments for the participants, must be provided, and in some cases a goat
or fowl is needed for slaughter.

Barrenness is a special case as far as payment
by results is concerned. Only two ng'angas took cash
at the time of treatment (they justified this unusual
practice by cynical remarks about people who run away).
Another two expected payment when pregnancy was confirmed, but the others only expected cash on delivery,
or even later; nine ng'angas waited until some months
after birth, expecting nothing if the child did not survive. They might, of course, come by some extra business through the need to cleanse parents in the event
of a miscarriage or a child death. A side effect of
this is that a couple who consulted several ng'angas
for their infertility would be required to pay all of
them if the woman subsequently conceived.

Ng'angas and orthodox medicine

At least by their own accounts most of these ng'angas
did not feel a great deal of antagonism towards orthodox

doctors and hospitals. It was widely reported, by twenty-four out of twenty-eight, that the commonest reason why the ng'anga was consulted was that 'others had failed' - usually specifically the hospital. Our interviews with ng'angas' patients confirmed this - nearly two-thirds had previously consulted private doctors, clinics or hospitals. Two ng'angas modestly attributed their being consulted to the fact that they were near, and that their service was private and available without queuing - all in contrast to the municipal clinic; another one, a newcomer, said 'anyone selling new fish gets customers' - an indication of the general applicability of the principle that a new doctor in an area soon collects the patients who are dissatisfied with his rivals and predecessors.

Although more than half said they never referred patients to other ng'angas, for whom they could not say a good word, all could think of circumstances in which they could advise patients to go to or to return to the hospital. Seven out of thirty would refer seriously ill patients. Some of these mentioned specific treatments which might be required, which personally they couldn't provide, such as blood transfusions; others were obviously more concerned to avoid the embarrassment of police enquiries about patients who died under their

care, or worse still, on their premises. A similar reason was that advanced by twelve, that if their own
treatment seemed to be failing, they would refer. Thir-
teen thought some diseases required hospital treatment.

For ng'angas and other people, orthodox medicine
obviously had high status; both seemed to expect that
it would usually be the first professional agency to
be consulted for most conditions. If after a period
(and sometimes this was brief) there seemed to be no
sign of a cure, then a ng'anga might be consulted.

Some ng'angas seemed to endorse the high prestige
of orthodox medicine by trying to combine aspects of
the old and the new in their own practice. One wore
a white coat for consultation, and several stocked chemists' medicines alongside their herbs, all in neat jars.
A man who was very much at the 'traditional' end of the
scale often employed scarification, tattooing, and rubbing herbs into the wounds - but he referred to the
treatment as 'African injections'.

As we have already remarked, the ng'angas seemed
further to endorse the expected behaviour when they
themselves became ill. About half said they would try
their own herbs, one quarter would consult another
ng'anga, usually a named one whom they respected, but
twenty-six out of thirty-one would probably consult

either a private doctor or the hospital. Our observations during the illnesses of three ng'angas, and close
relatives of two others, confirmed that they did indeed,
as they said they would, consult an orthodox doctor.

Conclusion

As many ethnographers since Evans-Pritchard (1937) have
pointed out, mystical theories are usually theories of
multiple causation. Horton, indeed (1967: 169), makes
this a major distinction between divination and diagnosis. The results of the present survey may tend to
obscure this fact, although it was apparent in observing ng'angas at work. Gluckman's celebrated review of
the Azande (1955b) applied here too, and while the disease might be attributed to various causes, witchcraft
might also be put forward as the explanation of why the
particular patient caught it at a particular time.
Witches, however, were named in category rather than
personal terms, 'someone at your place of work' or
'someone in your home village'.

A town like Lusaka throws up a wide variety of
healers with a wide variety of theories of disease and
misfortune. It is possible to seek to order such material, but the theoretical apparatus required to do so
is not a simple one; personal/impersonal, or African/

European, for example, are not adequate categories.
We are very conscious of deficiencies both in data and
in theoretical apparatus. In further publications we
hope to relate the traditional and the non-traditional
systems, or rather the African and the western, and to
see these in the context of patterns of morbidity and
mortality, and individual case histories, for it is
only by analysing the system as a whole that the workings of the parts will become clear.

REFERENCES

BALINT, M.   1957.   The Doctor, his Patient and the
   Illness.   London: Tavistock Publications.

BRADBURY, R.E.   1959.   Review of Fortes (1959), Man 59.

CARTWRIGHT, A.   1970.   Parents and Family Planning
   Services.   London: Routledge & Kegan Paul.

COSER, L.A.   1955.   The Functions of Social Conflict.
   New York: Free Press of Glencoe.

DOUGLAS, M.   1970a.   Natural Symbols.   London: Barrie
   & Rockliff.

-- (ed.) 1970b.   Witchcraft Confessions and Accusations (A.S.A. Monograph No. 9).   London: Tavistock
   Publications.

EVANS-PRITCHARD, E.E.   1937.   Witchcraft, Oracles and
   Magic among the Azande. Oxford: Clarendon Press.

FORTES, M.   1959.   Oedipus and Job in West African
   Religion.   Cambridge: Cambridge University Press.

FRANKENBERG, R. 1968. The beginnings of anthropology. Proceedings of the VIIIth International Congress of Anthropological and Ethnological Sciences, Tokyo, II, 73-7.

GELFAND, M. 1964. Medicine and Custom in Africa. Edinburgh: E. & S. Livingstone.

GLUCKMAN, M. 1955a The Judicial Process among the Barotse of Northern Rhodesia. Manchester: Manchester University Press.

-- 1955b. Custom and Conflict in Africa. Oxford: Basil Blackwell.

GOFFMAN, E. 1963. Stigma. Englewood Cliffs, N.J.: Prentice-Hall Inc.

HORTON, R. 1967. African traditional thought and Western science. Africa XXXVII, 1: 50-71, 2: 155-87.

LEESON, J. 1967. Paths to medical care in Lusaka, Zambia. (Unpublished Conference Paper, Dakar).

LOUDON, J.B. 1961. Kinship and crisis in South Wales. British Journal of Sociology 12, 333-50.

MARWICK, M. 1963. The sociology of sorcery in a Central African tribe. African Studies 22, 1-21. (Reprinted in Middleton, J. (ed.) 1967.)

-- (ed.) 1970 Witchcraft and Sorcery: Selected Readings. Harmondsworth: Penguin Books.

MIDDLETON, J. (ed.) 1967. Magic, Witchcraft and Curing (American Museum Sourcebooks in Anthropology). New York: The Natural History Press.

TURNER, V.W. 1960. Muchona the Hornet, interpreter of religion in Casagrande, J. (ed.) In the Company of Man. New York: Harper & Brothers. (Reprinted in Turner, V.W. 1967.).

-- 1964. Witchcraft and sorcery; taxonomy versus dynamics. Africa XXXIV, 314-24. (Reprinted in Turner, V.W. 1967.).

-- 1967. The Forest of Symbols: Aspects of Ndembu Ritual. Ithaca: Cornell University Press.

van VELSEN, J. 1964. The Politics of Kinship.
    Manchester: Manchester University Press.

WOOTTON, B. 1963.   The law, the doctor and the deviant.
    British Medical Journal, 2 (27th July), 197-202.

M. A. JASPAN

HEALTH AND ILLTH IN HIGHLAND SOUTH SUMATRA[1]

This paper elaborates a series of studies of the theory
and practice of medicine among the Rejang, a people
numbering about a quarter of a million who reside in
the foothills and mountain valleys of the High Barisan
mountain range in South-West Sumatra (Jaspan 1964a;
1969; in press). For those unfamiliar with this proto-
Malay Indonesian people, their ecosystem, social structure and key cultural values, I shall briefly summarise
this background.

The British, through the English East India Company, established contact with the Rejang in about 1685
(Sumatra Factory Records). In Bencoolen and Lais on
the West Sumatran coast they established some degree

1 I am grateful to the Wenner-Gren Foundation for
   Anthropological Research for a grant which has made
   possible further analysis of field material on
   Rejang medicine, traditional literature and belief
   systems. I am indebted for the term 'illth' to Dr
   Ivan Polunin of the Department of Social Medicine
   in the University of Singapore.

of hegemony over small groups of Rejang which had already been converted to Islam by the matrilineal Minang-
kabau of West Sumatra. These subject or protected
peoples were absorbed by means foul and fair into a
system of pepper cultivation for the world market, chan-
nelled through the East India Company's monopoly in this
part of the East Indies. The Company made several attempts to invade and control the Rejang Highlands,
principally in the early 19th century, when Raffles was
the Lieutenant-Governor, but these all failed. It was
believed both by the British and the Dutch, and not
without foundation, that Rejang country contained the
richest gold mines in all South-East Asia. In 1825 the
British exchanged Bencoolen, with its coastal plain and
hilly hinterland, for Malacca in West Malaya, which had
for about two centuries been ruled by the Dutch. The
Dutch then intensified their efforts to conquer the
Rejang Highlands, but several military expeditions ended
in marked defeat, until a well-equipped naval and land
expedition, organized in Padang, succeeded in conquering
the entire Rejang Highlands in 1859-61.

Until that time the Rejang had a loosely-knit,
acephalous, non-centralized political system, based on
four exogamous patriclans - Bermani, Jurukalang, Selupu
and Tubai - each settled in a discrete clan territory

in the original tribal heartland of Lebong. From the
16th to 18th centuries, further clan territories were
settled by sub-clans and patrilineages of the original
four clans, spreading the Rejang domain across the Musi
River Valley in the highlands to the east, and southward
across the Barisan watershed to the coastal foothills
and plains north and north-west of Bencoolen. Everywhere they went they maintained the original pattern
of localised clan territories, with an ideology based
on hill swidden farming and a social system that embrac-
ed prescriptive modes of courtship, marriage and ritual
affineship among the four 'pillar clans' of the tetradic
system. This, by extraordinary good fortune, was accurately described in 1783 by William Marsden,[2] a servant
of the East India Company, who resided among the coastal
Rejang for almost six years in the 1770s, and thereafter
published what is probably the finest anthropological
monograph concerning any non-European people in the 18th
and 19th centuries (Marsden 1783).

At that time, and indeed until the early 1930s,
the Rejang had a strongly entrenched patrilineal system

2   After leaving Sumatra Marsden became a Fellow, and
    later President, of the Royal Society. His princ-
    ipal observations on the Rejang social system were
    also confirmed in 1934, before the transition to
    matriliny, by the Indonesian Adat Law scholar
    Hazairin.

that underpinned their political, social and ritual-
religious organization. Marsden and subsequent Dutch
writers in the 19th and early 20th centuries have left
detailed descriptions - surprisingly free of the culture
bias of 18th century Europe - of the indigenous Rejang
ancestor cult and its syncresis of Buddhist, Hindu and
(since 1860) Islamic elements. Marsden also wrote a
few pages about Rejang medicine, particularly with regard to the folkdoctor or medicine man. What he there
described was valid in the 1960s when I carried out two
years' field research among the descendants of the same
people.[3] We are thus fortunate in having a datum in
field research and documentary sources almost 200 years
old. Rejang ethnohistory, magico-medical texts and
genealogies in their own ka-ga-nga syllabic script on
bamboo, buffalo horn, rattan and bark cloth, both con-

---

3   The empirical data on which this essay is based
    were collected in South Sumatra in the course of
    twenty-three months' fieldwork in 1961-3, whilst
    I was a Research Fellow in Anthropology at the
    Australian National University, Canberra. During
    this period I was apprenticed for approximately
    fourteen months to Man Aher, at that time the most
    renowned Rejang folkdoctor; he died in 1964 at
    about seventy-six years of age. A subsequent brief
    visit to the Rejang in 1969 was made possible by
    the Centre for South-East Asian Studies at the
    University of Hull. Other comparative studies of
    traditional medical theory in practice have been
    carried out in other parts of Indonesia, and in
    Cambodia, Malaysia and the Philippines from 1955
    to 1972.

firm and extend what Marsden and subsequent Dutch writers reported through an alien cognitive and descriptive
apparatus (Jaspan 1946).

From the early 1930s until about 1950, the Rejang
experienced a generation (about twenty years in their
domestic developmental cycle) of severe economic depriv-
ation and politico-social anomie caused firstly by the
world economic depression and later by the Japanese occupation (1943-5) and the six to seven years of revolut-
ionary warfare and disorganization that followed their
capitulation. Throughout this period it was virtually
impossible for anyone but the sons of the wealthiest
clan chiefs to accumulate the somewhat massive bride-
price (lékét; Malay-Indonesian jujur) which consisted
of gold, silver-sheathed daggers, silk scarves, blankets, buffaloes and cash, for a traditional marriage.
If the full bride-price was not paid, Rejang customary
law required the marriage to be semendo, i.e. a matri-
focal contract with prescriptive uxorilocal residence
and the recruitment of the children of the marriage to
the clan and lineage of their mother. When I first came
to live among them in 1961 there were already third and
fourth generation matrilineal 'fringes' of otherwise
patrilineal genealogies extending back twenty-one to
twenty-three generations, in an umbrella-like fashion

as among the Tiv of Nigeria, to one of the four sons
of Jang, the eponymous clan founder. The transition
from patriliny to matriliny has of course had profound
and complex consequences for the entire Rejang political,
economic and social system. These included a shift from
swidden to settled, irrigated rice farming, and a relax-
ation in the rules of clan exogamy. The Rejang are aware
of these changes, viewing them as part and parcel of
the process of their entering a wider national or world
society, though they do not always understand them. They
are likewise aware of changes in the manifestations of
health and disease, and in their medical practice, both
preventive and therapeutic. Their response to pressures
and new ideas from outside their own cultural frontiers
has been generally receptive-integrative, once their
traditional power structure and concomitant social system
had been displaced by new organizational forms imposed
or sanctioned by the Dutch.

Traditional environmental knowledge in relation to
concepts of health

The Rejang neither had nor have a distinctive body of
knowledge which might be called a theory of medicine
or pathology. In their world view or life view the
three principal biological crises in each person's life

- birth, reproduction and death - cannot be separated
from disturbances, actual or potential, of normal health.
These occurrences are common to everything in nature,
of which they conceive man an inherent, inextricable
part. He is not only affected in tangible or visible
physical ways by floods, drought, famine, lightning and
attacks by tigers, but through the less visible (though
for the Rejang not necessarily intangible) consequences
of the dispositions or actions of spirit beings, deities
and/or deceased ancestors, all of which they apperceive
as part of the natural order.

The matrix of their health-illth dichotomy, however, is akin or possibly derived from the Galenic concept of natural elements. Excess of heat/fire or cold/
wind are health hazards, whether pathogenic, morbid or
fatal in their effects on man. On the other hand, a
sustained lack either of warmth or of rain (associated
with cold and cooling), is believed to result in a failure in food supplies, and this in turn leads to a pleth-
ora of somatic and/or mental illnesses. Human beings
are not therefore a priori in control of nature, nor
have they any certain knowledge or procedures - whether
religious, magical or chemotherapeutic - with which to
modify it. The Rejang are not much impressed by assumptions and protestations by westerners that their scient-

ific technology has made possible in the west a dramatic reduction of the incidence and the mortality rates
of certain diseases that are still widespread in Indon-
esia. Western medico-technical success is regarded as
a good thing, and Rejang hope that by sending their sons
to medical schools they will soon have more direct access to it. Nevertheless they feel that the western medicine with which they have thus far come into contact
has an implicit and illogical arrogance in its assumptions about the causes of illness. In other words, Rejang
do not believe that most illness can be caused or cured
by material or technological media alone. They believe
that man must adjust himself as best he can both to nature's ordered seasons and its aberrations: to the excess
of heat in the dry monsoon when there are no fresh vegetables and epidemic diseases are rife; and to the wet
monsoon when head colds, broncho-respiratory and other
illnesses are most common. Thus heat and cold are both
necessary for man's survival, but when they occur in
excess or out of season they are deleterious, if not
disastrous. Is it then man's job, through either collective or individual action (or both), and especially
through the publicly delegated action of medical specialists, to minimise the effects of aseasonality or excessive seasonal manifestations, either through recog-

nized prophylactic procedures or through the proper medical therapy of the stricken.

In my experience, and in my attempted taxonomic
notation of presenting illnesses brought to the Rejang
folkdoctor (dukuen), heat is a greater source of danger,
infection and pathogenesis than the cold/chill-wind syndrome. These syndromes have much in common with Chinese
medicine. Thus 'wind' is seldom thought of in the abstract, as a process of temporary atmospheric movement
of measurable velocity, but as a cosmic life force that
actively resides (or at times hibernates) in space,
awaiting opportunities to enter human frames. The 'entry of wind' (masuk angien) is experienced through one
principal, invariable symptom - the patient's subjective
feeling of being cold, either in the head, the abdomen,
the joints or the extremities - and in a large and seemingly unlimited list of other observable somatic or
pathogenic symptoms.

The single most important symptom of 'cold entry'
in a patient is a sensation of pervading chill that no
amount of body covering (extra clothing or blankets) or
the heat of kitchen fires can alleviate. If such 'cold
entry' is accompanied by an absence of perspiration the
illness is regarded as serious, if not critical. The
folkdoctor therefore prescribes a febrifacient, for as

soon as the patient begins to sweat the sense of chill-
ing cold is diminished and it is believed that the crisis
of the fever or illness has passed.

It is important to stress that the Rejang and most
other Indonesian peoples do not differentiate as sharply
as does western medicine between observable or clinically
detectable and 'subjective' states of illness reported
or recounted by patients. Nor do they make such a sharp
distinction between soma and psyche, or between the ability to treat effectively the one without concomitant
treatment of (or its interaction upon) the other. The
reciprocal interaction of mind on body and body on mind
is much more taken for granted in indigenous Indonesian
medicine than in most western medicine. Nevertheless,
in terms of interaction between Indonesian medical systems and alien, western ones, there is a much higher
order of congruity in their respective ideas about nutrition and epidemiology than about therapy.

Illness presentation and diagnosis

Rejang folkdoctors are less confident than western doctors in exclusive chemical or physical diagnosis or in
treatment based on chemotherapy or internal surgery alone, though both are considered a useful part of the
total practice of medicine. They attach greater weight

to what might be described as holistic medicine, that
is, a process that embraces far more of the patient's
life-history - including his or her nuclear or extended
family history, not just his or her individual medical
history - than is usual in western medical practice,
and far more of the patient's spatial and temporal location within a broad natural ecosystem and metasomatic
world.

In carrying out diagnosis it is important for the
folkdoctor to know the circumstances of the patient's
birth, including sibling order; whether the patient's
mother's confinement was normal or abnormal; what was
the patient's state of infantile health; what is the
individual family and settlement history in terms of
affective social, economic, political and religious experience; and so forth. If he is a member of the village community, he will not usually need to ask any questions, for he already knows the answers. Only a specialist consultant from a remote area would actually put
such questions to a patient or to the patient's kinsmen.
The folkdoctor also wishes to know the degree of concern
that the patient's relatives have felt or shown in the
case, what action they have already taken, what they
propose or are prepared to do, and the extent to which
they are prepared to donate time and resources to aiding

him in treating the patient? This includes keeping the
patient in the closest possible contact with his respective natal and marital nuclear families, with his
other consanguineal and affinal kinsmen, and with his
neighbours, friends and other persons. He must not,
on any account, be left alone to brood in isolation or
to experience bodily or psychological needs that his
condition may either prevent him from expressing properly or which, because of his condition, it may not
be possible fully to satisfy.

For these reasons the folkdoctor expects the patient's kinsmen and friends to be in constant attendance
(though this does not require the same person or persons
to be present throughout the illness) and to so operate
some sort of unstructured rota that there is always a
small crowd beside the sick-mat, both by day and by
night.

In this sense, the folkdoctor directs a therapeutic programme in which he himself occupies a number
of diverse roles. First, he goes out to the rain forest
to seek the materia medica he requires for chemotherapy;
then he compounds the drugs and disperses them. Next
he steps in to direct and cohere a complex programme
of pastoral care involving two networks of personnel -
one living, the other dead. The patient might be

suffering from the effects of poisoning, sorcery, witchcraft, a spell, an involuntary breach of etiquette or
taboo (kesapo), the malignant thoughts or deeds of a
personal enemy, or failure to carry out ritual or ethical obligations to deceased ancestral spirits, living
kinsmen, friends or strangers. The folkdoctor uses a
far more open-ended diagnostic tool-kit, or (more aptly)
concept-kit, than the average western general practitioner or doctor-on-duty at an outpatients' clinic. Presenting symptoms are certainly important, and his examination is likely to begin with a visual and auscultat-
ory examination, which he regards as a necessary preliminary in the sense of first aid after an accident. But
he is more concerned with ascertaining more remote and
ultimate causes that have probably been building up over
a period of months or years in a disturbed psycho-social
or soma/natura binary relationship between the patient
and his human or biosocial environment. For this he
has a virtually ready-made working diagnosis, derived
from his life-long knowledge of the patient in his actual social setting. If there are lacunae in his knowledge, his patient's kinsmen see it in their own interest that their doctor should be fully informed, even
where this entails the communication of shameful or emb-
arrassing facts. This is generically akin to confession

in the Roman Catholic Church, or the voluntary communication to a psychoanalyst of previously suppressed feelings or ideas.

Presenting symptoms

Similar or homologous presenting symptoms may be common
to a wide range of somatic disturbances, but they are
generally regarded as being more specific to certain
demographic categories of sex and age differentiation.
Thus vaginal haemorrhage or discharge, pain in the
breasts and discomfort during pregnancy are regarded
as solely gynaecological ailments, and as such are almost
always dealt with by a traditionally trained village midwife (bidan).

        Nevertheless village folkdoctors, who are almost
always men, are not ignorant about problems of correct
diet during pregnancy and lactation, of taboos about body
posture and where or where not to go or sit during pregnancy, or about such obstetric problems as breach presentation in parturition. All the same, they prefer to
act as consultants to midwives rather than attend directly the pregnant or parturient mother. Such help may
take the form of invocations to ancestral spirits and
prayers to Allah, and to these may be added (with or
without the midwife's knowledge or consent) the admin-

istration of drugs believed to have an analgesic effect
or to hasten parturition. Likewise, an adolescent girl
suffering from dysmenorrhoea is more likely to be taken
by her mother or other senior female relative to a village midwife than to a folkdoctor. On the other hand,
disorders of the alimentary and digestive systems, persistent headache, high febrile states, diuresis, surface
wounds and lesions, skin ulcers and scabies are more
likely to be taken directly to the folkdoctor. Only
if his treatment fails is resort made to other village
doctors, or to more remote specialists renowned for their
competence in one or more specific fields of medicine,
such as chest ailments (often pulmonary tuberculosis)
or disorders of the skin. Current notions of tuberculosis causation and therapy are referred to below.

Apart from the dichotomy of symptoms and diagnoses based on sex, the next most important criterion
is age. For example, a foetus is believed to acquire
a soul and thus to 'begin to live' from the fourth month
of gestation. From then on its diet, both in the sense
of being fed properly nutritious meals in utero at the
same time as withholding from it physically harmful or
ritually deleterious foodstuffs, requires the closest
attention of the mother and other females in the household and neighbourhood.

The symptomatic presentations or cognition of illth in a person thus depend greatly on his or her stage of development in the individual life cycle. Illness presentations are therefore best considered in terms of an individual life cycle.

Early infancy

The most frequent presenting symptoms at this stage are (a) neonatal umbilical tetanus, (b) failure to breastfeed and (c) diarrhoea or dysentery. As the incidence of maternal and infantile mortality is relatively high this is regarded as a period of maximal health hazard for the puerperal pair. Access to the parturient mother's house or room is strictly limited to those directly concerned, such as the midwife and the puerperal woman's mother or sisters; otherwise generally speaking not even her husband may enter her quarters. The same applies in the first few hours after parturition, but once the placenta has been successfully removed and buried outside the front door by the baby's father, and the necessary ritual purification has been performed, the taboo on access is gradually lifted. The puerperal pair (i.e. mother and new-born child) may not however leave the house for some days, and the baby not for one week, until it is taken down to the river or to a bamboo shower for its first

ritual bath, supervised by both the midwife and a folkdoctor.

The sign of robust health most looked for in a
baby is a good appetite, initially in breast feeding
but soon thereafter in supplementary rice-gruel intake.
Secondly, its stools should be regular and well-formed.
Symptoms of illness are a poor, small or erratic appetite, vomiting, diarrhoea and fever. Crying, however,
even if excessive by western standards, is seldom considered a morbid symptom.

The incidence of one or more of these sickness
states requires maximal preventive care in terms of ban-
ishing, exorcising or neutralizing existing or potential
pathogenic forces. These are believed to consist mainly
of malignant spirits. To strengthen the baby against
them, it is 'smoked' soon after birth over the kitchen
fire and 'dressed' in one or more protective amulets
attached to a string and worn as a pendant over the
sternum or round the hips and over the navel or lower
abdomen. Generally speaking no clothing is worn until
the child is three or four years old, for the baby is
thought to feel more comfortable that way, and it is
not believed that babies feel or are susceptible to
cold. Nor is it realized that body chills are one of
the most widespread causes of infantile pneumonia and

consequent mortality.

     Most illnesses of infancy and early childhood
are given the generic name of bolon titik, which simply
means 'disease of infants'. Rejang folkdoctors consider
these diseases among the most serious that occur in
their society, and probably the most difficult to treat.
For this reason they tend to give great stress to what
might be called preventive epidemiology and public health,
rather than to individual therapy once children have fallen ill, particularly as it is recognized that the chances of recovery are small. Such preventive measures,
apart from smoking the newborn child and the ritual bath
after the navel stub has fallen off, consist in making
its birth known to its clan and lineage ancestors through
rites of invocation, and by simultaneously appealing to
them to help the newborn child to remain free of visit-
ations from harmful spirits. Apart from the first ritual
bath the baby should not be exposed to the elements, but
kept at home as much as possible, in a warm place next
to or near the kitchen hearthfire. If necessary it may
be taken to the fields strapped in a shawl to its mother'
back, but she must be careful that the baby is not out
of doors before about 8 a.m. or after 5 p.m., i.e. during
night-time or during the potentially dangerous psycho-
physical periods of dawn and twilight.

Diarrhoea and febrile states are treated either by known home remedies, or by the folkdoctor, but if the patient fails to respond its parents tend rapidly to give up hope in the belief that death has been ordained by Allah. This is expressed in the ritual formula bi sapeui adjea' ('he has reached his preordained destiny'). Nevertheless, pragmatic attempts to save the sick child are made right to the end, as evidenced in the parents' and the folkdoctors' continuing search for therapeutic drugs or magico-medical talismen, spirit invocations and sacrificial feasts, the making of vows and the maintenance of a solicitous non-stop vigil over the patient.

Later childhood disorders

These are essentially a continuation of those of infancy. However, if the child has survived the latter, there is considerably less chance of mortality in the 5-12 years age range. Fevers and alimentary disturbances continue to occur, and in some areas the risk of malaria, typhoid and other infection increases. All children have threadworms and other intestinal worms, and a high percentage have enlarged stomachs and spleens. However, there is little anxiety about a child's health as long as it gives evidence of an abundant appetite for rice - no other

comestible is regarded as 'real' food — and washes its
body in the river, or at a bamboo pipe, at least twice
a day.

When a child is off colour or seems poorly for
a few days, he is thought to be kesapo, that is, the
victim of an ancestral or other spirit's punitive action
for a breach of etiquette or adat (customary) law. The
victim is rarely conscious of when or where the breach
occurred, but a folkdoctor or diviner is called in if
the child's sickness persists longer than two or three
days, to discover the identity of the offended spirit
and what form of propitiation or sacrifice would induce
it to cease troubling the child. Kesapo is not however
restricted to childhood, but continues through adolescence to early adulthood. Attempted therapy is not confined to supra-natural resorts, however, and efforts
to relieve headache or other discomfort are simultaneously made through the use of herbal poultices on the
forehead or abdomen, by regulating the diet and by the
administration of herbal potions.

Puberty and adolescence

Septicaemia sometimes sets in as a result of male circumcision, the psychological trauma of which is believed
to be only slight, if not altogether negligible, among

the Rejang. The operation is performed between the ages
of 8 and 12; it usually takes the form of a collective
ceremony in that several boys are circumcised at the
same time in an atmosphere of initial solemnity and later
gaiety and festivity. Each boy is given a new sarong
and other symbols of maturation and initiation into adulthood.

Onset of menstruation and dysmenorrhoea in girls
is probably far more serious than the disorders of male
adolescents, though little has been reported on this in
the literature on South-East Asia. This is also a period
when goitre of the neck and throat first becomes manifest
in highland communities, though in the past few decades
it has been far more prevalent among females than males.
This is probably due to the greater spatial mobility of
boys and men who visit distant market towns more frequently than girls and women, and therefore have greater
dietary access to sea fish. Tuberculosis, mainly pulmonary or meningital, occurs increasingly from about
mid-adolescence onward; it is mainly attributed to poisoning or other forms of sorcery.

Young and mid-adulthood

Among younger adult men and women the most widespread
illnesses are tuberculosis and malaria, though there

are periods when cholera, smallpox and other epidemics
take a higher death toll. The link between the anopheles
mosquito and malaria is generally known, and most people
sleep under mosquito nets if they can afford them. However, the parallel link between certain mosquitoes and
filariasis is not recognized or understood. Once a malaria attack has set in, a patient is given quinine sul-
phate tablets, but their efficacy is known to be both
slow and uncertain, and the side-effects, such as a ringing sensation in the ears or partial deafness, are found
distasteful. More modern and effective anti-malarial
drugs are expensive and generally inaccessible.

Tuberculosis is far less often recognized as such,
and the term 'T.B.C.' carries a stigma introduced from
the cities by Europeans and westernised Indonesians.
It is more commonly regarded as consumption, almost in
the Victorian sense of wasting away, or as a result of
being poisoned or consumed from within by a malignant
familiar inserted and instructed by the victim's enemy.

The poisoning syndrome occupies no less time,
care and expenditure than such syndromes as the slipped
disc or neurosis in western societies. Nearly every
Rejang carries a mental stock of certain wayside rest-
aurants, or whole villages, or particular households in
his/her own village that should be avoided because of

the danger of deliberate and intentional food-poisoning.
Poisoning is not considered to result from food that has
accidentally or inadvertently become contaminated, but
from poisonous vegetable substances (such as upas or
ipuh sap, the fine miang hairs of bamboo, arsenic and
other substances that have been exhaustively studied by
Gimlette (1923)), deliberately inserted into food or
drink about to be consumed by an intended victim. Few
of these poisons are believed to take immediate effect
in the sense of killing within minutes or hours after
consumption. Most are intended to work their way slowly
through the victim's metabolism, gradually destroying
his inner organs, reducing both food and sexual appetite,
inducing lassitude and fatigue, and sooner or later resulting in emaciation, a yellowish dry skin, a rasping
cough, and ultimately in an unnatural death well before
old age.

In adult women death in childbirth, or long-
standing illness owing to complications of parturition,
are widespread. Village midwives are seldom able to
deal successfully with breach presentations, severe vaginal tears or post-parturient haemorrhage. The occurrence of these pathological states is often attributed
to some negligence in the observance of dietary, kinetic
or sexual taboos during pregnancy, or to some moral

shortcoming on the puerpera's own part or that of her
husband.

Old age

In a society where infantile and maternal mortality
rates are high, where tuberculosis and malaria cause
widespread morbidity, and where climate and work are
exceptionally demanding, men and women are considered
to be old once they have reached the 40 to 45 age span,
when most adults are already grandparents. From this
age onward no one is particularly surprised at the onset of severe or chronic illnesses, or if these result
in death. This is considered almost akin to death in
old age by natural causes, except that the exact time
of death is conceptualized as something preordained by
Allah for each individual. Sometimes it is said of a
sick man that 'his time has come for it is written in
the Book (Koran)', or in some other homologous formul-
ation. Nevertheless, each illness is treated on its
merits, in terms of its actual symptomology and known
methods of therapy and alleviation of pain. The prevailing philosophy is that man must be active, ingenious
and not sparing in his efforts to seek both relief from
pain and the prolongation of life. In many cases he
is successful, but where he is not this is due essenti-

ally to divine interception. From this it would appear
that there is a non-frictional area of uncertainty between man and god wherein men may search, often successfully, for more effective remedies, without anyone considering this an improper incursion into a realm that
is the proper or exclusive preserve of either Allah or
the ancestral spirits.

Conclusion

This paper has been concerned with a preliminary survey
of Rejang illness symptomology and concepts of disease
presentation. Such concepts are not separated in Rejang
thought from wider ideological and cosmological notions,
so that these have been referred to when necessary.
However, it has not been within the scope of this paper
to consider the immense range of Rejang or Malay pharm-
acology (see Burkill 1966a, b; Heyne 1927), or the non-
elitist and non-commercialized role of the Rejang folkdoctor (Jaspan: in press). The pathogenetic aspects
of Rejang sorcery and witchcraft have also not been considered in this paper.

REFERENCES

BURKILL, I.H. 1966a. Malay Village Medicine.
    Singapore.

-- 1966b. A Dictionary of the Economic Products of
    the Malay Peninsula (2 vols.). Kuala Lumpur:
    Governments of Malaysia and Singapore.

GIMLETTE, J.D. 1923. Malay Poisons and Charm Cures.
    London: J. & A. Churchill.

HEYNE, K. 1927. Nuttige Planten van Nederlandsch
    Indië (3 vols.). Buitenzorg.

JASPAN, M.A. 1964a. From Patriliny to Matriliny:
    Structural Change among the Rajang of South-West
    Sumatra. (Unpublished thesis, Australian National
    University, Canberra.).

-- 1964b. Folk Literature in South Sumatra (Volume I):
    Redjang Ka-Ga-Nga Texts. Canberra: Australian
    National University Press.

-- 1969. Traditional Medical Theory in South-East
    Asia. Hull: University of Hull Press.

-- In press. The social organization of indigenous
    and modern medical practices in south-west Sumatra
    in Leslie, C. (ed.) Towards the Comparative Study
    of Asian Medical Systems.

MARSDEN, W. 1783. The History of Sumatra (2nd revised
    edition 1811). London: Thomas Payne.

Sumatra Factory Records, 1685-1825. London: India
    Office Library.

VOORHOEVE, P. 1971. Südsumatranische Handschriften.
    Wiesbaden: Franz Steiner Verlag.

UNA MACLEAN

SOME ASPECTS OF SICKNESS BEHAVIOUR
AMONG THE YORUBA

The core discipline in social medicine is undoubtedly
epidemiology, an approach which implies the broad study
of disease in populations as opposed to the close-up,
clinical method of considering illness as it affects
individuals. It is, however, perfectly in order to apply
epidemiological methods to the study of attitudes and
beliefs about illness and this is an area in which social
medicine abuts upon medical sociology, social psychiatry
and social psychology. The anthropological method is
somewhat different, favouring prolonged observation as
against what must seem to some anthropologists a superficial, not to say flippant, concern with measurable data.
Each academic discipline has progressed to date by concentrating upon its unique viewpoint, and the tools and
special languages which have been developed have greatly
facilitated communication between the members of each
branch of behavioural studies. But we are beginning to

realise that our otherwise invaluable spectacles can
also have a distorting effect upon the topics at which
we are all simultaneously peering.

It would be invidious to suggest that anthropology is experiencing these difficulties but, as far as
medicine is concerned, it is undoubtedly the case that
the doctor's carefully nurtured powers of observation
can sometimes interfere with his complete understanding
of the very person whom he is trained to treat, namely
the patient. In medicine at the present time we are
faced with the fact that the prevention and treatment
of many pressing diseases depends upon the active co-
operation of people who may be patients and, in consequence, we are being forced to take seriously the patient's
point of view.

The signal successes of scientific medicine over
the past century have hitherto encouraged neglect of the
social and cultural factors which underlie the manifestations of disease and which are concerned in the recept-
ion by the community of people who are sick and impaired
We have been inclined to forget the distances which medical advances have created between professionals and the
public, between doctors and patients, between the provid
ers and consumers of the available medical services.
There is no doubt that anthropology can make a signific-

ant contribution to our current medical predicament,
since anthropologists have fostered an interest in societies as seen from inside and are ideally placed to prevent the medical profession from adopting the worst pre-
conceptions of outsiders.

My personal interest lies in the field of community attitudes to misfortune, taking misfortune in its
widest sense to mean anything which interferes with
peoples' pursuit of their chosen goals and tasks. Illness is subsumed as simply a special form of personal
misfortune, constituting an unwarrantable interruption
in human affairs which demands both explanation and action. The examination of different societies' reactions
to illness merges with reactions to deviant behaviour
generally. What is involved can possibly be regarded
as a categorization in terms of normal behaviour, illness
behaviour, mad behaviour and bad behaviour. However,
with reference to those forms of behaviour which are
classified as sickness, the question which next arises
regards the appropriate action to be taken by the sick
person and by those who are socially involved with him.

Let us first look briefly at the meaning of sickness for an individual, avoiding altogether the idea that
sickness exists independently of the person who makes
the definition. As far as the potential patient is

concerned, what he first experiences will be a subtle
change in his own self-image, an awareness of sensations
which are unusual or unpleasant. Thus he may feel hot-
ter, colder, or weaker than previously; he may experience
discomfort verging upon actual pain; the pain or discomfort may vary in kind and degree of intensity, manifested as a feeling of distension, throbbing, stabbing
and so on - for the language of pain is extensive; he
may have a disturbance of his normal appetites for food,
drink or sex; bodily processes of which he is normally
unaware may thrust themselves upon his unwilling attention, in the form of strange or excessive discharges from
sundry orifices; finally, as an alternative, or in addition to these experiences, he may be aware of an altered, a feeling of lethargy or sadness, a sense of anxiety,
agitation or dread; indeed he may at times dream strange
dreams and see visions and hear voices addressing him
in terms of entreaty or command.

        Any of these sensations, arising suddenly and un-
sought, demands two responses, action and explanation.
The action is directed to removing the unwelcome sensation and to restoring, as rapidly and completely as
possible, the former state. But the kind of action which
is initiated is inevitably closely bound up with the
explanation which the sufferer employs to account to

account to himself for his present state. His attitude
and subsequent actions will therefore depend upon previous experiences and knowledge, on the basis of which
he makes a rough and ready estimate of the probable outcome of the present discomfort. The process may be barely conscious, consisting at first, for example, in a
simple postural adjustment, going on to the use of hot
or cold applications, pressure, rubbing, covering or
binding some part of the body, or possibly taking a drink
or a meal. Common symptoms receive commonplace attentions in the expectation of early relief and it is only
their persistence or worsening, or the addition of further untoward symptoms and signs, which raise anxiety
to the level when a specific explanation becomes imper-
ative. Thus, someone who wakes with a headache may shrug
and press his temples, go on to place a wet rag on his
brow and then wait a little. But, if the pain gets worse
or is joined by other unpleasant experiences, like vomiting or shivering, the impact upon his daily round is
greater, increasing the need for explanation and further
treatment.

By this stage, something which started as an individual experience of disturbed sensations has acquired
social implications. Up to a point, illness or misfortune can be a purely personal affair but, as a rule, it

soon finds expression in disturbed behaviour, thereby
becoming visible and forming part of the experience of
others. The sufferer may give evidence of his sensations by simply complaining to someone about his feelings
but, in many cases, his altered behaviour is clear for
all to see, as he fails to get up or perform his expected
tasks or as he acts in a way which those who know him
deem unusual. As soon as a developing illness manifests
itself in limitations upon behaviour it has become a
matter of concern to the social groups to which the affected individual belongs, since his relative incapacity
or malfunctioning will necessitate alterations in the
programmes of others, as they adopt his usual tasks or
adjust for their non-performance. Action by the group
will generally be called for, similarly directed to a
restitution of the status quo. And the action or treatment which the group advises and supplies will, in turn,
be related to established cultural explanations and
expectations.

Treatment is always related to explanation since,
in the absence of some idea of causation, the response
to symptoms is arbitrary or irrational. The deeper
question put by patients everywhere, 'Why should this
happen to me?', demands a fuller answer than a mere re-
statement of the happening in an extended time sequence.

However, explanations may be proffered at different levels and those which intrigue a doctor may leave the sick
person perplexed. You may break your wrist after falling
off the bus but you may still wonder why you fell there
and on that day, having travelled safely by the same
route for years. Treatment may relieve your symptoms
but it will not entirely remove your puzzlement.

Illness always produces some degree of uncertainty, both in relation to cause and treatment. There are
always choices to be made between treatment or non-
treatment, between treatment now or after waiting to
see what happens, between self-treatment or treatment
by one or other medical expert. A society like that of
Nigeria, where the impact of modern medicine has been
growing during the last twenty-five years, presents many
opportunities to study the basis of decision-making in
the event of illness. Since the experience of modern
medicine which individuals and families have acquired
may vary greatly, there are possible conflicts and disagreements over what were once comparatively simple
choices. Since not only alternative treatment systems
but also alternative systems of casual explanations for
illness are available, the dilemmas facing individuals
and groups are considerable.

Before turning to some of the data which I

gathered in Ibadan and its surrounding district during
the mid 1960s, I would like to touch upon another aspect
of human response to misfortune, namely the action which
is taken with the object of avoiding misfortune alto-
gather. We doctors are sometimes inclined to regard
preventive medicine as a recent, sophisticated speciality, relating to vaccination, innoculations and other
such highly specific and scientific procedures. But in
fact people have been taking precautions against possible illness and disaster since the dawn of time. Given
our human capacity to envisage the future, it is not
surprising that we should seek to control it and, since
serious illness represents such a limitation upon our
plans, societies have developed elaborate avoidance mechanisms and rituals. Illness is not merely associated
with present uncertainty, but with the anxiety which relates to its possible fatal outcome. Prophylaxis and
protection are ultimately defences against death.

It is only when medicine has progressed to a high
degree of specialization that prevention becomes conceptually and administratively separated from cure. There
are good sociological reasons why this should take place
since, for the highly organized medical services of the
modern world, prevention involves dealing with whole
communities whilst treatment is still an individual

matter.

Furthermore, public health measures are liable
to involve some degree of limitation upon personal freedom, whereas the clinician usually feels that his first
duty is towards his patient. Where presentday West
African society is concerned the impact of preventive
medicine and public health regulations is slight and they
only enter occasionally into personal considerations
regarding illness behaviour.[1] But the impulse to avert
or forestall misfortune is in no way abated and the traditional culture affords ample means to this end.

One reason for the relative lack of prestige from
which modern preventive medicine suffers derives from
the fact that its triumphs consist in producing non-
events. It is successful in so far as an epidemic does
not occur, infant mortality is reduced, the rate of occurrence of a certain industrial poisoning falls, life ex-
pectancy generally increases. But, if people do not experience disaster they are less likely to attribute their
own luck to some far-off official health policy than to
the avoiding action which they have personally chosen
to adopt, such as taking a tonic or a regular cold bath
or using a protective charm. Traditional prophylaxis

---

1 For example, people are generally aware that smallpox
   should be reported but nevertheless often try to hide
   cases of the disease from sanitary inspectors.

may be demonstrably inefficient from the statistical
point of view, but it does retain a marked psychological
advantage.

Available systems of action

With these considerations in mind, let me describe some
of my findings among the Yoruba of Western Nigeria. The
social structure and religious beliefs of these people
have been amply documented elsewhere. They tend to live
together in very large settlements[2] and distinct echoes
of animism persist in spite of public declarations of
adherence to the predominant Moslem or Christian faiths.
Prominent among their beliefs is the Ifa cult, concerned
with divination and the actions advised to avoid an unwelcome fate. The influence of religious belief upon
reactions in illness and misfortune is still considerable and a close relationship exists between sickness
behaviour and the systems of explanations which the Yoruba have developed to cheat death and render life mean-
ingful.

        In the medical context, there are four main sys-
tems of treatment available, namely, traditional Yoruba
medicine; modern or 'European' medicine; Hausa medicine;

---

2 In 1962 the population of Ibadan was nearly half a
   million.

and, finally, what can for convenience be called 'faith healing', as practised by certain so-called apostolic cults. Each of these systems is based upon different sets of ideas about the nature of illness and the processes of disease. But the ordinary consumer feels at liberty to 'shop around' without thereby being conversant with or totally committed to the fundamental concepts behind modern medicine or the religion associated with Hausa medicine. In the case of faith healing there is more likelihood that usage will imply adherence to a cult.

My investigation began in the temple of modern medicine, among outpatients attending two large hospitals in Ibadan. Later the study extended outwards into the larger community and interviews were carried out among people living in an area of traditional housing; among families able to afford secondary education for their children, as well as with various categories of traditional medical practitioners from Hausa barbers, through Yoruba herbalists, diviners, circumcisors and sellers of local 'patent' remedies, to prominent faith healers.[3] I shall not be quoting many statistics but it may be worth mentioning now that a total of over

3   The methodology of these studies is described
    elsewhere (Maclean 1966, 1969, 1971).

1,100 people were interviewed in Ibadan. In addition,
data were obtained relating to the diagnoses arrived
at in relation to close on one thousand patients attending hospitals in the city during one particular month,
as well as information regarding the total attendances
at the three major local hospitals over the course of
one year.

One object of the last named investigations on
hospital attendance was to obtain some preliminary idea
of the extent to which hospitals were being utilized
by local people, since it was thought that families'
experience of this relatively new service would influence their subsequent sickness behaviour. It should,
however, be noted that the three hospitals in question
differed widely in staff and resources, being, firstly,
a large teaching hospital, secondly, an old government
general hospital of the type familiar to many who have
worked in developing countries and, thirdly, a smaller
Catholic mission hospital, treating only women and children. Just as the three hospitals could be ranked in
terms of medical specialism and facilities, so they
varied markedly in accessibility and general appearance,
from the tall, modern building on a prominent hillside
outside town to the shabby, low wards of the other two
hospitals, crouched in the midst of traditional compounds

and streets.

It appeared that the total number of Ibadan people
attending a hospital in any one year was very large indeed, being close to 150,000, or practically one-third
of the entire population of the city. This evidence
was amply substantiated in the course of subsequent interviews with local people in their own homes, when it
turned out that over 90 per cent of families had some
experience of hospitals. Since we are concerned with
illness as a social event, the experience of families
is more relevant than that of individuals.

Regarding the circumstances in which diagnoses
were made, the process was somewhat imprecise at the
government hospital, where all who presented were seen,
if somewhat cursorily, and quickly given prescriptions,
while the university teaching hospital employed some
pre-selection of patients, followed by much more careful
examination of those allowed to enter its precincts.
However, from all the information available, it was
possible to discover the main symptoms which took people
to both institutions. These included skin conditions,
fevers, coughs, injuries and gastro-intestinal disturbances of one kind or another.

Treatment for particular disorders

For the purpose of this paper, attention will now be
focussed upon what people declared would be the proper
action to take in the case of certain specific sicknesses-
es. The symptoms I shall first consider are fever, convulsions in children, jaundice and the rash of smallpox.
These conditions have been chosen for three reasons,
firstly, because they represent differing degrees of
severity from the medical point of view; secondly, because they include conditions known to be common in Ibadan; finally, because one of them, smallpox, constitutes
a grave threat not only to the individual but also to
society.

Fever is no more than a symptom of some illness,
but there are so many parasitic and bacterial infections
in this part of the world that it is a very familiar
experience. One elderly Ibadan man stated 'There are
eleven different types of fever', but he was not prepared to detail his own ways of dealing with all the
separate varieties. The great majority of people who
were interviewed had some idea of how to treat fevers
and, on the whole, European methods found most supporters. The effect of antimalarial drugs and of febrifuges
like aspirin is now well known and these are easily ob-
tainable locally. Most people declared that fever, in

common with headache and stomach ache, did not deserve
a hospital visit. The local treatments for fever were
numerous, the commonest ingredient of a popular infusion
being oruwo from the sapwood tree, the bitter bark, roots
and leaves of which are all employed. A powder made
from the dried leaves of a tree known as sepeleba (lit.
'curse the fever') could be mixed with salt and locust
beans and put into cornflour porridge; a special soap
containing onions, a type of yam and peppers was recommended by some; others suggested that melon leaves and
alligator peppers might be incorporated in a soap. As
compared with people from the traditional part of town,
twice the number of élite families preferred European
medicines for fever. But a proportion of them (20 per
cent) reported the use of both methods.

Naturally, interviews with traditional healers
produced the richest accounts of local fever treatments.
One hundred Ibadan herbalists were asked about the management of fever in children. Oruwo leaves were the
commonest single ingredient, but there were as many detailed prescriptions as there were prescribers.[4]

The faith healers were united in their opposition
to any specific treatment apart from prayer, although

---

4   Pharmacological analysis of this material has yet
    to be carried out.

one schoolboy, who came from such a family background,
confessed that he secretly visited hospital if he felt
very unwell.

Jaundice is another symptom, this time giving evidence of liver disease but, where it may simply indicate an infection (hepatitis), it can portend something
a great deal more serious. Cancer of the liver is the
commonest malignant tumour among males in Ibadan, striking down young or middle-aged men in a mere matter of
three months. Among the many possible aetiological factors which have been suggested is that of a prior liver
infection. Jaundice is known locally as 'yellow fever'
and is recognized by many lay people on account of the
staining of the whites of the eyes, together with changes
in the colour of stools and urine. Questions about personal familiarity with jaundice and possible treatments
for it might indicate, in a rough and ready fashion, the
prevalence of hepatitis.

Approximately equal groups of households in the
traditional part of town were reported to use local or
European treatments. However, about a quarter of those
who were questioned had no information to offer about
jaundice which was clearly, therefore, a less common
experience than fever. Prescriptions frequently contained the juice of limes or other citrus fruits and

the bark of the locust bean tree was another common ingredient. The same <u>oruwo</u> tree whose antifebrile properties were praised, was also mentioned in this context.
One informant said that oil or fat should be avoided
whilst the jaundice lasted, though whether this opinion
was part of folk knowledge or derived from a 'European'
source is not known.

Jaundice was much less familiar to secondary school
children than it was to the dwellers in Old Ibadan. It
is tempting to deduce that these children, coming from
homes with better sanitary facilities and a generally
higher standard of living, might be less likely to encounter infective hepatitis than people living in the
old style houses. But the difference could well be due
to their lack of illness experiences because of their
age.[5]

All the herbalists were able to prescribe for
jaundice, some of them specifically referring to a prior
fever remedy, but others describing liquid medicine to
be used both internally and externally. It was quite
clear that they were familiar with the urinary symptoms,
as many stated that the purpose of their mixture was
to 'make the dark urine come away freely and completely'.

---

5 It is planned to clear up this point by carrying
   out bacteriological investigations.

Convulsions are a common but alarming accompaniment of childhood illness in the tropics, by far the largest number occurring in association with a high fever. It was therefore not surprising to discover that four out of five households could quote a means of dealing with this sudden family emergency. Very nearly 50 per cent of Ibadan households were in the habit of employing a native medicine. The mixture used, and cited by very many respondents, is called agbo tutu, the cold medicine. This popular household remedy is prepared in a number of different ways but the two essential ingredients, urine and tobacco leaves, are known to everyone. The preparation involves no heating, the green tobacco leaves being steeped or marinaded in urine for at least twenty-four hours. Onion leaves are sometimes added. Though cow's urine is the commonest solvent, it was often said that human urine, particularly that of the child's mother, was preferable. Gordon's Gin may be added if the family can afford it. The liquid hangs in a large bottle or pot somewhere in the house for use as required. The recommended dose is one teaspoonful a day for a child and one tablespoon for an adult.

It is important to realize that agbo tutu is used to avoid convulsions as well as to treat them. They

are a symptom which is regarded with more apprehension
than either fever or jaundice; on the one hand convulsions involve loss of consciousness, so that the child
himself seems to be nearly lost; secondly, prompt action
must be taken and it is quite impracticable to make an
immediate visit to hospital; thirdly, it does seem as
if very large doses of what is, in effect, a solution
of nicotine, may be sufficient to sedate the nervous
system (although nicotine is initially a stimulant).

The mixture is recommended by hospital employees,
dispensary attendants and many of the well-to-do. Half
the secondary school children had no experience of fits
within their families but the remainder divided nearly
equally into those whose families would or would not
employ traditional treatment. Not surprisingly, the
herbalists produced prolific recipes for agbo tutu, as
well as other preparations for simultaneous external
application.

Convulsions occurring among adults (when they are
known as wárápá) are much rarer. They constitute what
we would call epilepsy or grand mal and are greatly
dreaded. This condition was frequently cited as one
which is totally unsuitable for hospital treatment.
The strange behaviour of the affected person both during
and after a fit, the violent movements, the loss of

bladder control and the subsequent loss of memory all
cause epilepsy to be associated in the popular mind with
sudden madness, another condition for which a multiplic-
ity of traditional and magical remedies were specifically recommended in preference to European medicine.

Turning now to smallpox, this is pre-eminently
the disease which arouses most alarm in the majority
of Yoruba. The investigation reported here took place
just six years after a major epidemic, but this disease
in epidemic form has long been part of West African experience and Yoruba ideas of causation and treatment
are only one of many which have been investigated. It
is still widely believed to be brought upon the community by the god Shopanna, who is also the source of madness, and many people were most reluctant to discuss
in detail such a dangerous subject for fear of attracting the unwelcome attention of the deity. Until British
legislation outlawed them, the priests of the associated
cult were responsible for the management of cases and
undoubtedly practised a form of variolation, using material from dried scabs for innoculation.

The treatments recommended comprise a mixture of
magic, herbal medicine and specific hygienic measures
which might well have been efficacious in reducing the
spread of the disease throughout the community. Palm

wine is ritually employed, together with sacrifices to
Shopanna and the use of particular incantations. The
floor of the compound containing an affected person must
only be swept with a green branch, which raises little
dust. Meanwhile public gatherings, and the drumming
which is their inevitable accompaniment, are forbidden.
A great amount of detail is involved in the recommended
medical and nursing care of a smallpox patient; he should
most definitely not be washed; he should be smeared with
smallpox ointment when the condition is past its peak;
later, when the pustules have all burst, a special soap
should be used.

Smallpox is the disease whose correct, traditional
treatment is most noticeably a male prerogative; one-
third of the women who were asked denied any knowledge
of how to treat it, whilst the rest were equally divided
amongst those preferring hospital or traditional treatment. Although a third of the men also recommended hospital, there were very few men who were unable to cite
some traditional measures for care.

Reactions to other conditions as well as the four
mentioned above were gauged in other sections of the
inquiry, when people were asked to state which illnesses
were especially suited to home treatment and, in addition, what conditions hospitals were capable of curing.

A small minority (6 per cent) were of the opinion that all diseases were curable by local means; not surprisingly, most of the herbalists and members of faith healing cults held to this view. Mild illness in general, headache, stomach ache and fever were regarded by many as not meriting a hospital visit. However, as the hospital evidence shows, such symptoms, when persistent and, presumably, resistant to simple measures, did affect most of the outpatients.

Some people declared that 'hospitals can treat all diseases except smallpox and madness'. Some members of the general population warned of the inadvisability of taking to hospital patients whose illness was 'due to the action of witches and wizards', and some prescribed prophylactic soaps to secure the goodwill of such potential evil doers. Virtually all the herbalists (some of whom were also diviners) claimed proficiency in this sphere.

The other main category of conditions for which traditional methods of treatment were clearly considered to be the most appropriate were those involving the reproductive system. Impotence, swollen testicles, disorders of menstruation and sterility were all repeatedly quoted in this context in the course of interviews with the general public, whilst abundant contributory evidenc

came from herbalists and from locally printed medical
pamphlets. This was pre-eminently the area for prophylactic measures to avoid possible misfortune. For example, there is a terrible disease known as máágùn, believed to be liable to affect a man who has seduced a
married woman. Potentially fatal, it can manifest itself either in sudden collapse or in a more gradual decline. However, someone putting himself 'at risk' to
máágùn can take the prior precaution of rubbing into
cuts around his waist a powder composed of tortoise
tail and the bark of a tree which had recently fallen
across a road. The tortoise in Yoruba mythology represents a whore, whilst the fallen tree may epitomise the
sinner or the barrier to his future which his transgress-
ion could cause.

Any number of magical prophylactics against miscarriage, to ensure an uneventful labour, to protect a
man against the ill effects of intercourse too soon after
the woman's menstruation, to increase virility, and so
forth, could be quoted. As the introduction to one medicine book explicitly declares, 'Guard this carefully,
because it contains prescriptions used by the ancestors.
They used it and proved it successful. Good fortune is
now within your reach. Take it and taste it, for it is
honey and salt'. Another literate herbalist writes,

'This book has been made for the use of all Yoruba, to
cure them and to protect themselves from the wrath and
machinations of wicked people'. He goes on to be even
more explicit: 'We should first find out what causes
any diseases, because most of the things we treat are
not the causes but the symptoms'.

There is one remaining large area of illness in
which prophylaxis and treatment are closely related and
this is childhood illness. The matter has already been
touched on in relation to childhood convulsions, but
it applies to a whole range of symptoms and signs, not
only indicative of illness but of failures to thrive
or develop in any way the mother considers proper. Thus,
there are medicines to help a child to talk or to bring
out teeth; to reduce the attentions of a child's spiritual companions, who are thought to be enticing him away;
to protect against every feared misfortune or possible
curse, as well as to treat the symptoms associated with
such postulated causes. Small children, in this society,
have generally had a tenuous hold on life and this has
required strengthening by every available means.

Reproduction, sex and sickness behaviour

So far this paper has dealt, firstly, with the patronage
of hospitals and secondly, with the action which people

report would probably be taken in the event of, or to
forestall, particular symptomatology. I should now like to
turn, briefly, to the influence of sex on sickness behaviour. Here I have in mind two aspects, one being
the universal African desire for offspring and the other
the way in which women are personally involved in the
management of illness.

The first aspect has been referred to above, namely the large area of traditional medicine which is involved in rendering circumstances propitious for conception and, once conception has occurred, ensuring that
all proper precautions are taken to try to secure a normal labour and a healthy infant. All the uncertainty
surrounding male sexual performance, the female menstrual
cycle and the initiation of labour itself makes this an
area where the precise efficacy of any particular item
of magical preparation or prophylaxis is exceedingly
difficult to gauge. But, far from decreasing reliance
upon traditional precautions, this actually increases
faith in them, since success will be attributed to their
use whilst failure can equally well be laid at the door
of inadequate observance. In other words, in the case
of matters to do with reproduction, there is such a long
time interval between biological cause and effect, that
all kinds of incidental and accidental events can appear

to relate to the ultimate issue. Hence the very powerful continuing hold of traditional medicines, magical
devices, prescriptions and proscriptions in this field.
Moreover, it is not without significance that the Yoruba
husband is held to be 'responsible' for his wife's pregnancy, in the sense that it is he who must arrange for
the correct medicines to be taken by her.[6] The anxiety
on the part of both parents to secure live offspring will
encourage the mother to participate readily in such measures. She will be anxious to leave undone nothing which
might help her to increase her family[7] and even what we
term failure may not diminish her faith. For example,
one Ogun worshipper, who had begged this potent deity
for children and had borne eight, had not ceased to worship him although they all died in infancy.

Among men in Ibadan one often hears it said that
women nowadays are difficult and disobedient. Apparently they are rapidly forming the habit of going to hospitals to be confined and taking their small children
there for treatment, whereas, formerly, they used always
to ask the husband's permission about such serious
matters. It is, of course, well known that Nigerian

---

6 Just as he himself will imbibe sundry aphrodisiacs
   believed to increase his potency and fertility.

7 Family planning campaigns in Ibadan have very
   limited success.

women are effectively responsible for the care and maintenance of their young children. Although they continue
to employ many prophylactics, using amulets and charms
and regular medication, they also have their own medical
specialists. Medical treatment is, in the main, a masculine prerogative (only two out of one hundred herbalists and diviners were women) but there are certain older
women who are famed for their knowledge about children's
ailments. Childhood illness and death is still an extremely common occurrence in Ibadan and traditional medicine is not very effective when illness does strike.
But in fact the uncertain hold which the young child has
upon life makes his mother all the more reliant on measures reputed to increase his resistance and fortify him
in advance against death.

So much for general uncertainty. It seems as if
the medico-religious system, largely a male construction,
has all kinds of preventive rituals to hand. But, when
an emergency occurs, action must be taken at once. So,
in the case of fits in childhood, the nearest remedy must
be immediately applied, and the traditional agbo tutu
is familiar to nearly everyone. A trip to hospital is
strictly out of the question in such an emergency; and
paediatricians seldom see such small patients until they
are already deeply doped.

Similarly, it is all very well to depend upon rituals
and tonic medicines during the course of pregnancy but,
once someone has gone into labour and is experiencing
difficulties, she, and her family, are unlikely to refuse European obstetrics if such is available within
reasonable distance. It is a branch of modern medical
practice which is, moreover, markedly successful, and
that in the most acceptable way possible, since it provides healthy babies for happy mothers. No wonder that
empiricism triumphs here and the demand for such services seems infinite. Even if men may claim to resent
the loss of some of their traditional rights to decision-
making in this area, since their desire also is for
healthy offspring they are easily persuaded to overcome
theoretical objections which are no longer functional.

It is appropriate to refer here to another aspect
of the Ibadan research, in which it was shown (in strict
terms of statistical significance) that the use of traditional medicines was inversely related to the educational level of the mother in the family. Where the
mother had been educated beyond secondary school level
she sought to approximate family life as closely as possible to the western model and this involved adopting
European modes of sickness behaviour. Local medicines
were looked on as dirty and disreputable and cast aside

along with the old gods. Moreover, in such professional
families, the Yoruba mother with an education equal to
that of her husband would have her natural female tendencies towards independence still further reinforced.
Since education also increased reliance on European medicines, regardless of sex, her husband would be likely
to agree with her personal determination to discard
tradition.

Conclusions

This paper has approached sickness behaviour among the
Yoruba from a sociological standpoint, concentrating
upon deliberate actions taken to maintain or enhance
health and to cure illness. These actions are taking
place against a cultural background which provides a
complicated system of beliefs and practices, evolved
to meet all the ills and misfortunes mankind is heir
to. But there are other medical systems simultaneously
to hand, namely, the western form of medicine, the rem-
nants of the Arabic tradition and, recently, the development of faith healing in association with apostolic
cults. An attempt has been made to analyze the factors
which influence people's behaviour regarding both prevention and cure, especially in relation to certain categories of symptom or disease.

It is difficult to summarize this complex situation, especially since the experience of households and of individuals, regarding both illness and particular remedies, is bound to vary greatly. However, it can be said that European 'hospital medicine' has now been present long enough for people to have formed some shrewd impressions of what it can and cannot achieve. Thus patients tend to go to hospital in the event of emergencies (surgical or obstetrical) and where a condition is clearly rapidly worsening despite local treatment. The great success of hospitals in midwifery and paediatrics is generally recognized, especially among the mothers who stand to receive most immediate benefit.

On the other hand, people are well aware that there are many conditions which hospitals cannot cure. For example, jaundice, which is common but largely self-limiting, is frequently due to a virus, for which there is no known antidote once the disease has taken hold, so the popular opinion is substantially sound. Epilepsy in adults is a condition which strikes dramatically and unpredictably, and European medicine is frequently at a loss regarding its cause, although the incidence of fits can be markedly lowered by regular sedation. It is a disease about which there is considerable alarm and awe in many cultures, including our own. Smallpox

can be regarded as a social misfortune as well as an
individual disaster, since it can rapidly kill off many
members of the adult population and is not curable, even
though eminently preventable by vaccination. So it is
not surprising to find an associated belief system with
a terrible smallpox god, ideas about preventing and lim-
iting the spread of the disease, together with numerous
prescriptions to ameliorate its dramatic and offensive
manifestations. Finally, mental illness, however defined, is deemed unsuitable for hospital care; here again, the local judgement of the capabilities of general
hospitals is justified. So there is undoubtedly a pragmatic element in the decisions regarding appropriate
care.

It should also be borne in mind that certain epis-
odes, by their very suddenness, call for immediate action at home; and home treatment is the norm for all min-
or conditions, among the Yoruba as in Britain and the
United States. The converse of this is just as true:
illnesses or failures of bodily functioning which are
associated with a high degree of uncertainty and where
it is not easy to discern a one-to-one relationship between cause and effect are eminently suitable for traditional, magical methods and for procedures which are
lengthy and complicated. This area of uncertainty is

especially associated with everything to do with pro-
creation. The production of children is a matter of
the greatest importance, both for the individual and
for the continuance of society. For all these reasons,
it is not surprising that so much reliance should still
be placed upon methods which have manifestly succeeded
in maintaining the Yoruba in existence since the beginning of their history.

I would maintain, therefore, that people's behaviour in sickness has certain common features everywhere.
Most treatment takes place in the family but, where that
is insufficient, people look for help to what has previously proved trustworthy. In a changing situation,
with many alternatives, western medicine has to prove
itself against venerable opposition and, whilst it is
notably successful in some respects, there are many misfortunes for which it can offer no help. As they still
feel themselves menaced by a great variety of ills, dog-
ged by bad luck, and enviously regarded by their closest
associates, ordinary Yoruba consider it wise to take
numerous precautions. If they remain well and success
comes their way, they feel they are to be congratulated
on their forethought; if the worst happens, then hospital treatment may be sought. Apart from fervent faith
healers and some elderly herbalists and diviners, there

are few who would not grant European methods an occasional trial. But tradition still affords a support which is both psychologically satisfying and socially sanctioned. Until the majority of the population are educated to the level of modern doctors some reliance upon traditional medicine, however modified, will remain.

REFERENCES

MACLEAN, U. 1966. Hospitals or healers? An attitude survey in Ibadan. Human Organization 25: 131-39.

-- 1969. Traditional healers and their female clients: an aspect of Nigerian sickness behaviour. Journal of Health and Social Behavior 10: 172-86.

-- 1971. Magical Medicine: a Nigerian case study. London: Allen Lane The Penguin Press.

HARRIET NGUBANE

SOME ASPECTS OF TREATMENT AMONG THE ZULU

My fieldwork was carried out among the Nyuswa-Zulu who
live at Botha's Hill in the Valley of a Thousand Hills
in Natal. Nevertheless, apart from local differences
of detail, I am confident that what I have to say about
the basic principles underlying the treatment of disease
holds true for all Zulu people who regard themselves
as following the traditional Zulu way of life. Throughout the essay I employ the terms 'disease', 'illness'
and 'medicine' in their Zulu sense; I must therefore
begin by explaining the ways in which the underlying
Zulu concepts differ from those implied by the use of
these English words.

     The English word 'disease' is defined as 'a con-
dition of the body, or of some part or organ of the body,
in which its functions are disturbed or deranged; any
particular kind of this with special symptoms and name'
(O.E.D.). In Zulu the word most closely approximating
to this sense of disease is isifo (-fa, to die; ukufa,

death); but there is also a notion of ill-health (<u>ukunga-phili</u>) which embraces the concepts denoted by <u>isifo</u> and also the general idea of a person being in a disordered state in relation to his environment, as a result of which he is vulnerable to all sorts of misfortune, including illness. Another usage which requires clarification is that of the word 'medicine'. In English the term denotes substances used with the intention of restoring health. Although the Zulu word <u>umuthi</u> (pl. <u>imithi</u>, tree or shrub) is usually translated as medicine, the two words are not synonymous, for <u>umuthi</u> may be used in attempts to destroy health as well as in attempts to restore it. There is medicine for healing (<u>umuthi wokwelapha</u>) and medicine for killing (<u>umuthi wokubalala</u>). While some <u>imithi</u> are always used for healing purposes and others for harmful purposes, there are in addition <u>imithi</u> which are used for both healing and harming, depending on the intentions of those using them. It will be shown how some <u>imithi</u> for healing purposes are believed to be potent in themselves and no ritual is observed in their administration, while others are symbolic and are accompanied by the performance of certain rites.

My knowledge of Zulu medicine is limited. In order to acquire a comprehensive knowledge in this field

I would have had to be apprenticed to an ethno-medical
practitioner for some time and according to the rules
of the profession's code it would be improper to make
such knowledge public. However, my interest is not in
the range of pharmacopoeia, but rather in the notions
and theories which govern the use of medicines. As this
is a complex subject, in this essay I will confine myself only to what are considered to be the basic notions.
I hope to demonstrate in broad terms how the Zulu treatment of disease is connected with the idea of causality.

Medicines are essentially of plant origin. The
widest and most extensively used form of plant life is
known as amakhambi, these being herbs, bark and roots
freshly collected from the veld. In addition a small
proportion of medicines are derived from animal sources.
Some amakhambi herbal decoctions and infusions are used
for healing purposes as household remedies and these
are common knowledge. There are also medicines which
can be prepared only by a trained practitioner who is
either an ethno-doctor (inyanga) - usually a man, or a
diviner (isangoma) - usually a woman. The diviner has
the same comprehensive knowledge of medical practice
as the ethno-doctor but in addition she is possessed
by her ancestors and has clairvoyant powers. However,
her two roles do not overlap. Her clients consult her

as a diviner in the first place, and, having found the cause of their trouble, they may decide to enter into a new arrangement, employing her in her capacity as a medical practitioner, or they may decide to seek the services of an ethno-doctor. Men may also become diviners; but since this is a woman's job, such men become transvestites for the rest of their lives as diviners.

There are also medicines which can be prepared only by specialists who are referred to as 'inyanga of such-and-such a disease' (e.g. inyanga yomhlabelo - the inyanga who treats fractures). Specialization is not restricted to either sex. Such skills are a family prerogative. The specialist passes on the skills to only one member of the following generation, so that even within the family such knowledge is limited to one or two people at a time. Some examples of specialised skills are: the preparation of snake-bite antidotes, dental medicines, the treatment of fractures and the anti-natal medicines. The inyanga or isangoma either buys the medicines or refers the patients to such specialists.

To understand and appreciate the Zulu treatment of disease it is necessary to examine briefly the prevailing notions of causality. Physical ailments which are believed to 'just happen' without association with

any personal malice are grouped together under a generic
name of umkhuhlane. It is impossible to translate this
very comprehensive term by any single expression in English. It includes minor ailments such as the common
cold as well as serious epidemics and diseases. The
contagious and infectious nature of some diseases of
this class is recognized. Some ailments are associated
with seasonal changes such as the common outbreaks of
diarrhoea in summer (isisu sehlobo). Others are associated with the malfunctioning of the body, such as
the excessive accumulation of bile (inyongo), believed
to cause biliousness, headaches, stomach ache and many
other bodily derangements. Others are further associated with heredity (ufuzo, lit. resemblance); these include epilepsy (isithuthwane), chronic chest complaints
(ufuba) such as asthma and chronic bronchitis, and also
an unhealthy skin condition (umzimba omubi, lit. bad
flesh) which is a tendency to develop sores, boils and
other forms of skin complaint.

On the whole umkhuhlane comprises illnesses which
are believed to be understood by a western trained doctor and to respond readily to his treatments. Although
a comprehensive term, the individual diseases that come
under it have particular names; for instance, measles
is isimungumungwane, malaria is imbo or uvuvatha, small-

pox is ingxabongo. Unless there is need to particul-
arize, I will refer to all illnesses that 'just happen'
as umkhuhlane. But in the rest of this essay I am concerned with what is regarded as ukufa kwabantu, the disease of the people, that is to say of Africans, which
can only be understood by African people because it is
based on Zulu cosmology.

Ukufa kwabantu and the notion of balance

The Zulu believe that there is a special relationship
between a man and his environment and that plant and
animal life somehow affect the environment. As different countries or regions have different types of plants
and animals, they therefore have different environmental
conditions. The people in each particular region are
adjusted to their surroundings, but if they were to go
to a completely different region they would become ill
as they would not be adjusted to the new environmental
conditions.

It is also believed that when moving, both man
and animals leave behind them something of themselves,
and absorb into themselves something of the atmosphere
through which they move. This 'something left behind'
in moving is known as umkhondo (pl. imikhondo). Because neither men nor animals are restricted to a par-

ticular region, when they return from far-off regions
which are markedly different from Natal and Zululand,
they bring back with them foreign elements which they
have absorbed in their travels. A man may even carry
foreign medicines and by so doing introduce a foreign
element to the region to which he has returned. Some
wild animals and birds travel long distances and on their
return may introduce something foreign. Poisonous snakes
also leave behind dangerous tracks. This is also the
case with lightning, particularly on the spot where it
strikes. Thus the atmosphere and the countryside are
believed to be riddled with dangerous tracks or _imik-
hondo_. Ironically, the situation can be aggravated by
some of the methods used in the treatment of disease.
It is believed that certain types of disease can be taken
out of a patient and be discarded as a definite material
object; having been discarded it may hover around in
the atmosphere or remain localized until it attaches
itself to someone else. In this way what is removed
when curing a disease is transformed into _umkhondo_ and
further pollutes the environment.

I must mention here that _umkhondo_ is a word used
more often to describe a visible track on the ground.
But it also describes the invisible track picked up by
dogs when hunting or when tracking a criminal. If such

a scent is floating in the air, the correct term of reference is imimoya rather than imikhondo. A person is said to inhale imimoya (uhabula imimoya) and he is said to step over imikhondo (weqa imikhondo). Usually an adjective emibi (bad) is added to differentiate between harmless and harmful tracks (imikhondo emibi). Since I use imikhondo in its harmful sense only I find it unnecessary to qualify it. Furthermore, because the word imimoya can also mean spirits, air, wind, soul, as well as an amicable disposition in people, I find it convenient to use imikhondo for tracks, whether they are in the air or on the ground.

Certain animal tracks are believed to affect babies, sometimes fatally. Owing to regular medication against imikhondo of the animal track type, a baby gradually develops immunity and as it grows into childhood it is usually immune. But an adult can be a carrier of the animal track type of imikhondo (imikhondo yezinyamazane). A nursing mother or a pregnant mother can pick up such imikhondo in her travels and her baby becomes sick as a result. Since young babies cannot walk, they do not step over imikhondo but they inhale them. Adults are said to step over (eqa) and the illness arising from stepping over any form of undesirable element in the environment is known as umeqo. It will be shown

later how umeqo plays a very major part in the causality
of illness. It must further be noted that some harmful
elements in the environment are believed to be localized, for example, in places where lightning had previously struck or where something considered harmful to
health had been buried. These are also regarded as
umkhondo, although they are not produced by something
in motion.

Illness owing to umkhondo may show itself in such
symptoms as nettle rash, which is said to be a result
of contact with fresh snake track. Fretfulness, crying
and depression of the fontanelle in babies are symptoms
recognized as caused by contact with wild animal tracks
(izinyamazane). Diarrhoea and dehydration in babies
is usually diagnosed as inyoni owing to contamination
from an area struck by lightning.

The environment is not only polluted by undesirable tracks, and by the substances that are thrown away
as part of a curing technique; it is also made dangerous
by sorcerers who scatter harmful substances along the
pathway or place such substances on the pathway of a
particular person so that on stepping over it he falls
ill with the condition known as umeqo. In order to survive despite such dangers in the environment, everyone
must be frequently strengthened to develop and maintain

resistance. In other words, everyone must establish
and maintain a balance with his surroundings. The balance is established not only between a man and his impersonal surroundings, but also between man and man.
If a person who has used very strong medicines to establish this balance meets someone who is not properly
strengthened the latter is overpowered by the presence
of the former and may become ill. This is known as uk-
weleka ngesithunzi, meaning 'to feel or suffer the weight
of someone's overpowering influence'. For this reason
people living together are strengthened at the same time
to keep up the balance between them.

There is no Zulu word which conveys the meaning
of the English word 'balance', but the notion is implied
in the word lungisa, of which the standard translation
is 'to put in order, arrange, adjust, set as it should
be, tidy'. It also means to restore order where there
has been disorder. I am therefore using the word balance
to mean moral order in the symmetrical sense with reference to the positions of people and their relations to
other people, to the environment, to the ancestors and
to the mystical forces which produce pollution. The
idea of balance in this sense should be understood to
mean symmetry or order rather than the more usual sense
of balance as the central pivot in a counterpoise situ-

ation. I have laboured this point of balance because
it is in fact the pivotal ideology around which revolve
practically all the notions which constitute what is
known as <u>ukufa kwabantu</u> or African disease.

Sorcery and sorcerers

Sorcery (<u>ukuthakatha</u>) is another cause of illness.
Three types of sorcerer may be distinguished. The first
type is that which approximates in many respects to the
conventional concept of a witch as described in many
African societies. Such a sorcerer is believed to have
been created or moulded with an evil heart (<u>wabunjwa
ngenhliziyo embi</u>). The stereotype of this sorcerer is
as follows. He harms people for no apparent reason.
He keeps baboons as familiars.[1] When he visits home-
steads at night he rides naked on these baboons, facing
backwards. He digs up corpses to use as zombies in till-
ing his fields at night while other people are asleep
in order to be more successful and gain advantage over
other people. He is mean, jealous and keeps to himself.

---

1   In this essay I have left out what is considered by
    the Zulu as 'new' and arising from contacts with
    other African groups in the current migrant labour
    situation. I am treating this elsewhere, where I
    aim to show how the 'new' is absorbed into the al-
    ready existing pattern of thought. This explains
    why I have not mentioned here the Xhosa familiars,
    such as <u>Tikoloshe</u> and <u>Impundulu</u> or <u>Umarmtsotsi</u>.

His chief technique is to scatter noxious medicines or bury them in the homes of his victims. Because he is so thoroughly evil-hearted on such nocturnal visits he also scatters harmful medicines along the pathways to harm anyone who passes by. He is a danger to the community at large and is feared. This type of sorcerer is a man. He may combine in himself the techniques of the two types of sorcery mentioned below, but this need not always be the case. Although he is said to have been moulded with an evil heart, he is aware of what he is doing and has conscious control over his actions. He always uses medicines and has no superhuman powers which would enable him to fly, or change shape, or perform such feats as many witches are said to be able to do. For this reason he is rather a sorcerer than a witch. There is no Zulu word which could accurately be translated as 'witch'. His aim, as his technique suggests, is to render the environment dangerous for his victims or to put the people out of balance with their environment.

The second type of sorcerer is the one who is supposed to use medicine to harm his opponents or rivals, or the people with whom he comes into conflict outside the lineage situation. He is not an habitual sorcerer but acts only in cases of personal animosities.

He may not be regarded by the community at large as a
sorcerer but only by those who are in conflict with him.
The main method said to be used by this type of sorcerer
is that of ukudlisa, which is to add harmful medicines
(including physically poisonous substances) to the victim's food. In addition he steals important portions
of a sacrificial beast, such as the gall-bladder (inyongo), the chyme (unswani) and the third stomach (in-
anmi). This action is calculated not only to nullify
the victim's sacrifice, but also to reverse the purpose
of a sacrifice; for example, if the sacrifice was calculated to enable the woman to bear many children, such
sorcery would make her sterile, or, when she bears babies, they die young. He may also use the technique of
placing harmful substances to harm someone who is his
enemy. However, the technique most commonly used by
this type of sorcerer is believed to be that of ukudlisa.
Both men and women may be found in this class of sorcerer, but women are believed to be in the majority. Such
sorcery is brought about by situations rife with competition, jealousy and rivalry such as may be found in a
polygamous or extended family situation among wives or
among co-workers.

Thirdly, there is the uzalo or lineage sorcerer.
Members of a lineage segment are descendants of a common

grandfather. Such agnates share sacrifices and have
certain ritual and social obligations towards one another. They are not supposed to practise sorcery of
the above-mentioned types against each other because
this would meet with the disapproval of the ancestors
who would cease to protect such a sorcerer. If members
of a lineage segment quarrel they must rectify it by
performing the ritual ukuthelelana amazi, that is, washing each other's hands, symbolizing the washing away
of anger in their hearts. This is followed by a slaughter of a goat and thus they are brought together by sharing in the sacrificial meal.

However, a man of this group can persuade the
ancestors to favour him and abandon one or more members
of the lineage. This is sorcery of a special kind which
can only be practised by one umnumzane or head of homestead against another of the same status within the lineage segment. In other words, it can be practised by
people who are in a position to approach the ancestors
in their own right and can therefore be practised by
men only. Its effects on the victim are that he and
his dependants are put into a condition of being without the protection and the good favour of the ancestors,
and are therefore exposed to all kinds of misfortune.
This condition can be partially inherited by the suc-

ceeding patrilineal generation in that the generation
would be without the protection of the ancestors of the
grandfather generation.

The following case is an example of accusation
of lineage sorcery which took place during 1971. One
umnumzane ('Y' in the accompanying kinship diagram) was
accused by insinuation by another umnumzane ('B'), whose
father ('A') died in 1969 and whose twelve-year-old daughter ('C') died in 1970. The accuser's father ('A') was
old and an invalid, whose state of ill-health was aggravated by drinking a locally distilled concoction known as
gavine. The accused ('Y') held a beer party at his home
to which the old man came and at which he was served with
gavine. He left the party that evening in a drunken state
but never reached his home. A search party was organized
by the accused who, being an inyanga, was the only able-
bodied man of his lineage at home, all the others being
migrant labourers.

The missing man was found dead on the third day
a few hundred yards from the accused's home. Across the
chest of the dead man lay a cord, which suggested strang-
ulation. In addition, the body had been mutilated. His
left leg had been amputated at the knee. His left eye
and his left testicle had been removed. The accused went
to report the matter to the police and also to break the

333

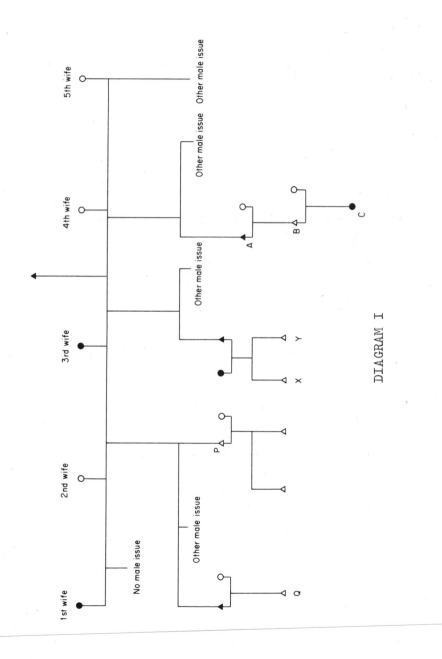

DIAGRAM I

sad news to his agnates in town. When the police arrived at the scene of the tragedy they mentioned that the
accused had reported that the dead man's body had been
mauled by dogs.

In 1970, the twelve-year-old daughter ('C') of
the accuser died. During her short illness (possibly
while delirious) she called out the name of the accused
and begged him not to kill her. She said she saw him
coming towards her, holding a spear as if he was going
to stab her. She was taken to hospital. While in the
bus to the hospital, she again repeated her accusations
in the hearing of the Nyuswa passengers in the bus. She
never reached hospital but died in the bus.

Her father began to ask himself why 'Y' always
seemed to be connected with his misfortunes. He had giv-
en gavine to the deceased man and never bothered to see
him safely home. He had chosen to tell the police that
dogs had mutilated the body; what dog would choose an
eye or a testicle for its meal? But the most damaging
factor was the dramatic death of the girl.

The accused in self defence pointed out that during the beer party on the night of the deceased's disappearance, he (the accused) had been called out on business to attend to a patient and left while the party was
still in progress. In his absence his wife served gavine

to the deceased and by the time of his return the deceased had left. He could not therefore have been aware of
his state of drunkenness. He denied ever telling the
police that dogs had mutilated the corpse. The accuser
was not convinced by such explanations. He approached
'X', the head of the lineage segment and a full brother
of the accused, to arrange with the lineage for an umhlahlo. Umhlahlo is a consultation with a diviner in cases of open accusations. Both the accuser and the accused
agree upon the particular diviner who is to be consulted.
It must be one who lives a good distance away and is
therefore not known to either. Her methods of divination
must be such that those consulting her give no clue; they
sit silent throughout the process of divination. Beside
the accuser and the accused there must be neutral observers representing the chief. These are chosen by the chief
himself and their duty is to report back to the chief and
also ensure that the antagonists do not fight. The accuser in this particular case had not made an open accusation, but had implied a great deal. When approaching
the lineage-head, he had merely mentioned that in view
of the unusual circumstances, he would like all the heads
of imizi (households) of his lineage to accompany him to
an umhlahlo. Seventeen lineage members went and two
neutral observers. The diviner chosen lived more than

one hundred miles away. Cars for transport were hired.

The diviner said the deceased man died of exposure because in his drunken state he slept in the open and, in any case, he was an invalid. Nobody killed him. But two men (whom she named) from a neighbouring tribe came upon the corpse by chance and mutilated it for their own nefarious purposes. The accuser had experienced a series of misfortunes because he was the victim of uzalo, lineage sorcery, directed against his father's home and now against his own house, not by the man 'Y' he had suspected but by 'P' and 'Q', respectively a classificatory father and brother, the latter being the prime mover, aided by the former. They had been cunning in their practice of sorcery in that they always used izicuyo or insila, the body dirt (such as sweat) of the suspected man; this explained why the dying child kept seeing the accused coming to kill her.

This was an unexpected turn of events. Usually any person accused at umhlahlo sessions is exiled together with his family, and this is enforced ruthlessly by burning down his home, looting, and beating him up; very often the accused barely escapes with his life. The umhlahlo decision in this case was so unexpected that the accuser 'B' refused to accept it. He maintained that 'Y' had used medicines to confuse the diviner. As a result nothing happened to the man who had been found guilty by the diviner. As soon as the party returned to Nyuswa the man originally accused went to the headman, who represents the chief, to lay a charge of libel against his accuser. The headman refused to consider the case, saying it was a lineage matter which should be settled at lineage level. It had not yet been settled in August 1971.

Ancestors and illness

The ancestors are also believed to cause illness. But, before looking into the activities of the ancestors, I want to consider the Beings in the 'other world' and inquire to what extent they come into the picture of health and disease.

In the beginning there was uMvelinqangi (the first Being.[2] At some point in time there was also uNomkhubulwane, or Inkosazane (the Princess).[3] At another point in time, a reed growing on the river bank burgeoned and gave birth to a man; but no mention is

---

2   See also Callaway 1884: 1-5; Krige 1968: 179-84.

3   Rituals for Inkosazane are occasionally performed within the Valley of a Thousand Hills in Natal. Although people know of a ritual for uMvelinqangi, I have never met anyone who has participated in it.

made of a woman in relation to the man. The people mul-
tiplied. UMvelinqangi sent a chameleon (unwabu) to tell
the people that they will not die. After some time
uMvelinqangi sent a lizard (intulo) to tell the people
that they will die. The lizard overtook the chameleon
which, instead of delivering the message, stopped on his
way to feed on ubukhwebezane, mauve berries that grow
wild. Later on the chameleon arrived with the message
that people will not die. The people refused to accept
the second message that people will not die, and decided
to stick to the first message delivered by the lizard
(sibambelentulo). Meanwhile the Inkosazane promoted the
fertility of the land, the people and the animals. Ideally, every year in spring certain rites should be performe
by married women and maidens to ensure good crops, more
cattle and more healthy babies. These rites are directed
to Inkosazane. UMvelinqangi is approached only in situations of catastrophe or impending disaster such as extreme drought, in which case both men and women participate. Both uMvelinqangi and Inkosazane are thought of
as living 'above' and they do not affect the health or
the life of an individual in day to day situations. It
is the ancestors that are closely connected with the
people.

        There are many words in Zulu which are used to

mean all-the-dead. These include amathongo, izithutha,
izithunzi, amadlozi, abaphansi. The last two are those
more commonly used by the Nyuswa. Abaphansi means 'those
who are below', for the dead are believed to live 'below'
The ancestors are primarily concerned with the welfare
of their descendants. They bring them the good things
of life and protect them from all harmful situations.
The ancestors withdraw their protection if the descendants offend them by failing to live up to their expectations. In this case they are said 'to face away from
and give their backs to the descendants' (bamfulathele).
This is the most common form of ancestral behaviour associated with illness and leaves the person concerned exposed to all misfortunes.

I have already mentioned lineage sorcery and the
type of sorcery which annuls a sacrifice. Both bring
the ancestors into play but within a sorcery context.
In cases of potential diviners, they become ill because
the ancestors who want to give them clairvoyant powers
want a recognition of their presence; such illness is
never expected to be fatal. The ancestors are, however,
believed to help those who help themselves. They cannot
be expected to protect a person who takes no precautions
against illness in the form of preventive and strengthening medicines. The ancestors will only endorse an

initiative once it is taken. When the ancestors cease
to protect a descendant owing to the reasons given above, such a person is said to be afflicted with umnyama
(blackness or darkness). Umnyama is a state of vulnerability to disease. The extreme form of umnyama, when
a person is at his lowest and unable to offer any resistance to disease, is associated with life crises such as
bereavement, menstruation, confinement and homicide.
These conditions produce umnyama of varying degrees of
intensity and duration. This type of umnyama is contagious and its victims are expected to avoid situations
which would bring about contagion not only to people but
to certain plants and cattle. The victims also observe
ukuzila behaviour pattern. Ukuzila covers such notions
as mourning, abstinence or moderation of pleasurable experiences, avoidance of certain things and the control
of the emotions.

　　　　Running through the notions of environmental disease or umkhondo/umego, of ancestor wrath and lineage
sorcery, and of umnyama due to life crises, is the principle of balance. In the case of environmental disease
the idea of balance is implicit because for a person
to fall ill because of umkhondo/umego is in itself suggestive of a diminished resistance. In the case of
ancestor wrath and lineage sorcery, the lack of balance

is explicit and recognized as _umnyama_, which is inevitable without the protection of the ancestors, and which
is a collective experience, that is, it affects a man
and his dependants. In the case of certain life crises,
the lack of balance is much more explicit and therefore
does not require to be diagnosed by a diviner. It is
treated accordingly as soon as people concerned experience the happenings. Since such balance cannot be demonstrated, and since it does not follow the natural
laws of cause and effect, it may well be regarded as
'mystical'.

There is another factor connected with the notion
of balance, namely, human activities. People are constantly making decisions and taking up responsibilities.
If a person does not strengthen himself he becomes an
easy target. This tacitly implies that it is his own
fault. When the ancestors are angry, the person involved is at fault. It can also be the fault of the sorcerer who disturbs the balance that people try to maintain.
Morality is an underlying principle in such cases. Morality, however, does not enter into the picture of an
imbalance arising from life crises. It must further be
noted that sorcery employing _ukudlisa_ deserves a special
comment. While it involves the personal action of adding harmful substances to the food, it is not regarded

in itself as putting a victim out of balance with his
surroundings. Although it carries a morality principle,
it has no mystical principle.

In re-examining the umkhuhlane class of disease
in the light of this, it can be said to stand apart in
that it implies neither the principles of morality nor
the principles of balance. Disease in this class is recognized as an inherent 'natural' process.

There is distinct treatment for the 'natural' as
against the 'mystical' symptoms of disease. The medicines reserved for the natural symptoms are believed to
be potent in themselves to cure the disease and they
are discarded for better ones if no improvement is effected. Their administration is accompanied by no ritual
and they are not regarded as symbolic. On the other
hand, the medicines used to cure mystical conditions
are accompanied by special rites, and colour is of symbolic significance.

The common method employed in curing mystical
diseases involves taking out the diseases (ukhiph' umnyama), discarding it (ulahl'umnyama), and substituting
good health (kingene ukukhanya izindlela zibe mhlophe).
This is expressed in a colour symbolism of black, red
and white.[4] It must be noted that in ritual usage 'black

4 The symbolic meaning of black, red and white does

means not only black but also all the dark hues such as dark brown, grey, deep green. 'Red' means red but also purple, mauve, light brown, sweet pink. 'White' means white, plus all very light hues such as cream or light yellow, and also includes transparent things such as water.

Black and red stand in opposition to white. They represent all that is bad, but they are also equivocal in that they also represent strength and power. White means all that is good. It represents whiteness, purity, as well as light. It is unequivocally good. Certain medicines, because of their colour, fit into this pattern of thought. There is a very rigid order in the usage. If all three colours are used in a sequence, black comes first, followed by red and then white. The sequence is never reversed. Usually, however, only two colours are used at a time, such as black followed by white, or red followed by white. White may be used alone, but whenever black or red is used, it must be followed by white. Black or red medicines are believed to expel the illness from the system but at the same time strengthen the patient against future attacks. What is expelled is discarded, but this does not mean that the

not extend outside the ritual setting. For instance, it is not important whether people are dark or light in complexion.

patient is healthy. He is in an intermediate state of
being neither sick nor healthy. To re-introduce health,
white medicines must be used.[5]

A good example of such treatment is that of the
black and the white treatment in extreme cases of misfortune believed to be caused by lineage sorcery (uzalo)
and manifested in various ways. A black sheep is killed
by suffocation (isimuku) and placed unopened in a hole
dug outside the home premises, preferably in secluded
bushy surroundings. The inyanga or isangoma prepares
black medicines. These consist of chopped-up fresh
roots, barks and leaves derived from a variety of plants.
A decoction of this is prepared in a clay pot. The decoction is dark greyish in colour and is known as amanz-
amnyama, which simply means black water. Before dawn,
the homestead-head stirs the decoction with a twig until
it froths. All the adult members of the homestead drink
their fill of this and vomit over the dead sheep. This
is repeated for three days. During the three days of
treatment the patients are considered to be deeply polluted and they follow the pattern of ukuzila behaviour

---

5 The black and red medicines in this context are also
   associated with heat and the white medicines with
   cold. Black and red emetics are decoctions, while
   white emetics are infusions. It must also be noted
   that the ancestors are addressed, silently or aloud,
   when the white emetic medicine is beaten to produce
   foam.

of polluted people. On the third day, what is left of
the black medicines is poured over the sheep and the
clay pot is broken over the sheep, after which the sheep
is well covered with soil and stones. The doctor then
prepares an infusion with white medicines in another
clay pot. A white goat is slaughtered in the manner
of sacrifice. For three days, early in the morning,
the patients use the white medicines to vomit, not at
one particular spot, but within the confines of the homestead. During the three days of white medicines the
meat of the white goat is eaten. This completes the
treatment, and the patients feel that they have been
rid of their misfortunes in a scapegoat (or, rather,
scapesheep) fashion and have had their health and the
good things of life restored to them by white medicines.

Ideally, such a treatment should be undertaken by
all the members of a lineage segment, but I have no record of an instance of such a case. It is, however,
accepted that the umnumzane may have the treatment performed for his umizi only, provided that he does not
use the treatment to harm his agnates. This could happen easily if, instead of destroying the clay pot which
had contained black medicines, it were kept and later
used to serve beer to those lineage members who had not
participated in the cleansing treatment with black and

white medicines. Indeed, this is how uzalo or lineage
sorcery would be performed.

The sheep in this instance is not a sacrifice;
in fact in this case it is the antithesis of a sacrifice. It must not cry out when killed, and blood is not
let out - the very two things which are important in
sacrifice. If a goat is sacrificed, the more noise it
makes the better. If it does not bleat at all when
slaughtered, the sacrifice is considered a failure and
another goat must be slaughtered. Blood must flow: this
is emphasized in the Zulu expression when the diviners
speak of kufneka kuchitheke igazi, meaning 'there is
need for the spilling of blood'.

I have never witnessed the treatment myself, as
strangers may not be present when it is performed; but
the account I have just given was collected from various
informants. There are, however, modifications to meet
present conditions. Some people complete the treatment
in two or three days - for instance, over the weekend,
as the men must go back to work most of them being migrant labourers. Some diviners allow the use of a black
chicken instead of a sheep if the people concerned cannot afford a sheep. In urban areas, where there are no
secluded bushy places, the patients vomit over a black
chicken in a pail and this is carried away by the inyanga

to be buried somewhere outside the premises.

I will briefly give two more cases of treatment with red and white medicines.

The elaborate treatment of the bereaved, particularly in cases of the death of a homestead head, provides a good example. The treatment is known as ukudla amakhubalo (the eating of red medicines). An emetic of red medicines is prepared, and in the morning following the death all the bereaved vomit outside the premises. On the same day, which is usually the day of burial, a goat is slaughtered and its entrails are cooked with bitter-tasting meat. On the day following the burial, the widow gets up at dawn and uses the remaining emetic medicine to sprinkle the entrance to the cattle byre as well as the entrance to the cattle byres of neighbouring homes. She also sprinkles the fields which are nearest to her home, as well as those of the neighbours, after which she washes her body at the nearest stream or river. On her return all the bereaved are given white medicines for emetics and they vomit within the premises.

Another example is that of ubulawu treatment. Ubulawu is used as an emetic to remove the type of umnyama known as isidina, which is a condition of being disliked for no apparent reason, or of being unpopular with people. It is an individual experience believed to be

the case by the patient. The condition of isidina can
be accidentally picked up in the environment or deliberately planted by a sorcerer. To correct this condition red ubulawu is prepared in one clay pot and white
ubulawu in another. The red ubulawu is used as an emetic performed outside the premises for three days, and
the white ubulawu is used as an emetic within the premises for three days following the treatment with red
ubulawu.

Although the black and the red medicines must be
followed by the white medicines in the treatment of mystical symptoms, the white medicines need not always be
preceded by the black or the red medicines. For instance, every sacrifice is accompanied by white medicines
of ubulawu type. There are also white medicines which
are believed to cancel the 'bad' and establish the 'good'
The generic name of such medicines is izintelezi. The
most commonly used of these is isiqunga or tambootie
grass (andropogon marginatus) which is kept available
in the home to be used if necessary by menstruating women, newly confined mothers or people who have been in
contact with death.

What I think is of particular significance is that
the somatic symptoms are always treated with medicine
in the scientific sense even if they are regarded as

mystically caused. To give an example of this: a woman
whose miscarriages are diagnosed to be either an outcome
of ancestral anger or lineage sorcery has the natural
symptoms treated as well as the mystical. During the
next pregnancy an infusion of pounded herbs is drunk in
cupfuls from time to time. Such medicines are known as
umsekelo, medicines calculated to prevent miscarriages.
This is a natural or scientific treatment which may be
administered concurrently with the mystical treatment.
Alternatively, instead of taking umsekelo medicines, the
patient may prefer to consult the western trained doctor
about her propensity to miscarry, but in addition she
will stick to the treatment with black and white medicines to correct the effects of lineage sorcery. In other
words, the western way of treatment is not precluded in
the schema of curing disease. On the other hand, the
treatment of mystical symptoms is unchangeable. It has
ritual and symbolic significance which conforms to the
principles of rites of passage in Van Gennep's sense,
that is, the patients are secluded while undergoing
treatment with black or red medicines, and are reintegrated into society after taking white medicines.[6]

6 The notions of black, red and white, and the rigid
   sequence of colours in usage, are frequently mentioned in literature on Zulu medical practice (see, e.g.
   Bryant 1970: 20; Krige 1936: 328; Callaway 1884:
   142). Although none of the literature gives an

Discussion and conclusions

What has been said so far can be reduced to the schema
shown in Diagram II. The causality and treatment of
disease as discussed in this paper and summarized in
the schema becomes much more significant if looked at
in relation to the mythology which explains death, mentioned earlier on. I do not pretend to explain the myth
as this is beyond my limited knowledge. But I do find
certain aspects of the myth interesting. That the people
are given contradictory messages, I believe, symbolizes
the right of people to make decisions and to take responsibility for their actions. It stands for the notions
of morality which set the human being apart from animals.
That the people, the animals (represented by the rep-
tiles – the lizard and the chameleon), and the plants
(represented by the berry bush) are brought together in
this story, symbolizes the relationship of the people
to their environment – it stands for the notions of that
which is Nature. That the people accepted orders from
a 'Being' presupposes the fundamental realization that
there are certain things that are beyond man's understanding, things that are controlled outside his sphere

---

analysis of the significance of such treatment, it
nevertheless indicates that such notions are neither
new nor typical only of Nyuswa-Zulu, but are part of
a general Zulu pattern of thought.

Morality	MORALITY	Morality
Idliso sorcery	The People and their:-	Failure in duty to the ancestors. Effect of lineage sorcery or of sorcery that produces isidina conditions.
	(a) Sense of responsibility, i.e. strengthening themselves to maintain balance.	
	(b) Intentions, i.e. sorcery to harm others.	
	(c) Decision making, i.e. discarding harmful substances with consideration for others.	
	(d) Duty, i.e. to the ancestors and to dependants.	

	Mystical	Mystical
	Lack of "balance", conceptualized in the notions of umkhondo/umeqo, isithunzi, ancestor wrath, lineage sorcery.	Misfortunes arising from lack of "balance". No biological symptoms.

Natural	Natural	
Biological symptoms arising from idliso.	Biological symptoms arising from lack of "balance".	

NATURAL OR SCIENTIFIC TREATMENT

MYSTICAL TREATMENT

MYSTICAL AND NATURAL TREATMENT

Natural		Mystical
Umkuhlane class of "diseases". Biological symptoms.		Umnyama arising from life crises. No biological symptoms.

| Natural or "scientific" treatment only. | | Mystical treatment only. |

DIAGRAM II

of action, and this constitutes the notion of the mystical. What I find particularly enlightening is the fact that the lizard, which is greyish-brown in colour, and therefore black in the ritual sense, is sent to deliver a death message. This conjures up the idea of black medicines believed to be used by the sorcerer to effect the illness or even death of his victims. The chameleon, known for its power of changing colour to suit its surroundings, is sent to deliver a life message. It stops on the way to feed on mauve berries, mauve being red in the ritual sense; this reminds one of the treatment with black, red and white medicines, red being in the middle, to be followed by white. Indeed, the chameleon delivered good tidings after it had been 'reddish' when feeding on red berries, like white medicines which introduce good health after red medicines. The message was a second one as indeed treatment with black, red and white follows the threat of death. However, with the realization that such a cure is only a temporary matter, and death is an inevitable end, the people refused to accept the message of immortality. What is symbolized here is that although people may attempt to control nature, they can only do this up to a certain point, beyond which mystical elements operate.

There are a number of paradoxical situations that

arise in the area of health and disease. For instance,
it seems paradoxical that the ancestors who are considered custodians of one's destiny are sometimes persuaded
by the very descendants they look after to abandon one
of their number. We have, however, a very suggestive
biblical parallel in the story of Isaac, whose younger
son Jacob used stealth to get the blessings which Isaac
had reserved for his elder son Esau. When later Esau
arrived for the blessing, his father Isaac had already
unwittingly given it to Jacob and could not retrieve it
to give it to Esau. This did not mean that Isaac did
not love Esau - only that Esau had been outwitted by his
brother Jacob. In the same manner, all things being
equal, the ancestors are believed to be good and loving
towards their descendants who all feel equally entitled
to their ancestral father's care and protection. But
in reality they realize that their fortunes are not the
same, in which case they feel cheated, not by their ancestral father, but by the wicked, envious or jealous
brothers who like Jacob get the blessings of their ancestral father by stealth.

To put it in a slightly different way - it becomes
difficult for a dutiful man to explain a series of misfortunes in spite of the ancestral protection to which
he is entitled. But if the ancestors have been made to

abandon him by the wickedness of mankind, the ancestors
are absolved from blame. The same may be said of sorcery, which involves the stealing of vital sacrificial
portions. Failure to achieve the purpose of sacrifice
is blamed on the sorcerer, not on the ancestors' inability to perform. If this observation is acceptable,
I would suggest that belief in sorcery and the Zulu
theory of its modes of operation are necessary for the
maintenance and internal consistency of the Zulu ancestral religion.

A further paradoxical situation worth considering is the dilemma that people face regarding the disposal of what they consider dangerous to health. Illnesses that are believed to be mystically caused are
believed to be cured by taking them out of the body
system as a substance which must be thrown away. Since
what is thrown away does not dissipate itself but could
be dangerous to other people the problem is, where can
one throw it away without polluting the environment?
How can one throw it away in such a way that there is
no danger of its reintroduction when the resistance
wanes, or in such a way that it does not affect other
lineage members and neighbours? The countryside within
reach is used for one thing or another - either as
fields, grazing ground, or provider of wood and herbal

medicines. There is hardly any area where people do
not walk around. How does one dispose of such dangerous
substances without harming other people or possibly oneself?

In an attempt to solve the problem, cross-roads
(enhlanganweni yezinglela) and highways (endleleni yom-
endo) are said to be the most often used areas for discarding undesirable substances, in the hope that these
are much more often used by travellers, outsiders or
strangers in the community to whom the illness might
attach itself and be carried away from the territory,
thereby diminishing the dangers in the immediate environment. But the problem is not quite solved. Such a
stranger may carry away the undesirable element, but
he may also introduce dangers which he brings with him
from a foreign territory. Although the problem may not
be solved, some balance is reached in that such a stranger, while taking away something undesirable, may leave
behind something perhaps equally undesirable. Without
such an equation, outsiders will probably continually
bring in dangerous elements in addition to the existing
and increasing dangers in the countryside.[7]

---

7   As an aside, I see the same dilemma regarding the
    disposal of pollution in the industrial centres of
    today. In the metaphysical sense, it seems to be
    an old problem demonstrated by the scapegoat notion.
    In the eighth chapter of the gospel according to

Another paradox is provided by the fact that kinsmen, who ideally must love one another, nevertheless have personal conflicts which may lead to hatred for each other. It is not conceivable that a reasonable man can kill his kinsmen - it would also be stupid because he would not expect any protection from the ancestors if he did so. To get round this hurdle, he persuades his ancestors by lineage sorcery to abandon his kinsman. Lineage sorcery is not primarily responsible for killing. It merely exposes the victim to all sorts of misfortunes - including illness. The lineage sorcerer does not do the dirty work of killing his kinsman, but other people or other factors find a suitable climate to do the dirty work for him. I see this as an attempt at reconciling a love-hate situation.

Luke, Christ is portrayed as facing the same dilemma when, after exorcizing the demons from a madman, he had to dispose of them by transferring them to pigs. In fact I see the very idea of redemption of mankind by Christ as based on the same concept of discarding the bad and disposing of it: Christ collected unto himself the sins of men.

REFERENCES

BRYANT, A.T. 1970. Zulu Medicine and Medicine-men. Cape Town: C. Struik.

CALLAWAY, H. 1884. The Religious System of the Amazulu. London: Folklore Society.

KRIGE, E.J. 1936. The Social System of the Zulus. London: Longmans Green.

-- 1968. Health, morality and religion among the Zulu. Africa, XXXVIII.

EVA GILLIES

CAUSAL CRITERIA IN AFRICAN CLASSIFICATIONS
OF DISEASE

This paper is concerned with classificatory ideas about
disease in a number of African societies, with particular
reference to causality. I shall argue that, in the wake
of Evans-Pritchard's statement (1937: 479) that 'Azande
attribute sickness, whatever its nature, to witchcraft
and sorcery', the conclusions drawn by ethnographers in
their accounts of ideas of disease causation have tended
to be rather too sweeping, and have not taken sufficient
note of discriminations made by the actors, both between
different kinds of illness and between the levels of aeti
ology and pathogenesis. In exploring the nature of some
of these discriminations, I shall also try to suggest
some reasons for this tendency.

The Ogori classification of diseases

I begin by considering my own none too exhaustive field
data from the village of Ogori in Kwara State, Nigeria;

the ethnographic present refers to 1965-66. Ogori is
a large nucleated settlement of about 2,500 people, situated a little southwest of the Niger-Benue confluence,
on the southernmost confines of the former Northern Region. The area is known to geographers as the Nigerian
Middle Belt, and is mostly derived savannah; but the
immediate neighbourhood of Ogori is well watered by several small streams, and there are still patches of hill
forest, as well as fertile swampland on the banks of
the streams. The annual rains fall from May to Nov-
ember; they are almost, but not quite, reliable, being
just uncertain enough to cause some anxiety to the predominantly farming population. The food staple is yam,
although other roots and vegetables are also grown; the
main cash crop is cocoa.

　　The Ogori and their neighbours the Magongo regard
themselves as Akoko (Bradbury 1957: 111, footnote 1),
but speak a language very different from those of the
nearby Akoko-Edo villages, and also from Yoruba and Igbirra, the languages of the two largest neighbouring
peoples. Their speech does, however, contain Yoruba,
Edo and Igbirra lexical elements, and all these cultural
influences are present, Yoruba being nowadays the predominant one. The Yoruba language is used for communication with neighbouring villages other than Magongo;

it is also the language of church and school, playing
a part not unlike that of mediaeval Latin in Europe.
The local system of divination, isiya, has affinities
with the better-known Yoruba ifa; the ruling potentate
has assumed the Yoruba style of Ologori. Nonetheless
there are still traditions of a time, in the second half
of the 19th century, when the people were grouped only
under sectional politico-ritual leaders whom I shall refer to as titlemen. These still exist, but are nowadays
much reduced in importance.

Despite the fact that land is becoming somewhat
scarce, Ogori is not by any means a poor village; this
is essentially because many of its people are working
elsewhere in Nigeria, earning salaries and sending money
home. The village has a high standard of education, and
its inhabitants were able to exploit their situation as
educated people in the old huge, largely illiterate
Northern Region very much to their advantage: at the
time of my stay Ogori had produced thirty-three University graduates and was, understandably, very proud of
the fact. The village has two churches (Anglican and
Roman Catholic) and, accordingly, two schools; also a
dispensary and a full-time midwife. Much of this somewhat self-conscious modernity can be attributed to the
fact that Christianity is, comparatively speaking, long-

established in Ogori, the first CMS (Anglican) mission
having been set up just before the First World War.
Before that, during the period of the Nupe-Fulani slave-
raids in the 19th century, the area underwent an Islamic
phase. At present the population of Ogori is, theoret-
ically, about 85 per cent Christian, 10 per cent Muslim
and only 5 per cent pagan; but, as elsewhere, many traditional beliefs and practices have survived the introduction of the world religions and come to co-exist fairly well with them.

This is particularly the case with underlying habits of thought such as come into play in dealing with
illness, both at the explanatory and therapeutic levels.
First of all, Ogori tend, like other peoples, to lump
disease together with other misfortunes into a single
category; by which I do not mean that there is, in this
case, a general native term that includes both, but simply
that people use the same procedures for dealing with
them. Secondly, divination is still, as with so many
African peoples, central to such procedures.

Two modes of divination are used. One, opopo, is
a form of witch-finding or blame-fixing, and is applied
exclusively to deaths for which an explanation of this
type is sought - i.e. the deaths of young or middle-aged
people, where it forms part of the funerary rites. The

death of the old, or of children, does not give rise
to witchcraft suspicions. More familiar in everyday
life is isiya, the local name for a much more widespread
system of geomantic divination (Bascom 1966: 409-10)
based on the same sixteen major configurations as the
more widely known ifa. It is isiya that is consulted
in illness, and also concerning the deaths of small
children. It is practised by elderly, highly-respected
part-time specialists (isiyaro) whom I shall refer to
as diviners.

Ogori distinguish, as many African peoples do,
between diagnostician and practitioner, i.e. between
diviner and medicine-man (omo). Both roles - the highly
prestigious, morally unimpeachable diviner and the socially and ethically much more dubious medicine-man -
are held by men; though elderly women often have some
knowledge of herbal simples and, of course, practise as
midwives. It is also usually old women who are suspected of witchcraft.

Adult Ogori witches, isoro, follow the normal West
African pattern, familiar from Field (1937, 1960) and
other authors: they fly about invisibly at night, meet
in covens and devour - spiritually and at first impercept
ibly - the invisible essence of their victims' internal
organs. Those attacked mysteriously waste away and

eventually die, so that it is only when death occurs
that one can be quite certain a witch has been at work.
The distinguishing characteristic of Ogori witches is
that they can afflict only their close matrikin, most
of all their own children or uterine siblings who have
'no other /i.e. non-witch7 mother to protect them'.
These are naturally the very people whom the witch should,
by prevailing moral standards, cherish and protect; so
that her activities are as monstrous and 'unnatural', in
Ogori eyes, as the deaths they cause - deaths of people
who should by rights be at their strongest and most vigorous. Witches are also held sometimes to cause barrenness in women. There is an additional category of child
witches, egbe, who also fly about at night doing mischief; but they cannot cause death, disease or barrenness, only things like minor accidents, breakages, bad
luck in bargains, and in general the kind of day-to-day
mishaps we ourselves would attribute to 'accident-
proneness'. Like adult witches, child witches can in-
jure only their matrikin. If people standing outside
such a relationship, e.g. jealous co-wives, wish to harm
one another, they must resort to magical-medicine.

      For medicine-men may practise two sort of medicine:
a non-magical (though traditional) herb-lore called utugbun or emen, some fragments of which are also known to

lay people; and magical-medicine, ogba, which involves
spells, invocations and the predominance of materials
of animal and human origin. Some medicine-men claim knowledge of herbal medicine only; others admit to practising
both. Magical-medicine, again, may be good or bad, depending on whether it is used defensively or offensively;
and this, of course, is where the morally somewhat ambiguous status of the medicine-man comes in.

Even quite innocent people may approach a medicine-
man directly, without having first consulted a diviner;
for not all illnesses are seen as calling for divination,
any more than all deaths are. For a number of diseases,
traditional Ogori have strictly naturalistic, even if
not scientifically correct, explanations. Thus malaria,
in common with other fevers, is regarded as a form of
sunstroke: all such fevers are known as eyigun, sun-
sickness. Hepatitis and yellow fever are similarly grouped together as iba, yellowness (a term which semantically
parallels our own 'jaundice'), and are believed to be
curable by non-magical herbal remedies. Gonorrhoea,
aaserenyan, reputedly a fairly recent disease, is known
to be caught by sexual intercourse; guinea-worm infection
isobiya, by drinking impure water. It is perhaps worth
pointing out that in West Africa many diseases are in
any case 'masked', clinically speaking, by malarial

fever or by worm infections.

None of these diseases are thought to require divination, any more than are such merely trivial everyday
complaints as indigestion, constipation, diarrhoea or
the effects of too much guinea-corn beer. The sufferer
will simply seek treatment, depending on his other attitudes, either from the dispensary or from a medicine-
man, who will sell him a non-magical herbal medicine.

There are, however, a number of diseases and other
afflictions which are attributed to deeper and more ambiguous causes, and concerning which, accordingly, the
help of a diviner is sought. We have already mentioned
the opopo witch-finding for the otherwise inexplicable
death of a young adult. For the death of an old person,
on the other hand, one who has lived to see grandchildren, no special explanation is sought; but then such a
death is not really regarded as an 'affliction' in the
Turnerian sense at all. There may well be private grief,
there is certainly quite stringent widow-mourning; but
people do not ask 'why?' or seek for someone or something to blame. It was time for the old man's or woman's
breath-soul to be united with the ancestors, and for
his or her shadow-soul to seek reincarnation: no other
explanation is felt to be necessary.

Diviners are, however, consulted concerning the

diseases and deaths of small children; but neither witchcraft nor magical-medicine are held responsible here.
Childish ailments are attributed to difficulties in the
emergence and identification of the shadow-soul. This,
as I have indicated, is transmitted by reincarnation,
usually of some recently dead person (though some children hold the shadow-souls of deities, or even of powerful
named magical-medicines). It may emerge at any time
during infancy or early childhood, and manifests its
presence through symptoms of illness. It is essential
for the child's restoration to health and its continued
well-being that the shadow-soul be correctly identified
and its holder trained in the appropriate food taboos.
The oracle is asked whether the child holds the shadow-
soul of So-and-so? or of Such-and-such? - naming by turn
all recently dead elders of both sexes on both sides of
the family; starting, where applicable, with some grand-
parent or collateral whom the child is thought particularly to resemble, or who died about the time of its
birth. If the oracle continues to answer negatively
(i.e. by throwing up inauspicious combinations) the net
is cast wider to include more distant relatives, remembered warriors or wise men of the past, deities, shrin
es and magical-medicines. But more usually the oracle
'assents' to the name of some recently dead relative;

and for the time being the parents go away satisfied.
Of course if the illness persists or recurs, the oracle
must have made a mistake: another shadow-soul seeking
reincarnation was trying to come out 'in front of' the
true predestined one and has thus confused the issue.
Efforts to identify the 'real' shadow-soul will continue
until the child either shows continued good health or
dies. If it dies, the matter becomes quite clear: the
child was an obafo.

Ogori share with a number of other peoples a belief in a class of mischievous spirit-children (corresponding to the Yoruba abiku) who never stay long in
this world, but die and return again and again to plague
their mothers. If a woman has had several babies die,
she, or her husband and relatives on her behalf, will
consult a diviner, who will advise on what is to be done,
the next time the obafo appears, to induce him or her
to stay. Generally, two diagonal cuts are made during
the child's first year, one on each cheek, below the
eyes and outwards from the nose, like very large 'circles under the eyes'. In the case of a boy obafo, moreover, circumcision, normally performed quite unritually
during the first year of life, may be postponed to the
second.

None of the explanations sought or given for any

of these phenomena invoke the active malevolence of
other adults. Small children - and this largely includes the child-witches mentioned earlier - seem to
be thought of as inhabiting a non-moral, presocial world
in which illness and other misfortunes may indeed require explanation, but nobody much is responsible for
them. In some sense, small children's illnesses and
even their deaths are accepted as forming part of the
expected order of things; just as are those diseases -
jaundice and gonorrhoea, fever and worm infections and
digestive upsets - for which divination is not required
at all. There is no need, in such cases, to go deeper:
no real moral or social issues are felt to be involved.

Of the diseases that do require a moral and social
explanation, most are attributable to what Evans-Pritchard
(1937: 74) calls a 'plurality of causes', and Horton
(1967: 170-1) 'converging causal sequences'. There are
one or two exceptions: insanity and tuberculosis, for
instance, are always believed to be due to magical-
medicine; and we may see in this, if we wish, the beginnings of a correlation between the nature of the disease
and the type of invisible agency brought into play (Horton loc. cit.). But most other diseases in this group,
which is a very large one, are attributable, at any rate
ultimately, to one of several possible causes rooted in

the patient's personal social, moral or ritual situation.

Thus the _immediate_ cause of leprosy is believed always to be the Earth, _Ije_, in her sacral aspect,'climbing up on a person'. But the Earth is here simply what Horton (1967: 53-4) calls the 'theoretical causal link' between leprosy and some human moral agency: she may thus afflict a man _either_ because he has offended her in some way, e.g. by undisclosed bloodshed or by incest, or simply by causing a titleman to fall to the ground; _or_ because someone has invoked her anger against him by a curse, or by magical means through the assistance of a medicine-man. Again, a man, feeling mysteriously unwell, may wonder whether one of his wives has used magical-medicine against him, even if only in the comparatively harmless form of a love-philtre. But quite possibly the diviner he consults will diagnose some quite different agency: he may say that some non-domestic enemy (who need not be a relative or an affine) is behind the bad magical-medicine; or that the sufferer is himself to blame for having offended the ancestors; or he may diagnose witchcraft in its early (and still possibly reversible) stages, in which case a uterine relative is involved; or say that the patient is under a curse.[1]

---

1   The distinction between witchcraft and cursing is

Thus in most cases the correlation is not between disease and type of afflicting agency, but between one of several possible agencies and the appropriate situation in the patient's own life. About this, the diviner normally already knows a good deal: his clients are familiar to him, and the more elderly and anxious will have consulted him fairly regularly on minor day-to-day problems, bad dreams, etc; what he does not know, he can usually elicit by skilful questioning, and his recommendation will vary accordingly. In most cases of recognizable illness, it will include sending the patient elsewhere for actual physical treatment: sometimes to the dispensary, more usually to a medicine-man. Of course, the client may also be sent to the medicine-man for protective magical-medicine; especially nowadays, when fewer people have compound shrines to protect them against bad magic.

But all this is seen as symptomatic treatment only. The diviner's main business is to get at the underlying moral and social causes of illness and to prescribe ap-

---

in practice largely a moral one, particularly where women are concerned. An old man, believed to converse already with the ancestors whom he is so soon to join, curses with their morally valid authority always behind him; but the old woman pronouncing a legitimate curse on undutiful offspring shades off almost insensibly into the witch. The assessment in each case will depend on the relationships and personal reputation of all concerned.

propriate action to remove or neutralize these. If
it appears that his client is innocent, i.e. that someone else, through witchcraft, magical-medicine or an
unmerited curse, is to blame for the illness, defensive
magical-medicine is generally the basic remedy: either
a charm from the diviner himself, or medicine, whether
from a compound shrine (preferably the client's compound
of birth), the medicine-man, or (in serious cases involving the possibility of witchcraft) from the local
anti-witchcraft shrine, whose cult the patient is then
advised to join.

Even here, the recommendation is often accompanied
by another, to patch up a quarrel with a spouse or heal
a kinship breach. But if the patient is himself to blame
for his illness - i.e. if agencies outside ordinary human
malevolence (ancestors, tutelary deities, in some cases
the Earth) are held to be involved - then the first pre-
requisite is that he put his life in order. This generally involves a sacrifice, but usually also a reconciliation and the renunciation, indeed as far as possible
the reversal, of previous unjust dealings, e.g. over
property. This kind of 'social therapy' has been described for a number of societies; aside from possible
symptomatic treatment, a disease is dealt with essentially by righting the patient's life-situation, his

relationships with the people with whom he is most intimately concerned. And it is the diviner who – often
by a process of trial and error, involving several consultations and several possible 'causes' adduced in succession – decides what that situation is and what must
be done to improve it.

   There is one important and dreaded disease, however, which is not traditionally regarded as suitable
for this type of private consultation with a diviner.
This is smallpox, which, together with other public calamities such as drought, calls for public consultation
of the isiya oracle by a titleman. Smallpox was formerly attributed to a goddess known placatingly as Iya
Okeka, the Great Mother, or Iya Osaka, the Rich Mother,
rather on the same principle as the Greek Furies were
usually referred to as 'the Gentle Ones'; the phrase
for catching smallpox was, 'The Great Mother has decor-
ated So-and-so'. Nobody was, in pre-European days,
blamed for the Mother's whims. Ogori shared with a number of neighbouring Akoko villages a system of common
information whereby, at any fresh outbreak of the disease, runners were sent out to the other villages with
a warning. In Ogori there was then a public isiya divination to determine both whether any offerings might
be made to appease the Great Mother, and in which ward

of the village she meant to 'decorate' a victim. A
young girl was then chosen, again by divination, from
that ward: the disease was believed to be 'softer' after
passing through a young virgin. She was escorted by
the messengers to the village where smallpox had broken
out, and there inoculated with lymph from a victim, a
small incision being made on the back of her left wrist.
When she returned to Ogori, all young children were sent
to be similarly inoculated from her; one such 'vaccination' being held to suffice for life.[2] This practice
gave way to western-style vaccination some thirty-five
years ago; the change can be fairly precisely dated from
the histories of different siblings in families. Concomitantly, belief in the Great Mother declined as a
result of Christianity. Nowadays, smallpox is referred
to as mizu (from English 'measles') and is usually, as
among the Igbirra and other neighbouring peoples, attributed to witchcraft. This was certainly the case during the epidemic which raged through the area during my
stay, but which never in fact reached Ogori - largely
because all children were immediately and compulsorily
vaccinated, by command of the Ologiri, with vaccine

---

2   It has been suggested to me that some of the local
    epidemics may not have been of variola major, but of
    alastrim (variola minor, Kaffir milkpox, amaas) which
    is usually non-fatal. Like cowpox, alastrim seems to
    result in a cross-immunization with variola major.

TABLE: OGORI CLASSIFICATION

EVENT		TYPE OF CAUSE SOUGHT	
		IMMEDIATE MECHANISM	ULTIMATE
Death of socially fulfilled person			'Will of God' 'It was time'
Trivial or Common Diseases of Adults	Colds		'Just happened'
	Digestive Upsets	Too much food or beer	
	Guineaworm	Polluted water	
	Jaundice		
	Fevers	Sunstroke	
	Gonorrhoea	Sexual intercourse	
Diseases of children			Emergence of shadow-soul
Deaths of children			Obafo children
Minor accidents and misfortunes			Child witches
Serious economic misfortunes			Ancestral punishment
Grave or uncommon diseases of Adults	Tuberculosis Epilepsy Insanity	Invasion of body	Bad medicine
	Mysterious illness Reproductive ills Serious accidents	Invasion of body or stealing of vital essence	Bad medicine or witchcraft or curse or ancestral punishment
	Leprosy	'Earth climbing up on person'	
Death of young adult		Stealing of vital essence	Witchcraft
Smallpox epidemic		'Decoration'	'Good Mother'
Drought or other public calamity			Displeasure of tutelary deities

OF MISFORTUNES

REMEDIAL ACTION	BLAME	CAUSAL UNIVERSE	TYPE OF DIVINATION APPLICABLE	DOMAIN
None	None	Expected order of things	None	Private
Non-magical medicine				
Identification of shadow-soul; Training in taboos		Pre-moral world of small children		
Marking of next child; Circumcision postponed				
Where possible, avoidance or appeasement of child witch				
Moral and ritual only	Self	Adult moral responsibility	Private isiya	
Moral and ritual action, magical and non-magical medicine as appropriate: Area of multi-level therapy	Others			
	Self or other: area of moral ambiguity			
Ostracism of witch until she joins anti-witchcraft cult	Others		Opopo	
Inoculation procedure: appeasement of 'Good Mother'	None	Deities	Public isiya	Public
Appeasement of tutelary deities				

brought from the nearby town of Okene, a measure which,
partly because of its recognizable affinity with traditional procedures, enjoyed general support.

It will be seen that Ogori traditional notions of
disease build up into quite a coherent system of classification, as demonstrated in the accompanying table.
At one end of the scale are illnesses accepted as 'natural' in the sense of being part of the expected order
and requiring a matter-of-fact explanation only: trivial
ailments, and a number of the run-of-the-mill non-fatal
diseases of adults, such as malaria and gonorrhoea.
Death in old age, for which no special explanation is
sought, should perhaps be put into the same category.
Almost equally 'natural', because so frequent, and accepted as it were as mere mischief, are the illnesses
and deaths of small children.

At the other end of the scale is the death of a
young adult, of somebody who by definition should not
have died; an anti-natural event which calls for an
anti-natural, horrifying explanation, namely, witchcraft among his matrikin. As we have seen, the mode
of divination attached to this event is a form of witch-
finding or blame-fixing, quite different from the ordinary isiya oracle. In between lies the area of competence of isiya, i.e. those diseases (and other mis-

fortunes) which are seen as mysterious in their origin
and outcome, which are serious enough and persistent
enough to worry about, but have not yet proved fatal:
troubles about which something could still be done if
one could only, by ascertaining their true cause, find
the right remedy. And these are of two sorts: individual non-trivial illness and misfortune, which requires
individual consultation of a diviner and the carrying
out of his recommendations whether material, moral or
ritual; and public calamities (e.g. smallpox), which
call for public divination and village-wide measures.
In each case, it is what is done that points to the
category to which a given disease is assigned.

Other African classifications

This is rather a different picture from the one so often
associated with African ethnographic material, in which
'Azande attribute sickness, whatever its nature, to
witchcraft and sorcery' (Evans-Pritchard 1937: 479), or
'The Ndembu, like the Azande /my emphasis7, consider that
calamities and adversities of all kinds are caused by
mystical forces generated or evoked or directed by conscious agents' (Turner 1964: 2). By comparison with
statements of this nature, the Ogori view of disease
seems much more differentiated, more flexible, less

implacably reductionist. Something may perhaps be attributed to the community's cultural eclecticism and its
somewhat self-conscious modernity; nonetheless, I believe
it would be possible to show that other peoples too are,
on the evidence of their own conscientious ethnographers,
less 'obsessively logical.... on the basis of mystical
premisses' (Turner 1964: 2) than we have come to think
of them.

The Ogori classification of diseases rests on a
number of dichotomous distinctions: diviner/medicine-
man; herbal-medicine/magical-medicine; good (i.e. curative) magical-medicine/bad magical-medicine; private mis-
fortune/public calamity; also, of course, between witchcraft within the matricentric group and sorcery (what I
have called bad magical-medicine) outside it. Some of
these distinctions are quite common in the literature,
from Africa and elsewhere, others considerably less so;
and, of course, in some cultures distinctions are made
that are not present in Ogori, e.g. between ritual and
lay healers, or between herbalists and specialists in
manipulative techniques. Disease classification is, after all, part of the total semantic arrangement of reality and must be expected to vary with it, in degree of
differentiation as well as in the content of the criteria
used. Yet the principles of semantic ordering, though

multiple, are not infinite in number; and some of the discriminations present in Ogori can be followed up elsewhere.

Commonest of all, perhaps, is the dichotomy between diviner and medicine-man, which, since in most societies consulting a diviner is expensive and carrying out his recommendations may be troublesome as well, usually brings in its train a preliminary, rough-and-ready classification of diseases into those that are, and those that are not, worth consulting a diviner about. To give only a few examples from the many that spring to mind:

> When a Zande suffers from a mild ailment he doctors himself. There are always older men of his kin or vicinity who will tell him a suitable drug to take. If his ailment does not disappear he consults a witch-doctor. In more serious sickness a man's kin consult without delay first the rubbing-board oracle and then the poison oracle, or, if they are poor, the termites oracle (Evans-Pritchard 1937: 488).

> Some sicknesses are so common that the element of the untoward which makes people immediately suspect sorcery or witchcraft is lacking. Nevertheless if these become exceptionally severe or protracted, suspicion grows....Thus it is usual for the relatives of a per-

son who has had a lengthy illness.... to seek out a
diviner.....But consulting a diviner and sponsoring
a curative rite are both costly and troublesome for
marginal subsistence-cultivators, and there are many
herbalists and lay-healers.... who claim to be able
to dispel /diseases7 (Turner 1964: 2-3).

Kalabari recognize many different kinds of diseases,
and have an array of herbal specifics with which to
treat them. Sometimes a sick person will be treated
by ordinary members of his family who recognize the
disease and know the specifics. Sometimes the treatment will be carried out on the instructions of a native doctor.....Sometimes, however, the sickness does
not respond to treatment, and it becomes evident that
the herbal specific does not provide the whole answer.
The native doctor may rediagnose and try another specific. But if this produces no result the suspicion
will arise that 'there is something else in this sickness'. It is at this stage that a diviner is likely
to be called in (Horton 1967: 60).

Gravity and prolonged duration are clearly very important
here. But there are other considerations: who suffers
the symptoms? are they dramatic in their suddenness?
alarming by their rarity? Ackerknecht (1942: 472), after

a somewhat Frazerian review of 'primitive medicine',
concludes that, aside from slight ailments such as colds,
very common illnesses like malaria, yaws, filiariasis
and venereal diseases are also fairly widely regarded
as 'natural' (in the negative sense of calling for no
magico-religious explanation); other candidates for this
category are children's diseases and diseases 'imported
by the Whites' (or, more probably, acquired through any
recent contact with people regarded as outsiders: gonorrhoea in Ogori, believed to have been 'brought here
by Igbirra women', would be a good example). Evans-
Pritchard (1937: 479) in fact mentions two 'diseases
of infants', kaza Amadi and Ngorombe, as 'the only serious illnesses which are, to my knowledge, not attributed in any degree to witchcraft or magic'. I think
it can safely be assumed, too, that no oracles are consulted concerning these; but we are not told to what
they are in fact attributed, or what therapy (if any)
is used.

The latter might have provided a clue to causal
classification, since a non-magical medicine, empirically specific in intent, would seem to imply a naturalistic explanation for the disease. I say this with the
greatest caution, fully aware that very few African medicines, if one takes into account the conditions of

their gathering and preparation, invocations, charms,
symbolic associations, etc., can be regarded as unam-
biguously non-magical. A lexical differentiation, such
as the Ogori utugbun (non-magical medicine) and ogba
(magical-medicine), seems to be the exception rather
than the rule; yet its absence should not lead one to
assume without question that no conceptual distinction
is made. Thus the Idoma have a single word, eci, for
magical and non-magical medicines alike; yet when Armstrong (1966: 2-4) questioned one of his informants,
an intelligent illiterate pagan about twenty-five years
old, the young man's answer differentiated very clearly
and at considerable length between 'disease-medicine',
'leaf-medicine' that one prepares, and the medicine that
one propitiates - for which one kills a cock or a ram,
to which one sings incantations. 'Because when a disease afflicts you, if you have propitiated medicine and
they have not prepared disease-medicine for you, the
disease will not finish'.

Here, it seems clear that both 'leaf-medicine'
and 'propitiation-medicine' are regarded as necessary;
but even this is not always the case. Thus, the Ndembu
treatment of otitis media (Turner 1964: 14) by dripping
warm herbal decoctions into the affected ear seems to
be strictly and prosaically empirical in intention: for

once, there is no mention of colour symbolism and

no explanation of the use of these vegetable medicines in terms of sympathetic or contagious magic were
forthcoming. I have known Ndembu, treated in this
way, who asserted strongly that they experienced an
improvement in their condition. It is possible that
these medicines are employed because they are objectively effective.

Such a treatment would presumably be administered by
one of the 'many herbalists and lay-healers in the villages, who claim to be able to dispel /diseases7, whether these are associated with spirits or witches or not'
(Turner 1964: 3). For the Ndembu are not certain that
such minor ailments as suppuration of the ear are really
sent by spirits or witches: some think that they are,
but only for 'little grudges' which are not worth consulting a diviner about, while others (Turner 1964: 2,
38) believe that diseases which are thought of as low-
order living entities 'motiveless in their malignity'
need not in every case be controlled by a higher-order
agency. Some illnesses indeed are explicitly 'not considered to be the result of witchcraft/sorcery or of
ancestral affliction' (Turner 1964: 40): thus smallpox
(whose treatment, though not objectively effective, would
seem to have no magical overtones either) is said to

'come to you in the air from Europeans', and seems therefore to be a 'contact disease' explained by commonsense
notions.[3]

A naturalistic explanation at the level of pathogenesis need not preclude notions about conscious afflicting agencies at that of aetiology; any more than
treating disease symptoms with 'leaf-medicine' precludes
ritual action to remove or neutralize a putative underlying cause. The Ndembu, with their 'diseases in their
own right', susceptible to 'strong' or bitter medicines
(Turner 1964: 2) but manipulable by higher-order afflicting beings, are a case in point; so are the Igala, who
believe

> diseases... to be manipulated or sent by mystical
> agencies, not created by them, and in dealing with
> illness it is therefore necessary to apply therapy
> at the physiological level as well as at the spirit-
> ual level (Boston 1966: 1).

'Physiological' therapy, for the Igala, is by medicines,
and 'the power of a medicine lies mainly in combining

---

3 Non-European commonsense notions of causation need
   be no wider of the mark than European ones: the Som-
   ali of Zaila seem to have attributed malarial fever
   to mosquito bites in 1853, well in advance of Ross
   and Manson. Burton (1856: 53) comments wisely in a
   footnote that 'the superstition probably arises from
   the fact that mosquitoes and fevers become formidable at about the same time'!

the right ingredients' (Boston 1971: 200). Invocation
is also used, but it is simple and informal and - unlike
the principal, and possibly magical, ingredient in each
medicine - is 'known to all Igala'. Yet Boston (1971:
203) came to conclude that in the last resort Igala medicine is a closed system:

> Medicines act primarily against other medicines. They
> do not directly affect the course of nature except in
> so far as natural processes are already being inter-
> fered with by other medicines. For instance the maj-
> ority of curative medicines are regarded as being the
> antidote... of different forms of sorcery.....Good
> and bad medicines are counterpoised.

If this were always so, we would here be in the presence
of a system where, despite the impersonal, non-ritualistic
character of the therapies used, no disease could have a
naturalistic explanation. Such a system would simply
not contain the category of 'natural illness'. The total
absence of this category would make the system far more
radically different from e.g. the Ogori classification
than such lower-order criteria as whether the category
itself is large or small, or whether it does or does not
include non-trivial diseases. But - as so often seems
to be the case in reports of this kind - Boston's statement is in fact a little less sweeping than at first

appears: it is only 'the majority' of curative medicines
that are seen as antidotes to sorcery. One cannot help
wondering: what about the others? for what complaints
are they used? what beliefs attach to them and how do
they fit in with other beliefs? We know no more about
these things than we do about Evans-Pritchard's two
'diseases of infants'.

How, why and who?

It is perhaps not the sort of question traditional social anthropology has asked; though cognitive anthropology might well do so. Evans-Pritchard (1937: 481)
has, with his usual forthrightness, voiced what must
be a very general feeling:

> Knowing nothing at all of pathology, physiology,
> botany and chemistry, I soon tired of the fruitless
> labour of collecting the names of innumerable dis-
> eases and medicinal plants, few of which I could
> render either into the English language or into
> scientific terminology and which remained therefore
> useless and unintelligible.

His own list of Zande diseases is frankly based on the
work of Father De Graer, 'a Dominican missionary at
Doruma' (Evans-Pritchard 1937: 481).

But the difficulty, all-pervasive but probably

enhanced in the field of medicine, of 'translating' indigenous category-terms into European ones (whether
common-sense or scientific), is not the whole story.
Evans-Pritchard is well aware (1937: 73) that 'belief
in witchcraft in no way contradicts empirical knowledge
of cause and effect'; but he was not very interested in
Zande ideas about cause and effect in the purely empirical realm. He was interested in their witchcraft beliefs: not in their account of 'how' disease or other
misfortunes occurred, but in their ideas as to 'why'
they happened to a particular person - their theoretical
aetiology rather than their common-sense pathogenetic
level of explanation. Other anthropologists have followed him in this; and it is not difficult to see why.
For the Azande, for instance, the theoretical level consisted largely of witchcraft and sorcery explanations,
in which the philosophical or metaphysical 'why?' (or
perhaps more accurately 'why me?') had become - as very
easily happens where theory operates in what Horton
(1967: 164) calls 'the personal idiom' - a sociological
'who?'. Now this 'who?' has a quite legitimate fascination for social scientists, which is why so many studies of witchcraft or sorcery are essentially studies
of the sociological spread of suspicion and accusation;
but it cannot be denied that this very understandable

professional interest has led to some neglect of the
'how?' question. It is illuminating that one of the
best studies of African medicine is Turner's (1964) of
the Ndembu: his main interest has turned from strictly
sociological problems to world-views, symbols and underlying patterns of thought.

'Who?' is, of course, a complex question. It need
not merely be a matter of who can bewitch or ensorcel
whom; ancestors and tutelary spirits, among the Ndembu
and many other peoples, can also afflict with illness,
in which case the disease is likely to be thought of
as a punishment for some moral or ritual offence or
omission. Usually, as in Ogori, it is for the diviner
to decide who is to blame; and what is to be done, at
the underlying-causes level, will obviously depend on
this. Typically, the correlation is made between the
patient's illness and his life-situation: different
situations bring different disease-controlling agencies
into play (Horton 1967: 169-70). Sometimes indeed there
are the beginnings of a more direct correlation between
type of disease and type of afflicting agency: e.g. the
Ogori believe that tuberculosis is invariably caused by
magical-medicine, and the Ndembu (Turner 1964: 10-11)
that leprosy is invariably a ritual sanction; but it
seems more usual for the diviner to have a free hand.

Aside from dealing with underlying causes he will generally, where his role is differentiated from that of
the medicine-man, send the patient to the latter for
treatment with medicines, whether or not these are mag-
ically conceived. This is the classic double therapy,
'at the physiological... as well as at the spiritual
level' (Boston 1966: 1), familiar from so much African
ethnography, in which both the 'how?' and the 'why?'
(or 'who?') problems are taken into account. Here too,
it is what is done that is the real criterion of belief.

Nonetheless, there seem in some cultures to be
diseases where this kind of two-pronged action is felt
to be inadequate. Ogori smallpox is an example: private
divination, however complemented by worship or repar-
ation or medicine, is simply not enough. The Good Mother
has manifested herself: both divination and action must
take place at the village level - action indeed going
well beyond this, to embrace other villages in the Northern Akoko world. The philosophical question 'why?' no
longer translates as 'why me?'; and the 'who?' question,
concomitantly, does not apply at all. The difference
is here no longer between commonsense and theory, but
between different levels of theory, invoked for phenomena of different magnitude (Horton 1967: 60-2).

There is some evidence for similar theoretical

leaps elsewhere; though, like naturalistic explanations
and probably for the same reason - the fascination exerted by the 'who?' question - they have been passed over
rather lightly by most social anthropologists. First
of all, the objectively effective action which in Ogori
is buttressed by belief in the Good Mother has been reported from elsewhere in Nigeria. Fox (1915), writing
of Djen on the right bank of the Benue, a community consisting of three 'towns' making about 4,700 people in
all, describes a similar process of variolization; but,
though he mentions those accompanying rites that have
a clear sympathetic-magical significance (a grain of
maize placed in the mouth to ensure large discrete pustules; a drop of honey to make the vesicular fluid clear
as honey) and tantalizingly mentions 'various' further
rituals, he is not, as a medical man, interested in the
beliefs justifying this action. Smallpox deities as
such are common enough in West Africa: the Yoruba Soponon
is the best known, but the Igbirra and Igala (Boston
1966: 7; 1971: 200) each have a smallpox goddess, and
so do various Dahomean peoples (Zwernemann 1968: 61-5);
often the association is with the Earth in her sacral
aspect (as with leprosy in Ogori). The Bambara of Mali,
as well as the Malinke, have a dreaded 'Good Mother'
eruptive epidemic; theirs, however, is not smallpox

but measles (Imperato 1969: 771).

But there are other possible ways of classifying
and explaining diseases that transcend the 'who?' level
of inquiry. It is accepted knowledge that the Azande
make wide use of the 'who?' level, and the various 'how?'
explanations that appear in Evans-Pritchard's list of
diseases (1937: 482-8) must, I think, be taken as proffered against a background ideology of witchcraft or
sorcery as underlying cause. But at the end of the list
comes the illuminating passage:

> Father De Graer says that certain diseases are re-
> garded as incurable: smallpox, sleeping sickness, and
> cerebrospinal meningitis. They attribute incurable
> conditions to Mbori, the Supreme Being, a word that
> accounts for whatever cannot be explained by other
> Zande notions and indicates their incomprehensibil-
> ity (Evans-Pritchard 1937: 489).

Here I think I am doing the text no violence by assuming
that the phrase 'cannot be explained by other Zande
notions' includes the meaning 'cannot be explained by
witchcraft or sorcery'; and I think it can safely be
assumed also that, when these diseases are recognized,
no oracle is consulted.

The Azande, in other words, do not, any more than
the Ogori, or, I suspect, other peoples, attribute all

diseases to witchcraft or sorcery. At one end of the
spectrum, infants' diseases, even where serious, fall
outside the scope of witchcraft explanation. At the
other extreme, incurable diseases (incurability rather
than epidemicity seems to be the Zande criterion of
classification here) are, in some sense, too grave a
matter to be explicable on the 'who?' level, just as
infants' diseases, and possibly some trivial ailments,
are not grave enough to warrant such an explanation.
In between, in the world of the 'who?' explanation, lies,
not all 'sickness, whatever its nature', but the serious
though potentially curable diseases of adults — those
about which, Azande believe, something could still be
done, if only one could identify the witch in order to
ask him to 'cool' his witchcraft.

The overall classification is, in fact, not unlike
that which I have given for Ogori; and the fact that it
can be shown to be implicit in the Zande material makes
one wonder whether comparable classificatory schemes
are not rather more widespread than the anthropologist's
professional interest in the 'who?' question would lead
one to suppose.[4] Such classifications of disease will

4 A comparable non-African classification is given for
   the Hindus of Hyderabad State by Dube (1955: 127).
   At one extreme, common diseases are curable by natural remedies; at the other, smallpox, cholera and
   plague are caused by the wrath of goddesses and

obviously form a part of more general ones, and must be
expected to vary with the religious and cosmological
beliefs underpinning them; nonetheless the analysis of
behaviour (including verbal behaviour) in illness might
well yield up the principles governing each such semantic
arrangement, and such principles could perhaps more easily be ordered in comparable form than the generalizing
statements of informants.   In our own traditional ordering of our subject-matter, such problems might well be
thought to pertain to cultural rather than to social
anthropology; but this particular boundary may be dis-
solving, and world views and cognitive maps are now held
by many to be as well worth studying as the sociological
implications of blame-fixing for misfortunes.

'worship' is the only measure taken. In between come
diseases and misfortunes attributed to 'supernatural
forces' (presumably of a lower order than the goddesses) where both propitiation and medicine are used.
Here too what is done points to the category in which
a given case of illness is placed.

REFERENCES

ACKERKNECHT, E.H. 1942. Problems of primitive medic-
    ine. Bulletin of the History of Medicine, XI, 5,
    503-21.

ARMSTRONG, R.G. 1966. Idoma traditional ideas of dis-
    ease. Unpublished paper presented to the Special
    Seminar on the Traditional Background to Medical
    Practice in Nigeria, held by the University of Ibadan
    Institute of African Studies in collaboration with
    University College Hospital, Ibadan, 20-23 April
    1966.

BASCOM, W.R. 1966. Two studies of Ifa divination: I.
    Odu Ifa: The names of the signs. Africa, XXXVI, 4,
    408-21.

BOSTON, J. 1966. Igala traditional ideas of disease.
    Unpublished paper presented to the Special Seminar
    on the Traditional Background to Medical Practice
    in Nigeria, held by the University of Ibadan Inst-
    itute of African Studies, in collaboration with Univ-
    ersity College Hospital, Ibadan, 20-23 April 1966.

-- 1971. Medicines and fetishes in Igala. Africa, XLI,
    3, 200-7.

BRADBURY, R.E. 1957/1964. The Benin Kingdom and the
    Edo-speaking Peoples of South-Western Nigeria. Eth-
    nographic Survey XII. London: International African
    Institute.

BURTON, R. 1856/1966. First Footsteps in East Africa,
    4th edition. London: Routledge & Kegan Paul.

DUBE, S.C. 1955. Indian Village. London: Routledge &
    Kegan Paul.

EVANS-PRITCHARD, E.E. 1937/1965. Witchcraft, Oracles
    and Magic among the Azande. Oxford: The Clarendon
    Press.

FIELD, M.J. 1937/1961. Religion and Medicine of the
    Gâ Peoples. London: Oxford University Press.

-- 1960. Search for Security. London: Faber.

FOX, H.A.   1915.   Inoculation of smallpox as a prophy-
    lactic measure as practised by the natives at Djen
    in Nigeria. Journal of Tropical Medicine, XVIII,
    255-7.

HORTON, R.   1967.   African traditional thought and
    Western science. Africa, XXXVII, 1: 50-71, 2: 155-
    87.

IMPERATO, P.J.   1969.   Traditional attitudes towards
    measles in the Republic of Mali. Transactions of
    the Royal Society for Tropical Medicine and Hygiene,
    LXIII, 6, 768-80.

TURNER, V.W.   1964.   Lunda Medicine and the Treatment
    of Disease. Rhodes-Livingstone Occasional Paper
    No. 15. Lusaka: Government Printer.

ZWERNEMANN, J.   1968.   Die Erde in der Vorstellungswelt
    und Kulturpraktiken der Sudanischen Völker. Berlin:
    Dietrich Reimer.

ANTHONY D. BUCKLEY

THE SECRET - AN IDEA IN YORUBA MEDICINAL THOUGHT[1]

The purpose of this paper is twofold. First I attempt
to give an ethnographic account of certain Yoruba beliefs about the causes of disease. Specifically I shall
look at the nature of the curse and of beliefs concerning two specific diseases, known to Yoruba herbalists[2]
by the names èelá and ètè. The second purpose will be
to understand how it is that these beliefs, at first
sight obscure and enigmatic to an outsider, are rational and valid within the context of generally accepted
Yoruba beliefs.

---

1 I wish to acknowledge with gratitude the financial
   assistance of the Leverhulme Trust and the Esperanza
   Trust who made this study possible, the support and
   encouragement of the late Dr R.E. Bradbury and of
   Dr Elizabeth Tonkin and, above all, the devotion and
   friendship of my field assistant and interpreter,
   J. Akintunde Ayandokun.

2 The Yoruba word oníseègùn may literally be translated
   as 'owner of the making of medicine', though, of
   course, 'medicines' are prepared for many purposes
   other than the treatment of disease. For brevity,
   I use the term 'herbalist'.

Part of the difficulty of understanding the beliefs
of Yoruba herbalists arises from the astonishing variety
of radically differing ideas which they offer. Herbalists do not agree about the nature of specific diseases;
still less do they agree about the effective cure. They
are sceptical, inventive and individualistic. When ties
of friendship and kinship are sufficiently close, they
will exchange theories of disease and, with less freedom, recipes for medicine, but, in private, they will
express a deep scorn for quite reputable ideas with which
they do not agree.

Faced with a number of reputable herbalists who
scarcely agree on any point of detail, the anthropologist must seek the shared structures of thought which
have allowed these essentially similar individuals to
arrive at substantially differing solutions to similar
intellectual problems. Following the work of T.S. Kuhn
(1962) I shall use the word 'paradigm' to identify this
shared structure of thought.

The nature of the paradigm

There are two kinds of problems which the Yoruba herbalist must solve. The first is to identify and explain
the nature of the disease. The second is to find a cure
for it. In solving these problems, he may use his own

expertise and imagination. More often, he will select from among the various solutions that other herbalists have offered him. However his conclusions are reached, he will demand of them that they be rational. He must feel that they enable him to cure the disease; but before he uses such empirical tests of their validity, he must feel that they are compatible with his general assumptions, his paradigms.

It is necessary to my argument to allege, though I cannot here adequately prove, that the particular paradigm explained in this paper may be perceived not merely beneath the structure of a few ideas expressed by herbalists about the nature of specific diseases, but as the basis of virtually every major Yoruba institution and belief. If this hypothesis is correct, the paradigm has provided Yoruba thinkers with a method of imposing categories, relationships and meaning upon the otherwise formless content of their world. Its structure has determined the method by which the Yoruba have fashioned and understood their political, social, religious and economic relationships. It is an unconscious blueprint applied to countless different situations and expressed in countless different ways. Expressed abstractly throu the medium of colour it summarizes the whole truth about the nature of man in the world. The paradigm consists of a theory about the composition of the human body.

In Yoruba thought the human body is formed by the
coming together of sperm and menstrual blood at the time
of conception. Sperm and blood are united within the
enclosure of the womb, where they remain hidden until
the time of birth (see Fig. 1). They then emerge, but
are still concealed by the black exterior of the body.

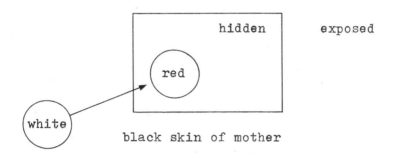

Fig. 1. Healthy conception

It is a simple theory, but from it the Yoruba have been
able to derive a number of categories which they have
imposed on the world. These categories are usually expressed through the medium of colour, as shown in Fig.
2. Yoruba words for colour do not readily translate into
English; even those Yoruba who have a good command of
English often have difficulty in this sphere. Yellow,
for example, is often confused with red, and blue is
sometimes mistaken for green or black. But this diffic-

dúdú	pupa	funfun
black	red	white
dark blue green	light yellow brown pink	colourless

Fig. 2. Yoruba terms for colour

ulty is more than one of translation, for in the Yoruba language there are only three major distinctions of col our. The three terms dúdú, pupa, and funfun embrace the whole spectrum of colours which in the English language are more finely differentiated. I do not suggest that there are no Yoruba words for yellow or green but rather that they are usually ignored; members of specialist trades, notably cloth dyeing, know many different shades by name. The three colours will be translated as black, red and white.

Starting with the colours red and white, we have already seen how the human body is a product of the un- ion of the red blood and white sperm. This duality is continued after birth with the existence of blood which remains inside the body and of water which, as urine, flows outwards (Fig. 3). Red and white also have cos- mological significance. In Yoruba thought, the sky is white and the earth is red. Our English minds naturally

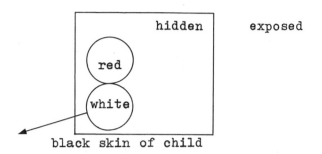

Fig. 3. Healthy child

think of the sky as being blue, but it is not at all
unnatural to think of it as white, since in West Africa,
as indeed in Britain, the sky is more often white than
it is blue. Additional proof of the sky's whiteness
is furnished by the flow from it of white rain and of
occasional white hailstones.

It is the brick-coloured subsoil which the Yoruba
call red. Above it, at least in the forest, is the rich-
er topsoil which is black (see Fig. 4).

In the three diagrams (Figs. 2, 3 and 4) which
illustrate three healthy relationships of red and white,
it is immediately apparent that elements associated with
the colour white - sperm, urine, rain water - flow normally and beneficially between areas that are hidden -
the belly, the earth - and areas that are exposed - the

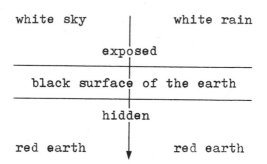

Fig. 4. The cosmos: fertile land

sky and the outside of the body. Elements associated
with red are only exposed with danger.

When, as in Fig. 5, there is no black soil and
the red earth is exposed the land is infertile.[3] Similarly, the blood in menstruation is considered dangerous, even though, like so many apparently evil things
in Yoruba thought, it has its beneficial side. Most
herbalists, for example, fear that the presence of a
menstruating woman will destroy the power of their medicines, and for this reason it is uncommon to find women
of child-bearing age practising medicine on any scale.
We cannot investigate every aspect of this complex subject here, but need to examine the relationship between

---

3   It may be that the term ilè gbígbó-ná, hot earth,
    which is an epithet of the smallpox god, Sònpòn-ná,
    is related to this. I have heard it said that water
    poured on to the hot earth brings with it the danger
    of smallpox.

disease and the forbidden practice of having sexual
intercourse during a menstrual period.

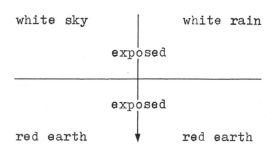

Fig. 5. The cosmos: infertile land

Two of the three major colours involved in the
paradigm have been discussed. The third, black, is of
great importance, for it is only in the context of darkness, which black represents, that red and white may be
mixed without danger. In religious symbolism, black is
used to indicate secrecy, and the colours red and white,
even when used together with black, imply a dangerous,
revealed secret.

Eelá and ètè

I turn now to an appraisal of the ethnographic data in
the light of the Yoruba idea which I have called 'paradigmatic'. I shall not pretend that all the information
to be presented fits simply and neatly into my hypotheses.

Certain types of data, such as myth or ritual, contain
within them an inner logic which leads to a high degree
of precision in their analysis. In assessing the meaning of information gleaned from an enormously complex
civilization and culture in informal interviews, one
must tolerate extraneous facts which seem contradictory
or which cannot be explained in a short space. One must
merely hope that, as the theory is developed in later
work, these facts will find a place in the general picture.

The diseases we must consider first are generally
known in Yoruba by the names èelá and ètè, though we
should make it clear at once that, just as Yoruba concepts of disease differ radically from those of European
science, so Yoruba herbalists differ one from another
in their categorization of symptoms and diseases. Herbalists disagree about the names given to different diseases, but on a deeper level they differentiate between
diseases in different ways. They are a lexicographer's
nightmare.

Speaking generally, my three informants, all of
them herbalists, agreed that èelá is a dangerous disease
affecting small children, the main symptom of which is
the appearance of red blotches on the body. The word
ètè is usually translated as 'leprosy', but it may well

be that there are other diseases which we would identify differently and which are also known by this name. It, too, is characterized by red patches on the surface of the skin, but it is distinguished by its unpleasant tendency to wither away the limbs of the sufferer. There, briefly, is the area of agreement; from here their patterns of beliefs diverge.

In addition to the names èelá and ètè, my informants used a third name, ara pupa, which means, literally, 'red body'. My first informant, Mr Babálólá, a babaláwo or priest of Ifá from Osogbo, identified ara pupa with the disease èelá. My second informant, Mr Fátóògùn, another babaláwo from the same area, used the name ara pupa as a synonym for ètè. My third informant, Mr Adébawò, who is not a traditional priest but an Ijèbu professional herbalist working in Ibadan, offered yet another and more complex categorisation;[4] he distinguished three types of èelá. The first, he said,

---

4 Most Yoruba men know at least a little about the preparation of medicines from plants and trees. The cult of Ifá has access to so many esoteric truths that its priests, the babaláwo, are usually able to administer medicines as part of their divinatory practice. The ordinary óniseègùn possesses knowledge of a number of aspects of Ifa and other cults, but essentially he is a tradesman practising a craft.

.... is called èelá inú (the èelá of the inside) in
which the general complexion of the child will become
red,[5] but the èelá itself,[6] will not appear on the
body. There is a type of infusion (àgbo)[7] which can
be used to drive the èelá out on to the surface of the
skin, where it can be cured. The medicine used on the
surface of the skin cannot be used to cure that which
is inside the body. There is another type of èelá
which the Yoruba people[8] call olóro-ǹtó. If this affects a child, he will pass watery faeces very frequently. This disease affects a male child more easily than a female, and it is much easier to cure a
girl. It is very dangerous because the child's legs
will swell up and the skin will start to peel.

Mr Adébawò told me that both these diseases were caused
by dirt or disease in the womb of the mother at the time
of conception. This is a common form of explanation
for diseases affecting young children, but not one with

5   That is, light in colour.

6   The distinctive patches of light-coloured skin.

7   Àgbo is of two kinds; one is cooked, the other is
    allowed to marinate.

8   The people from Òyó and related towns are called Yor-
    ùbá: Mr Adébawò is from Ijèbu and regards his area
    and dialect as, at least in one sense, non-Yoruba.
    To discuss whether or not the Ijèbu should be con-
    sidered a Yoruba people for the purpose of this paper
    would be tedious and irrelevant.

which we can concern ourselves here.

   More interesting in the context of this paper was
his explanation of a third type of èelá which he called
èelá ara pupa, and which he also regarded as a type of
ètè or leprosy:

> If a man should happen to have sexual intercourse with
> a woman while she is menstruating, she will give birth
> to a child with this type of ètè. This form of the
> disease does not cut the fingers and toes like other
> types, but people will still run away from the child.
> There will be black and red patches all over the body
> of the child.

This, he says, is the most dangerous of all the forms
of èelá.

   Mr Babálólá, on the other hand, believes that all
forms of èelá are caused by the parents having conceived
the child during or immediately after a menstrual period. He says:

> If a man has sexual intercourse with a woman on the
> same day that menstruation stops, and she becomes
> pregnant, the resulting child will be affected by èelá
> when he is three months old. This is because the blood
> has not finished coming from the womb; it will mix
> with the sperm and become èelá on the surface of the
> child.

In these two similar theories we have an example
of what Kuhn calls 'the articulation of a paradigm' -
the definition and solution of a problem using the structure of a widely held belief. Red and white should be
joined together in the secrecy of the mother's body
(Fig. 2) to produce a healthy child (Fig. 3) in which
red and white are again combined in the confines of the
concealing, black skin. But if the white sperm and red
blood combine in the open, outside the woman's body,
the child will not be healthy. The redness of menstruation is already moving into the open when it forms part
of the child (Fig. 6). 'The blood has not finished coming from the womb'. When the child is born he will be

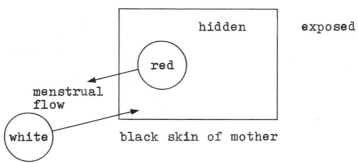

Fig. 6,   Conception of a child during
          menstruation

normal in so far as white urine will emerge from his
body in the approved manner. But the redness which was
still coming from the womb will not remain hidden; 'it

will mix with the sperm and become èelá on the surface
of the child' (see Fig. 7).

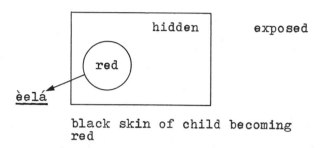

black skin of child becoming
red

Fig. 7.   The appearance of èelá on a child's
          skin

We have seen that there is a certain amount of
disagreement about the nature of the disease èelá. When
we consider the disease ètè, which we know as leprosy,
the disagreements become more pronounced; but let me
start with the area of agreement. All three of my informants agreed that, if a man lived in the same house
as a leper or wore his clothes, he would soon become infected by the disease. Similarly, everyone agreed that
it was possible to induce the disease in an enemy by using bad medicine, and Mr Adébawò seemed to regard himself as something of an expert on the subject:

  If we dip a stick into a certain kind of medicine and
  touch anyone with it, the place that the stick touches
  will be affected by ètè. In the eta ètè (i.e. the
  medicine thrown at a person to induce the disease),

they will soak alligator pepper (<u>ataare</u>)[9] in medicine
and use pincers to pick it up and to administer it.
If this medicine touches any part of the body or if
it is stepped on, that place will become diseased unless you can quickly find the antidote. Another kind
of medicine is called àtapà, which can be sent to a
person's house. It is usually projected through the
hole in a hoe (where the shaft enters the blade).
They usually use medicines for ètè against individuals, but if it is used the disease will soon spread
and become a disease of the whole family. For this
reason they always tell them at Leper Central Hospital
at Ogbomoso not to have sexual intercourse, for if the
wife of a leper conceives she will give birth to a
leper.

I dearly wished to find out the ingredients of the medicines which caused leprosy, but Mr Adébawò pretended
to know no more about them than I have already recounted. He once explained that he was unwilling to tell me
about bad medicines because it was illegal to pass on
such information in Nigeria and he feared that his

---

9 Ataare - literally 'good pepper', or, perhaps 'the
   good thing that stings' - known as 'alligator pepper', is used in medicine to 'give power' to the
   other ingredients. Its seeds are chewed for pleasure. It is not normally cooked but is perhaps the
   commonest ingredient in medicine.

enemies would betray him to the police.

We now come to the areas of disagreement. Mr
Fátóògùn stated that, in addition to the sort of explanation which I had already been given, ètè could be caused by burying a dead man wrapped in red cloth, and indeed this information is reflected in the literature
about the Yoruba people. There is an odù ifá recorded
by Professor Bascom which explains that white calico
and not red cloth is used to wrap the bodies of the dead
because it is believed that the deceased will be reborn
as a leper if he is buried with red (Bascom 1969: 238-
41).

This theory rests on a belief in reincarnation.
I once asked Mr Fátóògùn about this; let me paraphrase
his reply:

When a man is alive his head (orí) is really in heaven
and the man will worship his head because it is close
to God. Since it is in heaven, it can go to God and
petition on the man's behalf. When he dies, his head
will become the heart of the next child or grandchild
of the same sex to be born. Such a child will be giv-
en a name such as Babátúndé (father has returned) or
Ìyábò (mother has come) to indicate the relationships
between ancestor and child. The heart of the dead
man will go to heaven and replace the head which has

come to the world to become the heart of the child.
The child will then worship the heart of his dead ancestor which is his own head (see Fig. 8).

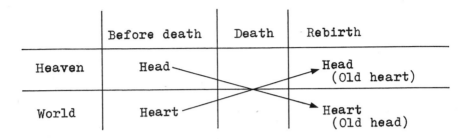

	Before death	Death	Rebirth
Heaven	Head		Head (Old heart)
World	Heart		Heart (Old head)

Fig. 8. Head and heart

This description of the process is not one likely to
be offered by the average Yoruba, or even by the average
Yoruba babaláwo; but Mr Fátóògùn is an exceptionally
gifted man whose opinions are always worth serious consideration.

Part of his theory is that it is only the head
of the person that is reborn. Because, in general, it
is only the elderly who are reborn, the head of the deceased will already be white with old age. It is possible, therefore, that the wrapping of the body in white
cloth signifies the integration of the whole physical
body with the existing whiteness of the head. Whether
or not this interpretation is correct, it is not at all
fanciful to compare the burial ceremony with the sexual
act, where the white sperm is enclosed in the blackness

of the woman's body where it mixes with red menstrual
blood. In burial the white body enters the grave where
it is hidden from view so that it may blend with the
redness of the earth. In both cases the results are
the same: red and white combine in secret to produce a
child.

In Mr Fátóògùn's theory about ètè we have one almost identical in form but not in content to our other
informants' interpretations of èelá and èelá ara pupa.
The red patches of èelá on the child's skin are caused
by that menstruation that belongs outside the woman's
body, so it tends to emerge from the body of the child.
In Fátóògùn's theory of ètè the same is true. Whiteness
should be mixed with the earth's redness that belongs
inside the grave. If the body should be wrapped in red
cloth outside the grave redness will emerge from the
body of the resulting infant.

I have said that not all informants would be likely to subscribe to Mr Fátóògùn's theory. Mr Adébawò
disagreed with it forcefully. Every family, he said,
had different ways of burying their dead which were generally kept secret, but red was not generally prohibited
in a burial cloth.

In the olden days, our forefathers used the red cloth
called aláàárì to bury their dead. Why did they not

become lepers? If this belief is correct, why is it
that Muslims and Christians, who generally bury their
dead in white cloth, are not reborn as white people?
The followers of the god Sango usually bury their dead
with red cloth. Why does not the family of Sango wor-
shippers have ètè?

No one will deny the force of these arguments. Mr Adébawò, who is a knowledgeable practitioner of medicine
and who, within the traditional framework, knows much
about the causation of disease, is here vigorously rejecting a widely accepted belief derived from my paradigm about the nature of the disease ètè. But we have
already seen that he himself derived his own explanation
of a type of ètè – what he calls èelá ara pupa – from
the very same paradigm. Here, as elsewhere, the paradigm does not furnish complete answers; it is merely a
starting point. From it, two different people may arrive at two entirely different conclusions.

The secret and the curse

Secrecy is a dominant feature of many Yoruba institutions and it is remarkable that it has never been explained satisfactorily. The best known Yoruba secret
organization is Ògbóni which, where it still flourishes,
is one of the most important religious, judicial and

political institutions of the Yoruba town. The other
dominant cult is that of Ifá, which is often called simply 'awo', the secret, and whose priests are called the
owners of the secret, babaláwo.

Aside from these well known examples, one may state
that in general anyone who possesses significant truths,
whether he be the leader of a cult-group or a craftsman
such as a master car-mechanic, will keep these truths
secret.

The greater the truth, the greater will be the
secrecy. In organisations where secrecy is the dominant
feature, Ògbóni, Ifá, Òrò, the truths which are concealed
and fostered are of overwhelming significance to the
community. The verses of Ifá strive to, and in principle do, embody the truths of all the Yoruba cults.
Morton-Williams says the same about Ògbóni; he emphasizes at some length the idea that leading members of
this cult understand and transcend the limited perspective of specific Yoruba truths (Morton-Williams 1960:
372-3). Secrecy is linked to truth; for the truth must
be hidden from daily view, to be revealed only when it
is needed.

The curse is an important idea in many folk cultures as an explanation of disease and misfortune. Among
the Yoruba, it is related to the ability to overcome

secrecy and speak the truth. I became interested in
the relationships between truth and cursing through an
Ibo friend, who had told me of a medicine for cursing
which involved the use of alligator pepper (ataare) and
another fruit, bitter cola (orógbó).[10] These fruits
had to be chewed together following a 'dry fast' of three
days during which time no food or water could be taken.
After this, I was told, anything evil that one chose to
say about anyone would come true.

At this time, I was interested in the god Sàngó
who was reputed to prefer bitter cola to the more common, segmented cola nut.[11] I therefore asked Mr Fátóògùn,
my babaláwo informant: 'Bitter cola is offered to Sàngó,
but it is also used in cursing – what is the connection?' He replied:

Bitter cola is eaten as a trustworthy fruit. You cannot split it into two like ordinary cola (obì) for it
is in one piece. Its power comes mainly from the root.
If you should chew the root of bitter cola for three

---

10   Orógbó (bitter cola) is a fruit with similar flavour
     to the popular cola nut (obì). Unlike most varieties
     of cola, it does not split neatly into segments.

11   Sàngó is generally believed to be a deposed king
     of Oyo who either hanged himself or 'did not hang
     himself' (kò so). He is said to hurl thunderbolts
     from the sky at those who deceive their neighbours
     by lying. Part of the story of T.M. Aluko's novel,
     One Man, One Wife, rests on this belief.

years (sic!) and then curse somebody, whatever you say
will occur, it will affect the person. This is why
Sàngó likes bitter cola; he hates dishonesty.

Leaving aside the complexities of bitter cola and the
cult of Sàngó, Mr Fátóògùn quite explicitly identified
the ability to curse with the ability to state what will
happen in the future, and related this to concepts of
honesty and dishonesty. Unlike the Christian tradition,
where dishonesty (i.e. not telling the truth) is unequivocally evil, Mr Fátóògùn is explicitly identifying telling the truth with the evil practice of cursing.

Mr Adébawò is very interested in medicines for
cursing. He is an Ìjèbu and once slyly told me, 'everybody knows that Ìjèbu are the owners of curses'. On
occasion he would say that he knew nothing about curses,
but I am sure that he did; he once showed me a medicine
for curses which he had made himself and which he hoped
to sell. He was always ambiguous about his knowledge
of evil medicine; but what information he was prepared
to give was always interesting. He began by discussing
some masquerade cults (egúngún):

In my town Òde Ògbòlú we have several important mas-
querades (egúngún), ekùn, moson, moji, agemon. Anyone who does not possess any curse (èpè) must not be
a member of their societies for they usually curse each

other even though it does not affect them because they
know how to avoid it. Olúgbohùn (a type of curse) is
owned by the òsùgbu (more often known as ògbóni). This
olúgbohùn must not be brought inside the house because,
when it is there, anything they say in the house will
actually occur. There are other kinds of curse (èpè)
that resemble olúgbohùn and no wise man will live in
the same house with it. I remember two women who quarrelled in the house of a man who owned medicine for
curses (èpè). One who was pregnant accused the other
of spoiling her property. The other said that her own
property would be spoiled. The pregnant woman mis-
carried twins. A medicine for curses (èpè) must be
kept away from the house because it is like a sword
which does not know or respect the person who made it.
The type of èpè that is called olúgbohùn is always kep
in the sacred grove of òrò (a secret cult) or in the
part of the forest where egúngún (the masquerade) appears or in the ògbóni lodge.... We do this because
the èpè must not hear bad things.

What emerges from this complexity is the clear and distinct belief that ability to speak the truth is dangerou
and perhaps lethal. Also, speaking the truth about future events is not a detached descriptive act but one
which is creative, actively transforming the future to

make it conform to the words of the prediction.

But what is the truth? It is revealed and created
in the verses of the Ifá cult chanted by the owner of
the secret (babaláwo). It is sometimes revealed and
created by the Ògbóni cult, and by countless lesser
cults, all of which possess creative knowledge about
aspects of the cosmos. In a less controlled and, therefore, more dangerous form, the truth is stated by the
owners of medicines for cursing. All that needs explanation is the danger which attends statements of truth.
It can be explained by means of the paradigm. If my
hypothesis is true, that Yoruba beliefs about the conception of the human body provide the paradigmatic
structure for most of the significant truths of Yoruba
culture, then the danger of revealing truth should be
self-evident.

Truth, like the human body, is understood as the
union of red and white in the darkness of secrecy. In
daily life whiteness may be seen without danger, but
revelation of the whole truth which embraces redness
involves inconvenience, disaster or death. Truth is
not to be revealed casually, without due care. Since
to reveal the aspects identified by the colour red is
to expose death, then death must be given a central and
controlled place in the ritual of revelation. It is

unthinkable that the truth should be ignored or kept in perpetual secrecy; but at least, through the sacrifice of an animal, or even of a man, death may be controlled during the revelation so that the life-giving side of truth may prevail.

In the curse, the truth about the future is spoken and created through the power of the medicine. When not in use, the careful owner will store it in a place where other truths are stored, in the lodge of the secret Ògbóni in the centre of the town; or in the hidden groves deep in the forest where òrò and egúngún emerge. If the medicine is not hidden away it will bring destruction to the owner as well as to his enemy.

Conclusion

My twofold intention in this paper was to give an accoun of the rather enigmatic statements of my informants abou certain origins of disease and then to synthesize them using a methodology based in Kuhn's idea of the paradigm

This second objective has proved much more difficult in the face of the overwhelming complexity of Yoruba culture. I have mentioned Ifá, Ògbóni, Sàngó, egúngún, òrò, all of them highly intricate strucures of belief and practice. Ultimately one must hope and, indeed, expect that the paradigm which has been outlined will provide a suitable tool to reduce this complexity to manageable proportions. For the present, there is only one choice - to select a theory which appears plausible and to develop it. This paper represents a first step in this direction.

REFERENCES

ALUKO, T.M. 1959. One Man, One Wife. London: Heinemann.

BASCOM, W.R. 1969. Ifá Divination. Bloomington, Pa.: Indiana Press.

KUHN, T.S. 1962. The Structure of Scientific Revolutions. Chicago, Ill.: University of Chicago Press.

MORTON-WILLIAMS, P. 1960. The Yoruba Ògbóni cult in Oyo. Africa, 30 (4): 362-74.

AUDREY BUTT COLSON

BINARY OPPOSITIONS AND THE TREATMENT OF
SICKNESS AMONG THE AKAWAIO

The majority of the Akawaio Indians live in the Upper
Mazaruni District of Guyana, in the northern Pakaraima
Mountain region of the Guiana Highlands. A small group
lives in the adjacent area of the upper Cotinga River,
in Brazil, and there are also a few mixed Akawaio and
Arekuna Indians in Venezuela, on the Wenamu River which
is a tributary of the upper Cuyuni, and on the Gran
Sabana. Altogether the Akawaio number about 2,700.
They are Carib-speaking.

The information in this article derives from two
periods of field research which took place from June
1951 to August 1952 and from April to September 1957.[1]

1 Financial aid from the American Association of University Women, the Colonial Development and Welfare
   Corporation, London University Central Research Fund
   and Oxford University, made possible my study of the
   Akawaio of Guyana. A grant from the Calouste Gulbenkian Foundation in 1963 enabled me to make a comparative study in Surinam and French Guiana, among
   the Wayana Indians. To the Social Science Research

To write fully of the treatment of sickness among
the Akawaio, with all its implications and ramifications
in their categories of thought and in social relationships at large, requires at least a book. There is, for
example, the shaman system (piai) with its primary aims
of fighting hostile spirits and curing sickness through
the aid of friendly spirits. There is the practice of
ritual blowing (taling) for the causation and cure of
sickness. In addition, there is belief in a system of
sorcery (edodo) which is an explanation of the phenomenon of death and its social implications. I have already published a certain amount of my data on shamanism
and ritual blowing.[2] Here I consider one theme only,
that of the basic principles which underlie and explain
the selection and application of medicinal substances
for the cure of sickness, but I shall refer to those
aspects of ritual blowing which illustrate the same basic
concepts as the medicines. To understand the operation
of the cures it is necessary, first of all, to consider
the mode of behaviour of the sick person during the
period of ill health.

Council I owe a period of research in 1971, in conjunction with Dr Neil Stevenson, in the Ica Valley,
Peru. To all of these I express my deep gratitude.

[2] For data on shamanism see Butt 1962, 1965/66; Wavell,
Butt and Epton 1966. For data on ritual blowing
see Butt 1956, 1961.

The onset of illness

Among the Akawaio the hammock performs the combined roles
of bed, settee and chair. Although a few jobs may be
carried out whilst relaxing in a hammock, mostly it is
used for resting. This can take the form of any degree
of lounging, whilst the occupant engages in informal
chatting and drinking or a quick snooze, or stretches
out full length. If complete rest or sleep is sought
during the day time the hammock sides may be folded over
the face in order to create greater privacy and to exclude light and sound and the troublesome attention of
stray flies or unexpected visitors.

However, the hammock is also a place of retreat
for a person experiencing any form of suffering. Children return to their own or a parent's hammock to sulk
or weep if they have been firmly rebuked for some mis-
doing. Adults preserve a stony silence or an aloofness,
lying out in their hammocks if they suffer grief of any
kind, or even a temporary depression or a jaundiced view
of life. The drawing of the hammock sides over body and
face then becomes eloquent of psychological withdrawal
from the social life of the household and the wish for
seclusion. An extension of this behaviour occurs with
the onset of a real, physical indisposition and illness.
When Akawaio feel indisposed, sick, suffer from pain, fee

weak or ill, they lie in their hammock in the house.
If at the time they are away from the house working, they
immediately make for home and hammock if still physically
capable of doing so, or they are carried there.

A sick person, reclining in his hammock, will frequently treat his relations and sympathetic enquirers
to detailed and graphic descriptions of the circumstances
in which the physical sensations of discomfort started
and their exact manifestations. Speculation on the causes
will also be included. These narratives may be repeated
each time there is a new arrival at the house. The
phraseology used to describe sensations is about as general as that used by people in Great Britain who have
no specialized medical knowledge when areas of pain and
discomfort are described and indicated. E'nek means pain
or hurt and phrases such as 'urö ezi e'nepe' - 'I am in
pain'; 'e'nepe upai ezi' - 'my head aches', are frequently repeated. If a feeling of more general sickness or
illness is described then the phrase 'urö ezi taköroke'
is used, taköro meaning sick or ill. A greater degree
of illness still is expressed by the phrase 'urö ipambe
ezi'. Akawaio possess a great variety of words to indicate the nature of illness from the most obvious symptoms. Some examples of the most common ones are adöng,
cough; arowdaima, whooping cough; engup, swelling of

eyelids and sore eyes; yatmansak, boils or any kind of
swelling or bump; walbaima, fever (which may accompany
all sorts of illnesses); amaliwakŏpang, fits; tulima,
yaws.

By taking to the hammock an Akawaio performs his
or her first action in the event of sickness of any kind.
If it is a mild indisposition, such as a temporary backache, headache or slight stomach upset, a few hours rest
may suffice and a return will be made to normal life as
soon as sickness passes. If it does not pass, then the
sufferer will continue to rest and will also begin to
curtail his food or to fast.

Jeruma - fasting and dieting

Jeruma (or seruma) means to fast or diet to the extent
that considerable hunger (iwam) may be endured. Akawaio
who knew a little English described the word as meaning
that 'they starve through going without food' or 'they
eat very little', meaning that they curtail their meals
severely. The association of resting and fasting as an
essential part of the treatment of sickness is so close
that it requires joint consideration as the basic reaction to ill health. Although fasting or diet curtailment
is not always associated with complete rest, it does mean
avoiding hard work and taking more rest than usual.

Although resting for any period of time because of ill health does mean diet curtailment, it does not always mean a complete fast.

The degree to which resting and fasting occur depends upon how serious the sickness is felt and judged to be and, to some degree, the length of time it lasts. If a person does not feel very well, but is not really sick, then he may spend much of the day in casual conversation and intermittent sleeping. He may sling his hammock in a place where he can watch what is going on without being exposed. He may get up and sit on a stool by the fire or in the doorway. He will not go out of the house except from necessity, because to be wandering around outside is to invite the unwelcome attention of spirits (akwalu) with such unfortunate consequences as spirit attack and soul loss. He will eat only a little and drink only a little. If he feels really bad, on the other hand, he will remain in the hammock keeping completely aloof. He will eat nothing at all and drink only water. Adults who are only indisposed will get the children to run errands for them. If seriously ill their few wants are catered for by their spouse or close adult kin. Children are cared for by their parents, grandparents, parents' siblings or their own older siblings.

The diet which is permitted during sickness which
is not serious enough to require complete fasting is
eki totsa. This is a cassava gruel or porridge. It
is made by breaking up lumps of cassava bread and steep-
ing them in water, usually warm water. Alternatively,
some dry, or lightly toasted, cassava bread in thin,
biscuit form, may be nibbled. Water is drunk, and sometimes a little lightly fermented kassiri, the regular
drink made from the bitter cassava (Manihot spp.). No
meat, vegetables or fruits may be eaten. When the patient starts to recover pepper pot, made of boiled fish
mush (from sardine-sized fish) and seasoned with a single
not very hot, pepper, may form a stew into which some
dry cassava bread is dipped. As improvement continues
the patient gradually eats more and increases the variety. Meat is usually the last item to be added and meat
of birds is taken before the meat of large animals such
as tapir, peccary and deer. If an illness persists the
patient will spend weeks eating only cassava bread and
fish pepper pot, with water and kassiri to drink. At
the same time, he will spend most of his time in the
hammock and around the house, doing very little.

An example of the belief in the ill effects of
relaxing diet restrictions during sickness occurred in
the case of a man with yaws (tulima) on his shoulders

and back. The local shaman had extracted a spirit stone
(wata) from him during a seance and he was getting better after the removal of this spirit intrusion. Then
he ate hog tannia, a very large cultivated root (Xanthos-
oma spp.), and so made the illness worse. The shaman,
who was called in again, remarked reproachfully: 'People
should eat very little when ill'.

     During the period of combined rest and diet the
patient will take various remedies (ibik, or dibik) in
order to try and effect a cure. These are administered
in the household and by members of the household, usually by close relations, although friends and more distant relatives who are knowledgeable may be called in
to help and advise. In particular, those who are expert
in ritual blowing (taling), and who have a word formula
appropriate to the case, may be called on to help effect
a cure. Recourse may be had to a shaman (piai'chang)
and if there is not one living in the settlement then
one who lives elsewhere in the river area may be summoned. The shaman will hold a seance and during the
course of this will seek spirit help. He works on the
fundamental spirit causes of the sickness and will go
on holding seances from time to time until either the
patient is cured or the enemy spirits triumph and death
occurs.

The order of **treatment of sickness is by no means**
rigid. Medicines, ritual blowing and shaman aid are
sought according to circumstances. If a shaman lives
in the settlement and is conducting a seance, even so
slight an indisposition as a headache may be tackled by
him. If there is no shaman readily available and the
sickness does not seem to be very serious, it is more
likely that the treatment will be confined to home remedies and ritual blowing. All modes of treatment can
take place in quick succession, during a few minutes,
or, if the shaman takes over, during a few hours. Thus,
someone may be blown upon, be subject to a seance and
take herbal baths all within a very short time. In no
respect does one form of treatment exclude another, although shamans may sometimes, with professional condes-
cension, proclaim in the seance through a spirit that
too many home cures and medicines have aggravated the
patient's condition. For the most part sick Akawaio
are willing to try any likely remedy, whether from a
shaman, a possessor of blowing or from a foreigner with
a store of pills and injections. Many Akawaio attended
the small hospital at the Government Station at Kamarang
Mouth, manned by a government-appointed dispenser and
an Amerindian nurse and medical rangers, although they
complained about leaving their settlements, travelling

whilst feeling ill, sleeping on beds and on receiving
strange food. Their basic objection, which could not
be met, was to the number of sorcerers (edodo) who were
thought to be in the vicinity. According to their way
of looking at it the occurrence of deaths means the presence and activity of sorcerers. Since several people
had died in the hospital it was plainly a dangerous place
to be in whilst ill and should be avoided. The dispenser
did not take kindly to the suggestion that his hospital
be turned into a mobile unit in order to avoid the attention of edodo! On the whole, however, I found the
Akawaio to be extremely broadminded about foreign remedies whilst adhering firmly to their own techniques as
well. Inevitably they added their traditional remedies
made from the resources of the local environment, the
knowledge of these being widespread and not in any way
secret. The actual preparation and brewing up of medicines was mostly a female activity - as a logical extension of food preparation and cooking preparations, it
seemed.

When a person is ill, and consequently resting
and dieting (jeruma), certain other members of his or
family are also affected. They should, in certain instances, also rest or at least perform a minimum of work.
They should also curtail their diet. Thus, husband and

wife will rest and diet if one or other falls seriously
ill. In particular, parents will jointly observe these
restrictions if their child falls sick. Brothers and
sisters can also be confined in this way. In addition,
the restrictions of jeruma may extend outside the nuclear family, to embrace close kin. Siblings of the
parents are affected, so that mother's sisters and father's brothers may be confined and also their children
who, as parallel cousins, rate as brothers and sisters.
Mother's brothers, father's sisters and their children,
the cross cousins, are not included in the category of
kin which may be expected to restrict their diet and
activities.[3] Since marriage with cross cousins is preferred, while marriage between parallel cousins is prohibited, it can be seen that those who are placed in
the category of affinal kin are not expected to observe
the jeruma restrictions at the time of sickness. These
restrictions only apply, therefore, to those who are
considered to be blood kin, as opposed to those who are
counted as affines. In practice, only very close blood
kin are normally affected, while the most crucial relationships entailing the curtailment of diet are those

---

3 I am greatly indebted to Mr Patrick Browne, a Makusi
   resident in England, for the information that the
   Makusi Indians (Pemon) of the Rupununi savannas have
   similar diet observances (referred to as esenma) and
   that the same categories of kin are affected.

of spouses and of parents and children, young children
in particular. Thus it is said that 'when a child is
ill the mother does not eat with other people at the
communal meals of the household or village'. If the
child is seriously ill both parents will eat just a
little cassava with water. They do no work but sit in
their hammocks and nurse the child, often taking it in
turns to do so. They should continue with their restricted diet and resting until the child recovers.

A good example of this type of behaviour occurred
when a baby fell sick with a bronchial infection. The
mother immediately stopped working and stopped eating.
She could be seen in her hammock, holding the child (perhaps one year old) to her breast and gazing at it sadly.
As the illness progressed the father stopped work too.
Then another crisis occurred, for the mother's milk dried
up because she had not been eating. Immediately, a host
of old women assembled to discuss the problem. The mother could not eat because if she did the child would die;
this they believed and this was their custom, they asserted. It was also thought that the spirit of the sickness would eat with the parents perhaps, and get strong,
so killing the baby. However, the child needed some
nourishment and plainly could not be given solid foods.
Nor would it feed from another breast when this was

tried. At this stage the anthropologist donated a tin of sweet milk and some sulpha tablets. Without this aid it is possible that the mother would have started eating again, but not without taking the precaution of applying charms or having the food blown on ritually in order to counteract any ill effects from the spirit world.[4]

Another example of similar behaviour was witnessed at Kataima village in October 1951, when the families associated with the village moved into their houses there in order to participate in a big dance and drink festival. Every day large communal meals took place and all the people of the village came to eat and drink, except the parents of a child ill with a bad cough. The mother stayed most of her time in the hammock, nursing the boy, and did not mix with the others or eat with them; nor did she perform the usual household tasks such as making supplies of cassava bread. At first the father carried on in a relatively normal manner, and even went hunting. However, he spent a lot of time with his wife and child. At this stage he ate at the communal meals, but on the outskirts of the assembly and slightly apart. His wife could be seen hovering nearby and watching forlornly. Then, as the child got more seriously ill, he

---

4   See Butt 1965/66: 162-6.

gave up work and all village associations. Both he and his wife strictly curtailed their diet and spent their time performing only the bare necessities of life while they jointly nursed their son.

There is very little in the literature on Guiana tribes concerning the behaviour which is prescribed for situations of illness. W.E. Roth, however, remarked (1924: 704) on 'a sort of routine treatment followed by the lay and medical fraternity in general'. Amongst the various treatments he mentions are restrictions in diet: 'The restrictions of diet may vary from the limitation of several foods to a cooked drink of cassava meal, often an absolute fast. But the curious part of the affair is that similar taboos may be, and are, simultaneously imposed upon the sick person's kinsfolk.' For the most part authors have frequently remarked on a general neglect of the sick and old. Roth (1924: 702) also summed up these assertions:

> There is one great failing which unfortunately appears to prevail among all the tribes – neglect of old persons and the sick. They are stowed away in a small corner of the house, neglected, and left to themselves; and, where weakness keeps them to their hammocks, perhaps often without the necessaries of life.

Whilst not denying that Guiana Amerindians have their

share of inconsiderate and selfish folk, my experience
of Akawaio behaviour suggests that casual observers have
probably been deceived by the operation of the restrictions imposed through resting and dieting into thinking
that the indisposed, weak and sick are merely neglected
and ignored. On the contrary, in the implementation
of these observances there is every evidence of concern.
Not only are the restrictions believed to create the
essential conditions for further treatment of sickness
and a subsequent return to normal health, but members
of the family can be said to be 'all in it together'
if the sickness appears serious. The charge of neglect
is particularly ironic in view of information on similar
practices among their Arekuna (Pemon) neighbours on the
Gran Sabana, west of the Akawaio: 'As for the concept
and practice, that the Akawaio call jeruma (resting and
fasting), it seems to be, as I see it, the same as the
Pemon Indians call esenmá - to care for oneself in a
very special way, not to cause oneself or to cause
others harm'.[5]

---

5   This private communication from R.P. Cesáreo de
    Armellada, for many years a missionary on the Gran
    Sabana and author of a number of books on the Pemon
    Indians, is as follows: 'En cuanto al concepto y
    práctica, que los Akawaio llaman jeruma, (descanso
    y ayunos), viene a ser, por lo que veo, lo mismo que
    los indios pémon llaman esenmá - cuidarse de manera
    muy especial, para no causarse or no causar daños a
    los démas' (my translation in the text).

It should be noted that resting and dieting (jer-uma) also occur on certain other occasions:

1. When a baby is born, and for the succeeding nine days approximately, both parents observe certain birth customs of which resting and fasting are primary; this has often been referred to in the literature as the couvade.[6]

2. When a person takes a succession of hunting charms, or a particularly powerful charm. Notably, this applies to young men when they are learning to hunt; the resting period may then be followed by intense hunting.

3. When a girl reaches puberty and undergoes a period of observing certain customary practices, at the time of her first menstruation in particular; the taking of special charms and the occasion for tattooing the face may be included here.

4. When a close blood relation dies, and during mourning.

5. When a shaman pupil is preparing for his first public seance and, to a lesser degree, before all suc-ceeding seances.

6. When curare poison is being prepared.

The period of resting and fasting is followed by the individual alone, or by certain kinsfolk in associ-

---

6 An article entitled 'Birth customs of the Akawaio' is in the press.

ation with him, according to the nature of the occasion.
I do not intend here to treat of the structural aspects
of the observance of the restrictions described as jeruma,
but merely note that they are obviously of importance
in any study of the interrelationships within the nuclear
family, of the relationship of blood kin to affinal kin
within the extended family unit, and of these to the
community at large.

Charms and cures

At the time of my field research the Akawaio were already,
in some instances, acquainted with the English word 'medicine', while a very few also knew the Spanish-derived
word pilota,[7] sometimes used by the Arekuna for medicine
in the form of pills. The Akawaio equivalent of medicine
is ibik, or dibik, but murang may be used instead. The
word murang means 'attraction' and can in this sense
be translated as 'charm'. Ibik means a 'cure'and its
verbal form, ibita, is used to mean 'heal'.

However, both murang and ibik occasionally involve
the use of the same or similar substances in the same
say. In such instances different qualities are evoked
according to the effects which are required. Murang,
as one informant explained, means 'medicine' in general

7 Pelota is a ball, or something round.

and, although mainly used in hunting activities, can
also be used in illness. When employed in this general
way murang is best translated as 'remedial substance'.
Thus, some remedial substances deal with problems of
health and others with problems ranging from lack of
hunting success to lack of a spouse. When attraction
and charming are the functions of a remedial substance
then the word murang is used to describe it. When curing is the function the appropriate range of remedial
substances may be specified by referring to ibik, a cure,
although the general term murang can still be used. At
a certain level, therefore, cures and charm substances
are merged as 'remedial substances' or 'medicines' in
the broadest, unspecialized sense of the word.

In this essay I am mostly concerned with cures,
that is, healing substances. To avoid confusion I refer
to them only as ibik. When referring to charm substances
I use the word murang, disregarding the fact that, being
a broader and more general category, it can also be used
to refer to healing substances.

Curing medicines and their preparation

Curing medicines (ibik) can be of either animal, vegetable or mineral origin (my classification). Of these,
animal products are very little used for making up

remedies, the Akawaio only utilizing ants for regular curing purposes. As possessors of powerful and potentially dangerous spirits, animals can be utilized safely only at the spirit level of existence, and then only in certain ritual conditions as, for example, during a seance when a shaman has control. Of the mineral products certain kinds of earth, fire ashes, smoke and soot are used. Stones, frequently believed to contain powerful spirits, are used by shamans. In particular, they manipulate quartz crystals, both to attack an enemy and to cure a friend.

Plant products form the basis of the bulk of Akawaio cures, as might be expected of people living in an area with a highly concentrated and varied plant life. They are able to draw on tropical forest, highland savanna, mountain tops and escarpments, rivers and river sides and also their own garden clearings. As the latter are abandoned and re-seed themselves with the aid of birds, they rapidly turn into a jungle of shrubs, herbs and grasses characteristic of incipient secondary growth. Akawaio make their cures from leaves, bark, seeds, fruits roots and wood of trees, shrubs and forest creepers. Grasses, caladiums and a variety of small plants such as ferns and reeds which invade gardens and forest clearings, or which are found amidst the sparse vegetation

of small, sandy savannas, are transformed into medicines. At least one type of fungus is used.

Although certain cultivated products may be utilized, such as tobacco, pepper and ginger in particular, wild forest plants with similar properties, or
the wild variety in the case of tobacco, are always regarded as more powerful. They belong to Imawali, the
order of forest spirits, or to Piait'ma, the mountain
spirit order, if they grow on high ground.

Infusions are made by adding water to leaves,
bark, roots, seeds, etc., and the resulting liquid may
be drunk or used externally as a bath or wash. Sometimes cold water is added and the vegetable ingredients
squeezed, grated or shredded as the case may be. Sometimes warm solutions are made by heating ingredients
in a pot over an open fire. They may be drunk warm or
applied externally while warm. More frequently,
infusions are made and not decoctions, which involve
deliberate boiling down to a more concentrated solution.[8] However, pots containing medicinal leaves are
frequently re-heated or lightly boiled a second or third
time so that the initial infusion becomes progressively

---

8   The sorcerer (edodo) is believed to boil up plants
    until the water has evaporated and only a powder is
    left, which he uses to cause sickness or to aid his
    nefarious work by sending his victim and companions
    to sleep.

more concentrated and could be said to end up as a decoction.

Direct application of plant substances is also made when the juice or sap of the plant, fungus or grated root or bark, is applied to the infected area, a skin wound, a sore or to the eyes. For example, fern leaves (ipaipigi - unidentified) were squeezed with a little water and the juice applied to a cut in order to stop the blood flowing and for quick healing. Similarly, cotton leaves, kŏdŏkwa (Gossypium barbadense),[9] yield a reddish juice which I saw squeezed directly onto foot sores. Sometimes a plant may first be warmed or charred on the fire and then used, or simply burnt to give off a smoke. A part of a plant may be eaten without any preparation. Another method is to cut the skin with bottle glass or make a scratch, and rub in the appropriate plant juice, usually from the root. This method is used for a cure (ibik) but is even more regularly used for applying charms (murang). Many Akawaio are to be seen with slight scars, on legs, arms and back in particular, where they have treated themselves in this way.

---

9 Fanshawe: unpublished.

Categories of cures (ibik)

Many Akawaio curing medicines are divided into hot or
cold remedies. Sometimes they are categorized in this
way because of their intrinsic qualities. For example,
pepper and ginger are considered to be hot (a'nipe) substances without any treatment being given to them. Some
substances are considered to be cold (komipe) by their
very nature; for example, river bank clay, dew, fungus
juice. However, many plant products can be assigned
to the hot or cold categories by means of various treatments. Boiling, roasting, baking or charring are processes which add heat to a substance, while washing in
a river, exposure to cold night air or leaving the substance in its raw state may place it in the cold category. Some remedies are warmed only; they are made 'a
little hot' to provide an intermediate category which
does not clash with the patient's condition and so 'make
the sickness angry'. Some heated remedies may be left
to cool before being taken.[10]

Hot cures and the hot category

Akawaio state specifically that 'hot things are used

---

10   After some field experience in 1971 among Quechua
     speakers in Peru, where an intermediary temperate
     category (templado) is also very important, I real-
     ize that further investigation of Akawaio concepts
     relating to such a category might be rewarding.

for curing sickness'. For example, wanowboima, lemon
grass (Andropogon citratum),[11] is boiled in water and
drunk for a cold (adöng). Powijimö (Aristolochia dae-
moninoxia)[12] is a forest creeper with a pronounced aromatic smell: the seeds and its long pods, the leaves,
roots or bark are boiled in water; it is strained and
then drunk as a remedy for a cold, for stomach disorders
or, in another instance, 'to stop a woman getting a
baby'. Kobari (Peperomia spp.)[13] is a creeping plant
with small, fleshy, pear-shaped leaves, found growing
on tree trunks and fallen branches during the wet season; it is boiled in water for coughs, including whooping cough, but alternatively a leaf may just be chewed
raw or squeezed in water. The leaves of makui (unidentified),[14] belonging to a creeper, may also be used for

---

11   Fanshawe's unpublished list gives wanauböma.

12   Fanshawe's unpublished list gives paui-semu. Fan-
     shawe 1950: 44, has the following: 'Aristolochia
     daemonioxia. Boyari. A reputed antispasmodic good
     for tuberculosis, bronchitis, bad coughs, bad bow-
     els, dyspepsia and indigestion. A coiled section
     of the rope kept in the bedroom is believed to act
     as a contraceptive charm. A decoction of the leaves
     with leaves of Muniridan, Bamboo, Sweet Sage, Lemon
     Grass, and Lime is used to sweat out fever. The
     decoction is highly aromatic and dark brown in col-
     our'. Here the reference is to the use of this
     plant in Guyana generally.

13   Fanshawe's list gives the Akawaio word as kobare.

14   Makui is possibly Stigmaphyllon fulgens (tentative
     identification by Mr Rufus Boyan, of the Forestry
     Department, Georgetown).

colds; they are boiled until soft and the liquid then
used as a warm wash. However, this remedy can also be
a cold one if required; the green leaves are then simply
soaked in cold water and the resulting infusion drunk.
Arailŏ (Duguetia decurrens)[15] is known as yarri yarri
on the coast of Guyana and is a cough medicine. When
required as a hot cure the bark is scraped into water
and drunk hot; when the cold category is needed then
it is drunk in cold water. As a 'fever' remedy (walbaima dibik) the seeds of the powa tree (unidentified)
are boiled and drunk. In addition, the seed pods may
be strung round the neck and worn as a necklace.

Pepper fruits, pumwi (Capsicum frutescens),[16]
are important in the hot category of cures. They may
be squeezed in water and the juice sniffed up the nose
to cure headaches. Very small gourds, kagiok, about
four inches long and cut in half to make a ladle, are
employed for this purpose. The pepper juice (or other
medicines or charms as the case may be) is put in the
ladle and the juice is dripped through a small hole in
the stalk, which can act as a handle as well as a
spout.

A child, already seriously ill with whooping

---

15 Fanshawe's list gives the Akawaio word as araira.
16 Fanshawe's list gives the Akawaio word as pŏmŏ.

cough, developed stomach disorders and pains. To deal
with this additional affliction the boy was stretched
out over the laps of his parents, face down, while his
grandmother applied the remedy. This consisted of pepper bush leaves squeezed and dampened in water, then
enclosed in a small leaf sachet and put on a smoulder-
ing fire. When heated, the inside leaf mass was removed, dipped in a little water and squeezed into the
anal passage. It took some twenty minutes to apply
this remedy, the aim of which was to get the hot juice
to the stomach where it was to cure the pain.[17] For
another condition of this type an ointment called ka-
bakta ibik was made consisting of a mixture of pepper
leaf and soot from inside the house roof. It was smeared in the child's anus. Both these forms of pepper
treatment failed, for both children died soon afterwards
from whooping cough, of which the stomach and intestinal
symptoms appear to have been a final stage. The ultimate cause of death was identified as sorcery (edodo).

Ginger, kwarötnai (Zingiber officinale), is also
important as a hot cure. Juice from the root is sniffed
up the nose to cure colds. Also for a youth with a

17 In a further effort to relieve the stomach pains
    leaves were placed on the child's stomach shortly
    before he died. Unfortunately I did not note what
    these leaves were.

cold, ginger and a black powder (said to be gun powder)
were made into a paste and rubbed into cuts made at the
knees, ankles, arms, wrists, elbows and shoulders. It
was stated that the gun powder might 'shoot the sickness'
which was causing aches in all the joints.

Tobacco, tamu (Nicotiana),[18] is believed to have
strength and power which is mobilized when it is smoked.
It is then a vehicle for the spirit power or will of
the smoker, for it is said to carry or send his spirit
(akwalu), or his words - especially ritual blowing words
(taling). Tobacco is also hot, for when tobacco smoke
is inhaled 'it goes to the heart' and people inhale it
when they are ill because it keeps the heart warm.

Some degree of heat may be applied to foreign
medicines for curing. For example, sulpha tablets given
to cure a baby with a bronchial infection were always
put into warm water: 'The medicine should be given warm,
otherwise the sickness may get cross with the child'.
However, this could have been an example of an intermediate category, between hot and cold.

The generalization has been made that 'hot things
are used for curing sickness'. Specifically, it was
said that 'peppers are used because they burn'. More
specifically, it was said that 'peppers may be used to

18 Fanshawe: unpublished list.

burn the eyes' (that is, to make them smart) or 'pepper
juice may be sniffed up the nose and the sickness goes'.[19]
One informant stated: 'Sickness does not like hot things'.

Not only are peppers grown in gardens used, but
'things from the bush'; that is, those forest plants
which are hot, like peppers. For example, wawicha dibik
(unidentified) is a cure taken from a forest tree with
an oval-shaped seed pod, yellow when ripe. Inside the
pod is a white centre, spotted with small, black seeds.
These are hot like pepper when tasted.[20] One of these
seeds may be taken as a cure for walbaima, a feverish
condition with aches and pains in the head, neck, shoulders and other joints. The prototypes of hot remedies
are pepper and ginger, especially the former, although
ginger is also said to burn.

Which sorts of illness are these hot remedies
believed to cure? Certainly the group which includes
colds, influenza, bronchitis, pneumonia and whooping
cough may be treated at certain stages with hot remedies
and warm washes: 'Things that burn like pepper are used

19 Onions, with which Akawaio are now acquainted, may
    also come into the hot category. One woman asked
    me for an onion and, on receiving it, rubbed it into
    the eyes of her sick dog.

20 Akawaio use the sense of taste, of bark, fruits,
    etc., in order to identify forest trees. In par-
    ticular, they often differentiate between similar-
    looking plants by tasting them.

as medicines for colds'. Headaches, toothache, the aches
and pains associated with certain conditions of fever,
stomach pains, diarrhoea, ulceration and inflammation
of the rectum, itching, irritation and swellings - all
these get treated with hot remedies.

Conditions of abnormal coldness of the body associated with certain stages of sickness such as cold
fevers get treated by hot remedies. Any feelings of
cold, as when people start to shiver, receive the same
treatment. If the patient is lying ill in a hammock,
a hot fire is kindled underneath or just to one side;
hot medicines follow. An interesting example of combating cold was when a young man, not in any way ill but
in order to keep himself warm when exposed to a cold
breeze in a boat on an open stretch of river, scraped
a ginger root and rubbed the chippings on his arms and
shoulders. Ginger also 'gingers one up' and is a cure
for lassitude. Laziness, especially in the young, is
corrected by squeezing ginger juice in the eyes or in
cuts on legs and arms. It is also used as a general
hunting charm (murang), by grating the root and rubbing
it in cuts in the arm where it causes burning sensations.

These uses of ginger to provoke energy lead to
situations in which it is difficult to place it in the
category of a cure (ibik), as opposed to that of a charm

(murang). In such instances it is a remedial substance of a more general nature and for this reason, as I have shown, is frequently referred to as a murang. The following example serves to show how a ginger treatment can fulfil two related functions. A girl aged about fourteen or fifteen had had a bad fever,[21] but it eventually disappeared. Nevertheless, she did not return to her customary good health and when I saw her she had been indisposed for four months. She had been resting and dieting during the whole of that period, eating (I was told) only cassava bread and drinking only kassiri. She was very thin and wan and had scars on the back of her hands and on her arms where ginger juice had been rubbed in. The cause of the fever was thought to be evil-intentioned blowing (taling). A young man had got cross with her when she refused to be his girl friend and he had retaliated in this way. The indisposition had, however, continued, and ginger had been used in an attempt to revive her vitality.[22]

---

21 'Fever' is a general term covering a wide variety of illnesses. Temperature change and aches and pains are the main symptoms leading to the use of the term.

22 The girl was eventually treated by the government dispenser, who found her to be very anaemic and in need of feeding up. She was put in the Government Station hospital and was soon reported to be recovering strength and demanding to eat only corned beef!

Both ginger and pepper may be used as hunting charms for people and for dogs. Ginger juice and water is poured into a dog's nose to make it an energetic seeker after game. A cut ginger root was rubbed into a puppy's eyes because it slept in the daytime but stayed awake and squealed at night. Pepper water is similarly poured into the noses of the hunter and his dog.

It appears, therefore, that the hot category, which is used to counteract the coldness of certain forms or stages of sickness, is also the one which generates energy. Heat and energy are therefore associated and, in this latter respect in particular, the hot category is suitable for hunting, hard work and activities of all kinds.

Frightening away sickness

The power which is contained in the hot category is suggested by its association with the use of gun powder for 'shooting the sickness'. In addition, it is reflected in the practice, frequently reported in the literature, of rubbing pepper or tobacco in the eyes at the sight of dangerous falls and rapids and of great mountains. Thus Roth (1915: 298) wrote:

The temporary occlusion of vision, as with tobacco and peppers, on the occasion of visiting for the first

time any strikingly peculiar landmark of natural scen-
ery, especially in the way of mountains, or even on
entering a new region, would seem to have been a custom
very prevalent among the Indians. From the examples
which I propose here submitting it will be seen that
the procedure specially concerns the particular Spirit
with which such landmark or region is connected. Its
object, partly perhaps to placate this Spirit, and so
turn aside the sickness or any other evil it might
otherwise choose to send, is mainly to prevent the
visiting individual attracting it towards himself.

Among the Akawaio the rubbing of peppers in the eyes on
such occasions is said to keep off sickness which might
come from strong and angry spirits believed to be inhabiting certain landmarks.

For similar reasons ginger or pepper may be applied to the eyes of a person suffering from fits (amali-
wakɵpang). In the case I encountered it was believed
that the sickness was caused by an evil spirit which
had entered the girl. 'Probably', said an informant,
'she saw a ghost (akwalupɵ) when she was a child and it
entered into her'. When a fit came on and she began to
fall out of her hammock and to struggle, pepper was put
in her eyes. This seemed to bring her round, for the
glazed, unconscious stare disappeared and she returned

peaceably to her hammock to rest.

A distinctive set of remedies, which the literature has referred to as counter-irritants, but which
Akawaio say are applied to scare away sickness, are the
ant remedies. A number of ants are collected and dex-
terously sandwiched in a lattice of wood splinters (sawra)
which has been bound with cotton. The ants are posit-
ioned in such a way that all their heads are on one side
of the lattice and their abdomens on the other. An alternative method is to select a particularly large type
of ant and place it in a small cleft stick. The wriggling, infuriated creatures are applied to those parts of
the body which ache - the thighs, legs, shoulders, arms
and neck. They are frequently applied for the rheumatic
conditions of the elderly, which seem to occur mostly
at the approach of the rainy seasons. They are also
applied for the aches associated with bad colds and feverish conditions (walbaima). Thus a frame of ilak[23]
was applied by a grandmother to two small children with
colds. Indignant screams and yells, crying and wriggling,
occurred as the stings took effect and there followed
several minutes of scratching and grumbling. The ant

23 Various other ants are utilized besides the ilak,
    a black ant known generally in Guyana as the monori.
    Maba, a red ant, is used as a cold cure, for example.
    I have not been able to identify them individually.

remedy is said to ease the pain of the sick person. It
is also asserted that 'the sickness does not like the
sting'.

     As well as the ant _ibik_, the ant cure, there is
also the ant _murang_, a hunting and energy producing charm
Like the ants, which rush out early to get food (such
as flies) and return with the meat quickly to the nest,
so the hunter and his dog who have taken this charm will
go out early and quickly seize their prey to bring home.
The _kobala_ ant is used as a hunting charm in general,
but some ants, such as the _ilak_, may be used both for
hunting and for curing.[24] In the latter instance it is
frequently referred to as a _murang_ in the sense of being
remedial in general; for example, Roth noted (1924: 566)
that ant bites may be inflicted on lazy children. The
indications are, therefore, that the biting of ants can
be placed in the hot category which, with its energy-
giving component, serves both to dispel sickness in the
form of aches and pains and to galvanize the hunter into
activity. The same underlying principle serves two
functions.

---

24 When used as hunting charms ants are sometimes
    rubbed in cuts in the hunter's arm or may be
    sniffed up the nose on a cotton string and drawn
    out through the mouth.

Bitter cures

Many cures combine a bitter principle (i'nipe) with a
hot principle (a'nipe). Toothache, for example, is
treated with ginger and pepper put on the tooth together,
but an alternative treatment is the application of the
scrapings of a bitter nut from a tree called kŏrŏng-
pimbiu (Ormosia coutinhoi).[25] The cure for 'ground
itch', paleda, is another instance; this is the name giv-
en to severe itching and swelling of the feet resulting
from some skin infection.[26] At one Akawaio village the
cause of the itching was attributed to a small, spreading
weed which covered the paths and part of the compound
and was used as a deer charm (usali murang) by hunters,
the leaf of the plant having a point at the end remin-
iscent of the shape of a deer's ear. As hunting charms
are said to cause itching sensations when used by a hunter, the itching of the feet was directly attributed to
the operation of the same qualities when the plant was
trampled on. To cure the ground itch, leaves of the
bitter cassava plant, eki (Manihot utilissima), were

25 Fanshawe's unpublished list gives the Akawaio name
    as kurumbenbeo, but in Fanshawe 1950: 48, its pop-
    ular name is given as korokororo: 'A boiling infus-
    ion of the bark is used to induce sweating. The
    inner bark is applied to joints to ease rheumatic
    aches and pains. The seed is used to treat toothache'.

26 'Ground itch' has been said to be due to a hookworm
    infection.

taken, squeezed and rubbed in a little hot water, and applied to the feet. Then more cassava leaves were rubbed in hot ashes from the fire and the mixture applied vigorously to the feet. Finally, the feet were bathed in hot water. Bitter cassava is considered to be a very bitter plant — the roots contain hydrocyanic acid — and has to undergo a very long process of preparation and cooking before it is rendered safe and palatable for eating.

It is believed that bitter substances have the power to cure certain illnesses. These include stomach disorders, diarrhoea (kwasök), dysentery (möngaima) and fever (walbaima). A certain illness called witnarök,[27] the symptoms of which are described as a redness (inflammation?) and biting (ulceration?) inside the anus and lower rectum, is treated with bitter remedies, although it is said that death follows within a day or so of the appearance of this sickness. One remedy is mörairai bark (unidentified); the bark is boiled and the patient drinks it or is bathed in it. The taste is supposed to drive away the sickness because it is very bitter. In particular, bitter and astringent barks are used as febrifuges by Akawaio.

---

27 Witnarök may be the form of sickness referred to in the literature as 'Buck sickness' or 'Caribisi sickness'.

Bitter medicines are taken to stop, or at least reduce, the blood flow at menstruation.[28] A well-known example is called kodak, or kotak. It derives from the greenheart tree (Ocotea rodiaei),[29] the bitter seeds of which provide this 'women's medicine'. An extension of this line of thought can be seen in the practices associated with the onset of puberty among girls. At the time of first menstruation a girl is slung in her hammock, often high up under the house thatch, away from the men who would have no success in their hunting if they had contact with her. She is partitioned off either with the leaves of the greenheart tree or with those of the purpleheart (Peltogyne spp.) or of the crabwood tree (Carapa guianensis). The purpleheart leaves are bitter, as are the greenheart leaves, while the crabwood tree has a bitter bark and seeds which yield an oil with an intensely bitter taste. The latter is used on the skin as an insect repellent and on the hair to control

---

28 The desire to reduce the menstrual flow is said to be because women are ashamed of menstruation and because it is inconvenient, especially when travelling.

29 Fanshawe's unpublished list gives the Akawaio word as kot. Fanshawe 1950: 48, has the following information: 'Ocotea rodiaei. Greenheart. Bibiru. The seeds contain at least 2 alkaloids, bibirine and sipirine used to treat dysentery, diarrhoea and malarial fever. The light yellow decoction of the bark with a nauseating bitter taste and a sickly odour is also used as a febrifuge'.

lice; it is said to prevent itching.[30] Whilst fasting
(jeruma), the girl is given kodak and water to drink
in order to lessen the flow of blood.

After the birth of a child bleeding must be similarly reduced. Father and mother share the birth customs and both must rest and fast. They may, if all goes
well with the baby, eat a little pepper pot consisting
of the stewed leaves of the bitter manioc with a pepper
to spice it. Alternatively, the pepper pot may be made
of kata, the boiled juice of the bitter manioc roots,
which contains hydrocyanic acid in its original state
but is made into a palatable gravy through boiling. One
pepper is added to spice it. A little cassava bread may
be dipped into either of these stews and eaten. Paia-
waru, a lightly fermented drink made of toasted cassava
bread, may be drunk by the mother. Kassiri may be drunk
by the father.

Just as significant is the list of foods which
are forbidden during this crucial period. Not only meat
and fish have to be avoided, because they have powerful
spirits which may harm the vulnerable spirit of the baby
but there is a prohibition on certain kinds of garden

---

30 Fanshawe 1950: 45, states: 'Carapa guianensis.
    Crabwood. A decoction of the bark is used for
    dressing ulcers, curing diarrhoea and relieving
    rheumatism'. He describes the bitter qualities
    of the seeds on pp. 39-40.

produce, as on wild forest fruits, because they are sweet, a'seku. Sweet foods, it is asserted, 'cause blood', which is itself classified as sweet. Salt is also classified as sweet. For these reasons maize, bananas, sugar cane, pineapples, root crops, salt, etc., must be avoided, as also any sweet, unfermented drinks, including the unfermented cassava drinks.

The cold-sweet category

Blood is classified as especially cold when associated with menstruation and birth, so that cold liquids and foods must also be avoided in order to avert an especially cold condition of the body. It is said that 'the stomach must not have cold things'. Again, 'all food must be warm; cold food would kill the mother'.

The opposition of cold to hot and of sweet to bitter, opposing but complementary categories, can be seen in a whole range of medicines in which the stated purpose is 'to cool down the sickness'. For example, there is chilikö itagu, star spittle, or dew. To acquire this cure a cup with a little water in it is put outside the house during the night to collect the dew; the contents are drunk the next morning as a cold cure. 'Water is cool from a star and therefore cools down sickness.'

Piait'ma is the order of mountain spirits, and

each mountain is believed to have a family of such spirits living there. Piait'ma is associated with cooling
cures, as are other, lesser, mountain spirits, for mountains are cold places, where rain falls and mist gathers,
where rivers have their sources and cold water falls from
the summits. Thus, Piait'ma manadu (literally, Piait'ma
breast milk) is a small fungus which may be found growing on rotten branches which litter the forest floor.
The fungus has the shape of a long, pendulous breast
and contains a milky white juice. It is associated in
Akawaio thought with the long flapping breasts of Piait'm
women and the cooling medicine which they bring down in
shamans' seances to cure the ills of their grandchildren,
the Akawaio. The image is of cold water flowing from
the breast of the mountain on to the hot lands below.
There is also an association with sweet breast milk.
The sick person nips off the tip of the fungus and squee
es the juice into an infected eye. In particular, this
is the treatment for blepharitis, swelling and infection
of the eyelids due to small flies, called engup. Akawai
say that engup is cooled down by this treatment.

Piait'ma mömbödöpö,[31] (literally, Piait'ma after-

---

31 Mömbödö = womb. The suffix -pö signifies 'past' or
    'former'; mömbödöpö therefore means 'former womb'.
    The Akawaio associate the appearance of the after-
    birth with the end of the blood flow, for women

birth) is a dank kind of clay from the river bank. Mixed with cold water it, too, can cool down a sickness.
It is given in the form of a cold bath as a remedy for
bronchitis or bad colds and as treatment for a person
sick with headache who is feeling thin and weak. 'Piait'ma is a good cooler', one informant aptly remarked.
Various other clays are similarly used, such as aboi-
doima, a black clay, and tawa, a clay used for pot making. Tawa is mixed with water and drunk for a cold cure.
'The earth cools down the sickness.'

A number of herbal remedies can be classified
as cold when taken in a raw state or with cold water.
I have already referred to those which, like kobari and
makui, can also be made hot by boiling and then drunk
as warm decoctions or infusions. Oba bipa (unidentified) is a tree bark which is squeezed, may have sugar
cane juice added, and can be taken as a cure for colds.
The same principle of cooling down sickness has f rther
extensions. For example, onoli wata is literally the
'tiger bird spirit stone'[32] used by the shaman to cool

----

use a plant called mömböda (unidentified), the root
of which is grated, squeezed and the juice drunk,
just before menstrual periods: this remedy is said
to stop menstruation.

32 Beebe 1917: 139, identifies the onoray or 'tiger
bird' of the Akawaio as the Guiana green heron (Bu-
torides virescens). The stone which I saw had a
projection which was likened by its shaman-owner
to the beak of the bird.

down sickness because the tiger bird lives at **river**
sides, which are cool places.

Numerous references in the literature bear wit-
ness to the underlying assumption that women's blood
(mɵng) is cold and sweet, and will neutralize male activities in food getting. Thus, curare arrow poison used
in hunting is bitter and hot; bows and arrows, blow pipes,
darts and the poison, have to be removed from possible
contact with menstruating or pregnant women because mɵng
would 'cool' the poison. Sexual relations come into
the sweet category, if certain bawdy remarks by a Piait-
'ma mountain spirit at a shaman's seance are to be trust-
ed.[33] All these conceptions explain why, when an Akawaio
couple saw their hunting dog consorting with a bitch,
they hastily mashed up peppers and put them in the dog's
mouth as a deterrent. However, it is in the various
prohibitions traditionally placed on the curare poison
maker that the oppositions of hot-bitter and cold-sweet
are most apparent. Richard Schomburgk (1922: 353), who
witnessed the making of the poison among the Makusi in
1842, gives a list of the ingredients used and remarks
that 'all the ingredients that the Macusis employ for

-----

[33] It was stated that the reason why a hunter should
     avoid women at the time of taking charms (murang),
     and why young women in particular should not handle
     the charm substances, was because his charms might
     attract women (sweet) instead of the meat (by
     implication also sweet).

the manufacture of the poison are uncommonly bitter'.[34]
He notes that the mixture was slowly boiled for twenty-
four hours and that ritual blowing was employed at one
stage in order to increase its strength. Finally, the
concentrated liquid was exposed to full sunshine for
several hours. Waterton (1903: 39), also among the Makusi of the northern Rupununi savanna, noted in 1812 that
besides the wourali vine (a root with a very bitter
taste) there were also included two species of ants with
powerful stings, the strongest Indian pepper and the
pounded fangs of two of the most poisonous snakes, one
being the dreaded labarria (Trigonocephalus atrox). The
entire process involved the use of the most bitter, biting and stinging ingredients, which were further treated
by boiling, by exposure to hot sun and by ritual blowing
to increase the strength.

The observances associated with the manufacture
of poison were clearly designed to keep away from it
anything which would counteract the qualities which had
been carefully created. No woman, certainly no pregnant
woman, could go near the site of activities; and the
curare maker's wife, if pregnant, inhibited the manufacture of the poison. It was believed that anyone who

34 The Makusi, although belonging to the Pemon group
    of Indians, are very similar to the Akawaio, who
    are of the Kapong group.

had eaten sugar cane would cause the poison to lose
strength if he came near it whilst it was boiling. The
curare maker himself, according to Schomburgk's account
of the Makusi procedure, 'must submit to a stringent
fast both before and during its manufacture'. Waterton
specified that 'he who makes the poison must eat nothing
that morning, and must continue fasting as long as the
operation lasts'. Quelch (1895: 262-3) added the information that '... the greater the abstention from food
on the part of the piaimen, the greater the virulence
of the Urali, its action being supposed to be deadly
in correspondence with the degree of hunger of the maker'
Finally, the poison maker believed himself to be sick
for some days after preparing the poison. These observations indicate that the poison maker undergoes an extensive fasting period of the type which the Akawaio
refer to as jeruma. After the poison making, if not
before, fasting is combined with resting.

The Akawaio, who now no longer make curare, re-
call that curare makers could not eat sweet things, othe:
wise the curare would not kill, for the bitterness would
be taken away. They could eat only kumagi or kasarip,[35]

---

35 The juice expressed from bitter manioc roots con-
    tains poisonous hydrocyanic acid which can be rend-
    ered harmless by boiling. When lightly boiled a
    thick, creamy gravy results, which the Akawaio call

the poisonous juice from the bitter manioc which is boiled down to make a dark sauce, together with peppers and
cassava bread. Salt was also forbidden at that time,
in addition to cane juice. The antidote for snake bite,
the bite of spiders and ant bite, is frequently reported
to be sugar or salt rubbed into the wound, though Awakaio
sometimes maintained that there was no cure other than
fasting and resting and ritual blowing treatment. Early
travellers were told by Amerindians that sugar or salt
rubbed into a wound made by a curare-coated arrow or dart
would effect a cure. Some cold treatments have also been
reported in combination with these. For example, Waterton (1903: 51) noted the assertion that if the wounded
animal was held for a considerable time up to the mouth
in water the poison would not prove fatal. All experim-
ents failed to justify these antidotes. The Carib-
speaking tribes were thinking along other lines, those
of the sweet and the cool, when employing these remedies.
A good example of their type of cure occurred when an
Akawaio child stepped on a monori (ilak) ant and was
badly bitten in the foot. The mother first rubbed in
salt, scraping it in with a knife; then she followed this

---

kata, and into which they dip cassava bread. When
boiled further, kumagi, a dark gravy, in Guyana
called kasarip, results; this is a preservative.

with the juice of the root of a snake bite cure, its
long stalk mottled like a snake's skin.

A striking association between cold and sweet
is made with reference to madness possessing the sorcerer (edodo), especially one who has killed for the first
time. He is regarded as sobai, mad, because of the powerful charms he has taken to enable him to kill in a
particular way. In this state of derangement and heat,
engendered by the use of his poison charms, he may run
wild; he seeks graves in order to cool himself down.
Bones and the remains of corpses (not necessarily his
own victims) are said to smell sweet to him and he is
believed to insert a hollow cane into a grave in order
to suck up the juices from the corpse; or he may even
dig it up. An informant added: 'If you are mad you can
walk under the earth and see many things, you can go
under the water and suck the camudi - the camudi can't
catch you if you are mad. You can see the water spirit
(Lato) and others, and so an edodo can take his cure
for sobai from them'. Thus water, the water camudi,
which is a constricting snake (Boa murina), the water
spirits and under the earth - are all regarded as cold;
so also, it seems, are decaying flesh and bone. In this
context, I was also told that if an edodo goes mad at
the start of his career as a killer he has to be blown

upon by his relatives, who are also likely to be sorcerers, in order to recover. Should this not be done then
he may drown himself - presumably seeking the enveloping
cold of the water and of death.

Another activity which seems to be regarded as
having cooling properties is that of scratching. A girl
at the time of puberty has a small stick tied round her
neck which should be used instead of her finger nails
when she wishes to scratch herself. If she does use
her nails then it is said that permanent white marks
will be left on her skin. Similarly, if a woman scratch-
es herself at the time of giving birth her hair will
fall out. This could also happen at puberty. Itching
is said to follow the taking of charms (especially some
caladium charms), and it also follows on the application
of ant frames as cures or charms. It would appear that
the Akawaio regard such itching as the sign of heat and
energy, or a force unleashed, and that to scratch at
such times, without due precaution, is to cool down at
a time when heat is the crucial category.[36]

Binary oppositions in ritual blowing

This is a ritual process whereby the spirit (akwalu) of

---

36 It is said that when a hunter mixes the juice of a
    charm plant with his blood the itching arouses a
    corresponding itch in the animal he seeks, so
    attracting it within reach.

of the blower (<u>taling genak</u>) is sent out in the breath
and, in combination with the spirit forces invoked by
a special set of words appropriate to the intention,
achieves a particular effect, socially good or bad. The
blowing words may call on any aspect of the physical and
natural environment, such as climatic phenomena, sun and
stars, animals and plants. They may also invoke cultural objects. All are personified. Some blowing words
clearly refer to and manipulate the major categories of
hot-bitter versus cold-sweet, both for curing and killing, but they are not expressed simply as abstract categories. They become qualities intimately associated
with the personifications conjured up in the blowing
ritual, and through this they have the additional vitality deriving from the spirit forces characteristic of
animistic belief.

    The first phrases of the blowing words used for
curing often describe the sickness of the patient and
its causes. There may be mention of the hot condition
of the patient. Then follows the invocation of various
helping agents which will cool down and so cure the sickness. For example, the following formula[37] is used to

----

37 Many of the words used in blowing formulae are diff-
    erent from everyday speech. In addition, the two
    formulae I reproduce, although used by an Akawaio,
    were acquired by him from his Arekuna mother-in-law

cure <u>witnarök</u>, inflammation and ulceration of the rectum:

Melemwimö	yumbösak,	parakowalimö	wasinimö
Poison name	is poisoned,	<u>parakowa</u>	<u>wasi</u> poison
(used by		poison	
edodo)			

yumbösak,	uröbölimö	yumbösak,	<u>tesangya</u>	yumbösak,
is poisoned,	uröbö	is poisoned,	owners	is
	poison			poisoned,

Arambödongkongya	yumbösak,	wubökokya	yumbösak,
Aramödong people	is poisoned,	forest	is poisoned,
(i.e. <u>Imawali</u>		people	
people - owners)		(owners)	

mangik	ebiakösak,	parakowa	yalelöke	mangik
child	is aching,	<u>parakowa</u>	with leaf	child
(the patient)				

ebiakösak.	Mölowya	mangik börotmega,	mangik
is aching.	That is it,	child is sick,	child

eketötrumba,	mangik	ingöwaitlöngba,	mangik egatnönga,
falls	child	gets headaches,	child feels bad,
unconscious,			

mölögingsatnö.	Pönöpang	köbökwaitö!	Witnödilimöke
it is like	Cool down	do it!	With cool
that.			medicine

kowönalimöke	pakalalimayak.	Pönöpanggowyadö
with menstruation	in shoulder bag.	Cools down
blood		

mangik	pönöpang	köbök! Legingsatnatö,	urö	kingsatnö
child	cool down	do it! I alone,	I	am

mötö,	pakalamök,	menurökong,	biatö,	töpebong,
that	shoulder bags,	shoulder bag	help,	shoulder
one,	(rectangular)	ones (of		bag ones,
		'tiger' skin)		(with
biatö.				cover)
help.				

---

in exchange for some of his own. However, similar thought processes underly both Akawaio and Arekuna formulae.

The formula makes it clear that the sickness is
the result of sorcery. The sorcerers have not made a
full-scale attack, which inevitably brings death, but
have poisoned the patient by using various charm plants
which include <u>parakowa</u>,[38] <u>wasi</u> and <u>urɵbɵ</u>,[39] all well-
known sorcerers' charm substances made secretly from
plants found or grown specially in the forest. Informants described how, for example, the <u>parakowa</u> leaf and
root would be burnt and made into a powder which, when
put on the victim, would make him fall sick. The sorcerers are vaguely referred to, in this particular word

---

38 <u>Parakowa</u> is a large caladium about four feet high.
    Everything done to prepare this plant denotes poison-
    ous heat. The roots are roasted, ground into powder
    and kept in a tightly closed container. If someone
    'comes cross' they put a little powder in his drink
    and he is poisoned. Sometimes pepper is put with
    it and then, when the victim eats peppers in the
    pepper pot, he gets hot and feverish and dies. It
    is so powerful that it makes the skin itch. This
    plant is grown by the sorcerer deep in the forest
    at a river head, amongst the trees. I saw such a
    plant, identified by the Akawaio as <u>parakowa</u>, growing
    in a swampy habitat in the forest in the Amokokupai
    area of the upper Kukui River.

39 Dance 1881: 332, mentions the Akawaio poison <u>hurubu</u>,
    which he describes as being similar to the hog tannia
    plant (that is, the Xanthosoma spp.). He says that
    'the root is grated and placed in water to get the
    starch, which after being dried is used on the point
    of peels (arrows) for large birds. A little pressed
    in between the extremity of the thumb and the thumb
    nail, and thus conveyed to the paiwari or kasiri
    bowl, is said to poison the drinker'.

formula, as being forest people. Aramödong is the 'spirit name' for Imawali, the order of forest spirits, and
one which is often used in shamans' seances. They are
the owners of the poison charms in this instance.[40] The
victim feels pain all over, is sick, gets fever and headaches and finally falls unconscious - 'sleeps all day
without opening the eyes' as my informant described it.
The sickness is hot and has to be cooled down and so
taken away. For this, cooling medicines have to be used
and there is a reference to menstruation blood, which
is regarded as the essence of coldness. Three types
of shoulder bags are called on for assistance: they will
take out the sickness, as this will be shut inside them
with the cooling medicines which will counteract and
nullify the poisonous heat which the charms of enemies
have engendered. The shoulder bags are the pakala - a
rectangular, basketry one, the menuru - one made of the
skin of one of the cat family, and the type töpe - which
is shaped like an envelope of basketwork with a flap.
Men take these when out hunting to hold small items of
essential equipment, including hunting charms.

A similar blowing formula, used for a feverish
cold cure, is as follows:

---

40 That these are the owners of the poisonous plants
    which are grown in the forest is indicated by the
    subject indicator -ya.

Mermaimö parakowalimö   wasinimö,   tatnödimöya
Sickness parakowa poison   wasi poison,   you get hot

mangik,   awonomba   tatalumba;   mölögingsatnö.
child,   get cough   itching of   it is like that.
(the patient)   throat;

Pönöpang   köbökwaitö!   Witnödilimöyak,   kowönalimöyak,
Cool down   do it!   In cooling   in menstruation
                      medicine,   blood,

pakalalimayak,   manadilimöyak,   wöboimödatlöging.
in shoulder   inside breast,   inside mountain.
bag,

Tatnödilimö   tatnödimö,   Pönöpang   köbökwaitö!
Get you hot   get you hot.   Cool down   make!

Urö legingsatnö,   mötö,   Chöwilögong,   biatö,
I am   like that,   that one,   Piait'ma people,   help,

Adai'taigong   biatö,   Bökkagong,   biatö.
Piait'ma people   help,   Praying mantis   help.
                         ones,

The various poison charms are blamed for the bad cough which the patient, referred to as 'child', is suffering from. To cool down the sickness the mountain spirit order, Piait'ma, is invoked for help. Adai'tai and Chöwilö are names which are frequently used for Piait'ma in a ritual context. In addition the praying mantis (normally referred to as awabölö) is called on for help because the mantis 'has his own medicine to cool down sickness and helps Piait'ma to take the sickness away'. The medicine referred to is called menstruation blood and the sickness is to be put in the shoulder bag of

Piait'ma,[41] inside her breast (which contains cooling
medicine analagous to sweet breast milk) and inside the
mountain (which is a cold place).

In both the examples of blowing formulae I have
given, the cooling agent kowönalimö is referred to as
menstrual blood, my informant having translated it so.
However, he also explained that kowöna 'is water dripping from a mountain which never dries up, even in hot
weather, when all the other streams are dry. It is always cold - you can call on it to cool down sickness'.
Perpetual coldness and dampness is thus called upon to
counteract the heat and dryness of the sick person, but
at the same time it is identified closely with the cold
stream of women's blood which is also the epitome of
coldness. My informant maintained that the blood referred to was not real blood; he went on to say that, just
as menstrual blood cools poison, so the blood called

---

41 It is no accident that Piait'ma has a shoulder bag
    which is the pakala (or pakara) type and which is
    rectangular. The mountains of the Guiana Highlands
    where the Akawaio live are called Pakaraima, the
    'big pakara' mountains, being of the rectangular,
    flat-topped, mesa type, of which Roraima is the
    most famous example, and it is appropriate that the
    mountain spirit should have such a shoulder bag.
    There is thus a complicated set of associations in
    which the rectangular, mountain-shaped shoulder bag,
    the breast of the mountain, the cool streams from
    the breast which fall in a frothing, creamy stream,
    combine in elaborate symbolism.

on (that is, the medicine), will destroy the efficacy
of the urᵫbᵫ poison used by the sorcerer to cause the
patient's sickness. 'The same name is used for the medicine as for blood, both having the same effects.'

Excess, imbalance and disharmony

An extreme condition of any sort, whether achieved inadvertently or imposed by the evil motivation of enemies
is a basic cause of sickness and likely to disrupt the
constitution to the degree that death occurs. A number
of beliefs and practices illustrate this fundamental
assumption. For example, extreme heat can wither or
poison a person: there is a blowing (taling) formula
in which the sun spirit is called on because a very hot
sun withers and dries up life;[42] the hot midday sun can
make a person ill, especially when they are mourning
and should be resting and fasting. The starchy mush
from suruwa seeds (Cunuria glabra)[43] has to be boiled
from early morning to late afternoon and then soaked
in water and washed free of poison during the night;

---

42 In spite of the withering power of the sun in this
    context, it must be remembered that the sun is also
    believed to be the place where light (akwa) is and
    thus the source from which comes vitality and
    strength for everything alive on earth: see Butt
    1954.

43 Fanshawe lists the Akawaio name as suruwai.

it should then be eaten early in the morning, preferably with banana or sugar cane juice, for if kept and
eaten at midday, or near a fire, it is believed to be
poisonous and to cause a headache. This is an example
of the belief that temperature differences according
to the time of day affect the qualities of a substance.
I have already noted that the application of heat to
various remedies transfers them from a cold to a warm
or hot category. Similarly, other substances, especially those closely associated with a person, can be affected: thus, people are advised to throw away hair
clippings or to bury them because burning the clippings
in a fire will make the head hurt.[44] One of the many
stories about the doings of _Piait'ma_ mountain spirits
tells of one such spirit who killed his wife by frying
her footprint on a baking pan. I was told at the time
of hearing this that one method of killing a person was
to take a footprint and put it in the fire to burn. A
person sick from evil blowing can take two or three drops
of blood from himself and fry the blood on a hot baking
pan. Through this the blower, whose spirit will have
gone out with his breath and entered his intended victim,

---

[44] Akawaio are not particularly careful about hair
clippings. I have seen pieces of hair discarded
in the settlements, although some people take theirs
and, presumably, dispose of them more carefully.

will himself fall sick while his victim will recover.

Too cold a condition will also cause sickness. Excessive exposure to cold winds is dangerous in this respect. Too much blood can cause headaches, pains, laziness and other ills. The remedy is to let some out (batögö - bleed). For persistent headaches the vein of the temple may be pinched up and pierced with a dried sting-ray spine. As the blood flows out the pain is relieved. For pains in the legs cuts are made and the blood let out. Women, old and young, will cut legs and arms with bottle glass and put in special remedies to stop blood at the time of menstruation, believing that if they do this there will be less menstrual flow. If people sleep too much or are lazy, and also when they have headaches, sala or razor grass (Scleria spp.),[45] is pushed up the nostrils, the sharp edges of the grass making them bleed inside. The literature shows that Amerindians in general have used bleeding as a cure for weariness, pains or stiffness in the limbs caused by fatigue.[46] Bleeding is presumed to give greater strengt especially in arms and legs. On the other hand, too little blood can be fatal. In the story of the origins of Hallelujah, the syncretic religion of the Carib-

---

45 Fanshawe lists the Akawaio name as sara.

46 See Roth 1924: 706-7.

speakers of the Guiana Highlands and Rio Branco savannas, the Makusi founder was attacked by sorcerers. After several miraculous recoveries, aided by heavenly medicine, he eventually died because, as one narrator put it, 'must be, blood finish'.[47]

Harmony and balance through the use of binary oppositions

Many authors have commented upon various medicinal practices of the Carib-speaking peoples, usually with extreme disapproval. Richard and Robert Schomburgk, famous nineteenth-century explorers of the interior of British Guiana, saw numerous cases in which conditions of heat during sickness were treated by cooling measures. Among the Makusi of the Rupununi savanna, Robert Schomburgk (1836: 282) remarked:

> We found whole families afflicted by fever when we returned in January from the upper regions of the Rupunoony. The measles likewise committed great havock amongst these aborigines, who, when covered with the disease, and warned by us not to expose themselves to cold, considered nevertheless that the best remedy for allaying the insufferable heat was to plunge into the water.

47 Butt Colson 1971: 39.

Richard Schomburgk (1848: 240, 265) also commented that
the Makusi 'drench the smallpox patients during the most
acute febrile stage with water, a procedure from which,
in spite of all our protestations, we could never wean
them'. Later, he noted that steam baths and cold river
bathing occupy the chief place in treatment.

> No matter the nature of the complaint, the bath as I
> have already said, comes first. In the height of fever
> and with no strength left to take him to the river,
> the patient will be just as soon drenched with cold
> water as enveloped in steam: the latter is produced
> by quartz or pebble-stones made glowing hot, placed
> under the hammock and water then poured over them.

Roth (1924: 705-6) quotes a number of references whereby
hot fevers were counteracted by the patient standing
in the river up to the neck in water or immersing himself in cool mud, having had his spouse pour a calabash
of water over his body. The steaming treatment, on the
other hand, seems to have been used for cold fevers or
the cold condition of women after confinement.

The manipulation of remedies based on a categorization of the hot (a'nik) and the cold (komik), the
bitter (i'nik)[48] and the sweet (a'seku), hot-bitter and

---

48 A closely related category is the sour, karapang.
    Drinks which have undergone long fermentation are
    said to be sour, also some unripe fruits.

cold-sweet, is plainly outstanding in the attempts to
cure sickness made by the Akawaio and their closely related Carib-speaking neighbours. That they aim at a
balanced state is further suggested by the fact that
a particular illness is not always consistently treated
by one category of cures. It is the state of cold or
heat of the patient which is important at any time, so
that feverish complaints which make the patient feel
temporarily cold are treated by the hot-bitter category
and a good fire is maintained under the hammock of the
patient who is resting and fasting. If the condition
changes to one of heat then cooling remedies are sought
while the fire is extinguished or left very low. Plant
remedies in use may be converted to hot or cold to ac-
commodate the changed condition of the patient.

The power of spirit activity

Another important facet of the treatment of sickness
and states of imbalance relates to the spirit sphere
which, as already pointed out, is dominated by the shamans who are spirit experts. Danger can be avoided, or
at least reduced, by not hunting and not eating meat
or large fish. Animals have powerful spirits[49] which

49 The spirit of anything which is alive is that which
    gives strength (merundö) for living. It is described

are unpredictable in their actions and which cause harm
when aroused. At certain times people are particularly
vulnerable to these forces, notably when in some state
of transition or imbalance. The state of well being and
health is when a person's own spirit is sovereign in the
body, or with a friendly spirit supporting it. If an
ill-disposed spirit, or spirits, are inside doing mischief then remedies have to be used to frighten them out
or other, stronger spirits have to be invoked by the sham
an or a possessor of ritual blowing to assume control
and force a return to normality. Sickness itself is
spoken of in animistic terms. There is a measles spirit,
a whooping cough spirit, a 'fever' spirit, amongst many
others.[50] An enemy may send a sickness spirit to maim
or kill. Such an enemy may be another human being or
may be a nature spirit of some kind. For example, Nias,
son of Abraham of Kataima village, Mazaruni River, was
said to have died from whooping cough (arowdaima) and
also because the father had killed a jaguar shortly

---

as akwalu; without it a person or thing is dead
and has only a ghost, akwalupö.

50 My impression was that spirits of sickness are
    especially associated with infectious maladies.
    However, it is a vague term and can be used to
    mean also any spirit which has caused a person to
    be sick, whether by direct attack or by sending a
    particular sickness.

before:[51] members of the cat family have powerful and
angry spirits and when hunted retaliate by causing sickness and making spirit attacks.

All the curing activity I have described and the
attempts to restore or maintain a temperate, balanced
state of health by utilizing certain categories, do not
invalidate the belief in the ultimate, spirit cause of
sickness. During a whooping cough epidemic all the Akawaio houses contained numerous remedies, pots of infusions of roots and leaves and barks in particular. Parents were busy warming up or cooling down their offspring,
rubbing on ointments, shooting sickness and applying ant
frames to frighten away the sickness with hot, bitter
and biting remedies. They engaged in ritual blowing,
calling on the wandering spirits of the sick to return
to the body. They attended shaman seances night after
night. In addition, patients manfully downed the most
vicious-tasting, black, whooping cough medicine forward-
ed by the local government dispenser in response to my
urgent request for help. They did so without a murmur
- after having made me give several demonstrations of
its harmlessness! Everywhere in the territory people
were busy at curing, utilizing all the methods they

---

51   The government dispenser had said earlier that the
     child was suffering from malnutrition.

knew to bring back the norm of good health. The underlying cause of the whooping cough sickness was not ascertained immediately. The blame was at first put on the
Arekuna, Carib-speakers living immediately to the west,
on the Gran Sabana in Venezuela. It was at first sur-
mised that they had sent the whooping cough spirit to
their old enemies, the Akawaio. The Arekuna probably
got to hear of this allegation through relatives in their
easternmost village, Paruima on the Kamarang River, where
they had intermarried with Akawaio. They denied it,
pointing out that they themselves were suffering similarly. They passed on the blame, asserting that it was
a people further over, the Kamaragadok (Kamarakoto),
who were the culprits. The Kamarakoto were hungry, lacking food, and they wanted to kill off the Akawaio and
take their land, which was better than their own for
gardening since there was more forest in Akawaio country.
'The Kamarakoto are sending bad spirits and sickness
to the Akawaio and when the people have died and there
are no more Akawaio they will move in here and take the
food and gardens.' Every illness is believed to have
been sent by some bad-intentioned person, though 'who
it is we often do not know: illness kills, but the illness is sent by someone behind, who is responsible'.

        If the theme of basic evil intent is removed then

such an explanation was not far wrong in scientific,
medical terms. The whooping cough in this instance had
indeed come from the Gran Sabana, brought, it seems,
by Arekuna when visiting their relatives at Paruima on
the Kamarang River. Thence it had spread down the river
and into the Mazaruni River settlements, eventually passing into the tributaries of the Mazaruni to affect all
the Akawaio settlements to some degree. No doubt it
had come to the Arekuna from the very similar, Carib-
speaking Kamarakoto, further west still, and, one might
guess, had originated in the Venezuelan settlements of
the Caroní and Orinoco, or been brought in from even
further afield, perhaps from Caracas, by a passenger
on one of the flights to the Gran Sabana missions.

    Beliefs concerning the spirit causation of sick-
ness are complex, spirit action being related to opportunities for harm which ensues when people's behaviour,
states of being and interrelationships render them vulnerable, either as individuals or as members of particular social groupings. Similarly, complex and complementary procedures have to be taken to effect the cures.
Although cures of vegetable and mineral origin work chief-
ly through the action and counter-action of their essential qualities, hot-bitter, cold-sweet, they are linked
to the spirit elements which are an essential and funda-

mental part of the premises of belief. This can be seen
in the fact that the range of remedial substances (<u>ibik</u>)
are spoken of as affecting the spirit components of the
illness. Thus, hot and bitter remedies are so unpleasant
to the sickness spirit that the latter is driven out.
The sickness spirit 'does not like' the hot, bitter remedies, or, in another phraseology used to describe the
effect, the sickness 'does not agree with' the remedy
and so goes away. Similarly, gun powder, ant bites,
etc., 'frighten away' the sickness. This close association of the categories of cures with spirit vitality
is also clear in the blowing formulae. Certain spirit
spheres are associated with a particular category, so
that mountain spirits, inhabiting a cold place, have
cooling properties, and so likewise have water spirits.
Forest spirits, on the other hand, are frequently associated with the hot category.

By analysis I have isolated two sets of concepts,
one relating to spirit activity and the other to the
categorization of substances through binary oppositions.
Together they make up one system of thought, being inter
related to the degree that complete separation is difficult and unrealistic. Several informants agreed that
'all remedies have spirits and a good remedy has a good
spirit which will make a cure'. One shaman said he had

seen _ibik_ spirits when he had been conducting seances
and it is certainly the case that the spirits of various
cures and charms come and attend seances, speaking through
the shaman. Shamans in particular tend to attribute all
energy and power to animistic forces as this is their
main professional sphere of interest and activity. On
the other hand, several other informants denied that
cures (_ibik_) and charms (_murang_) had spirits. In trying
to explain the efficacy of remedies two of this latter
group said, hesitantly, that remedies had 'a sort of
people in them', and they then added that they were not
sure how these things worked, they simply believed that
they did - that was all!

In practice, therefore, I found that many Akawaio
observances could be explained, in their own terms, either
by their beliefs relating to spirit forces or by the
categories, the binary oppositions, which I have described. Most often, as in the case of the whooping cough
epidemic, the two are found in close combination in a
general pattern of thought. At the same time, much of
what has been described in the literature on Guiana Amerindian ritual practice can be understood more readily
once these basic thought patterns are comprehended.

Hot and cold in Latin America

In a notable article on the hot-cold syndrome and symbolic balance, Richard Currier stated (1966: 251) that in
contemporary Mexico and Spanish-America one important
aspect of folk medical belief and practice is a simplif-
ied form of Greek humoral pathology, which was elaborated
in the Arab world, brought to Spain as scientific medicine during the period of Moslem domination, and transmitted to America at the time of the Conquest.

> According to this classical pathology, the basic funct-
> ions of the body were regulated by four bodily fluids
> or 'humors', each of which was characterized by a com-
> bination of heat or cold with wetness or dryness (blood
> - hot and wet; yellow bile - hot and dry; phlegm -
> cold and wet; black bile - cold and dry). Proper bal-
> ance of these humors was considered necessary for good
> health, and any imbalance resulted in illness. Curing
> of disease consisted of correcting such imbalances by
> the addition or subtraction of heat, cold, dryness or
> wetness.... In Latin America today, most foods, bev-
> erages, herbs, and medicines (and some other substance
> as well) are classified as 'hot' (caliente) or 'cold'
> (fresco or frío). This classification is usually in-
> dependent of such observable characteristics as form,
> color, texture, and physical temperature, and it is

descriptive only of the effects which a substance is thought to have upon the human body. As in classical humoral pathology, illness is often attributed to imbalance between heat and cold in the body, and curing is likewise accomplished by the restoration of proper balance.

But, Currier points out, there is no corresponding classification of substances as 'wet' or 'dry', nor do the concepts of wetness or dryness appear in folk medical belief and practice. Why, he asks, has the hot-cold syndrome persisted for centuries as the basis of folk medical beliefs, while the wet-dry syndrome, equally important in classical theory, has long since been lost?[52]

Resorting to a psychological interpretation, Currier's hypothesis is that

In the process of weaning, the Mexican child is subjected to a prolonged period of acute rejection. As a result of this experience he forms strong subconscious associations between warmth and acceptance or intimacy on the one hand and between cold and rejection or withdrawal, on the other. In adult life these associations appear in those beliefs intimately concerned

---

52 Categories relating to wet and dry do not appear to have any special significance in the concepts of the Carib-speaking tribes I have studied. This is in spite of the fact that there are pronounced wet and dry seasons to act as an environmental model.

with the problem of personal security: theories about
nourishment and about the prevention and cure of disease and injury. On a conscious level, then, the hot-
cold syndrome is a basic principle of human physiology,
and it functions as a logical system for dealing with
the problems of disorder and disease. On a subconscious level, however, the hot-cold syndrome is a model
of social relations. In this case, disease theory
constitutes a symbolic system upon which social anxieties are projected, and it functions as a means of
symbolically manipulating social relationships which
are too difficult and too dangerous to manipulate on
a conscious level in the real social universe (1966:
251-2).

Currier then proposes 'that the individual's continuous
preoccupation with achieving a balance between "heat"
and "cold" is a way of re-enacting, in symbolic terms,
a fundamental activity in social relations'.

My main criticism of this interesting proposition
lies in the fact that the opposition of hot and cold is
found, within my knowledge of the South American area
north of the Amazon, amongst Amerindian tribes which
extend from French Guiana through to the Andes, including in the latter settlements of Quechua-speakers in
the Ica Valley. So embedded is it in the languages,

the concepts and practices of all these peoples, that
it could scarcely have been borrowed, Moreover, Spanish
and Portuguese influences have been very slight in those
areas of the Guianas where Dutch, French and British
contacts have predominated since the first settlement.
Some of the Amerindians possessing these concepts have
only in recent years been in regular contact with set-
tlers while the influence of the latter has been superficial, even in the most receptive spheres for borrowing, such as that of material culture. Added to this
is the fact that observations and descriptions of first
contacts reveal practices which can best be explained
by reference to the underlying categories of thought
which refer to the complementary oppositions of hot-
cold, bitter-sweet. These practices, as for example
in curare making and the use of remedial substances for
curing, appear to have continued to the present day without significant change. So far as it is possible to
judge from the present literature, the bitter-sweet oppositions do not extend to the Andean cultures. They
appear to be tropical forest in their extension, but
a great deal more research requires to be done, or published, to ascertain the distribution of this category.

        While Spanish influence may have affected Mexican
and other acculturated areas by its hot-cold syndrome,

my suggestion is that owing to its indigenous origins,
which its presence in the tropical forest area of South
America argues, it was probably already strongly entrenched before the Conquest. Incoming concepts may have har-
monized, modified and even strengthened the syndrome.
Alternatively, the contrary may have occurred and imported concepts, already weak, were fortified by the corresponding, indigenous Amerindian ones. Unless this were
the case I doubt whether imposed concepts, of considerable subtlety, could have lasted and become so deeply
entrenched - any more than the wet-dry syndrome has done.
To attribute the power of this binary opposition to a
'subconscious model of social relations' is therefore
unnecessary. It is also invalid, unless one produces
a universalistic doctrine to the effect that, wherever
there is a concept of hot-versus-cold medical categories,
there is a particular set of social relations. If this
were to be so, then not only most of aboriginal South
America and presentday Latin American peasantry had, and
still have, this set of social relations, but also the
ancient Greeks, mediaeval Europeans, right through to
the Burmese of both the past and the present, and probably many other peoples as well. I therefore find this
correlation difficult to accept and, in any case, too
general to have much value for the anthropologist.

The mediate state

The mediate state is one which has frequently escaped
attention, yet the basic treatment of all states of excess, imbalance and abnormality shows that a mediating
range exists between opposites. In the Andean area this
intermediate condition may be referred to as templado,
from the Spanish word templar, which has the meaning:
to moderate, to temper, refrain from excess, etc. Among
the Akawaio it is manifested in the behaviour of a person
observing the resting and dieting period, jeruma. The
diet during this period, at its simplest and most stringent, is eki totsa, cassava gruel eaten luke warm, or it
can be thin cassava bread, eaten dry and accompanied by
a drink of tepid water. Cassava bread (eki) is made
from bitter manioc root, from which poison has been extracted after a long cooking process of peeling, grating,
squeezing, sifting and baking. With water it is a taste-
less mush, said to be harmless for 'old time people got
accustomed to it'. This innocuous diet, together with
rest in the hammock and seclusion from general community
life by confinement within the immediate circle of close
kin, provides a neutral, safe condition for the person
who is sick or in any way vulnerable. At the same time,
the observances of the jeruma period isolate such a person from others who might suffer harm from a dangerous

configuration of forces and circumstances around him
or her.

Treatments of an appropriate kind are put into
operation when a sick person enters this neutralizing
state. First, the deliberate avoidance of 'strong' foods
has the effect of removing contact with the powerful,
potentially angry and harmful spirits associated with
animals which are normally hunted and eaten as food.
As already remarked, close blood relatives must not anger
animal spirits for fear of rendering their sick kinsman
vulnerable. Contacts with the most dangerous aspects
of nature are therefore broken off, so leaving the ritual
experts, the shaman (piai'chang) and the possessor of
blowing (taling genak), a clear field for manipulating
their special control over the spirit world to the benefit of their patient.

The condition of the patient is inevitably judged
to be one of imbalance, otherwise the sickness would
not exist. Diagnosis based on pronouncements in the
shaman's seance, and also the observable physical condition of the patient and the symptoms reported, suggest
which conditions have become exaggerated to the detrimen
of health. As we have seen, when a condition of cold,
weakness and lassitude is diagnosed, hot, bitter, energy
giving remedies are sought to restore a proper vitality

and to force out the sickness. When a burning heat, fever and restless discomfort predominate, sweet, cool and soothing remedies are applied as the complementary opposite.

In certain circumstances the mediate condition is also designed to isolate one set of opposites from another, so that the shock of a confrontation of contradictory elements can be avoided. Thus the heat, energy and poisonous power of the male hunter can be isolated from the cold, weak, sweet but enervating experience of women at puberty, at times of menstruation and at childbirth. If this isolation of opposites is not maintained at crucial periods hunting is spoilt and young children and women are rendered vulnerable. It is believed that the spirit world will retaliate on both. The basic assumption here, therefore, is that of danger becoming operative in either sphere of opposites and its spirit associations unless appropriate precautions are taken.

Thus the mediate condition is one in which that which is inappropriate, dangerous or in excess may be avoided, or it is that condition in which an imbalance may be counterbalanced, mitigated or rectified by special treatment. However, it is also a condition in which an imbalance, or an intensification of certain categories, may be deliberately created, under control, for

specific purposes. It is the condition requisite for
the building up of energy and power for such ends as
the re-charging of the hunter, the preparation of the
shaman for his breach of the spirit world during trance,
equipping the curare poison maker, endowing women with
qualities of sweetness in the preparation of strong
drinks. The mediate state, represented by the practice
of jeruma, provides the setting for the control and manipulation of the different forms of power and energy
for certain ends. Contradictory forces have sometimes
to be separated, and sometimes to be combined, for creative purposes or to avoid destruction of the individual
and his society. The ultimate aim is the attainment of
a new synthesis or equilibrium appropriate to the circumstances. In the case of the sick this is the return
to a balanced and harmonious condition which is the norm
of good health. To achieve this the mediate state of
jeruma is an essential preliminary.

Conclusion

I have considered the categories of thought which explain the selection and use of certain remedial substances, particularly those deriving from plants, and
which are used for healing. I have also shown how the
same categories may operate in ritualized forms of

healing, such as in the ritual blowing formulae, and how these combine with animistic beliefs. Without going too far from my central theme I have tried to indicate how the same categories also underlie the use of hunting charms, poisonous substances, treatment of some foods and various practices relating to states of transition, notably that of a girl's puberty and the time of giving birth, when the basic categories of hot-bitter and cold-sweet are considered to be in extreme polarization. I have tried to investigate these binary oppositions carefully, on the assumption that all but the sub-human can appreciate oppositions such as light and dark, up and down, hot and cold, etc. In themselves these universalities mean little - as little as the 'biological needs' or 'social needs' of the early Functionalist School now mean to us. What is important, on the other hand, is to find out which oppositions are selected, categorized and actually used, that is, to discover which ones are operative in any system of thought and action. Only by careful ethnographic research and documentation can one avoid the danger of seeing binary oppositions, enthusiastically but indiscriminately, everywhere.

Finally, I have sought to show how mediation occurs through the practice of _jeruma_, when conditions are created which are favourable for attempts to restore the

balance or health of the individual and the community,
or to endow him or her with an increase in the appropriate qualities for the achievement of some particular
sphere of work. This intermediate, bounded state also
ensures that the qualities possessed, being acquired or
utilized by the individual, and sometimes his near kin,
and which are considered dangerous in their excess for
the rest of the community, are both isolated and controlled.

Evidence from the tropical forest Amerindians
suggests that the major categories of opposition, hot
and cold, as well as that of the intermediary and the
notion of a balanced norm, date from pre-Columbian times
and were not merely introduced into the Americas at the
time of the Conquest by the Spanish or Portuguese.

Can the Akawaio be said to possess medicine? The
Concise Oxford Dictionary defines medicine as the 'Art
of restoring and preserving health, especially by means
of remedial substances and regulation of diet, etc., as
opposed to surgery and obstetrics'. In terms of this
definition the Akawaio certainly have medicine, and if
one simply considers the role of their curing substances
for combating ill health then the matter could rest there.
However, curing may be a primary aim in other spheres
of activity, notably among the Akawaio in the shaman

system and in ritual blowing, so that immediately a broad question is posed as to the interrelationship between a medical system and spheres of ritual in general. When the whole field of medical endeavour is investigated, therefore, a great vista appears for research which plunges the anthropologist once more into the old and familiar problems of the nature of religious belief, of magic, of notions of causation, of danger and power, of the interrelations of all these to each other and of all, together or in part, to social systems. In my opinion, a breath of fresh air may be infused into these hoary problems by looking at them from the angle of ethno-medicine.

REFERENCES

BEEBE, W., HARTLEY, G.I. and HOWES, P.G. 1917. Tropical Wild Life in British Guiana. Vol. I. New York: Zoological Society.

BUTT, A.J. 1954. A Study of the System of Beliefs of the Carib-speaking Akawaio of British Guiana. Timehri, Journal of the Royal Agricultural and Commercial Society of British Guiana, 33. October.

-- 1956. Ritual Blowing. Taling - A Causation and Cure of Illness among the Akawaio. Man, 48.

-- 1961. Symbolism and Ritual among the Akawaio of British Guiana. Nieuwe West-Indische Gids, No. 2, December.

-- 1962. Réalité et idéal dans la pratique chamanique. L'Homme, II.

-- 1965/66. The Shaman's Legal Role. Revista do Museu Paulista, n.s. Vol. XVI. Sao Paulo.

BUTT COLSON, A.J. 1971. Hallelujah among the Patamona Indians. Antropologica, 28. Caracas: Fundacion la Salle.

CURRIER, R.L. 1966. The Hot-Cold Syndrome and Symbolic Balance in Mexican and Spanish-American Folk Medicine. Ethnology, 5. 5.

DANCE, C.D. 1881. Chapters from a Guianese Log-Book. Georgetown.

Fanshawe, D.B. 1950. Minor Forest Products. Forestry Bulletin, No. 2 (n.s.). Georgetown: Forestry Department.

-- unpublished. Akawaio Indian Plant Names.

QUELCH, J.J. 1895. The Materials of the Urali Poison. Timehri, Journal of the Royal Agricultural and Commercial Society of British Guiana, Vol. IX (n.s.) Pt. II.

ROTH, W.E. 1915. An Enquiry into the Animism and Folklore of the Guiana Indians. 30th Annual Report of the Bureau of American Ethnology. 1908-9. Washington: Smithsonian Institution.

-- 1924. An Introductory Study of the Arts, Crafts, and Customs of the Guiana Indians. 38th Annual Report of the Bureau of American Ethnology. 1916-17. Washington: Smithsonian Institution.

SCHOMBURGK, Richard. 1922. Travels in British Guiana, 1840-44. Trans. W.E. Roth. Vol. I. Georgetown.

-- 1848. Travels in British Guiana, 1840-44. Vol. II, Leipzig.

SCHOMBURGK, Robert. 1836. Report of an Expedition into
    the Interior of British Guayana, in 1835-6. Journal
    of the Royal Geographical Society, Vol. VI. London.

WATERTON, C. 1903. Wanderings in South America, the
    North-West of the United States and the Antilles in
    the Years 1812, 1816, 1820 & 1824. London.

WAVELL, S. (Ed.), BUTT, A.J. and EPTON, N. 1966.
    Trances. London: Allen & Unwin.

N. J. ALLEN

APPROACHES TO ILLNESS IN THE NEPALESE HILLS

In the course of eighteen months field research among
the Thulung Rai of east Nepal[1] the subject of illness
arose frequently, but I found it particularly difficult
to distill clear or coherent conceptions from the mass
of information. Some of the difficulties were of a commonplace kind - language problems,[2] less than ideal rap-
port with the most knowledgeable informants, and so on.
But one source of discouragement, as I now think, was
the mistake of looking for clarity and consistency in
directions where they were not to be found. In discuss-

1 I acknowledge with gratitude the financial support
of the Social Science Research Council and the long-
term encouragement of Professor C. von Fürer-Haimendorf
and Dr R. Needham.

2 All Thulung speak Nepali as second language and it
has for two centuries been infiltrating, modifying
and increasingly replacing the Tibeto-Burman tribal
language. Nepali expressions used in this paper are
labelled on first mention with an 'N'; their spelling
and meaning have been checked in Turner (1931) and
Sarma (1962), though the glosses given are my own.
Thulung has not previously received serious study.
Thulung words (unlabelled) are written in a modified
form of an orthography based on a phonemic analysis
which I hope to publish.

ing what the Thulung think and do about illness, this
paper pays particular attention to some of the dimensions
of variability and vagueness in the data.

There is very little literature on the Thulung
or on the other (linguistically defined) Rai sub-groups
but it will be useful to refer to comparative evidence
from other parts of the country. It is conventional to
stress the immense diversity of the peoples of Nepal,
and in certain matters (ecology and language for example)
this is undeniable. However, in other contexts, distinctions such as Hindu, Buddhist, animist and Bon[3] are
of little relevance and in thinking about the hill peoples
the attitude one tribe/one culture is a positive hind-
rance.

'Illness'

The picture of the incidence of illness given by Worth
and Shah (1969) applies in broad outline to the Thulung.
My own impressions are too unsystematic to deserve detailed record. Malnutrition is not a major problem, respiratory disease is the commonest complaint. However,
the lack of precise knowledge of the objective public

---

3 Bon is used to refer both to Tibetan religion as it
   is thought to have existed before the arrival of
   Buddhism and to the greatly modified contemporary
   continuation of the same tradition.

health situation hardly affects the questions we shall
be posing.

A fundamental problem is how far the English category 'illness' is applicable at all to the situations
the Thulung experience and deal with. It cannot be assumed without analysis that we know exactly what the English term means (broken legs, senility, alcoholism are
borderline instances), but for the sake of argument we
can define 'medical illness' as 'what the doctor deals
with'. In that case the nearest Thulung equivalent is
'what the dhāmi N deals with'; Thulung who had served
in the British or Indian armies commonly referred to the
dhāmi as hāmro pahāri dāktar N, 'our mountain doctors'.
We shall discuss the office later, translating it meanwhile as 'officiant'. The following list gives an idea
of how the officiant himself may describe his field of
action.

lama gang	coughs and colds (related by one informant to the Buddhist lamas who might cause them)
kuyepma mayepma	(peṭ ko surtā N), deep anxiety, as about death
pla-ari nakhliri	tears (pla) and snot (nakhli) of mourners
nacerwa nayerwa	(ris, ḍāhi N), anger, envy

sukuri tamari	evil spirits
babari bapcari	" "
khlamyami teoyemi	curses, very evil forces caused by someone's anger
rangli budiumo	a particular ghost (bhut N) who steals grain
boksi N daini N	witches
sungkarma angkarma	anger, envy
sasiciu saksiciu	thorns of the chestnut, i.e. sharp pains
granggrangciu kepcimo	scratching and clawing pains (informant gestures vividly)
somori salari	illnesses of all sorts
hoktiumpar moripar	skin diseases and boils
buysangma daysangma	headaches
darciumo seoki	fevers and coughs
khara[4]	particularly severe cough

The same list occurred with minor variants six times in a hutpa rite performed by the officiant Dan Bahādur (DB) of Mukli village, and in some of his other rites. A comparable list was chanted by Dimajit of the same village

---

4   The recording actually runs: lamanga hepto ganganga hepto...angkarma hepto, sasiciu salto...salari salto, hoktiumpar ghrimto...kharanga ghrimto; the -nga is for scansion rather than sense, the verbs repeated after each noun mean respectively 'ward off', 'pick out', 'close up as of wound'. The tense ending is first person past, i.e. the act is presented as a fait accompli.

in two rites directed to the minor gods Rangkime and
Limbu Deutā:

ciciri babari	evil spirits
oyebu sabdebu	" " (?) of those killed in the jungle
bleakcebu cerkebu	evil spirits of those killed by lightning
hiwasam mamasam	evil spirits of those who die through falls on the steep hillsides and of women who die in childbirth
nacerwa nayerwa	envy (as above)
boksikhlamya dāinikhlamya	the anger of witches
selekhlamya muktiukhlamya	" " " seleme, a variety of officiant (v. inf.)
sungkarma angkarma	anger, envy (as above)
khole hepnimi	all of them ward off (imperative?)

Typically each of the six recorded lists differs to some
degree, some for instance including rangli budiumo as
in DB's list, or jori pāri N 'rivalry'. Comparing the
transcript of one hutpa rite in Lokhim village with the
performance of the same rite by the same officiant a week
later showed clearly that such variations are without
significance. Each officiant develops his own style from

the stock of elements he comes across, and treats his
sample as though it were equivalent to the totality of
possibilities.

Many of the glosses given are inadequate. Only
about half the roots have recognizable cognates in the
current language and where they lack them, informants
can rarely convey any clear notion of their meaning.
Indeed comparison of such ritual vocabulary between one
village and another showed vividly how easily a ritual
expression can pass from being a transparent and often
richly poetic coinage, through a stage of vague meaning-
fulness, to end up as an effectively unintelligible formula, appropriate in a context but semantically empty.
But in spite of the difficulties of translation the texts
give at least an impression of what the officiant claims
to be dealing with. The connotations of 'medical illness' are of course quite inadequate; those of the word
'ill' would be less so because of its wider (if somewhat
archaic) use in expressions like 'ill-will', 'an ill
wind', 'it has gone ill with him'. Seoki is the everyday word for cough in Thulung, as is par for all skin
conditions including erosive cancers and traumas, and
it is clear that for the Thulung officiant, as so often
in non-western societies, medical illness is to be placed
on the same level as other forms of evil and affliction.

I am not claiming of course that medical illness
cannot be differentiated by Thulung from other forms of
evil which to us appear of a different nature. For one
thing, even those who have not been in the army are familiar with the Nepali words rog, bethā, bimāri, all of which
are close equivalents of medical illness.[5] We need not
consider the less straightforward linguistic evidence in
Thulung, since the point concerns not the possibility of
making the distinction but its social importance. Certainly it is not one that has traditionally been embodied
in any institution such as a specialist role or a particular type of ritual.

Health

An alternative approach to a global comparison of the
English and Thulung categories 'illness' could start by
defining it as the opposite of health and comparing the
two cultures' views of the latter. In practice this approach seems harder, and there is probably a good reason
why it should be so. Health, in English, is a more general term than illness, for whereas one can have good or
bad health, an illness is never absolutely good. To use

5   All the same, it is perhaps interesting that the word
    have a learned ring about them, the first two being
    loan words from Sanskrit, the third from Persian via
    Hindi (Turner 1931).

the linguists' term, health is unmarked, illness marked;
it can apparently be predicted from this (Clark 1970:
276-8) that in word association tests the stimulus illness will elicit the response health more frequently than
vice versa. The asymmetry of the opposition is reflected
in morphology in that unwell and unhealthy are not balanced by unill, unsick or the like. This points to a
fundamental unhappiness in our second definition of illness, which is not so much the opposite of illness as a
departure from it.

This perhaps explains why we should not expect
the Thulung officiant to recite a litany of the blessings
he hopes to produce, parallel to the list of evils he
hopes to prevent. It is enough if he succeeds in disposing of whatever threatens the natural order, of which
health is one aspect.[6] Thus normal health and positive
good health are seldom distinguished. Physical vigour
and a good build are naturally admired and moṭo N, literally 'fat', or seo baṭpa, literally 'having flesh', are
compliments, quite without the pejorative overtones of
obesity in English. But Thulung adults (unless in the
army) play no games or sports, and have no call for a
special concept of fitness in an environment where hill

6 No doubt, then, it will always be harder to describe
an ethno-physiology than an ethno-pathology. As to
the former, some Thulung claim that intestinal worms
aid digestion.

walking is an everyday necessity.

In the west, in contexts such as greetings, wishes
for medical health are often conflated with wishes for
economic, social and psychological success, and it sometimes proved helpful among the Thulung to recognize a
comparably broad conception. For instance, when asked
the reason for such and such a custom, informants commonly replied that those who ignore it 'do not do well'
(phāpdainan N). Further questioning sometimes elicited
more specific sanctions, say stomach aches, but these
were more in the nature of speculations than of beliefs
widely held in the society.

The chants of officiants such as DB sometimes stat
their aim as seor tharmu, reor tharmu, 'to set up, or
establish firmly, someone's seor' (reor being used only
as an echo-word to seor). In trying to understand the
word seor I collected the following Nepali translations,
among others: graha 'planet', karma 'lot', śakti 'streng†
āt 'courage', phāp 'growth, prosperity'. The combinatior
of neutral and positive senses is paralleled by the English word 'fortune', and other contexts confirm that to
a first approximation it is not an entirely misleading
translation. One may say of a rich couple enjoying good
health and a large family that 'their seor has turned
out harmoniously'. A daughter leaving home at marriage,

or a sick man for whom everything possible has been done,
may be told that 'from now on they must make for themselves their own seor-chela' (chela being from ches- 'to
look lively').

However, the provisional translation only helps us
up to a certain point. One informant offered a definition of seor as 'the god within a person'. The Thulung do
not have any general belief in individual tutelary spirits, but what he was trying to express in Nepali is clar-
ified by other suggested translations, pitri N 'patrilineal ancestors', and kul N 'lineage'. One may jokingly
ask a child who comes out with a surprisingly adult expression, 'Did your seor teach you?'. The seorlung (lung
= stone) are the three hearth stones sacred to the ancestors. A legendary forbear ends the tradition of inter-
marriage with a neighbouring subtribe by symbolically
planting a stone by the bridge to their territory and
saying, 'Our seor is no longer one', meaning 'We have
become a separate community'. The seorriya or seorrip
(riba = rope) was translated simply as āyu N, 'life';
if it is not there you die. It is also the name of the
rope which in certain rites leads from the fireplace
through the roof of a house to a tall pole planted in
the courtyard and symbolizing the route both to heaven
and the ancestors. Thus the health and fortune of an

individual Thulung and his relationship to his ancestors
are fused in a single concept. It is true that an Eng-
lishman's 'fortune' may also be inherited; however, not
only is this subject to the whim of the testator, but
the word in this sense has a material, reckonable ring
(as '80,000 acres of rich Wessex farmland') which is
entirely alien to seor. Until about a century ago new
jungle for bringing under cultivation was so plentiful
that social ranking among the Thulung due to differences
in inherited property seems to have been of little importance.

So just as medical illness is but one aspect of
affliction, health is only an aspect of a concept of
good order which embraces the properly cooperative ancestors. It is not easy to enter into or analyze alien
metaphysical ideas and it is comforting as well as interesting to compare the Gurung data from Pignède (1966:
375-6). Some informants there considered the two principal divinities to be chaname, the spirit of long life
(connoting good health), and plehname, the spirit of
abundance or riches. According to certain officiants
they were the lineage gods of the household (kul deutā N)
and the representatives in the home of Wainabarnaje, who
(p. 367) is the centre of the world. As with other pair-
ed spirits we shall meet, it appears uncertain how far

the two are differentiated. They are represented in
each house by two birds modelled in rice dough. Sometimes in cases of illness or threatening economic circumstances it seems that one may leave the house and
need to be ritually recalled without the other (pp. 325,
331, 361); on the whole, however, they behave as a pair
(pp. 361, 376) and it is even stated that 'cha est tou-
jours lié à pleh' (p. 325). So the Gurung conception
of an individual's health cannot be understood any more
than the Thulung one, without taking account of his economic well-being and of his situation in life as a member
of a household which continues an ancestral line.

Tribal priest and spirit medium

The term for 'mountain doctor' (dhāmi N, nokcho) is applied by the Thulung to two types of officiant who at
first sight present a straightforward contrast. The
dewa dhāmi we shall translate as 'tribal priest'. Always
male, he is the son or close agnate of a previous priest
from whom he learned the traditional tribal ritual chants.
In principle, a single line of priests serves one group
of patrilineal clans within one village. In all Thulung
villages the priests are also responsible for collective
agricultural rites (bhume pujā N); several priests may
combine to perform them at communal shrines within the

village on a fixed number of occasions per year related
to the farming calendar. When a person dies in the ordinary way of illness or old age, the priest acts as psycho
pomp, accompanying the spirit on his journey past named
landmarks to the hill of the ancestors (which lies on
the map some twenty miles to the south-west). At fixed
periods after a death or, occasionally, in fulfilment
of a client's vow made during an illness, he may perform
one of a series of ancestral rites (pitri N). At a wedding he introduces the bride to the ancestors of her new
family and invokes for the fertility of the match. He
does not go into trance nor does he have the individual
tutelary spirit of those who do. His rites are accompanied if at all by cymbals and by the type of drum (dhol N)
which is suspended by a string from a post or round the
neck, never by that which is held by one hand and struck
with a baton in the other (the dhyāngro N). When I arrived in the area and expressed an interest in the histor
(itihās N) and culture (sanskriti N) of the Thulung, thos
who understood such high-flown vocabulary directed me at
once to the priest. According to tradition his office
was originally closely related to that of the petty prin
es who ruled at least in Mukli before the Gorkha conques
of the early 1770s, when the whole area was incorporated
in the newly founded political state of Nepal.

The contrasting type of officiant will be rendered
as 'spirit medium'. In Thulung he is called seleme, while
in Nepali he is indifferently either dhāmi tout court,
or jhākri, or bijuwā; local usage does not distinguish
the latter pair, nor does Sarma (1962), but English sources
based on experience with the Gurkhas (Turner 1931, Ministry of Defence 1965: 84) connect the bijuwā specifically
with the Rai.

One man cannot be both priest and medium. The
initiative in the recruitment of mediums is ascribed not
to the humans involved but to some spirit. The typical
sequence in the area is for someone to become possessed
in the course of a seance and on receiving this sign of
his vocation to seek instruction from another medium,
his guru, who need not be of the same caste. At least
twice a year at full moon he must worship the spirit or
spirits who possess him. He commonly does so at large
gatherings or 'fairs' (melā N), where numerous mediums
(some female) assemble from a wide area and dance at sacred spots, situated usually on high ground away from villages. This is the only communal occasion in which mediums take part and there is no evidence that they do it
to benefit the collectivity. Crowds gather overnight to
enjoy the festival with its attached temporary bazaar,
but if they too worship at the shrine it is their own

individual affair.

The medium's main activity is as diviner and exor-
cist at nocturnal seances (cintā N, literally 'meditat-
ions') held in ordinary houses. He does not deal directly with the client's ancestors (though he sometimes diagnoses them as the cause of an affliction); indeed his
shrine in a client's house includes some bamboo splinters
(rapa, from rap- to fence off), which according to some,
explicitly serve to separate him from the ancestors'
hearth stones. Many mediums are held to have inherited
their gifts from relatives on the father's or mother's
side, or better still, on both, but there is no regular
relationship between medium and clan. A Thulung can call
on a medium of any tribe or caste, being influenced only
by his local reputation for efficacity. The services
of a medium in place of a priest are obligatory at deaths
classified as bad, i.e. unnatural or untimely, as those
of an infant, of a mother in childbirth or of the victim
of an accident. Such souls are guided on a journey to
a destination quite distinct from that of the good dead,
though laymen are uncertain of the details. The medium
usually (invariably at the fair) uses only the one-handle
drum, and when doing so wears a special outfit with feath
er head-dress, robe, rudrāksa N bead necklace, etc. (for
details see Macdonald 1962).

Thus on the one hand stands the tribal priest, concerned with collective welfare and social continuity, natural death, and such afflictions as the neglected ancestors may cause. On the other stands the medium, not necessarily tribal, who deals on a household level with unnatural death and other afflictions typically ascribed to non-ancestral spirits. The contrast (whose origin incidentally is entirely obscure) is not only the anthropologist's; one or other aspect is frequently made explicit by informants. But the more information one takes into account, the more it becomes necessary to recognize how easily the opposition can be blurred.

First of all, both types of officiant can occur in what we may call etiolated forms. Though no one can replace a priest at an agricultural or ancestral rite, if it happens at a wedding or death that the priest is ill or otherwise engaged, any male with sufficient knowledge of the invocations may substitute. A priest usually officiates with one or two assistants at his side who accompany him or chime in with occasional invocations and in this way learn enough for the role of substitute. In Mukli, Dimajit often stood in for DB, but when doing so he had no well-recognized or unambiguous title.

Among mediums a distinction is occasionally drawn between those who dance and drum (nācne dhāmi or dhyāngro

bajāune dhāmi N), and those who only drum on a metal
plate (thāl bajāune dhāmi) and become possessed sitting
in cross-legged position, without dancing or wearing special clothes. The seances of the former are the more elaborate, use a greater variety of techniques and last
longer into the night, or right through it till after
sunrise; they are usually for more serious conditions
and would be essential after a bad death. The distinction
indicates a significant polarity but does not offer the
basis for a hard and fast typological division, either
of officiants or of seances. A well-recognized drum-
playing medium (such as the remarkable deaf and dumb Sim-
buri of Mukli) may decide that the lesser procedure will
suffice for a particular occasion and there appears to
be nothing to stop a plate-playing medium acquiring the
accoutrements of the other role. The two instruments
are often played simultaneously. This is not the place
for full examination of the question and I can only suggest (following Hitchcock 1967) that the situation in
the Thulung area arises from a blending of two mediumistic traditions of distinct historical origin: one is
closely related to classical Central Asiatic shamanism
and uses the drum, symbols of flight and mimetic dancing
(e.g. imitating birds or the paddling action of a ferry-
man), while the other is closer to Indian traditions,

uses the brass plate, and relies heavily on possession.
The caste of the officiant is, however, no sure guide
to the techniques he will use.[7]

It is worth raising the matter since Lewis (1971:
50) has expressed doubts about Eliade's evolutionary
interpretation of the relationship between the techniques
of shamanic flight and of possession and it will be clear
from what we have said that Nepal offers a good testing
ground for the issue. It does indeed appear on present
evidence that the former technique is there being infil-
trated or replaced by the latter (or by other types of
ritual), whereas the converse is not occurring.

If the role of full-scale medium shades off into
the etiolated one of plate-player, this in turn merges
into the even less demarcated role of someone who performs a simple exorcism (jhār-phuk N). Sarma defines·
the word as (to translate): 'the treatment of the sick

---

[7] Informants affirmed that mediums could be found in
any caste, even Brahmans. Of the seances I attended
in the Thulung area, the officiants were Thulung in
eight, Kāmi (Blacksmith) in three, Gharti in one.
Kāmis appear disproportionately represented. Hitchcock (1967: 152) found fourteen Kāmi mediums to four
Magars and two of other castes in an area where there
were as many Magar households as Kāmi ones. Funke
(1969: 56, 60) found to his surprise a Kāmi succeeding
a Sherpa in the role. Further research is needed to
conform whether we have here a real caste specialization, and whether the apparent deficiency of Damais,
the lowest caste, is related to their auspicious quality - they are a saguni jāt N, whose music often
accompanies Brahmanic rites.

by the recitation of mantras according to the tantric
scriptures and by the use of kuś grass, brushes, ash,
water and so on'. In the Thulung area materials used
for making passes around the patient's body include husk-
ed rice, an egg, a chick, rosaries of rudrākṣa beads, a
hat (ṭopi N). Some non-Thulung mediums possess Nepali
books of mantras, for instance a Chetri in Tingla village, or Baunne, a blacksmith in Mukli. The latter, apart
from a considerable practice as diviner and performer
of exorcism, also officiates at seances with a drum,
though he danced only for the briefest period and did
not wear the robe which is the usual concomitant of the
drum. Although he is treated like any other medium, he
points out with pride that his knowledge is 'reading science' (paḍhibigyān N), i.e. derived from books alone,
and that he did not study with a guru. Mediums who use
the exorcism techniques at seances may also perform them
without elaboration in the day-time, but the activity
is not confined to them. It would be out of the question
for the priest DB to perform a seance, but he is often
asked to do a quick exorcism on a sick baby when he drop
by at a house. Indeed there is nothing to stop the ordinary person trying his hand at it, even if in his ignorance he is unlikely to be very successful. My host in
Mukli was certainly no recognized variety of officiant,

but one evening when his sister on a visit became feverish and it seemed too late to send for an expert he made
some passes with his hat, invoking in Thulung,[8] and the
next morning she was better.

Exorcism, though it may be performed by the priest,
is essentially the activity of the medium, but there are
other minor rites that are not easily allotted. According to some the hutpa rite is the 'youngest' (kāncho N),
i.e. smallest of the five ancestral rites, and in Tingla
it is held to be properly the job of the priest. Three
hours away, in Mukli, it is now performed only by the
priest and on behalf of the collectivity (cf. the text
on p. 504). However, four hours further east still, in
Lokhim, it is only performed by mediums, and often constitutes the first part of a nocturnal ritual strictly
equivalent to the seance, though usually called there
by the imprecise term 'household rite' (nem pujā).

An obvious way to emphasize the structural opposition of two roles is through their accoutrements. At
the major ancestral rite in Tingla the priest wears in
principle an old style of jacket made locally by the

---

8 He used language very like the invocations quoted.
   Whereas Thulung ancestors should only be addressed
   in Thulung, other spirits can in general be addressed
   in Thulung or Nepali, depending on one's knowledge
   of an appropriate invocation. Even the priest DB
   uses Nepali in his annual collective rite to Sansāri.

Thulung several generations ago and not found among other
castes. The medium, there as elsewhere, wears the robe
and feathered headdress, and the two uniforms neatly
symbolize the contrast. Elsewhere, however, the priest's
jacket is obsolete (if it was ever current) and at the
major agricultural rites in Mukli, and at the nagi ancestral rite in Jubu, the priest wears the medium's outfit.
Similarly, the contrast between the drums of priest and
medium breaks down in Lokhim, where both instruments
are used in the household rite. The most striking instance of blurring occurred in the Jubu nagi rite, when
to the beating of a plate the priest became possessed.
Mukli informants had denied that this could occur and
were surprised when I played a tape in which the priest
went into trance (signified by the usual shaking, and
audible because of the bells on his belt), and prophes-
ied in answer to questions concerning future deaths in
the neighbourhood, the marriage prospects of two youths,
and other such matters, exactly in the manner of a medium.

       One method of searching for order in all these
local variants would be to describe a distinct subcult-
ure for each village. But if this approach were carried
to its logical conclusion there would be no stopping
at the village. The settlement pattern is highly diffus

the Thulung living interspersed among immigrant tribes
and castes in administrative villages of up to 3,000
inhabitants, which may take three hours to cross, and
it is possible that relationships between specialists
vary as much within villages as between them. The Thulung themselves have a strong sense of sharing a single
culture, based on their common language and their historical dispersal from the single original settlement
at Mukli. Moreover it is only necessary to attend a few
ceremonies, especially of the priest, to realize how much
discussion and disagreement takes place among the Thulung
themselves as to the correct procedure; although they
are apt to claim that each ritual is age-old and immut-
able, in fact every performance represents a creative
development (or degeneration) of its tradition, and variation is not an occasional accident but a normal and essential feature of a rite. It is necessary, therefore,
to recognize frankly that this is not a society that is
interested in maintaining the sort of precise contrasts
and demarcations that would make it easy to describe with
accuracy. The next section proposes a historical explanation for this lack of interest.

The changing balance of specialists

The contrast sketched in the last section, and its

blurring, are by no means peculiar to the Thulung area.
The medium, as we have stressed, is not a particularly
tribal role, and officiants of the same general character have often been described in the literature. The
classic account of the Nepalese medium (jhākri) is Macdonald (1962), based on research in the Darjeeling area,
but other sources are Hosten (1909) on the same area,
Macdonald (1966a: 47-8; 1966b) on various parts of Nepal,
Hitchcock (1967) on the traditional Magar area; diviners
and mediums bearing a strong family likeness but non-
Nepali names include among others the bombo of the Hel-
ambu Sherpas (Schmid 1967), the lhawa of the Khumbu Sherpas (Fürer-Haimendorf 1964: 254ff), the minung of the
Solu Sherpas (Funke 1969). Clear equivalents of the
Thulung tribal priest have been less often described,
but Chemjong (1961) distinguishes the Limbu phedāngmā =
purohit N 'priest' from the yābā = (1) bhutyāhā, dhāmi,
(2) bijuwā, jhākri, both pairs being translated 'exor-
cist'. Sagant (1969: 122) confirms that the phedāngmā
is only rarely possessed, and if so, less violently than
the yābā, and contrasts their respective association
with good and bad deaths (ibid.: 115-17). Further south,
however (Caplan 1970: 110), the Limbu priest has many
of the attributes we have described as characteristic
of the medium. Secondly, among the western Tamang (Höfe:

1969) the 'shaman' (bombo), with the usual medium's drum
and nocturnal seance, contrasts with the hereditary 'village priest' (lambu), who is concerned particularly with
the collective cult of the sipda deities of the soil,
though he also helps in some illnesses. Fürer-Haimendorf
(1955-6), though not mentioning any distinction among
the eastern Tamang officiants (dhāmi), confirms that the
sipda cult may be equated with the Thulung agricultural
cult (shipda = bhumi, ibid.: 173).

Alerted to the nature of the contrast, it becomes
possible to recognize it a third time among the Gurung
in the persons of the klihbri (or gyabring), the priest,
and the pucu (or poju); the latter, although he is never
possessed, is rendered in Nepali by the Gurung themselves
as jhākri, i.e. medium (Pignède 1966: 293). The former's
calendrical, collective non-Hindu agricultural rites
(ibid.: 307-10) are performed at ancient stone shrines
(ibid.: 301), analogous to the Thulung priest's bhumesthān
and the eastern Tamang shipdathān. Like the Thulung
priest he is said to have had a strong association with
the local rajas of the period before the Gorkha conquest
(ibid.: 296, 302). The Tibetan gods painted on his crown-
like headdress contrast with the medium's feathers.

The Gurung contrast is useful for the diachronic
perspective it suggests. The number of mediums there

is if anything increasing, while the priests are in the
process of disappearing (Pignède 1966: 389-90); in a
more recently settled area near Pokhara they are not
found at all and the poju is the only tribal officiant
(Macfarlane 1972). Among the Thulung there is nothing
pointing to the imminent disappearance of the priest
but his influence is certainly waning. His ancestral
rites are less and less often performed and in spite
of the dancing that follows them attendance at his agricultural ceremonies is recognized to be falling off.
The number of priests remains barely constant, while
here too informants considered that the number of mediums is rising.

In both areas the main cause of the priest's decline is no doubt the spread of religions based on sacred texts. Nowadays there can be few if any groups or
areas in Nepal so isolated that they have remained un-
affected by contact with either Hinduism or Buddhism
or both. The Thulung meet with at least four types of
officiant belonging within the literate traditions.
Occasionally they have recourse to a Buddhist village
lama, e.g. to make amulets for infants,[9] and most vil-

---

9 Amulets (buti N) contain dawāi N (the general word
   for medicine), such as shavings of tigers' bones,
   wrapped in paper on which spells and diagrams are
   drawn. Most people wear them prophylactically,
   changing them around the Nepali new year, but they

lages have a household of the caste called Kammar Jogi,
whose Sanskrit mantras, uttered twice a year at each
house, are supposed to protect the inmates against epidemics. Of much more importance are the Brahmans, who
are employed as astrologers, for annual or occasional
merit-making ceremonies, and sometimes instead of the
tribal priest at weddings and at the death rites following the burial. Over the last generation Brahmans have
been meeting increasing competition from Sadhus, local
Rai householders who vie with them in the pursuit of
purity in the Hindu sense and use written texts to perform very similar rites in the same circumstances.

　　　　Though it is not surprising that the leaders of
Thulung society should prefer the more prestigious literate specialists, it is not immediately clear why the
area of illness should remain firmly in the hands of
the non-literate medium (non-literate, that is, with
regard to his role); the translation 'tribal priest'
tends to obscure the fact that this officiant, too, is
concerned with illness. The answer must be complex, and
part of the general evolution of religion, but much of
it can be summed up in the inherently conservative character of the tribal ancestors. Ancestors belong within

---

may be prescribed as treatment at a seance._ Both
the priest DB and the mediums Simbure and Baunne
make them.

the traditional social structure and expect to be addressed in the language to which they are accustomed,
even if it is quite unintelligible to the priest himself
(as among the Gurung - Pignède 1966: 297). As caste society infiltrates the clan-based villages of the once ter-
ritorially segregated tribe, as temporary contractual
relationships tend to replace hereditary ones, and as
the national language displaces the tribal, the cult of
the tribal ancestors becomes more and more peripheral.
It is another aspect of their conservatism that the ancestors are closely associated with the unmarked category
of continuity and good order (cf. pp. 506-511); the afflictions they send are thus expected to be merited rather
than showing the apparent capriciousness typical of an
illness. This is equally true of the Bhagawān (God) of
the Hindu and neo-Hindu officiants and although Brahman
and Sadhu are said to perform a rite called sosti-sānti
N ('good fortune-tranquillity') on behalf of the sick,
few would think of turning to them before consulting a
medium. So even apart from life-cycle ceremonies, the
emphasis of the tribal priest's activities is closer to
that of the literate officiants than is the medium's and
it is he who faces the more direct competition.

The medium's spirits lack the ancestors' continuity with the tribal past and the medium's role is cor-

respondingly more open to change. The relative adapt-
ability of the two specialists is well illustrated in
their payments. The priest typically receives beer and
portions of the pigs killed in his rituals; only when
invited to officiate at a wedding does he receive cash,
and then it is the fixed sum of half a rupee which inflation has rendered little more than symbolic. The
medium, though he may receive payment in kind as well,
nowadays expects a fee (basanti N) of several rupees.[10]
This is not to say that the Thulung priest cannot adapt
at all. But since he can hardly hope to approximate
himself to the encroaching literate priests, his best
chance of survival lies in adopting elements from the
still very lively tradition of the medium and the blurring discussed in the last section is the result of this
process.

Classification of afflictions and their causes

Western medicine, having distinguished illness from
other afflictions, sets up classifications both at the

---

10 The officiants employed by the Thulung are all
    primarily subsistence farmers and it seems unlikely
    that they undertake the exhausting nocturnal work
    of a medium for conscious and purely economic mo-
    tives. Ostensibly they do it in obedience to their
    possessing spirit and many claim that they would
    rather lead a normal life.

level of symptom (e.g. for pain, location, duration, pre-
cipitating factors) and at the level of cause (infective,
allergic, neoplastic, etc). Some non-western societies
also approach illness with more or less elaborate and
systematic taxonomies which have a direct bearing on
therapy (cf. e.g. Frake 1961). Nothing like this is
found among the Thulung. No importance here attaches
to the precise discrimination of symptoms and their terminology is correspondingly vague. Little would be gained by listing Thulung and Nepali terms for fever, diarrhoea, abdominal lump or colic, wasting ('drying up')
or oedematous ('swelling') conditions, and so on.

In the more casual efforts at exorcism, diagnosis
may be omitted, but usually a divinatory procedure is
used, the choice of method varying with the practitioner.
Often the diviner is said to 'see' the cause of the affliction; to aid him he may hold to his forehead some
object with which he has made passes over the patient.
At seances the spirit that possesses him speaks through
him, in which case he will usually (but not always) be
willing or able to discuss afterwards what the spirit
has said. Here it is impossible to know the process
by which the decision as to the cause is arrived at and
one can only, like the Thulung layman, take account of
the result. Sometimes a mechanical divinatory procedure

(jokhanā hernu N, 'look at the omens') precedes or re-
places a consultation under trance. To take one method
as an example, Bāunne casts handfuls of rice onto a brass
plate and pairs off the grains to obtain a yes-no answer
to his binary questions according as the number of grains
turns out to be odd or even. The invocations he makes
while doing so are not intelligible to ordinary listen-
ers, and are no doubt not intended to be, but it was
suggested that he was putting questions such as: is it
a spirit?, is it a witch?, is it the ancestors?

     General questions to ordinary people do not elicit
systematic answers concerning the possible causes of
affliction. The agencies and classes of agency that
may be held responsible are indefinite in number and
only somewhat less so in characteristics. One can attempt, as we do below, to pick on particular agencies
and explore their properties, but to start from some
totality of possibilities and try to subdivide it would
be to impose a system alien to local patterns of thought.
Thus an approach which might seem natural would be to
take the list of afflictions from the texts quoted above
and pigeon-hole them under headings such as (a) named
spirits, (b) classes of unnamed spirits, (c) forces orig-
inating from the living. But as we suggest towards the
end of this section, this sort of classification is per-

haps an example of what the anthropologist must transcend
if he aims for an imaginative entry into Thulung categories. It is interesting, however, that the texts do seem
to segregate symptoms from potential causal agencies;
lexically, too, Thulung distinguishes <u>seoki beṭngiri</u> 'I
have a cough' from <u>boksi lāge</u>- N <u>diusta</u> 'I am suffering
from witchcraft', whereas Nepali uses <u>lāgnu</u> in both sorts
of context, much as in English one can 'have' indiscriminately a virus or the sore throat it causes. But let
us examine some particular causes.

Here is a translation of a story tape-recorded
from my host in Mukli:

Rajime's daughter (? niece) had gone off to get married,
I don't know where the place was. Later, they say,
her cattle, buffaloes, oxen and whatever fell ill and
they all came out in skin troubles and swellings. The
medium performed a divination and announced the cause
of the trouble as Rajime <u>leom</u>. 'But the man they call
Rajime is my father, why has he caused the trouble,
he's alive, he hasn't died,' she exclaimed. 'Well in
the omens it's Rajime <u>leom</u> that comes down, your father
or whoever he is, it's Rajime <u>leom</u>. If he's your
father, one of these days go and appease him,' said
the medium. 'Take with you a cock, some ceremonially
prepared beer, and a measure of grain.' So she got

together the things he'd said and went off to her father.
'What have you come for, my dear?' he asked. 'My cattle
are ill, father, that's why I've come.' 'What's the
matter with them?' 'It's their skin, it's all peeling
off, they've come out in swellings and boils. The medium said it was my father Rajime leom, that's why I've
come.' 'But what on earth?' said her father. 'I'm
not dead, I don't understand, if I were dead I might
have become a leom, I suppose, but I'm not.' 'They
kept saying it was you, father,' she replied. So she
gave him the beer and all the other offerings she had
brought. 'Well, it seems I must have been the cause
of your cattle being ill like that with boils and peeling skin. If so, let them recover, let them become
just as they were,' he said. The woman went home and
her cattle all got gradually better.

Since Rajime died, his leom has spread all through the
villages all over the place round here, affecting both
men and animals. When my children were ill and they
(i.e. mediums) said it was Rajime leom, the offerings
and rites that were necessary - I've not done them,
what's his name, Mandras Pap (the priest DB), does the
sprinkling like this with water and invokes with all
the ritual names and so on. After his sprinkling, up
till now the children have always recovered. As for

the cattle, so far leom has not attacked them. That's
all I know, that's the lot.

This story illustrates how, as we have stressed,
the ordinary route from symptom to treatment lies through
divination. As often, one agency, here leom, can cause
two types of affliction, human and veterinary.[11] The
continuity between an evil influence classifiable as
witchcraft and one that counts as a dead spirit is very
clear; as among the Sherpas (Fürer-Haimendorf 1964: 265)
witchcraft is considerably less often implicated as the
cause of affliction than are evil spirits or gods.

An interesting question is the degree of differentiation or individuality ascribable to Rajime. The
story is not particularly well known even in Mukli, and
was quite unknown to the most celebrated medium in Lokhim.
On other occasions the story-teller stated that leom was
in fact Gelbu, the Sherpa wife of Mapa Raja, culture hero
of the Khaling Rai, who live to the north of the Thulung.
But this remark taken literally does not square easily

---

11 At rites performed at cattle shelters for sick animals
    (goth puja N) offerings may be made to the following
    groups or pairs of spirits, some of whom also afflict
    humans, and who are worth listing as corroboration of
    our comments later on the identity and patterns of
    association of spirits; in Mukli - Naran, Cirkan,
    Gosain, Gosaini, Gaidu; in Deusa - Kulunge Sitakhau,
    Harikarne Deuta/Bijuwa; in Tingla - Harikarna and
    Krosyuban, both Bijuwa; in Lokhim - Sitakhau and Purbe
    Aitaware and Sansari, and Harikarne Dasekarne Bijuwa.

with the Rajime story, nor with the fact that the <u>hutpa</u>
rite frequently addresses Gelbu Rājā Gelbu Rāni.[12] In
any case, as the story implies, there were <u>leom</u> before
Rajime and no doubt they will continue to afflict humanity after his name has been forgotten. People who knew
of no named <u>leom</u> translated the word as <u>bāyu</u> N or <u>pisāt</u>
N, meaning simply evil spirit. This suggests that the
life cycle of a named evil spirit is as follows: he is
recognized as a cause of affliction usually after his
death, when a diviner first implicates him. If he catches
on, he may enjoy a certain local vogue before his individuality is merged with that of other named spirits or
lost in the swarms of potentially harmful anonymous spirits. But the story may be more complicated, as the next
example shows.

Limbu Deutā can cause shooting pains in the head
and barrenness of cattle. A Limbu once came from the
east to Rai territory to trade in ornaments, as his people
still do. He went hunting with a Sotang or Kulung Rai
(neighbours of the Thulung, living to their north-east).
The hunters were caught in a snowstorm, perished and became evil spirits (<u>bāyu</u>). A medium, called in to see a
sick man, had a vision of the pair and diagnosed their

---

12   The name Gelbu comes via Sherpa from Tibetan <u>rGyalpo</u>
     'king', the gender evidently being neglected.

evil spirits (pret N) as the cause of the illness, which
cleared up after an appropriate rite addressed to them.
When Dimajit performed this rite he addressed the Limbu
as Athanni N (referring to the eight anna coin necklaces
he would have traded in) and constructed for his compan-
ion the left-hand half of the shrine where the offerings
were addressed to Sitākhāu Purbe. The point of all this
is that in spite of the apparently strong local roots of
the story the cult of the couple is in fact very widely
spread; in Assam they are called Purbiyā Athanne and homo-
logues with varying names can be identified in Darjeeling
and Tibet (Macdonald 1962: 138-9).

One final example may be given from the non-literate
tradition of a spirit who is feared among other things
particularly for the giddy spells he sends. The Ban Deutā
N 'forest god' is instructive in several respects. His
nomenclature, Rangkime in Mukli and Lokhim, Rangkeni in
Tingla (cf. Rākebhūt in Sarma 1962), shows the variability
typically found in Nepal in the names for gods and spirits. Like Limbu Deutā he appears in several other guises;
in Thulung as Broanum Sokmonum 'the one from the cliffs
and jungles', in Limbu as Tāmphungnā = 'spirit (bhut N)
of forest (tāmphung)' (Chemjong 1961), in Gurung probably
as Toh Kleh 'maître des bois' (Pignède 1966: 338). Like
Limbu again he shares his shrine with another deity,

Bureni in Lokhim, Sansār Māyā in Mukli. Like Sitākhāu
(cf. note 11), neither of the companions is confined to
the relationship. At Darjeeling Bureni is regarded as
a cause of convulsions in children (Barnouw 1956: 266),
and may take seven forms (Macdonald 1962: 123-4); Sansāri
Mātā or Sansāri Māi is a well-known Hindu goddess associated with Kāli (e.g. Barnouw loc. cit., Ministry of Defence 1965: 77). The pairing tendency of gods has already
been noted with regard to the Gurung birds of long life
and good fortune and the Gelbu 'couple'. Similarly, the
Limbu jungle spirit, though she may be glimpsed by humans
as an old and ugly female, is addressed as Tāmpungmā Hāng
Tāmpungma Hāngmā, i.e. as constituting a royal male-female
couple (Sagant 1969: 111-12, 114).

Traditionally Rangkime's rite is performed regularly twice a year by each household, but increasingly
such prophylactic rites directed towards ambivalent spirits are being replaced by regular annual rites performed
by Brahman and Sadhu, and if the trend continues Rangkime
will only receive attention when specifically diagnosed,
as he sometimes is. Comparison of his rite in different
villages showed some of the dimensions of variability in
its performance. In Tingla, two brothers, neither ritual
specialists, carried it out in Nepali almost surreptit-
iously in a patch of jungle with myself as only onlooker.

In Mukli, Dimajit was called in one evening to officiate
in a field near the house and to share the sacrificed
chicken with the household. In Lokhim, half a dozen
neighbours accompanied the householder and a medium to
the edge of the jungle and shared in a morning picnic
there.

As a group, all these potentially harmful spirits
are sharply distinguished from the gods worshipped by
Brahmans and Sadhus inasmuch as they demand animal sacrifice (bhog khānchan N), a practice from which the literate priests strongly dissociate themselves. The tutelary deities of mediums (sikāri, nāg, banjhākri, banes-
khandi, to mention some of their commoner Nepali names)
undoubtedly belong to the blood-eating group, so it is
puzzling to find that questions addressed to possessed
mediums always begin and end with Parmeśura N, Parameswar
being a literary word for the Creator god, who is certain
ly not carnivorous. An element of flattery may be involv
ed, but the classification of spirits is in general highl
imprecise; a being such as Limbu or Rangkime is referred
to indiscriminately as a bhut 'ghost' or deutā N 'god'.
Similarly, Pignède (1966: 357) suggests with more cautio
than necessary that the limit between a dead person or
ancestor and god (Tibetan la) or godling (Gurung kleh)
is not a sharp one.

Comparable difficulties surround the distinction we have emphasized between good and bad deaths. In principle the ordinary spirits (sāto or hamsa N, pel) resulting from the former are accompanied to the ancestral home by the priest and, suitably propitiated, continue from there to maintain the health and prosperity of their descendants. The evil spirit (munang) resulting from a bad death is disposed of by the medium. In practice the clear contrast is not maintained, any more than that between the two officiants. If pushed the Thulung would no doubt explain that there is always a chance that the failure of the priest would result in an evil spirit. But the deeper reason is perhaps simply that the distinction of good and bad death, for all its importance, can readily be ignored in the face of the overriding badness of all death.

An example occurred one evening after I played through a tape recording of a perfectly ordinary priest's funeral rite and the housewife described her terror at the possibility that the munang would appear and cause harm. Similarly, at an ordinary burial the dead person's weapons are blunted before being put in the grave beside the corpse, 'lest he become a pret /ghost7 and use them against us'. In spite of their Buddhism and its clear doctrine of reincarnation the Sherpas use similar vague

concepts. The common word shrindi covers both malignant
spirits who have never been human and 'in casual speech'
those resulting from bad deaths, and even those who, whatever their mode of death, are afterwards diagnosed as having become malignant (Fürer-Haimendorf 1964: 252, 265-6).
In Nepali, too, the various terms are used interchangeably
According to Spaight (1942: 137), 'Some Gurkhas say that
bhut, pisāc and pret are different names for the same
ghost, but the majority agree that there are three different species'. This remark illustrates the westerner's
search for a sort of precision that is simply not there.

When the need is realized, it is easy enough to
accept the insignificance of certain discriminations with
in the realm of supernatural beings; as the Thulung often
answer when pressed on points of detail or inconsistency,
how can you be certain of what you cannot see with your
own eyes? It may seem less natural to find 'the envy of
mediums' or unallocated 'anger' placed side by side with
symptoms, named spirits and classes of spirits in the

---

13 The word appears to be the same as Sherpa shen-dre,
    Tibetan shi-'dre (Snellgrove 1957: 290) and Funke's
    chendi (see his index - probably also the same as his
    chende and sende). Chendi is summarized as 'Schatter
    seele' and is said to accompany a man through life as
    well as causing harm after his death. Cf. also Höfer
    sinde 'ghosts of the recent dead'. The Thulung recog
    nize Sindi as a dangerous Sherpa god and either offic
    iant may perform rites to him. Thulung munang appear
    to belong to a similar family of cognates, cf. Funke
    mung (Tibetan mu), Pignède's moh, Höfer's and Chem-
    jong's mang.

officiant's list of afflictions. But of course in any manifestation the spirit is expressing his envy or anger, a property which is ascribed either to his intrinsic nature or to his bad death; moreover, as the *leom* story showed, death does not necessarily affect the evil activity of a person's spirit. It may in fact introduce a spurious precision if one distinguishes between the motive of an angry being or force, the being itself, and the means by which it expresses its nature. Fürer-Haimendorf (1964: 263) translates the Sherpa word *pem* as 'witch' and talks of them as harming others 'through the invisible influence of their mind (*sem*)'. Funke, in contrast, talks consistently of the *pem*, even when its effects are evil, as the 'nicht körperlicher Teil des Menschen' (1969: 343), never uses it to refer to a role, and suggests that it is not clearly to be differentiated from *sim* or *sem* (p. 140). Even if this represented a local variation in lexical usage, it would confirm our point about the fluidity of the distinctions involved. In a similar way it is difficult to avoid talking in terms of a causal chain: accidental bad death results in angry spirit, who causes symptoms. The Nepalese often use this language, and other links still may be suggested; according to Pignède (1966: 371), the bad death is often preceded by extraordinary circumstances or socially reprehensible behaviour. But the

abrupt juxtapositions of the officiant's list are best
understood not as jumbled links in a chain but as samples
falling under a more abstract notion of interruptions to
the natural harmony of life.

This section has explored some of the difficulties
in making definite yet general statements about the classification and identity of the causes ascribed to illness.
Here are some of the possibilities not mentioned so far.
Toothache, as in many parts of the world, is ascribed to
a worm of unspecified nature. The moon is said to punish
with tuberculous neck glands those who point a finger at
it. In many Thulung households the ancestors would afflict the senior members with stomach ache if they touched goat's meat. If the shrine for agricultural rituals
is defiled the community will come out in sores. Those
who fall ill after a journey ascribe it to a poison calle
hartāl N (yellow orpiment) alleged to have been introduce
into their food by ill-disposed people encountered en
route. The evil eye of jealous onlookers (cokhe N) caus
indigestion. Certainly a Thulung would regard it as a
hopeless undertaking to attempt an exhaustive taxonomy.

Treatment strategies

Three centuries ago dense jungle covered the whole Thulu
area apart from a handful of clearings for villages and

swiddens. Even now that most land below 7,000 feet has
been permanently cleared for intensive cultivation, visits
are often made to the forest for firewood and other purposes and older men know many Thulung botanical names.
Some Buddhist lamas are supposed to be very knowledgeable
herbalists and an official publication describes 393 medicinal plants to be found growing in the country (His
Majesty's Government of Nepal 1970). Yet in the Thulung
area I met no acknowledged experts on herbal lore and in
spite of enquiries on the subject collected the names of
under a dozen plants used as specific remedies. Only a
handful were at all widely known, let alone used. It is
not clear whether the Thulung have always been so unconcerned with this possible use of the environment or whether with the ecological change the knowledge has simply
and rapidly disappeared, without as yet being replaced
by the literate Ayurvedic tradition that the government
is fostering.

        Among the Gurung, Pignède (1966) describes numerous
rites in which an individual's spirit or the household's
birds of life and fortune are lost, or captured by evil
spirits, and have to be recovered by the officiant. Soul-
loss is recognized as a risk by the Thulung after a fall
or a shock, or in any ritual where potentially dangerous
spirits are involved. In either case the errant souls

must be summoned back; the individual does this by tap-
ping metal on stone, the medium by dancing with a scoop-
ing gesture, ringing a bell, drumming, and/or invoking.
The concept is certainly available to the Thulung but it
is not often brought up in the explanation of illness.
Symbols suggesting capture are common enough in the medium's seances, for instance a sort of glue made by soak-
ing Machilus leaves in water, and a mystical substance
chit-khoa which is likened to bird-lime or a spider's
web; but their ostensible purpose is to catch evil spirits, not the patient's spirit. However, interpretations
of symbolic motifs are often more labile than the motifs
themselves, and further field work might give a picture
closer to Pignède's. As he says (p. 360), the freeing
of the lost spirit of the patient is concomitant with
the subjection (preceding the driving away) of the spirit
that captured it. The close relationship of the two processes provides for easy shift from one to the other.

Treatment is thus for the most part a matter of
expulsion or removal. Laymen do not know of straightforward relationships between diagnosis and therapy, any
more than between symptoms and diagnosis, and are usually
content to follow the recommendations of the medium or
the spirit who speaks through him. In one case, however,
the god made the unreasonable demand of a five-year-old

white cock (no one would keep a bird so long without eating it), and the next day the householder blamed the medium for incompetence and went to put his problem to a
different one at a neighbour's seance. Details of procedure vary greatly and here we can only mention certain
strategies without describing their realization. Commonly, several are applied in turn. It might be held that
one spirit could only be removed by a combination of methods, or alternatively that since one method might fail
several are needed for safety. Again, the variety might
be to cover alternative possible diagnoses, for a medium's
failure is sometimes explained by his having recognized
only one out of several afflicting forces.[14] But it did
not seem that mediums, let alone clients, were interested
in distinguishing such possibilities.

Often the approach to the personified evil is direct. In a simple exorcism he is brushed down off the
patient (jhārnu N 'cause to descend') and blown away (phu-
knu N 'blow'). He may be exhorted with ordinary language
or constrained with mantras. In the priest's rites he

---

14 It may be said, for instance, that sikāri N chostam,
    the verb chos- meaning to 'mix in', as when whey is
    diluted. The sikāri are a particularly protean group
    (cf. Hitchcock 1966: 28-9; Macdonald 1962: 120-1).
    Apart from being the tutelary deities of mediums they
    may as kul sikāri translate the Thulung sāse, bilat-
    ally inherited household gods, represented by baskets
    of grain and gourds of alcohol, and occasionally
    implicated as the cause of illness.

may be frightened away with shouting and the brandishing
of weapons (risaunu N 'be angry, threaten'), or wafted
away with a winnowing fan. His passage may be blocked
by burying a ploughshare point down and out (lam krip-
'cut the path'). Very often, objectified rather than
personified, he may be extracted from the patient, either
by sucking or with the aid of a wand (phurke N), a process called somo that-, or bhed jhiknu N: the verbs both
mean 'extract'. The nouns refer to a small material object, a piece of grit or some unidentifiable fragment of
animal or vegetable origin, which is produced by the medium's manipulations and handed round on a brass plate
amid applause, as proof of his success.[15] At the same
time, of course, they refer to the disease or its cause.
Phed has a variety of dictionary translations, including
'piercing, cleaving, fragment, secret essence, witchcraft'. Clearly no single English word can be appropriate to the complex of ideas we are exploring; the term
'witchcraft' in particular introduces an implication (that
the cause of the trouble is living) whose irrelevance we

---

15 Somo is related to the somori of the hutpa text. A
    schoolmaster assistant, sceptical about this partic-
    ular procedure, dismissed it with the English word
    'magic', effectively reversing his intended meaning,
    which was 'conjuring'; jadu N is ambiguous between
    the two, allowing room for an interesting semantic
    shift.

have noted above.

Most seances include elements whose theme is the
luring of the evil away from the patient, typically via
a thread, and its localization in some object which is
then cut down, burnt, or discarded a minute or so's walk
from the house. Particularly common is the element called graha-khadgo sārnu N ('planet-disastrous conjunction
shifting', mentioned also by Pignède 1966: e.g. 361).
I am not sure how far the Thulung are aware of the abstract and impersonal astrological forces symbolized in
this rite by model animals (in principal nine, sometimes
called hāti-ghorā N 'elephants and horses'), made from
potatoes with bamboo slivers for legs. These models ex-
emplify the scapegoat approach to evil forces[16] and have
equivalents in a large number of rituals reported in the
Himalayan literature. The Gurung offer a particularly
instructive example. The ostensible object of the death
ritual is to get rid of the spirit of the deceased who
will otherwise afflict the living. One element in a lengthy ceremony is the killing of a certain sheep, which
corresponds to the deceased in sex and is said to imitate
his or her habits. It is seated and offered food

---

16 In popular usage the term 'scapegoat' often blurs
    the important analytical distinction between someone
    or something that is incorrectly supposed to be res-
    ponsible for an undesired situation and someone or
    something that is ritually made to symbolize evil
    without being mistaken for its cause.

and drink, and is supposed to weep when the mourners do;
ultimately it is killed and its blood is discarded some
way off (Pignède 1966: 356, 371; Ministry of Defence 1965:
74). Nothing could be more straightforward than the interpretation of the army handbook, that the sheep represents the dead person, and it is unnecessary to look further afield at the confirmatory evidence from other Himalayan death rituals. Yet in spite of all this Pignède's
informants expressly denied that the sheep was possessed
by the spirit of the deceased and claimed instead that
it served to 'open the route', i.e. that it was an offering to the spirits who might block it. Further details
of Pignède's account need not concern us since the point
here is how easily a direct expulsory or eliminatory approach to evil can shade into an indirect, prestational
or contractual approach. It would be worth investigating
the hypothesis that changes of interpretation rarely or
never occur in the converse direction.

Even when a sacrifice is recommended there is usually scope for two interpretations. Macdonald (1962: 125
comments cautiously on 'un flottement...concernant la
qualification de certains esprits comme bons ou mauvais',
and Pignède (1966: 360) notes a 'contradiction' between
an offering to certain spirits to make them help with
harvests and the fact that elsewhere they are always

treated as evil. But are not spirits essentially ambivalent? An offering given to him in his evil aspect to
keep him away can as well be interpreted as given to him
in his good aspect to persuade him to act as protector
against other evil spirits. This duality is well seen
in the Fierce Divinities of Hinduism who have been accepted into the Buddhist pantheon as Protectors (Snellgrove
1957: 78). The Rangkime rite is certainly intended primarily as prophylaxis against that deity, but all the other
sorts of evil listed in Dimajit's text are to be warded
off simultaneously, and apparently through his help.

Sacrifices recommended in the course of a seance
are not usually performed during it but are left to the
householder to perform another time with or without assistance. A particular animal, or more usually fowl, is
singled out and may be kept for months before the promise
(bhākal N) is carried out. Another deferred strategy,
but addressed to the non-carnivorous gods, is a vow of
abstention (barta basnu N); thus a girl who fell ill vowed
to eat no salt on Sundays for one year in honour of Surje
(the sun).

One common strategy called 'raising the head' (sir
uthāunu N) is directed to no particular spirit but is
conducive in a general way to health and prosperity, much
like the western blessing or the Hindu tikā N. From what

has been said earlier, such a procedure might seem likely
to fall within the province of the priest, but in fact
I met it performed only by Lokhim mediums and by the
priest-substitute Dimajit, both at nocturnal rites. Although the latter does not possess a tutelary spirit or
go into trance, the rite was called a seance and his invocation was accompanied by the beating of a brass plate.
This will serve as a final example of the difficulties
of arriving at general but true statements of the form
'such and such a Nepalese tribe has such and such a custom, office or belief'.

Final remarks

Though the data discussed have been limited geographic-
ally and in subject matter, the theoretical preoccupation
has been with a difficulty that must have troubled many
anthropologists: that of writing ethnography that is not
(to quote Hubert and Mauss 1964) 'falsified by the exact-
ness of our languages'. To know the overt distinctions
generally recognized in a society and to form models of
its structural oppositions provide a necessary framework
for understanding it, but really to feel at home there
it is just as important to be aware of the ways in which
one social representation shades off into another, without recognizable margins or thresholds. A realistic

picture needs its obscurities no less than its highlights.
Analytically, too, it may be helpful (if not novel) to
focus attention for instance on the vague and fluid transition between a spirit who is warded off as evil and one
who is appealed to as helper, much as, in a more sophisticated way, a linguist (e.g. Lyons 1968) can usefully
focus on the easy logical transition between transitive
and ergative case systems. Of course a reported vagueness
may arise from the observer's misapprehension rather than
from the society's indifference, but more positive reports
are not immune from similar risks. The term vagueness
is itself uncomfortably vague and it would be interesting
to attempt an analysis (in the manner of an Empson) of
the distinctions and affiliations between the various
senses in which it applies to ethnographic material; this
paper has provided illustrations, but not expositions.

The analytical notion of classification is helpful
up to a point since by definition a class disregards some
distinctions; so we may say that witches, ghosts and anger
come together in an implicit class of interruptions to
the natural harmony of life, or, since we are translating
into English (which like Nepali lacks such a unified concept), that ancestors and fortune are explicitly classed
together under the term seor. Other sorts of vagueness,
for instance those surrounding the individuality of

spirits, hardly yield to such an approach and are perhaps characteristic of the subcontinent. There is no reason a priori why cultures should not differ in the emphasis they place on precision in such matters as much as they do, for instance, in the richness of their symbolism; if I expected more clarity and uniformity than I found, this was a preconception of just the kind that field work is supposed to break down. But the most interesting instances of vagueness seem to me not so much those where the transition involved is logical but those that offer scope for explanation in terms of large-scale diachronic trends Examples we have met include priest versus medium, shamanic journey and soul-loss versus possession and invasion by hostile force, and scapegoat versus prestation. All of them, however, need further investigation.

REFERENCES

BARNOUW, V. 1956. Some Eastern Nepalese customs: the early years. Southwestern journal of anthropology 12: 257-71.

CAPLAN, L. 1970. Land and social change in East Nepal. London: Routledge & Kegan Paul.

CHEMJONG, I.S.   1961. Limbu-Nepali-English Dictionary.
    Kathmandu: Nepal Academy.

CLARK, H.H.   1970. Word associations and linguistic
    theory. In Lyons, J. (ed.) New Horizons in Linguist-
    ics. London: Penguin Books.

FRAKE, C.O.   1961. The diagnosis of disease among the
    Subanun of Mindanao. American Anthropologist 63:
    113-32.

FÜRER-HAIMENDORF, C. von.   1955-6. Ethnographic notes
    on the Tamangs of Nepal. Eastern Anthropologist 9:
    166-77.

-- 1964. The Sherpas of Nepal. London: John Murray.

FUNKE, F.W.   1969. Religiöses Leben der Sherpa. Inns-
    bruck-Muenchen: Universitätsverlag Wagner.

HIS MAJESTY'S GOVERNMENT OF NEPAL. 1970. Medicinal
    Plants of Nepal. Kathmandu: Ministry of Forests.

HITCHCOCK, J.T.   1966. The Magars of Banyan Hill. New
    York: Holt, Rinehart and Winston.

-- 1967. Nepalese shamanism and the classical Inner
    Asian tradition. History of Religions 7: 149-58.

HÖFER, A.   1969. Preliminary report on a field research
    in a Western Tamang group, Nepal. Bulletin of the
    International Committee for Urgent Anthropological
    and Ethnological Research 11: 17-31.

HOSTEN, H.   1909. Paharia burial customs (British Sikkim).
    Anthropos 4: 669-83.

HUBERT, H. and MAUSS, M.   1964. Sacrifice: its nature
    and function. London: Cohen and West.

LEWIS, I.M.   1971. Ecstatic Religion. London: Penguin
    Books.

LYONS, J.   1968. Introduction to Theoretical Linguistics.
    Cambridge: Cambridge University Press.

MACDONALD, A.W.   1962. Notes préliminaires sur quelques
    jhākri du Muglān. Journal Asiatique 250: 107-39.

-- 1966a. Les Tamangs vus par l'un d'eux. L'Homme 6:
    26-58.

-- 1966b. Le Népal. In Le Monde du Sorcier. Paris: Editions du Seuil.

MACFARLANE, A. 1972. Personal communication. See also: Population and Economy in Central Nepal: a study of the Gurungs. Unpublished Ph.D. thesis: University of London.

MINISTRY OF DEFENCE. 1965. Nepal and the Gurkas. London: H.M.S.O.

PIGNÈDE, B. 1966. Les Gurungs. Paris: Mouton.

SAGANT, P. 1969. Tāmpungmā, divinité Limbu de la forêt. Objets et Mondes 9: 107-24.

SARMA, B.C. 1962. Nepali Śabda-Koś. Kathmandu: Royal Nepal Academy.

SCHMID, T. 1967. Shamanistic practice in Northern Nepal. In Edsman, C.M. (ed.) Studies in Shamanism. Stockholm

SNELLGROVE, D.L. 1957. Buddhist Himalaya. Oxford: Cassirer.

SPAIGHT, W.M. 1942. Gurka Ghosts. Royal Central Asian Journal 29: 136-40.

TURNER, R.L. 1931. A Comparative and Etymological Dictionary of the Nepali Language. London: Kegan Paul

WORTH, R.M. and SHAH, N.K. 1969. Nepal Health Survey 1965-1966. Honolulu: University of Hawaii Press.

JEANNE BISILLIAT

VILLAGE DISEASES AND BUSH DISEASES IN SONGHAY: AN

ESSAY IN DESCRIPTION AND CLASSIFICATION WITH A VIEW

TO A TYPOLOGY[1]

Q. 'I am asking you for the names of these diseases
    because I make no distinction between them.'

A. 'It is you who mixes them up. Since I have told
    you what the first disease consists of, you ought
    to ask me what constitutes the second. They have
    the same name but their patterns are different.'

This essay is a study in description and interpretation

which, while making considerable use of hypotheses, faith-

fully follows the teaching given to me by a Songhay-Zarma

healer, the zima Moussa Parsident, in twenty recorded

sessions of about two hours each. The exchange quoted

above is a translated extract from one of these lessons

which, conducted in the Zarma language, form the main

body of my material. As a parallel text I have chosen

another series of interviews, conducted and recorded under

the same conditions, with another healer, the sonance

---

1 Translated from the original French by J.B. Loudon.

Yaye. I also employed direct observation. The evidence
has not been used to favour either the cult of possession
- with which a zima is concerned as a religious healer -
or the practice of magic - a sonance being a magical healer specializing in diseases brought about by sorcery.

I have tried to show how the healer sees and con-
ceptualizes disease. In order to do this, I have copied
out, analyzed and rearranged some of the descriptions
given to me. My selections were governed by a desire
to understand the classification employed by the healer
himself, to elucidate the coherent mechanisms invoked
and to demonstrate some of the principal notions which
are central to his learning. Some of these notions were
presented quite explicitly; others have been deduced and,
where this is so, I have indicated as much.

I only allowed myself to embark on this kind of
investigation after five years' work in the field, which
has I hope enabled me to tackle the material with some
understanding. The study was undertaken in order to contribute to the working out of a typology. The results
obtained are still uncertain and incomplete on some issues. Nevertheless I feel justified in presenting them
in the form of a working hypothesis.

The design of this paper reflects the distinction
made by the healers themselves between village diseases

and bush diseases. This antithesis raises a few problems
which are examined in the third and final section. At
the same time it is not impossible that further research
might reveal more important classificatory concepts.

I   Village diseases

When the healer is discussing village diseases, he analyzes them as a series of standard mechanisms, variously
related to one another according to the illnesses under
consideration. So far I have been able to identify only
three which seem to account for all the relevant facts.
They reveal three varieties of movement: movement of the
blood, movement of heat (whether associated with coolness
or not), and movement of the disease itself. These movements take place between one region and another along
routes which, like the healer, I shall call 'pathways'
(chemins).

The lay-out of these routes is not the product
of extensive anatomical knowledge. We know that dissection is not carried out and that the examination of the
bodies of slaughtered animals provides the only basis
for analogies. Investigation of patients is undertaken
through observation and verbal exchanges. No auscult-
ation takes place. The use of touch is confined to taking hold of the wrist, in the case of fever, and of the

arm in the case of madness.

The movement of blood

It is not legitimate to speak of circulation, either
partial or general. It is more a matter of a system of
balance in the amount of blood present at any given moment in a particular part of the body through a to-and-fro
non-circulatory movement.

This movement takes place in two types of ducts,
the functions of each being quite distinct. On the one
hand, there are small veins, invisible to the eye and
hidden under the larger ones: they take blood to and from
the organs. On the other hand, there are large veins,
visible to the eye, which take blood into and out of the
flesh. Blood also moves between flesh and skin but, in
this part of the body, its movement is less clearly described and its function is not apparent.

It is taken for granted that the quantity of blood
is not the same for each individual and that it very prob
ably varies according to circumstances for any particular
individual. The liver is believed to be responsible for
regulating the amount of blood available for the body as
a whole. It is the 'navel' of the blood, 'it is in the
blood', but it is not a container filled with blood. Per
haps, together with other organs (the kidneys), it is the

source of blood.

There is nowhere, therefore, that the blood is
stored, but it is to be found in small amounts within
the organs. The heart itself only contains very little
blood when the body is in a healthy state. In fact blood
surrounds the organs without it being possible to say
whether this is by means of a special system of veins.

A disturbance of this state of affairs corresponds
to the presence of serious illness. Blood may then accumulate in excess around the organs or even invade them
as far as their 'belly' (heart, lungs, abdomen, intestines, bone-marrow, joints), sometimes causing death. Regarding the heart, it is said that 'the blood has a right
to go to the heart but God does not tell it to go there;
it only does so in serious illness'. In contrast, other
parts may see the blood withdraw, which may, in serious
cases, bring about dessication of the organ concerned
(e.g. the liver).

Movement of the blood is not brought about by the
beating of the heart. Nowhere did I find any mechanical
notion to explain it. The meaning of this movement is
ascertained by its function. Its task is to help the
organs by going to them. It is the small veins, whose
strength comes from the heart, which stimulates the blood.
The large veins conduct blood into the flesh in order to

moisten it. In the event of illness they balance the
local distribution of blood by taking away excessive
quantities that have accumulated around an organ and re-
distributing it throughout the flesh. There is no link
between the two systems of veins; they do not communicate with each other and are always distinct from one
another.

The notion of 'large quantity' is often used to
express the role of the large veins; the notion of 'small
quantity', associated with that of thinness, transparency,
purity of liquids, is often used in descriptions of the
role of the small veins. The latter convey not only blood
but also air, healing vapours, heat, coolness, the poison
of diseases, liquids, fear and the disease itself. It
is also in the small veins that blood is transformed when
it is mixed with various liquids. The small veins have
openings which appear to be open when the body is in good
health and temporarily closed if disease passes through
them. These openings, which are never localized by the
healer, do not bring about bleeding.

Blood normally moves in both directions, whether
towards the openings of the veins or towards the organs;
but certain illnesses cause a reversal of its movement.
Illness is not linked, therefore, to the idea of direction but to that of a reversal of normal flow. In a way

that seems strange to us, disease does not go through
an open opening but through a blocked opening.

In the description of diseases, the notion of
obstruction reversing the movement of the blood is very
frequent. In good health blood flows towards a particular organ; it meets, moving in the opposite direction
and within the small vein, a modificatory liquid or a
disease. Contact between these two elements produces
a blockage which temporarily obstructs the vein. En-
countering an obstacle which it has in fact helped to
create, the moving blood retraces its steps and resumes
its progress in the opposite direction. The obstruction
is then removed and the element introduced into the vein
may follow the blood on its return movement or mingle
with it and thus arrive at the organ which, as a result,
will be affected.

Sometimes the blood stops, and that always happens
in particular places. Such a stoppage brings on (or is
an element of) an illness. Once it has stopped the blood
spreads throughout the system, but by what means is not
known. The intestine is the favoured site for this phenomenon. Sometimes the blood becomes restless (a feature
of illness) or its flow becomes more rapid (under the
influence of fear).

The movement of heat and coolness

The temperature of blood is not constant. Illness may
be accompanied by a heating or a cooling of the blood -
a notion which might seem to correspond to that of fever.
It would be rash, however, to try to equate one notion
with the other. There are three separate words denoting
fever, heat and coolness.

On the other hand, heat - the pathological and
symptomalogical role of which is important - also ful-
fils a specific function in the healthy body; carried
by the slender veins from the heart to the blood, it is
the source of the power which ensures the movement of
the latter. No mention is made of the phenomenon of
dilatation to provide a mechanical explanation. On the
other hand, it is held that if heat does not reach the
blood the latter stops flowing and becomes black, which
is either a sign of illness or a cause of illness.

Coolness is also supplied by the heart to the
blood by the slender veins. Its role in the movement
of the blood is clearly defined. The movements of heat
and coolness in the blood seem to be identical. Coolness, a notion symmetrical with that of fever, is also
a cause or a consequence of illness. Organically it
appears to arise in the lungs. Heat and coolness must
both be able to circulate as freely as blood. When their

pathways are blocked, they come back to the heart and
disease breaks out; reciprocally, disease itself blocks
these pathways. From these observations emerge the following principles:

Cessation of movement of blood	)
	)
	)
Closure of openings of blood	) Causes and
	)
	) consequences
Cessation of movement of heat or coolness	)
	) of disease
	)
Closure of openings of heat and coolness	)
	)

Not all diseases, however, are accompanied by changes
in temperature.

The notions analyzed above come into the description of blood, viz: (i) at normal temperature and in normal flow, blood is red; (ii) fever causes a cessation
of movement of blood and all stationary blood becomes
black; (iii) any reversal of the flow of blood is accompanied by an alteration in its appearance - it becomes
black or like water; when this reversal is accompanied
by mingling, the blood may take on the appearance of fat
or froth; as this reversed flow leads blood to organs
(especially the heart) this altered blood accumulates
around them; a similar phenomenon occurs if blood, in
its reversed flow, brings coolness back to the heart.

The notion of pathway

The various itineraries of the blood and of heat are
indicated by the healer through the use of the word _fondo_,
which corresponds to any kind of road, route or path,
as also to symbolic pathways. This notion covers not
only the movements of blood, of associated liquids, and
of heat/coolness, but also that of breathing (the pathway
of breathing being that of heat). Lastly, in a quite
general way, it serves to describe the progression of
disease in the body.

It would appear that in every case a pathway may
be traversed in both directions, one being that of health,
the other that of disease. But the correspondence is
not invariable. Medicines, in order to cure disease,
sometimes borrow pathways that are traversed in the same
direction by the disease itself (e.g. emetics and purges)
Certain extremely serious diseases operate in both directions, with a devouring action in the return direction
(for example, _dankanoma_ - certain diseases of the intestine which travel down towards the anus and then, rising
again to the stomach, bring about the death of the patient). It seems, therefore, that in this process, whatever the initial direction, it is the return movement
that is regarded as a pathological phenomenon. It often
involves the rupture of an organ or the destruction of

flesh.

At the present stage of my investigations it appears impossible to establish the existence of a continuous network of pathways. However, it is already possible to question whether such a continuity exists. For it is around essential organs, and between one organ and another, that these pathways are said to exist. Furthermore, the healer probably does not always describe every stage of a particular disease. Thus one may travel directly from sexual organs to eyes without including in the description of the disease (nikataw) an account of the itinerary, as also in the case of passage from stomach to head (dankanoma) or from stomach to the rest of the body (yeeni falku). Certain organs might be likened to road junctions, which must necessarily be passed through by many diseases in the course of their journey. Thus the heart leads at one and the same time to the head, the stomach, the lungs, to the space between flesh and skin, to the whole body. The stomach leads to those same places and also to the joints; such a list is not exhaustive. We should note that certain organic routes (such as the digestive tract) do not seem to be followed by diseases in any preferential way; quite the contrary. Few links are found between the stomach and the intestines. The healer is well aware, however, of the passage

of ingested food and of intestinal diseases, though his
description does not follow what for us might seem the
obvious route.

The organs in which the pathways of the diseases
intersect are also often those in which they come to a
head: stomach, heart, head, the region between flesh and
skin. But we must single out the joints, where large
numbers of diseases settle but where very few of them
arise. The liver, so closely linked to the movement of
the blood, is passed through only by a small number of
pathways (cantu).

The movement of diseases in the body is not always
described in terms of an itinerary leading successively
from one place to another. A different process seems
very frequent, above all in diseases in which heat plays
a large part: the illness starts from a particular point
(head, abdomen, heart) and scatters, apparently simultaneously, throughout the whole body, sometimes enlisting
the support of the blood and nerves.

Lastly, it should be noted that disease does not
take these routes unconcernedly. Once dankanoma has
arrived at the anus, it wishes to rise again inside the
body in order to devour the flesh on its way; once fever
has assembled in the heart, it wishes to reach the head
in order to escape; blood wishes to help or wishes to

make ill.

In itself, the pathway is not of great importance
in diagnosis; the stages of the disease are what hold
the attention of the healer or, in cases of dispersion,
the distribution of arrival points. In certain diseases
the route involves halts which are regarded as so many
symptoms (yeeni fare).

This conception clearly compares the body taken
as a unity ('the whole body', 'between the flesh and the
skin') with the body regarded as an aggregate of regions,
each identified by the presence of an organ acting as a
thoroughfare, as a point of concentration and as a centre
for diffusion. For example, disorders of the flow of
blood may affect one or other of these centres; blood
settles perhaps in the heart or in the intestines, and
it is only secondarily, as fever, that distant centres
may become affected.

Description of a village disease: binlutey

Let us take an example of a village disease in which the
system of ideas presented above may be seen at work:
binlutey (bin = heart, lutey = attack of breathlessness).
It is right to say something at this point about my attitude towards the naming of these diseases. I will not
attempt to show any correspondence between the diagnosis

presented here and the diagnosis possible according to
European medicine. On the basis of my research, however,
one can say that term by term correspondence would be
rare. Furthermore, a single Songhay name for a disease
would often need to be rendered by a whole series of des-
ignations. A deeper study of this problem must be postponed until later.

Binlutey is a disease 'which induces heat'. It
arises in the head and enters the brain (the 'navel' of
the disease), which it then proceeds to melt. A liquid
separates out and goes into the veins. Three analogies
help the healer to explain the process and its consequences: making butter, filtering a liquid, and kneading a
ball of uncooked millet. The first emphasizes the separation of a precious fat, the second the release of a
refined liquid, the third the formation of a liquid distinct from a mass and of impurities distinct from the
liquid.

As descriptions applied to the body, these metaphors are interpreted as follows: the precious fat is
the value of the brain; the purity of the filtered liquid
is the physical nature of the fluid which enters the
veins; the liquid oozing from the millet is the liquid
which separates out from the brain. Its characteristic
quality, as distinct from the 'dirt' that floats to its

surface, is the purity of the liquid released in contrast to the dirtiness of the diseased brain. In short,
the following oppositions can be identified:

$$
\text{comparisons}
\begin{cases}
\text{butter} & \text{worthless/valuable} \\
\text{filter} & \text{unrefined/refined} \\
\text{millet} & \text{solid/liquid} \\
& \text{'dirt'/purity}
\end{cases}
\begin{cases}
\text{relevant} \\
\text{character-} \\
\text{istics of the} \\
\text{pathogenic} \\
\text{element}
\end{cases}
$$

One may be forgiven, I hope, for laying so much stress
on these three examples; they illustrate, in an element-
ary way it is true, the problems of understanding the
metaphors by which the healer explains and probably de-
fends his analysis of disease. The conceptual coherences
are a reality but may well arrange themselves on the
basis of a selection process the principles of which we
do not grasp. The same component may be portrayed in
ways which are different and, at first sight, seem ir-
reconcilable. Such problems crop up continually and at
all levels.

        Let us return to the course of the disease by
considering the liquid that we have just described. Having arrived at the slender veins, at the exit from the
brain, it meets blood moving upwards (closing of the
vein). This brings about a return of blood to the heart
(opening of the vein). The liquid follows the blood to
the heart by the pathway thus opened up. The blood and

this liquid accumulate round the heart and mingle together to form a froth. This state of affairs brings
on shortness of breath, fainting and even loss of consciousness; if it persists – and note incidentally the
notion of time – the disease becomes established and
intervention becomes necessary. Treatment is carried
out in two stages. At first medicine is administered
with the object of making the froth disappear in three
different ways: it devours the disease in the form of
froth and it brings about the elimination of the disease
through vomiting and through defaecation (diarrhoea).
When all the froth has been got rid of, a little untaint-
ed blood begins to appear in the vomit. The patient then
recovers. For this treatment to be effective, the disease must not have lasted too long before intervention
takes place, otherwise death will supervene.

Although the 'navel' of this disease is in the
head, the organ which bears the brunt of the attack is
the heart which, once affected, is vulnerable to the
effects of another exacerbating disease: yeeni falku.
In his description of diseases the healer compares binlutey and yeeni falku by the action which each has on
the heart. The former, by enveloping the heart for an
extended period, causes the shortness of breath already
mentioned; the latter closes the heart, which probably

means that it makes this shortness of breath worse.

Despite their association, however, these two
diseases are quite distinct from one another.

Yeeni falku

Yeeni falku (yeeni = coolness, falku = mucus) arises in
the stomach and ends up in the joints. Leaving the stomach, the diseases 'wishes' to go to the heart; having
arrived there, it succumbs to the attraction of the liquid
contained in every healthy joint. Both in the stomach
and in the joints the disease manifests itself through
the presence of mucus which is 'neither red nor white'.
To the healer's mind its presence in the human body is
proved by what can be seen in the carcase of old animals
- tremulous mucus on the stomach, the liver and the intestines. Another sign, this time visible, is that the
patient's abdomen swells and 'trembles as if there was
a child inside'. The treatment is only aimed, however,
at eliminating mucus from the stomach. Once that is
gone, the mucus in the joints will also disappear. To
bring this about a medicine is used which promotes 'defaecation' of the disease.

This disease is accompanied by a sensation of
cold. On the other hand, it is known that it affects
subjects who have plenty of blood. It would seem, there-

fore, and this is confirmed by other facts in other diseases, that the idea of an abundance of blood is not
directly linked with the idea of heat.

In my description I have left on one side a phenomenon that may be significant: although the disease is
attracted to the liquid of the joints, it also brings
blood down into the same joints, an invasion which is
abnormal, following the rule that the invasion of an
organ by blood equals disease. By way of hypothesis,
the formation of mucus can be explained as the meeting
of blood and of the liquid, 'yellowish and like a sauce',
which, according to the healer, is to be found in every
healthy joint. In fact, the following combinations have
been noted: blood + liquid from the brain = fatty froth;
blood + another liquid from the brain = sperm; blood +
liquid introduced into the foetus = brain. To these
one can therefore add: blood + liquid from the joints
= mucus ('neither red nor white').

Regarding modifications of blood through the introduction of foreign substances, a brief digression
may be appropriate. If every substance introduced into
the blood causes its modification, how is it that medicines absorbed through the mouth and nose which then pass
directly into the blood-stream do not bring about a similar alteration (as is the case in the example of poison,

the intake of which brings about death by immediate invasion of the blood)? This question leads to another
concerning the mode of action of all medicines which,
somehow or other, come into contact with the blood.

When prescribing treatment, the healer does not
intend it to act upon the blood. This he states quite
categorically: 'one does not meddle with the blood, the
blood is the man'. One might think that here we have
a therapeutic principle. It leads to the conclusion
that medicinal substances introduced into the blood-
stream are regarded as active, that is to say, actually
present, only when they are in contact with the disease.
Otherwise they are a neutral and inert element.

Yeeni fara

Yeeni falku is not the only yeeni known. The healer
links his description of it with that of yeeni fara
(yeeni = coolness, fara = to prick or hurt the bones),
which likewise affects the joints. The name of the two
diseases also demonstrate another similarity, that of
the feeling of coolness experienced by the patient. In
fact, however, the two descriptions seem to indicate
entirely different diseases.

Yeeni fara first establishes itself between skin
and flesh; it never affects the abdomen and never threat-

ens the heart. It passes directly from the superficial areas into the **veins**, which lead it to the joints. Having 'stopped' there, it concentrates on the marrow of the bones; in time it may 'even reach' the vertebral column. The blood is black and at rest, though one cannot say where. <u>Yeeni fara</u> affects those who have little blood. The patient remains lying down and groaning. This sign, seldom exhibited, should be specially noted as a significant feature; its meaning can be better appreciated if one bears in mind that resistance to physical suffering in this culture is such that any public expression of pain arouses other people's disapproval and mockery, and hence a feeling of 'shame' on the part of the patient. It must therefore be understood that this disease which 'pricks the bones' causes a pain acknowledged as being unbearable. The pain is linked with a feeling of heat, though this does not exclude the coolness already mentioned. The disease is treated by the application of paste to incisions made at the site of the swollen joints.

The common and the distinguishing features of the two diseases may be set out as in Tables I, II and III.

Table I : COMMON CHARACTERISTICS

Yeeni fara Yeeni falku	origin: weyno	feeling of coolness	affected joints	curable

Table II : INTERPRETATION OF THE DISEASE

	Predis-position	Movement	Pathway	Blood	Swelling
Yeeni fara	Little blood	- continuous - uninterrupted course - from the outside to the inside	Flesh-skin: veins: joints: marrow: spinal column.	- at rest - black	Joints
Yeeni falku	Plenty of blood	- discontinuous - course with marked interruptions - from the inside to the outside	Abdomen: joints.	- not at rest - red	Abdomen

Table III : ELEMENTS OF THE DIAGNOSIS

	Temperature of the body	Posture of the patient	Pain
Yeeni fara	Coolness - Heat	Lying down	In the bones (with groaning)
Yeeni falku	Coolness	Not lying down	

Two facts emerge from these tables. The first concerns the course of the diseases, they travel in opposite directions - inside/outside and outside/inside. Yeeni fara combines a peripheral course with a final deep course. The second fact concerns the idea of time in the development of the disease. While yeeni falku progresses continuously, yeeni fara proceeds discontinuously in successive stages, since it fully establishes itself in each new affected area before resuming its progress according as the disease gets worse.

These two diseases on their own do not make up a separate category; they are linked to a generic disease known as weyno (weyno = sun, heat). In fact weyno gives rise to numerous diseases often connected with the abdomen, the heart and the liver, at the same time retaining its own identity. What concerns us here is not weyno in all its complexity but the links established by the healer between the series of diseases grouped round it.

Weyno, strictly speaking, is a universal 'disease', if
one can speak of a disease in such circumstances. A
'little' of it is present in every body. It may be
aroused by bad food, bad water, by meals postponed for
too long or by the hardship of excessive work. Its primary location is the abdomen, while its main effects are
exerted through the network of veins leading to the heart.
It never gets into the flesh.

It is when it lasts for a very long time that
weyno produces specific diseases. Derived from it in
particular are the two forms of yeeni just considered
and also binne doori (heart pains) and dankanoma (a Hausa
word).

New diseases appear through a process of division.
Weyno, divided into two, produces yeeni and dankanoma.
When yeeni, in its turn, is divided into two, yeeni falku
and yeeni fara are produced. Clearly what we have here
is a system of classifying diseases by binary oppositions,
the application of which could only be worked out after
a sufficiently far-reaching study. For example, yeeni
fara is linked to yeeni falku by coolness (yeeni) and
they are distinguished by 'pricked bones', in one case,
and by mucus, in the other. If we now take the example
of weyno, we see that weyno and yeeni, viewed by the
healer as being in a way analogous, are opposed at the

level of vocabulary: <u>weyno</u> = sun, heat; <u>yeeni</u> = coolness.
This arrangement may be represented in the following way,
letting A and B stand for the names in opposition:

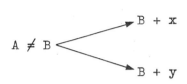

$$A \neq B \begin{cases} B + x \\ B + y \end{cases}$$

From one point of view diseases A, B, B + x, and B + y
are all the same; the healer sometimes uses A to denote
B, and B to denote B + x or B + y. At the linguistic
level there is nothing <u>a priori</u> by which to predict such
a classification. The evidence is based on the characteristics of the disease which transform one into another.
The relations between generic diseases and specific diseases are among the most difficult to elucidate.

     In the field the complexity grows when one moves
from one healer to another. According to different informants, the same disease may be denoted by words borrowed from the Hausa language and sometimes from the
Songhay language. That is to say, in the same system
of classification the terminology varies from one healer
to another. This is the case with the particular form
of <u>weyno</u> that is called either by the Hausa term <u>dankanom</u>
or by the Sonhay descriptive term <u>weyno beri</u>, the great
<u>weyno</u>. Ordinary people, however, refer to the whole ser-
ies by the generic term <u>weyno</u>.

Let us express in a simple diagram the oppositions of the whole <u>weyno</u> group studied here.

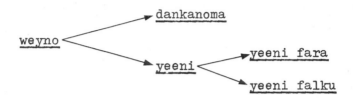

Note the generic term at the second level: <u>yeeni</u>. Does this refer to a disease? Healers declare that <u>yeeni</u>, like <u>weyno</u>, is present in the body of everyone and only produces one of its two specific forms after a lapse of time. But they also speak of <u>yeeni</u> in a general way, borrowing elements of either <u>yeeni fara</u> or <u>yeeni falku</u> in order to describe it. But, as we have shown, the symptoms are not necessarily common to the two diseases.

The same division into two is found in the description of <u>fafasa</u>:

in the description of <u>cantu</u>:

and, in a much more complex way, for that of <u>curo-curo</u>, which we shall discuss later. The healer makes just as free use of the unqualified terms as of the composite descriptive terms. However, it should not be thought that the position of the word yeeni is analogous in this system with that of the words fafasa and cantu. For these two I have not yet found a primary disease filling the same role as weyno. Nowhere do healers suggest that fafasa and cantu lie dormant in the body.

It will be clear that any conclusions based solely on terminology without studying the descriptions of the diseases themselves are likely to cause confusion. At the lexical level the construction of the nomenclature is marked by great freedom of association and borrowing. These phenomena have been little studied and existing Songhay vocabularies are too limited or inaccurate. Systems of disease are those requiring study, not lexical systems. As things are at present there is little balance between nosology and semiology.

II   Bush diseases

All bush diseases presented as such by healers are 'spiri diseases'; that is to say, spirits are thought of as bein at various levels, the direct cause of these diseases.

I shall exclude from this study the group of disorders whose treatment is the preserve of the cult of

possession found among the Songhay-Zarma. These appear
to form a distinct category, at least in terms of treatment. Here I am only dealing with those diseases brought
about by spirits in which the latter do not set out to
possess an individual in order to hag-ride him, and the
treatment of which involves the use of medicines. When
the terms 'spirit disease' or 'bush disease' are used,
they should be understood to refer to this particular
group of diseases to the exclusion of all others.

       The approach of the healer is not the same when
describing a village disease and a bush disease. In
order to explain a village disease, he tries to make
out the pathways of the illness and the distinct regions
at the same time or in turn affected by it, whereas in
bush diseases the healer considers the body as a whole.
The notion of pathway, so important for the first group,
disappears almost completely for the second. The blood
is as often mentioned, but particularly to stress its
normal or abnormal state rather than its movements. It
does not encounter those pathogenic agents which reverse
its flow or alter its composition; it is active or passive, black or red, according to a general condition:
fever. The general symptoms most often mentioned are
those connected with heat, coolness, movement, sleep,
fatness or thinness, tiredness — all of them phenomena

affecting the whole of the organism.

Disease is here seen as an aggression. The spirit
attacks the head and the abdomen, regarded here as centres
of dissemination. In fact, they are the two origins of
fever. The heart is not directly affected, it seems,
whereas in village diseases it is one of the centres of
heat.

Attack by a spirit is usually thought of as a physical act. It shoots a poisoned arrow; it puts an iron
cap over the brain; it sucks blood; it strikes like a
snake; it fells one to the ground like a bull. In the
shape of a night-bird it utters a terrifying disease-
bearing cry; it enters the body in the guise of a smell.
In other words, spirits penetrate the body through a number of orifices: eyes, ears, nose, flesh, the pores of
the skin - this list is probably incomplete. Even a
foetus may be affected, for if the spirit-bird passes
over a pregnant woman and drops a few grains of sand on
to her abdomen, this will give the child a disease which
develops after its birth. Thus the patient suffers either because the spirit is there, present and active, or
because the spirit has left behind the essence of disease
that will develop in its absence. In some of these diseases the spirit comes and goes, each visitation being
the occasion of an outbreak.

Leaving the abdomen or the head, the heat immediately spreads through the whole body and causes behavioural disorders: in time it may alter consciousness and
often leads to madness.

Fear seems to play a crucial part and is closely
bound up with heat, of which it is the cause. At times
it appears in another form of the same thing, that of
disease left in the abdomen by the attacking spirit.
Fear could well be itself the subject of special research.
It is true that important work has already been devoted
to it, but here it seems necessary to approach it from
the particular point of view of the medical culture of
local healers. We know, for instance, that fear has several origins: djinns, good spirits, evil spirits, sorcerers. On the other hand, it is very often linked with
the disappearance of a person's vital principle: the
biya (the 'double' or replica of a human being, invisible
except to magicians or sorcerers, without which life is
inconceivable). It is only when we know all the various
forms of fear, their psychosomatic consequences and the
way in which healers distinguish between them and classify them that we may hope to understand the crucial importance of fear in Songhay-Zarma culture. Such research
should equally involve a study of the status of the sick
person, as much in relation to himself as in relation

to phenomena acting on his perception and his imagination. Fear, therefore, can only be understood when the
unity of the medical socio-religious system has been
clearly established.

Bush diseases are not indicated by the same set
of characteristics as village diseases. Among the names
of the latter one generally finds a word designating an
organ linked to a qualifying or determinative word. In
bush diseases, the names of organs are absent; what appears is the family name of the spirit-donor or of its
incarnations. Thus there are diseases of Hausa spirits,
of Hargu spirits or of Karente spirits and, on the other
hand, the disease called curo-curo, caused by the incar-
nation of an unidentified spirit. These diseases may
be regarded as having no specific names. What one finds
is the existence of large classes within which various
disorders are arranged, the healer carefully distinguishing one from another by their symptoms.

A bush disease: curo-curo

The best description of bush diseases given me by the
healer concerns a group of maladies that he classifies
as curo-curo (the name of a night-bird) and among which
he distinguishes six specific diseases according to the
mode of classification by binary oppositions, as in the

case of the village diseases:

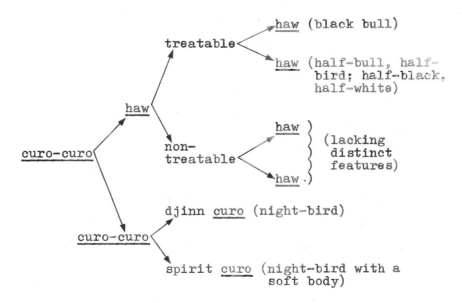

At no time does the healer display this classification as a unified system, but he uses it by making a
series of oppositions, distinguishing first between haw
and curo-curo, then between the four haws of the two
curo-curos. He repeated several times that the pairs
in question denote diseases which have the 'same shape'
and yet are quite distinct. If one were to sum up the
oppositions that he himself made, one would come to the
conclusion that the six diseases are both very similar
and very different. In his explanation his approach was
as follows:

$$4 + 2 = \text{same shape}$$

$$4 \begin{cases} 2 = \text{same shape} \\ 2 = \text{same shape} \end{cases}$$

Table IV   CURO - CURO

	Haw (black bull)	Haw (half-bull, half-bird) (non-fatal)	Djinn-curo (bird 1)	Spirit-curo (bird 2)	Haw Haw
General characteristics	Treatable Same form Disease in crises No disease without crises Untreatable if long-lasting Disease with a will of its own Disease attacks children by preference		Same form Sorcerer: fear: small child if not treated: curo - curo later		Untreatable (fatal) Same form Chronic disease Disease attacks everyone
Symbolic description of the attack	The child { Sees the bull which charges him. Is gored. Is felled to the ground. Loses consciousness. No longer sees the bull.	The patient { Does not see the flying animal. Is not gored. Is felled to the ground.	?	The child { Hears the cry of bird. Is afraid	
Description of the manifestations	Tremors from mouth and nose { discharge which looks like blood but is not blood. Staring eyes	Lies face downwards Contractions of the leg (single movement) Eyes closed	Stiff (stiff arms) does not move, except the heart, as if dead Eyes open	Fingers { outstretched / bent Stiff (arms stiff) Spasms Eyes blinking	Continuous madness Pale red blood discharged from mouth and nose.

	Howling	Moaning (groans)	Groans from time to time	
Descriptions of the manifestations	Tongue { protrudes, moves from left to right or is held between the teeth; Heavy breathing { violent exhalation, short inhalation; Hot like fire	Vomiting; Pains (heart) }; Suffocation	Mouth open; Difficult breathing; Suffocation	Hot and cold Feels ill in whole body; Difficult breathing
Sign of end of attack	Onset of disease – urine; Developed disease – urine and faeces		?	?
Treatment	Inhalations and applications		Drink inhalation applications	Drink inhalation applications

Table IV presents all the relevant characteristics of these six diseases.

In this table, with a few exceptions, probably due to forgetfulness on the part of the healer, all the data belong to systems of oppositions, whether it is a matter of describing symptoms or of making classificatory distinctions. The healer provides neither an overall view of the disease, nor a catalogue of disorders, nor a list of symptoms. He demonstrates by making a series of comparisons.

One feature scarcely appears in the table, probably because from the healer's point of view it is not discriminatory. This is what may be called the latency of the disease. I was given four examples of this. Two of them describe a brief latency of definite duration, the other two a long latency of indefinite duration.

Brief latency: I – a child goes into the bush, passes through a herd of animals and there contracts a form of illness with no detectable manifestations and whose nature is unknown. The child goes back to the village and only then shows symptoms of an attack by haw of the black bull.

II – someone goes into the bush, looks into an old disused well or into the hole of a zunku (unidentified creature). He returns to the village and an attack of the half-bull, half-bird variety of haw comes on.

Long latency: I - the bird of the spirits, <u>curo</u>, drops
a few grains of sand onto the belly of a pregnant
woman. Later on the child will fall ill.

II - a sorcerer frightens a small child;
the fear is not treated. Such a child will later
on become afflicted with <u>curo-curo</u>.

Cases of brief latency involve two opposite cir-
cuits of orientation and nature. Human beings make the
village-bush-village journey, whereas disease-spirits
move in the bush-village-bush direction. One of these
routes is registered in measurable human space, the other
in symbolic human space. As regards time, there is an
objective criterion - that of the human being's journey.
Cases of long latency, on the other hand, only involve
a single circuit - that of the disease-spirit - and time
is no more than an imaginary factor.

For the six <u>curo-curo</u> bush diseases just examined,
no spirit name was given. Other bush diseases, however,
correspond to the families of spirits responsible. The
Songhay pantheon has already been studied by Jean Rouch,
but from the particular point of view of spirit-possession
cults. From the point of view of our approach it seems
that a series of different or more subtle distinctions
may be necessary to account for the classifications encountered. Since such a study has not been carried out,
this point cannot be developed here.

One might suggest, however, that disease manifestations are different depending on whether named or nameless spirits are responsible. Diseases brought by named
spirits are characterized by fever, fatigue and inertia;
those brought by nameless spirits are accompanied by
convulsions, sometimes very severe, or by continuous
madness which is often fatal. The latter, which cannot
be treated, cuts the patient off from society completely.
In the case of the others, the institution of a possession cult makes it possible to treat them and thus re-
integrate the individual into society. Moreover, it seems
that the more definite the identity of the spirit responsible, the more specialized is the disease: for example,
a particular spirit of a particular family destroys the
right hand and the left leg at the same time, while a
different spirit destroys the left hand and the right
leg.

III   The bush-village distinction

On examination the dichotomy represented by village diseases and bush diseases has proved valid and a basis for
organization. Now, however, we must stand back from
this viewpoint and ask the question whether the actual
make-up of the diseases (including their development)
does not require a more unitary view. Or, to be more

accurate no doubt, perhaps we should discern in this
division, which seems to be made spontaneously and a
priori - following the categories of nature and of the
mind - other principles of understanding which go beyond
this dichotomy and form the basis of it. Were this the
case, the bush/village opposition would account above
all for the constitution of the field of activity of
both healer and disease; it would be practical and would
enable us to see (symptoms) and to act (medicines). But
behind it, an explanation of movement itself would be
possible. To the dynamic of disease which acts on the
level of facts would correspond a dynamic of medical
acts, situated on the metaphysical plane.

   Let us return to our initial question: can one
understand a disease in all its complexity by placing
it in one or other of these categories? Let us take
the example of yeeni presented as a village disease.
Yeeni, which is to be found 'a little' in all bodies,
comes from weyno, which is also to be found 'a little'
in all bodies. But its origin can be grasped not only
at the physiological level; the heat put into the abdomen
is the fear which produces it and this fear is a spirit
which has put it there. Fear appears at the point of
articulation of two worlds: those of the body and of
spirits. Fear is the passage of the spirit into the

body; it is the invasion of the village by the bush.
In the complete description of a disease, the two worlds
of bush and village are no longer in opposition, but are
complementary, no longer distinct but superimposed on
one another.

The consequences of this superimposition do not
always appear in an immediate way. Time forms part of
the disease (<u>weyno</u>; <u>yeeni</u>; <u>curo-curo</u>). When the organic
disease begins, it brings latency to an end; the bush
ceases to wait in the man's body.

The healer, then, must face the two realities of
the body and the bush in the same disease. If, in order
to classify his knowledge, he must arrange the diseases
in two opposed series, when he treats them he is led to
regard the continuity of the two modes of causality as
dependent upon one another and as acting together. Diagnosis and treatment takes place, therefore, on two levels, each level having its own coherence; the disease
itself is a whole with several aspects, a polymorphous
unity, but a unity nonetheless.

If the disease is a dynamism which brings the
bush into man, it can be expelled only by the action
of a symmetrical dynamism which also leads the bush into
man, but this time mastered by man. That is why the
healer must go into the bush to collect a few elements

of it (medicines are not only made from plants) and to
bring them together in a therapeutic order which is no
longer that of wild nature. This operation may be regarded as the initial mediation. A second mediation
occurs which is added to the action of the first, namely,
that of the cultivated bush, owned and dominated by man.
Wild plants, in effect, are associated in medicinal compounds with bases such as millet, milk, butter, the fat
of domestic animals and their blood. Thus the movement
that balances that of disease is closed again.

The conclusions and hypotheses that emerge from
this study do not, of course, make it possible to establish a typology. One can see a mass of information still
to be obtained from healers:

-- A more complete list of these diseases.

-- A description of these diseases.

-- A more complete list of the medicines.

-- A more complete and more coherent nomenclature.

-- A list of magical procedures and their organic,
   and possibly psychical, consequences.

On the other hand, it is desirable that the pantheon of
spirits already known should be studied systematically
and from a nosographical point of view. I have been able
to touch neither on this topic nor on that of diseases
brought about by sorcerers who eat biya (the 'double'

or replica of a human being, invisible to all but magicians and sorcerers, and without which life is inconceivable).

On the other hand, the absence from this paper
of certain themes, such as that of poison or of divination linked with disease, simply indicates the small
part played by such factors in the diagnostic scheme.
Healers mention them infrequently or not at all.

All this suggests that great care must be taken.
I hope that once the information required has been collected according to the main outlines described here,
it will be possible for us to consider developing a theory
of the classification of diseases.

What I have tried to establish is the order of
the thinking behind medical discourse; I feel sure from
the fragments elucidated that such an order exists, that
the healer is aware of it and makes effective use of it
in teaching sessions. Nevertheless, an analysis of this
discourse as such has not been attempted here. It might
be thought that this particular form of seeing knowledge
in layers laid out in a purely conceptual space derives
from my investigation. In learning or in teaching, the
healer does not often seem to encounter such a state of
affairs, and his medical thinking does not take this
form. His activity is one of discernment. The first

time he identifies; next time he discriminates. The
same or another. Outside medical action, **weyno** is a
classificatory entity; at a factual level, it is presented as something found in all bodies. In what form?
The question is probably meaningless. For, as soon as
its form appears, it 'divides' itself and gives rise
to series of discrete symptoms that will define specific
and observable diseases. The same applies to yeeni,
binlutey, cantu, fafasa. As for curo-curo, it gives
rise, as we have seen, to six distinct forms which, the
healer insists, are all the same. We encounter this
balance again at another level. When the spirit which
lives in the bush enters a person's body, it is called
fear. In its pathogenic abundance, fear is called fever.
Is disease therefore the bush in the village? Is the
patient Man and Other?

INDEX OF NAMES